First published 2014
by Lifeworlds Learning, 15a-17a Getliffes Yard, Leek, Staffordshire, ST13 6HU

Typeset in Myriad Pro
Printed and bound in China by Shanghai Ouyang Printing Limited Company, 128 Delixi Road, Jiading District, Shanghai, China 201802.

ISBN13: 978-0-9929780-0-6

Credits:

Editor: Trevor Higginbottom

Advisor: Rob Bowden, Lifeworlds Learning

Design: Rob Bowden, Lifeworlds Learning

Cover design: Wang Ke, Xiehe Education Group

Photographs/Illustrations: All photographs/diagrams/illustrations in this publication have been submitted by the authors/editor and remain the copyright of those contributors. We are grateful for their permission to include the images in this publication. We would like to thank the British Council for permission to use illustrations in Fig 3.2 - 3.5 (chapter 3) and Fig 1 (chapter 7.2) taken from Connecting Classrooms materials available at www.britishcouncil.org/connectingclassrooms-pd. If you believe we have used materials for which you hold the copyright, please contact rob.bowden@lifeworldslearning.co.uk to ensure that the proper credit is added in any future editions.

Website:

A website supporting the English language version of this book and promoting related content and events can be found at:

www.eastmeetswest.lifeworldslearning.co.uk

Developing Global Schools in China
'East meets West': learning together

Editor: Trevor Higginbottom

Advisor and Designer: Rob Bowden

'I believe East and West shall meet by virtue of each moving in the direction of the other. They may contribute to a blended world where social and cognitive aspects of both regions are represented but transformed – like the individual ingredients in a stew that are recognisable but are altered as they alter the whole. It may not be too much to hope that this stew will contain the best of each culture'.

Richard E. Nisbett, *The Geography of Thought: How Asians and Westerners Think Differently ... and Why.*

Lifeworlds Learning

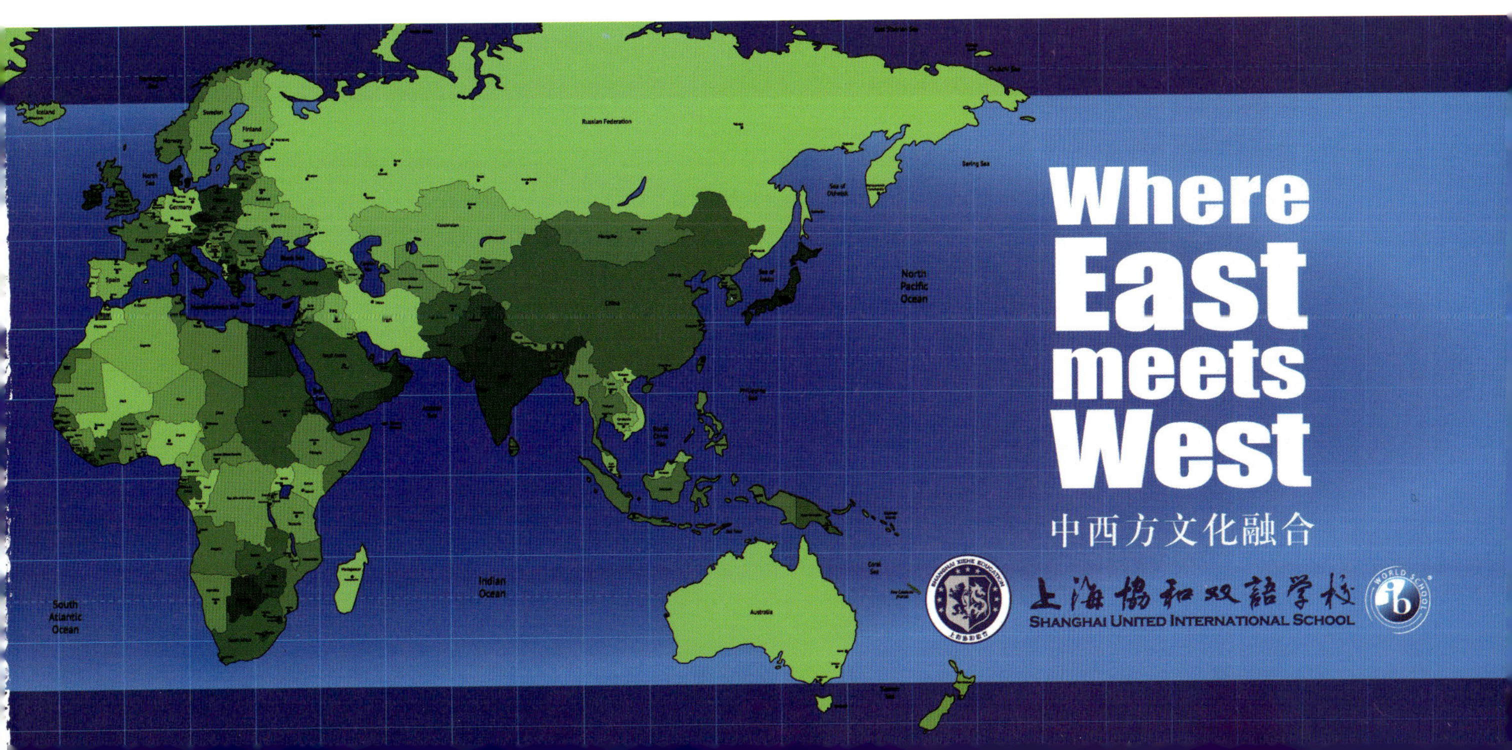

This book is dedicated to Xiehe's teachers
for their hard work, commitment and professional creativity.

'It is teachers who, in the end, will change the world of the school by understanding it'.

Professor Lawrence Stenhouse

'The driving force of China's growing influence as a global power remains its rapid economic expansion. The world has never seen its like before: a country possessed of a huge population combined with a double digit growth rate that has been sustained over three decades. It is this that is transforming the global order at such remarkable speed. Alas, much of the world, particularly the developed countries - the United States, Japan and perhaps above all Europe - find it almost impossible to grasp either the nature of this transformation or its speed.'

Martin Jacques

Acknowledgements

Editor's acknowledgements

I am grateful to Christine McGough, Publication Administrator and Cathy Wang Yi, Publication Co-ordinator Shanghai Xiehe Education Group, for their hard work and professional commitment. Without their support this book could not have been published.

Thanks, also, to Ann McGough for her thorough proof reading and to Wang Jin (Ellen), Xiehe, for her extremely efficient administrative support in Shanghai.

The following have been particularly helpful: Wang Shi Fu , Tan You Kang , Zhang Fu Zhi, Qian Feng, Zhang Hong, Mason Lee, Dr Roger Morgan, David Walsh, Zheng Li Da, James Waldron, Martin Donnellan, Wu Ping, Zho Liang, Rosie Wilson, Richard Eaton and James Morris.

I will always be indebted to both the teaching and non-teaching staff of the Shanghai United International School (Hong Qiao) for their remarkable pioneering work in creating Xiehe's first Dual Stream School. They are too numerous to mention but know who they are.

I wish to acknowledge the colleagues who have had a particularly marked influence on my professional development in the latter stages of my career. Wang Yi, Du Ling, Maxine Lu Hui Wen, Shi Ping, Vivia Xu, Angel Lin and Vivian Xiaoyun Chen. All of these colleagues have significantly enhanced my understanding of Chinese education. Professor David Hopkins and the staff of the 'Improving the Quality of Education for All' (IQEA) Project at the University of Nottingham, England, reminded me that it is what happens in the classroom that really matters in schools. George Jacobs, Singapore, greatly influenced my views on co-operative learning. Clive Belgeonne, Rob Bowden, Helen Griffin and Rob Unwin, all visionary English global educators, have significantly enhanced my understanding of this key curriculum dimension.

Finally, my special thanks go to Professor Hu Wei, founder of the Shanghai Xiehe Education Group, a visionary who always makes things happen.

Advisor's acknowledgements

I am grateful to Rosie Wilson for her support, patience and critical eye in bringing the design of the book together. I feel indebted to Trevor Higginbottom for the opportunity to contribute to such an interesting and important piece of work. I would like to thank my partners at Oxfam, British Red Cross, Practical Action and Think Global for their support in developing the ideas around values and global learning, and Robert Chambers, Roger Hart, Neena Joseph, Gill Allbutt, Rosie Wilson, Helen Hunter, and Jackie Zammit for their continuing influence on my own learning journey.

Contents

Editorial introduction

This book is concerned with both comparative education and global learning. It tells the story, in educational management, curriculum, professional development and quality assurance terms of some of the developments within the Shanghai Xiehe Educational Group's seven global 'East meets West' schools over the last decade. Five of these schools are Dual Stream, with a local (Chinese) stream and an international stream; two are cross phase (one 2-19 years, the other 6-19 years). The key aim in all of them has been to maximise the interaction between Chinese and international students and teachers.

These school organisation models are felt to be particularly significant in an educational world which now sees preparation for global citizenship as a key learning aspiration for students. The fact that the Xiehe schools are located in China, a country which might well have a very marked impact on the future lives of all students, worldwide, adds to this significance.

The aim over the last decade has been to ensure that the schools described in this book are learning communities for teachers as well as students. The *'East meets West'* dialogue has greatly enhanced this process. Testimony to the professional creativity of Xiehe teachers is their major contribution to many of the chapters which follow. Overall, the book is in part a celebration of global learning by both students and teachers.

The *'East meets West'* philosophy permeates all aspects of this book, within six main themes.

- How management, both centrally within Xiehe and at the school level, has supported this global approach.
- The development of many curricula (for example the Chinese National Curriculum, the English National Curriculum, the International Baccalaureate, the British Columbian Curriculum, the American High School Curriculum, a hybrid *'East meets West'* 'Pioneer' curriculum) across both the streams and the phases.
- The ways in which these curriculum developments have supported global learning, in particular.
- The related professional development activities for teachers.
- The constant search for ongoing improvement, with school self evaluation as a key strategy.

This book is, deliberately, very practical in content. In this respect it is hoped that the book will be used in both initial teacher training and continuous professional development. Additionally, individual chapters might well provide a catalyst for school based curriculum development. This is regarded as particularly important given that a key dimension of Xiehe's educational philosophy is that teachers should be given maximum scope for professional creativity.

Hopefully, educational organisations worldwide will find the book a useful vehicle for comparing the various dimensions of their work with Xiehe's strategies, for example with regard to issues such as educational leadership, the relationships with their schools, cross phase curriculum continuity and policy development.

The Shanghai Xiehe Education Group does not pretend, in any way, to have the 'right' answers with respect to the various educational themes raised in the book. It is very keen to engage in dialogue on these with both individual schools and other educational organisations

Trevor Higginbottom
Editor

(trevorconsult@cbits.net)

Biographies

Professor Hu Wei graduated from the Department of Education, East China Normal University, Shanghai in 1983. From August in the same year, he started work in the Shanghai Education Science Institute. In 1987, he completed his MA in Education in the Department of Educational Management in Shanghai Normal University. In 1992, he was accredited as the youngest Associate Professor Researcher in Shanghai by the Teachers' Professional Title Accreditation Committee of Shanghai. Later, the Shanghai Education Science Institute invited him to be its Professor Researcher. In December 1995, he established the Shanghai Non-governmental Education Research Institute. As the founder of Shanghai Xiehe Educational Group, he has established 30 kindergartens and seven primary and secondary schools. He has undertaken a wide range of research studies on non-govenment educational development in China. As a member of the China Association for Promoting Democracy and the CPPCC, he has attempted to combine his professional work with his political aspirations to improve the quality of education in China.

Trevor Higginbottom is currently Academic Director and Inspector, Shanghai Xiehe Education Group and an International Consultant in School Improvement/Global Education. Formerly, in the United Kingdom he was a geography teacher, a Member of Her Majesty's Inspectorate for England and Wales, Director of a National Geography Project and Chief Education Adviser for the Barnsley Local Education Authority. In Hong Kong he was Senior Education Officer with the English Schools Foundation and National Co-ordinator of a Primary English as an Additional Language Project for the Hong Kong Government Education Department. He has written more than forty student textbooks and numerous educational articles in various publications worldwide.

Cathy Wang Yi is a researcher in the Shanghai Academy of Educational Sciences. She has close professional relationships with the Shanghai Xiehe Education Group, taking the role of Principal Assistant of SUIS and an executive group member of the Stars Project. Her contributions have made a significant impact on the process of school self evaluation within Xiehe, as a key strategy for ongoing improvement.

Rob Bowden is founder and co-director of Lifeworlds Learning, a social enterprise in England specialising in critical learning and strategic creativity with schools, organisations and communities. Their focus is on engaging values, building young people's resilience, and encouraging an enjoyment of learning. Alongside this role, Rob is an author, photographer, designer and publisher of non-fiction books and resources focussed on global and environmental issues, and the producer of professional teaching and learning opportunities for a wide variety of organisations. Prior to this, he worked as a lecturer in three UK universities teaching geography, development and environmental studies.

Partner Organisations

Shanghai Xiehe Education Group - is an independent, non-governmental, non-profit organization whose remit includes strategic educational planning, school management and teacher training. The Xiehe Education Group manages a number of independent local and international schools across the full age-range; disseminates best practice based on educational research; promotes advanced models of educational management; makes full use of the experience of educational experts; ensures that all Xiehe schools strive continuously for educational improvement; and provides quality control to ensure a high quality international education which combines the best of Chinese and Western educational practice in a bilingual environment.

Lifeworlds Learning - Lifeworlds Learning is a community interest company (CIC) based in England but working locally, nationally and internationally. Their team of skilled practitioners work directly with students, teachers, and leaders in schools, but also with a range of educational organisations and local and national authorities. Lifeworlds specialises in crafting opportunities that engage in values, build individual and organisational resilience, and make learning enjoyable. As a CIC they also support a number of learning communities (including *Learning Through Values* and *Global Learning England*) that encourage multi-sectoral dialogue to create innovation in the theory and practice of learning.

DEC(SY) - The Development Education Centre (South Yorkshire) is a member organisation and a Charitable Incorporated Organisation (No. 1153377) and was established in 1984. It works with teachers and others involved in education throughout South Yorkshire and beyond promoting education for global citizenship through the school curriculum. DEC(SY)'s work focuses on building an understanding of the interdependence of global issues and people's own lives. Using active learning methods based on enquiry into issues and ideas, DEC(SY) aims to help people develop the skills and commitment to work together to bring about a more just and sustainable world. Work on cultural diversity and race equality is seen as integral to this work on the global dimension.

Institute of Education, University of London - Founded in 1902 as the London Day Training College, the Institute of Education's (IOE) original purpose was to train teachers for service in London's elementary schools. The IOE is now the UK's largest school of education and one of its biggest centres of social science. It undertakes world-class research and consultancy in both areas alongside the initial training and on-going professional development of teachers and lecturers for all phases of compulsory, further, adult and higher education. The IOE's international reach extends to some 100 countries. Its research, consultancy and collaborative partnerships brings the IOE into contact with governments, international and national agencies, institutions and organisations in every continent. The IOE's Internationalisation Strategy commits it to research and scholarship that has a global perspective; international partnerships that bring mutual benefit; with partners to find ways to reduce global inequalities through education; encouraging an international orientation in staff and students; responsible and sustainable international student recruitment; and an internationalised curriculum.

East China Normal University , School of Education Science - The School of Education Science of ECNU was set up in 1980. It was the first such school in Chinese universities on the initiative of former-president, famous educator and scholar, Prof. Funian Liu. At present, the school has a research focus, combining theory and practice, research and teaching, pre-service and in-service training, undergraduate and graduate students for 25 years. The School has eight departments and centres, 196 faculty members (including 49 professors and 61 associate professors), 610 undergraduate students, 1089 masters degree students, and 365 doctoral students. At present, the school has two first-rank disciplinary doctoral programmes; 2 post-doctoral mobile stations; 20 second-rank disciplinary doctoral programmes and master programmes; and three undergraduate programmes. The school also has two state key research bases for humanities. The school boasts a stock of over 130,000 volumes of Chinese and foreign books on education and psychology, more than 400 periodicals in Chinese and 130 periodicals in foreign languages.

UK Geographical Association - The Geographical Association (GA) is a subject association with the charitable object of furthering geographical knowledge and understanding through education. It is a thriving community of practice with over a century of innovation behind it and an unrivalled understanding of geography teaching. The GA was formed by five geographers in 1893 to share ideas and learn from each other. Today, the GA's purpose is the same and it remains an independent association. The GA provides support for geography educators through its journals, publications, training events and other activities. It gives a voice to geography education and exerts a significant influence on public debate and policy relating to geography and education. The reach of the GA across the geographical education community internationally is a key strength. The Association has members in 60 countries right across the world, and its website is visited by individuals from over 200 countries each year.

Think Global - Think Global is a national education charity, and the hub of a community of schools, NGOs and businesses in England which care about global learning and development. Its goal is to help create a more just and sustainable world, through the power of global learning. Established in 1993, its members now include 10,000 teachers and school leaders, and 140 organisations including international and national non-governmental organisations, universities, faith groups and unions, all of whom believe it is possible to create a world which is both just and sustainable. This belief drives the Think Global community. It runs the Global Dimension Website for teachers, works with policy makers to improve the opportunities for global learning both inside and outside of school, and promotes good practice amongst charities, schools, businesses and educators.

Explanatory Notes

East meets West - 'East meets West' has been adopted as the mission of the Shanghai Xiehe Education Group to summarise the concept of involvement/collaboration between its Asian (predominantly Chinese) and Western (predominantly North American, European, British and Australian) students and teachers in its schools.

Dual Stream Schools - The Xiehe Dual Stream Schools were established with the key aim of promoting the East meets West mission. Every attempt is made to encourage dialogue between both students and teachers across the 'local' and 'international' streams.

Explanation of Global Schools and SUIS - In the English version of this book, the word 'Global' is used rather than 'International'. However, in the Chinese version, 'International' is preferred to 'Global'. This is because in Mandarin 'Global' may imply an undermining of nationalism. All seven Xiehe schools have the title 'Shanghai United International School' (SUIS), with a specific additional reference to their location. Eg. SUIS (Hong Qiao).

Book Format

All chapters in the book have the following common sections.

An introductory quote - A brief quote on the chapter theme is included as a stimulus to both initial thought and to introductory discussion.

Editorial introduction - The editor summarises the main content areas included in the chapter.

Talkabout - At the conclusion there is a Talkabout box containing a number of key questions which could provide a basis for professional dialogue on the key issues raised in the chapter.

1 Developing a global education organisation

Professor Hu Wei

In this introductory chapter, the founder of Xiehe describes how the Organisation was first established and how it has developed over the past 20 years.

> ***'Every outstanding school I have worked with in my fifty plus years in education has benefitted from high quality external support and networking provided by an educational organisation. A key factor has been the willingness of such schools to accept new ideas and to ensure that there is not 'innovation without subsequent change, particularly at the classroom level'.***
>
> Trevor Higginbottom

The Shanghai Xiehe Education Group was formally established in 1993. Its development can be divided into three stages.

Stage 1: 1992 - 1996, initial establishment.

The Group started in 1992 for two main reasons. First, as a result of Deng Xiaoping's speeches on economic reform during his inspection tour of South China when he stated that it was essential to make economic construction of the country a central task. Secondly, because China's private education had entered a new stage of development: from non-academic to academic education and from the original cramming schools of SAT tutors and English courses to formal basic education.

As a result of Deng Xiaoping's influence, rapid urban construction began in the Pudong District of Shanghai. Many residential buildings were established but people refused to move there: the saying 'better a bed in the Puxi District than a house in the Pudong District' was coined. Kindergartens were therefore established in Pudong to persuade people to go there. The leaders of the Pudong Social Development Bureau asked the Shanghai Institute of Educational Sciences (the predecessor of the present Shanghai Institute of Basic Education Academy) to establish kindergartens and offered to provide 400,000 RMB start up funding in each case. The Institute, however, felt that such a venture was too risky. I therefore decided to open a kindergarten myself with the support of Qian Zaisen, the former President of the Shanghai Institute of Educational Sciences and with foreign capital funding.

My team worked day and night and put their hearts and souls into the preparations. The new kindergarten was opened in August 1993, in quite chaotic circumstances with a variety of vehicles blocking access to the building.

At that time we responded very much to market forces and tried hard to meet the diverse educational

demands of parents. We learnt a great deal from others, including how to create a development plan, write a new calendar, formulate a curriculum framework and obtain relevant textbooks. We also had to establish a new management system.

The number of Xiehe Kindergartens gradually grew. During this time we learnt, in particular, to internationalise our education with the introduction of advanced management concepts and methods, the employment of foreign managers and teachers and the development of international courses. Our aim was to create the best international kindergartens in China.

These early experiences, combined with our passion to reform local education, provided a firm foundation for the future development of the Shanghai Xiehe Education Group. Since then we have pursued an internationalised, technological and resource-sharing path.

Stage 2: 1996 - 2003, independent working based on a recognition of early errors.

On 1 February 1996 the Pudong Social Development Bureau authorised the establishment of the Pudong Xiehe Early Childhood Education Group. Three years later, the Bureau approved the 'Shanghai Pudong Xiehe Education Early Childhood Education Group' and this was subsequently renamed as the 'Shanghai Pudong Xiehe Education Group'. From 1999 onwards, following the requirements of the Pudong Social Development Bureau, the Group expanded on an experimental basis and created further high quality private kindergartens by means of management innovation.

In 1999 we helped to create an experimental school in Shanghai's Fengxian District, under shared management. Initially we chose to follow the same educational policies as the Shanghai Municipal Government schools with, for example, an emphasis on traditional whole class teaching and an examination orientated curriculum. In 2002, however, we decided that this was not the route to take and left the management of the Fengxian Experimental School to establish the Shanghai Xiehe Education Group.

Over this seven year period, Xiehe gradually developed its own approach to education and its management. Along the way mistakes were made and there was confusion as to whether or not the local or international educational route should be followed. In summary, we were gradually becoming more independent in our thinking and attempting to learn from our errors.

Stage 3: 2003 - 2013, the development of a unique, mature educational organisation.

In September 2003, the Group opened the Xiehe Bilingual School in the Hong Qiao District of Shanghai. This was Xiehe's first Dual Stream School with its local and international stream, the former for Chinese students and the latter for foreign students. Here we were attempting to combine local and international education.

The opening of this new school was partly influenced by the Local Municipal Government's demands for high quality private education for both local and foreign students and partly by the involvement of Trevor Higginbottom, who had previously had senior educational management experience in Hong Kong and the United Kingdom. The school's management structure reflected Xiehe's new *'East meets West'* approach, with the appointment of Trevor and a very experienced Chinese colleague as co-principals. *'East meets West'* reflected an attempt both to combine and implement, at the classroom level, the best of Chinese and Western education pedagogies.

The Xiehe Dual Stream model is described in detail in **Chapter 2** which follows. This new approach to school management in many ways reflected the philosophies of Xiehe's already established kindergartens, as described above. The Dual Stream model has enabled the Group to develop very distinctive characteristics as an educational organisation. This is now reflected in terms of Xiehe's curriculum, management, human resources, professional development and marketing strategies.

The Organisation now has 30 kindergartens and 7 schools operating within a common overall educational philosophy.

Summary of the twenty years development

Xiehe's overall philosophy is that of a central organisation attempting to achieve two key aspirations: *'One centre, two basic aims'.*

Aim One

Chinese education focuses very much on subjects such as maths, Chinese, English, physics, chemistry and biology, with an under-emphasis on music, art and physical education. Xiehe favours a much more broadly based education with an emphasis not only on basic academic subjects but on moral, physical, social, aesthetic and global education. We should focus not only on the lower end of Bloom's 'cognitive pyramid' but on the upper end (see **Chapter 5.4** which follows). Xiehe believes in a 'rounded education' for all its students.

Aim Two

Our aim is to encourage the development of students as individuals, not to measure them by a ruler and to create them all as one 'standard' type. We aim to allow our students to develop their own personalities and potential in a 'freer' manner, not to cover them in 'red tape'. In these respects we are attempting to combine the more human orientated Western education with the subject/knowledge orientated Chinese curriculum: hence, our *'East meets West'* philosophy.

During recent years Xiehe has placed particular emphasis on raising educational standards with respect to a broad range of both cognitive and affective learning targets and on sustainability/environmental awareness issues with respect to school building design and construction. Also, we recognise the need for education to meet the aspirations of our students as both national and global citizens. The era of large-scale industry and volume production has gone; there is now a new stage of personalisation and customisation.

Previously our students were prepared for, very often, one career role in life under the influence of an examination orientated system. Now they might switch to various fields during their careers, for example in finance, education, business, non-governmental organisations or individual projects. For example, in 2012, of Hong Kong's 334,000 companies, 97 per cent had less than 100 employees, 94.7 per cent less than 20 employees; 220,000 were one-member companies. All this suggests that Xiehe students should be offered a broader, more liberal education and one which prepares them for significant change during their future lives.

The Group is strongly committed to changing teaching and learning methodology, away from 'duck-stuffing' approaches. In the past, there has been over emphasis on rote learning, focussing on accuracy, rather than encouraging students to think independently, to make judgements and to take risks in their learning. We are determined to create genuine education reform, rather than to merely pay lip service to it. With this in mind, we have adopted transdisciplinary thematic approaches to learning across all streams in our schools. These focus students on real life issues which can rarely be tackled by studying a single subject and which require analysis through inquiry based learning.

Xiehe is moving away from a highly centralised form of management to smaller group management, from micro to macro planning through the 19 departments which provide professional services for our kindergartens and schools.

Challenges ahead

Xiehe currently faces three key challenges.

- To establish and properly handle the relationship between the Group and the schools. In doing this, to learn to let go and to manage this new approach effectively.

- To draw lessons from the past by not blindly introducing external experts, but by developing our own staff internally. Hence the importance of the 'Stars Programme' (see **Chapter 9.1** which follows) in supporting our talented young colleagues on their pathways to management positions within Xiehe. Those with experience of the Organisation's education culture/mission and an understanding of its history can meet our expectations particularly effectively. These young colleagues will contribute to our future, be the driving force for change and Xiehe's heroes. Further reforms relating to the curriculum, school management, quality assurance and professional development will rely very much on this new generation of managers. The Shanghai Xiehe Education Group has been constantly innovating for the last 20 years: *'a journey of a thousand miles begins with a single step'.*

- To face a period of uncertainty, challenges and constraints. There are very few Government school policies that have explored the road of globalisation, which bring us both challenges and opportunities for development. The pace of change within the Group has been incredibly fast: we have launched a new school almost every year over the past decade and currently great educational diversity exists within them. The Government's preferential policies for schools are increasing with higher configuration. Since there are more and more globalised schools in our organisation, we must have a more 'globalised' management team. There is, however, currently a shortage of talent in this field. Senior management within our schools is often uneven in quality, therefore realisation and achievement of the Group's central mission is not always achieved. On occasions, logistics such as resource allocation, the school bus system, school meals and sanitation cannot keep pace with international standards.

All these challenges will be tackled by Xiehe as we enter our third decade.

Talkabout

- *List ten ways in which you feel an educational organisation can best serve its schools in order to maximise their students' achievement.*
- *Compare the challenges being faced by Xiehe with those, currently, in your own organisation.*
- *Highlight three of your current challenges and discuss how they might be tackled most successfully.*

2 The Xiehe Dual Stream School Model

Trevor Higginbottom

This chapter describes the Xiehe Global School Model and its development over the last decade.

> ***'Global education is important because we are all part of one world family'***
>
> Zheng Li. Xiehe Local Stream student, aged eight years.

There are currently two main types of international school models in China:

'National' international schools (schools with a very strong national dimension, eg British, American, Japanese, Singaporean, Korean); and

'International' international schools (schools which combine 'eastern' and 'western' approaches by means of an international stream and a 'host' Chinese stream).

The Shanghai Xiehe Education Group pioneered the latter by opening, in 2003, the Dual Stream Xiehe Bilingual School. By January 2013 Xiehe had five such schools. Their 'local streams' consist almost entirely of Chinese students following the Chinese National Curriculum: their 'international streams' consist of students from many different nations, following, for example, the International Primary Curriculum, the International Baccalaureate, the British Columbian Provincial Curriculum and the English National Curriculum. This chapter will explain the benefits of Dual Stream 'international' schools and the ways in which they can most successfully be established.

Advantages for Students

Across the two streams, the Chinese and international students learn from one another: this helps to prepare Chinese students for their adult roles in a rapidly emerging powerful contributor on the 'world stage', and international students to understand and appreciate China's new role, in this respect, in the world. These Dual Stream Schools, therefore, help to prepare both sets of students to become well informed and caring global citizens and can make a very significant impact in terms of global education.

The Model has been found to have an extremely positive impact on the language attainment of the students: notably in English (the international language) and in Mandarin (the language spoken by almost a quarter of the world's population). The expertise of the English Department in the international stream and the Mandarin Department in the local stream is shared across the school as a whole. (This advantage will be appreciated by any readers who have tried to recruit either high quality Mandarin teachers for conventional, single stream international schools or high quality English teachers for local government Chinese schools).

The staff, Chinese and Western, provide role models for the students in terms of the need to understand and respect similarities and differences relating to our common humanity. The parents of the students in both streams are encouraged, at all times, to adopt similar values and attitudes. Clearly, if the parents are influenced in this way, this impacts on their children.

In summary, this *'East meets West'* approach enhances both the cognitive (academic) achievement of all the students, as well as their affective development in terms of values and cultural awareness.

Advantages for Teachers

These schools become learning organisations for the staff as well as the students; they are 'educational laboratories' in which ideas on all aspects of the curriculum and its management are exchanged between Chinese and Western teachers. There is an *'East meets West'* approach to professional development.

A particularly significant dimension of the schools is the emphasis on team teaching. Xiehe believes that the most practical and effective way of ensuring teacher collaboration is for 'Eastern' and 'Western' teachers to teach together in the classroom, as equal and mutually valued partners. The team teaching approach is adopted in a variety of curriculum contexts across the school as a whole, notably in English, Mandarin, maths and thematic/inquiry work.

There is much educational research evidence, world-wide, to suggest that the most effective teachers are those given maximum opportunities for professional creativity in their work. This exists, in abundance, in these Dual Stream schools and has a positive effect on the morale of the teachers overall and, as a result, on their effectiveness in the classroom.

Impressively, Xiehe has encouraged variety in the various types of curriculum on offer, both within and across the five Dual Stream Schools. As well as the Chinese National Curriculum the schools have implemented, for example, the English National Curriculum, the International Primary Curriculum, the International Baccalaureate and the British Columbian Provincial Curriculum. This emphasis on a variety of curricula approaches has greatly enhanced the range of professional dialogue.

Global diversity at SUIS (Hong Qiao)

Fig 2.1: Lessons learnt within the Dual Stream Model.

What the international stream staff have learnt from the local (Chinese) stream staff.	What the local (Chinese) stream staff have learnt from the international stream staff.
Whenever necessary, how to create a formal disciplinary atmosphere in the classroom, with high student concentration levels.	Whenever necessary, how to create an informal classroom atmosphere which enhances learning.
Whole class teaching and learning strategies.	Group work and individualised learning strategies as the basis for supporting the individual learning needs of students.
Competitive learning strategies which enhance discipline and motivation.	Co-operative learning strategies which promote an important value in any child's education.
How to ensure that the children develop a firm foundation of factual knowledge and skills in their learning.	How to develop more inquiry based, investigatory, problem solving and creative approaches in the curriculum.
The use of textbooks to create a foundation/ framework for learning.	Creative approaches which build on/adapt the use of the text book eg experiential learning.
Subject approaches to curriculum content.	Integrated/thematic approaches to curriculum content.
Ways of enhancing a child's understanding of his/ her nationalism.	Ways of enhancing a child's understanding of his/ her future as a global/international citizen.
How to focus more on the outcomes of the learning, through assessment.	How to develop (formative) assessment techniques which create less pressure for children.
How to develop a rigorous approach to evaluation and teacher research, including open lessons.	How to use evaluation as a key strategy for teacher self reflection and development.

A very significant outcome from these 'educational laboratories' has been the emergence of hybrid curricula, being developed with 'pioneer' experimental classes designed to combine the best of Chinese and Western educational practices.

These new curricula illustrate how 'international' international schools can have a very fundamental impact on curriculum developments in the host country in which they are located, in this case with respect to the Chinese National Curriculum.

The writer's experience suggests that both 'national' international educational organisations and their individual schools can easily become 'educational enclaves' in their host countries.

It is, surely, vital that the two worlds of 'international' and 'national' education interact in terms of curriculum development, in order to benefit all children being educated in the host country, whatever their social background.

Chinese and Western teachers learning from one another

In the pioneer Xiehe Dual Stream School there has been much evidence to show how teachers across the two streams have learnt from one another, particularly in terms of teaching and learning pedagogy. Some of this evidence is summarised in the table on page 7 (left).

Chinese New Year in a Xiehe Dual Stream School.

Developing the Dual Stream Model in practice

1. Establishing A Dual Stream School Culture

The Dual Stream Schools are encouraged to establish a clearly articulated 'school culture' (defined as 'the way we do things around here') relating to the *'East meets West'* model. A typical example is included in **Fig 2.2** (page 9).

A summarised version of this mission statement is displayed prominently in the entrances to both the Chinese and Western sections of the school.

There are displays of inter-stream student and staff activities across the school as a whole. Some of the most prominent displays are bilingual (English and Mandarin) in content.

It is now recognised that, in order to ensure that the school has a shared common school culture across the two streams, it is important to have the following.

- A whole school policy on the Dual Stream Model which is developed, implemented, shared and constantly evaluated by the staff as a whole.
- A high level of social interaction between colleagues in both streams. The schools are recommended to have:
  - an inter-stream committee which organises staff social events;
  - an inter-stream student council, which includes representatives from each grade in each stream;
  - inter-stream activities such as staff and student choirs, orchestras and sports teams.

Obviously, a significant barrier to developing a Dual Stream School is language. With this in mind, some schools now provide 'taster' courses in both English and Mandarin for their staff which are led by language specialists in the school. This helps to enhance staff communication but also, most importantly, demonstrates to the students that (i) the staff themselves are aiming to be bilingual; and (ii) in learning a second language from one another, they are showing mutual respect for their respective cultures.

Dual Stream School Mission Statement

'In our Dual Stream School, the Chinese and international students learn from one another: this helps to prepare the Chinese students to be potential leaders in a rapidly emerging world superpower, and the international students to understand/appreciate China's new role, in this respect, in the world. Our school also helps to prepare both sets of students to become well informed and caring global citizens.

In our Dual Stream School all the staff are role models for the students in terms of racial diversity. They understand and respect similarities and differences relating to our common humanity. We try to ensure that the presence of both Chinese and international students in our school enhances both their academic achievement as well as their affective (values) education. The parents of our students are encouraged, at all times, to adopt similar values and attitudes.

We believe that language is a particularly important dimension of our Dual Stream School curriculum, overall; notably English (the international language) and Mandarin (the language spoken by almost a quarter of the world's population). We celebrate that we have considerable professional expertise in the teaching and learning of these two languages within our school as a whole and ensure that this expertise is shared across the two streams. We believe that this greatly enhances the bilingual development of all our students, compared with single stream (international and Chinese) schools.

Our school is a learning organisation for staff as well as students; it is an educational laboratory in which ideas on all aspects of the curriculum, and its management, are exchanged between Chinese and Western teachers. We believe that this constant exchange of professional ideas between the teachers across our two streams enhances the quality of education in our school, for all our students, both Chinese and international'.

Fig 2.2: An examplar mission statement, common to all Dual Stream Schools.

2. Management strategies which support the Dual Stream Model.

A key factor in implementing the Model is the commitment of the principal and staff to this approach. When any member of staff is interviewed for a post in a Dual Stream School they should be given, beforehand, copies of (i) the school's mission statement; and (ii) its whole school policy statement with respect to the Dual Stream Model. In their interview, candidates should be questioned and judged on their understanding of and an empathy with this approach to school management. For all senior management posts, applicants should be required to give their views on the Model as part of their verbal presentation to the interviewing panel.

Once appointed, new members of staff should be given an opportunity to discuss the school's mission statement and whole-school policy on its Dual Stream Model during their induction. A key point which should be emphasised at this stage is that, although the key dimension of their work in the school is to teach a specific stream curriculum (eg the IB, the Chinese or English National Curriculum) the teaching and learning of this curriculum can be considerably enhanced by both student and staff (professional) contact with the other stream, in terms of both academic and affective (values) development. As such, they have an additional professional responsibility in the school, which should prove in time to be extremely rewarding for them. (For example, in terms of their own professional and linguistic development). During the induction process it should be emphasised that the school fully appreciates the time demands on newly appointed members of staff. Also, that the inter stream contacts need to be paced realistically.

It is helpful to appoint a Dual Stream Co-ordination Group consisting of the two deputy principals responsible for inter-stream co-ordination and the

Heads of English and Chinese in each of the streams. This Group should meet regularly to review inter-stream curriculum, extra-curricular and professional development issues. The Group can also be responsible for the development, implementation and ongoing evaluation of the school's policy on the Dual Stream Model. This policy should explain how the school's mission statement is put into practice. For example, relating to shared curriculum and extra-curriculum activities, language learning and the *'East meets West'* approaches to professional development. This is a useful 'overview' document which is particularly helpful for, for example, new staff, the School's Advisory (Governing) Group and parents. Its content can be adapted for marketing purposes.

Whole school policies obviously strengthen the partnership between the two streams. Two particularly relevant policies are:

- Generic teaching and learning processes

This policy could be formulated in terms of indicators of excellence and observable features relating to various aspects of the schools generic teaching and learning. This format would support the evaluation process. The policy's content could emanate from, for example, the outcomes of inter-stream lesson observations, analysis of lesson videos and school-based research undertaken by colleagues. It would demonstrate the advantage of the school as a learning organisation for staff as well as students.

- School self-evaluation

This policy could summarise the evaluative criteria used to determine the success or otherwise of the various dimensions of the school's Dual Stream Model and would be closely related to its existing policy document on this theme. The policy could incorporate shared good practice across the school's two streams, in this case relating to evaluation strategies and individual/group teacher research.

The main aim of each policy should be to ensure consistency of practice across the school with respect to a particular curriculum dimension.

In order to promote inter-stream communication and collaboration, it is helpful to locate the senior managers responsible for each of the streams in adjacent rooms. There should be Inter-Stream Management Group meetings to deal with whole-school administrative, management and any relevant curricular and extra-curricular issues.

Developing global education in the Dual Stream School

Interaction between students across the two streams can promote the development of global education objectives. For example exploration of similarities and differences between their cultures, customs and traditions; understanding that they have different values, attitudes and perceptions of those from differing countries; developing positive attitudes towards diversity; learning to co-operate.

Inter-stream interaction between students can be achieved in a variety of ways:

Inter-stream 'sister' classes

Inter-stream classes can work together on thematic studies, particularly in inquiry based work. (eg Inequality: a Grade 5 study of how the Chinese Government is attempting to support poorer communities in the west of the country. Co-operation: an inquiry based study of how people were helped with respect to the Sichuan earthquake. In home-room/social education, a topic about how students can deal with differences between themselves. (Grade 2); in English with poetry being written by the students, on the 'global family', promoting respect between cultures (Grades 6-10)). (See pages 15-16 which follow).

Thematic Days

Classes across both streams can develop themes during, for example, 'International Women's Day', 'Senior Person's Day', China 'National Day', the Mid-Autumn Festival, through blocked timetabling.

Collaborative curriculum projects

- For example through inter-stream planning of a theme on sustainable development, with an exchange of student work between students in the two streams.

- Inter-stream English and arts festivals; visits and assemblies; bringing visiting speakers into the school; student 'global citizenship awards'; and inter-stream observation of

'East meets West' in the Local Stream of SUIS (Hong Qiao).

the international stream's Nativity play and the Chinese stream's Chinese New Year celebrations.

Also, on various global topics such as Western fiction and non-fiction from diverse cultures and traditions, and scientific topics about the effects humans have on the world and the need for diversity and protection.

Whole-school charity event

For example relating to a UNICEF Project in Africa, for which bilingual materials may be made available.

Inter-stream house systems

These help to promote global learning objectives such as diversity, interdependence, empathy and a sense of common humanity.

Chinese cultural rooms

In two Xiehe Dual Stream schools these provide an invaluable learning resource for students from both schools.

Inter-stream extra curricular activities

These take place on a very regular basis. (See **Chapter 5.2**)

Inter-stream professional collaboration between the staff

The sharing of professional practice between Chinese and Western colleagues in a Dual Stream School can take place in a number of ways:

- Through inter-stream whole-school self evaluation

During each academic year there are many opportunities for staff from the two streams to observe and analyse open lessons. Additionally, each year in some of the schools, inter-stream Evaluation Working Parties mount whole school evaluation exercises on a particular theme (eg meeting individual student needs; group work; EAL). The Working Parties produce an Evaluation Report based on the outcomes of the exercise, which is analysed and discussed at staff meetings in both streams. Senior Managers have undertaken comparative 'student pursuit' exercises in the two streams to review and analyse the educational experiences which the Chinese and international students are receiving in particular grades. Two-way windows in one school enable lessons to be observed anonymously.

- Through teacher research

There has been a strong tradition of individual or group teacher research, on an annual basis, in the local (Chinese) stream; additionally many teachers in the school are involved in research relating to First, Masters, or Ph.D. degree courses, as a result of the visionary developments within the Shanghai Xiehe Education Group. Regular *'East meets West'* whole school professional development seminars are held to enable colleagues to give feedback to their peers on the outcomes of this research. On occasions, again due to the visionary approach of the Shanghai Xiehe Education Group, teacher training students from overseas universities undertake teaching practice in the schools. Their views and professional experiences are communicated to the staff.

- Through participation in inter-stream curriculum development initiatives

There are a number of inter-stream curriculum development initiatives in these schools relating, for example, to thematic studies and the Virtues Project. (See **Chapter 5.2**). This is a very practical form of *'East meets West'* professional collaboration.

- Through teacher 'exchanges' between the two streams

Local (Chinese) and international stream teachers, on occasions, transfer streams to support the teaching and learning in the other stream. (Eg international stream English teachers to the local (Chinese) stream; local stream (Chinese) Mandarin teachers to the international stream).

- Through contributions to the local (Chinese) stream 'Experimental' or 'Pioneer' Classes

These classes follow a curriculum which draws on the best of Chinese and Western educational practice. The experiment reflects the professional collaboration which has been undertaken between Chinese and Western teachers in the schools and is regarded as a particularly significant development. Local (Chinese) and international stream teachers are often involved in both the curriculum planning and the teaching and learning with respect to the experimental classes, which provides the schools with another form of professional collaboration. (See **Chapter 5.5**).

- Through team teaching involving Chinese and Western teachers from each of the two streams

Team Teaching is a particularly helpful model of professional collaboration in the schools. (See **Chapter 5.1**).

The inter-stream senior management teams in the schools try to ensure that these various *'East meets West'* professional collaboration strategies lead to ongoing school improvement.

Some potential implications for educators worldwide

Xiehe's journey in the ongoing development of its Dual Stream Schools over the last decade is not yet over. Experience within the Group suggests that full implementation of the model, as described in this chapter, takes many years. In September 2013, inevitably, the schools are at different levels of development. Arguably, however, some significant claims can already be made for this educational innovation, as follows.

- Enhanced individual student academic achievement in English, Mandarin and mathematics.
- Enhanced individual student self-awareness in the affective domain.
- Enhanced individual student awareness/ understanding of their roles as global citizens.
- For international students, a greater awareness/ understanding of a country (China) which is likely to play a very key role in the future global society in the remainder of this century.
- For 'local' (Chinese) students a greater awareness/ understanding of their (potential leadership) roles in a National society which is likely to have significant global influence in the remainder of this century.
- For the staff, considerable opportunities for professional development in an *'East meets West'* working environment.
- For interested educators worldwide, consideration of:
  - an example of the Dual Stream Model of international and national education;
  - the outcomes of a significant educational experiment involving Chinese and Western educational pedagogies;
  - the curriculum and professional development processes being developed in this type of school.

Conclusion

There is a paucity of information on the Dual Stream School Model, both in general education literature and research papers. Dual Stream Schools, containing 'local' and 'international' streams, do exist in some parts of the world, notably in the Middle East. In many of these schools, however, the respective streams usually form very separate entities with little dialogue between either students or teachers.

The writer's view is that significant opportunities are being missed in terms of global education for students and global curriculum and professional development for teachers. The potential of the Xiehe Dual Stream Model as an exciting and relevant early twenty-first century educational initiative is explored in the remainder of this book.

Team teaching in the Xiehe Dual Stream School.

Experiential language learning

Talkabout

- *Consider whether it would be possible to establish Dual Stream Schools in your own educational organisation.*
- *What would you see as the main advantages of such a development?*
- *What would be the main constraints and how might these be overcome?*
- *What criteria would you use to evaluate the success, or otherwise, of your Dual Stream School(s)?*

Global Learning in Action:

Sister Classes from the International and Local Streams learn together in a Xiehe Dual Stream School

Qing Yao Xu

Why have Sister Classes?

Inter stream sister classes have been established in Xiehe Dual Stream Schools in subjects such as English, the Virtues Project and Thematic Studies. The aims are to:

- promote cross stream dialogue between both students and teachers;
- develop all the students involved as global citizens;
- enhance the students' social skills;
- encourage team work; and
- enhance the students' English language abilities.

Physical education activities were used for ice-breaking

What happened?

- Grade 2 students from a (Hong Qiao) International Stream English National Curriculum class combined with a Grade 2 Local Stream Pioneer Curriculum class.
- Fifty students were team taught by four teachers: two Western and two Chinese.
- There were eight 60 minute lessons, held at fortnightly intervals.
- This was an inquiry-based lesson aimed at creating a robot.
- The students worked together in teams of ten, supported by individual teachers.
- The lessons were planned collaboratively by the Western and Chinese teachers.
- Each lesson was team taught in the English medium.
- The finally created robots were displayed in the school foyer.

Collaborative lesson planning

Students from many different countries learn together

Students are introduced to the topic through a story: 'Wendell's Workshop'

ABOVE: *Preliminary design planning*

RIGHT: *The raw materials are collected*

Excitement mounts as the robots near completion

RIGHT: *A designed robot*

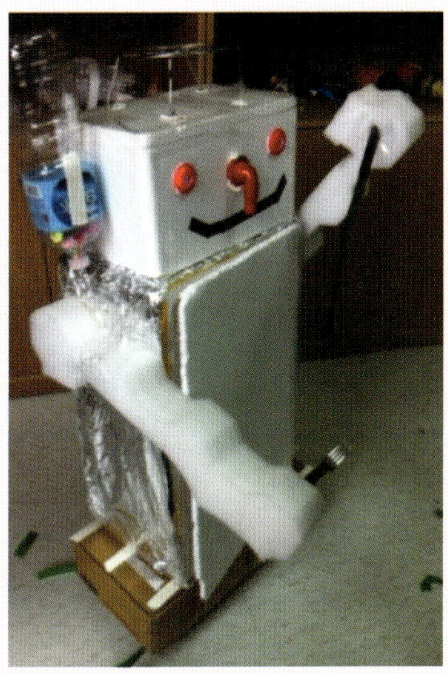

Assessment takes place by means of group presentations

What were the outcomes?

- Students from both streams enjoyed their creative experiences.
- There was very strong parental support on a social media site, after the posting of classroom activities by a participating teacher.
- Student motivational levels were very high.
- Teachers felt that planning was very collegial. Also, that their team teaching skills had been enhanced.
- There was evidence of significant English language enhancement.
- Lasting cross stream student friendships were established.
- Enhanced cultural understanding resulted for both students and staff.
- Some staff queried the choice of the theme, the staff leadership model and the timing.
- It was felt that more controversial lesson topics such as those included in **Chapter 5.2**, relating to values education, might further enhance inter-class student dialogue.
- Sister class activity clearly provides an excellent focus for school self evaluation, both relating to intercultural issues and teamwork/collaboration.

3 What is 'Global Learning'?

Rob Unwin

Before considering the concept of the 'Xiehe Global School' we must first try to define the nature of 'global learning'. This is important because much research on curriculum innovation tells us that change at the classroom level often fails because those involved are unclear about what they are attempting to achieve.

> *'Certainly, global citizenship is not determined merely by the number of languages one speaks, or the number of countries to which one has travelled. I have many friends who could be considered quite ordinary citizens but who possess an inner nobility: who have never travelled beyond their native place, yet who are genuinely concerned for the peace and prosperity of the world. I think I can state with confidence that the following are essential elements of global citizenship: the wisdom to perceive the interconnectedness of all life and living; the courage not to fear or deny difference but to respect and strive to understand people of different cultures and to grow from encounters with them; and the compassion to maintain an imaginative empathy that reaches beyond one's immediate surroundings and extends to those suffering in distant places.'*
>
> Daisaku Ikeda

This chapter seeks to describe briefly the rationale and background to global learning with the example of the recent development of an 'Education for Global Citizenship' framework for the British Council, now used in the Connecting Classrooms international school partnership programme[1]. The potential opportunities for implementing global learning within the National Curricula of England and China are then considered.

This leads to a short exploration of how global learning might relate to the differing philosophies and systems of thought in the East and West and how it could benefit from being reconceived by more explicitly drawing on the best of both traditions.

'The globalisation of trade [and our impact on climate change] converts us [unavoidably] into participating in the lives of people we have never met and are never likely to meet. We are as complicit in their lives as if they sold us their produce over the garden fence. The ties that bind are [...] chains of cause and effect that prompt obligations of justice rather than sympathy, pity or beneficence.'

Andrew Dobson [2]

What is Global Learning?

Few would deny the need to prepare young people everywhere for a complex, globalised, plural, fast-changing world with an uncertain future.

Among the consequences of globalisation that might be embraced are the widening of peoples' horizons, the greater access to knowledge and the products of science and technology, the value of multiculturalism and intercultural views, an increase in personal and social development opportunities and the possibilities of sharing ideas and joint action towards the solution of common problems[2].

The challenges mainly relate to increasing numbers of people in poverty, a growing gap between privileged and excluded people both within and between countries, forced migration, human rights violations, exploitation of vulnerable groups, racism and xenophobia, conflicts, insecurity and growing individualism, climate change, pollution and the loss of biodiversity and the exhaustion of natural resources[7].

Global learning can be conceived as aiming to implement *'the vision required to move to a model of partnership between peoples, cultures and religions at micro and macro levels to tackle the many challenges facing humanity and the natural world.'*[3] It can be seen as *'an active learning process, founded on values of solidarity, equality, inclusion and co-operation. It enables people to move from basic awareness of international development priorities and sustainable human development, through understanding of the causes and effects of global issues to personal involvement and informed actions.'*[4] It is an holistic *'education that opens people's eyes and minds to the realities of the world, and awakens them to bring about a world of greater justice, equity and human rights for all. It is understood to encompass development education, human rights education, education for sustainability, education for peace, conflict prevention and Intercultural Education; being the global dimension of education for citizenship.'*[5]

Education for global citizenship, global and development education and global learning are terms that are increasingly used in school mission statements in England. *'...in the last decade of the twentieth century, and the first of the twenty-first, schools increasingly valued development education approaches as communities became increasingly multicultural and globalisation demonstrated the interconnectedness of people's lives around the world.'*[6]

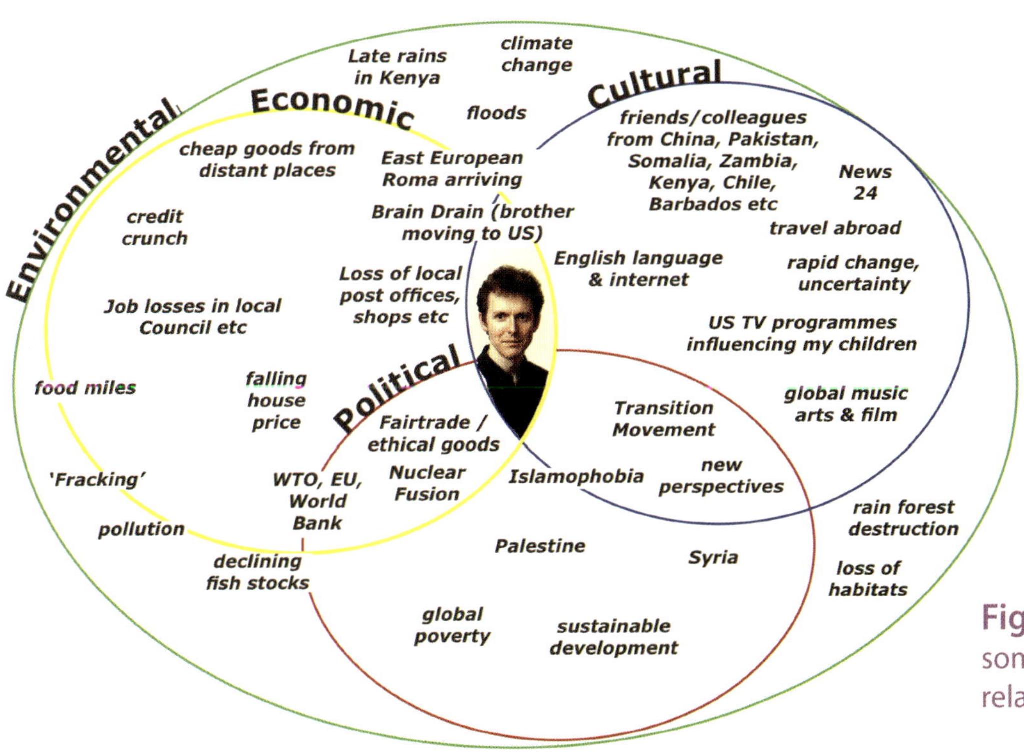

Fig 3.1: Diagram illustrating some faces of globalisation in relation to an individual.

How did Global Learning come about?

'Cosmopolitan [Global] citizenship should not be assumed to be a modern phenomenon; the beginnings can be traced to the Greeks, Confucianism and even Hindu philosophy'.[7]

In the 1960s and 70s global learning (or development education as it was mostly known) *'typically consisted of efforts by the charities to get increased funds for their own projects or, more generally, to influence public opinion to support more foreign aid for the Third World.'*[8] The impression left by such messages may have been that the 'problem is all out there' caused by internal factors, nothing to do with people in the North who can only provide more aid to help. These 'Charity' approaches, often based on 'modernisation' theories of development, were rejected by most development educators by the 1980s because they were seen as inaccurate and as *'reinforcing a harmful stereotype in which the Third World is presented as backward and hopeless.'*[7]

They were largely replaced by 'Interdependence' approaches influenced by the Brandt Report that emphasised a North-South[9] co-operation towards development, ranging from, for example, the poverty reduction strategies of the European Commission and Irish Aid, through to messages of development NGOs in areas like the effects of Northern trade policy on the Global South. They are based on the human development paradigm where development is seen as 'expanding human freedoms'[10] and focuses on building people's capabilities through social provision in areas such as education and health. These approaches, still influential, often recognise the need to challenge inaccurate stereotypes and prejudices held by the North about the South. However the approaches have been criticised for sometimes obscuring *'the exploitation inherent in the present system'*[7] as well as the conflict in interests between rich and poor.

A third strand of development education, influenced by Freire, liberation theologians and postcolonial theory, and increasingly popular since the 1980s, has been the 'Empowerment' approach. This views the poor as 'protagonists rather than partners', emphasises North-South solidarity, but has been seen by some as being overly politicised.[7]

Teachers trying out Global Learning activities in Chongqing.

What teaching and learning methods are used?

Different pedagogies are employed by each global learning approach, ranging from information giving (often more associated with the 'Charity' approach) to experiential learning, critical skills development and organisational skills or 'mobilisation' for campaigning (the latter is often more associated with 'Empowerment' approaches).

A more recent pedagogy 'dialogical learning' aims to encourage those from the North to challenge their own perceptions and cultural baggage before being able to communicate on a more equal footing with people from the South. This ties in closely with the 'Empowerment' approach, but because it does not treat the views of oppressed groups of people from the South uncritically, is perhaps less open to the accusation of being politicised.

An example of a dialogic learning approach is Philosophy for Children (or P4C). This is covered in more depth in **Chapter 5.3** but will be briefly introduced here.

P4C[11] draws on the theoretical work of John Dewey about the need for democracy in education and to bring morals into *'the average affairs of everyday life'.*

He argues that children in school should be involved in 'active construction' rather than 'absorption' of knowledge and be given opportunities to gain the power of judgment through the exercise in 'forming and testing judgment'.

P4C is designed to allow *'children to learn to ask questions of a variety of stimuli, each other and the teacher; to give reasons for their opinions; examine their own values and tease out their own and other's assumptions about an issue... Alongside this critical engagement, P4C encourages an openness to other people's ideas and perspectives.'* [12]

Another reason why the process can be appropriate for sensitive topics is that it gives children a high degree of control so that they do not feel the views of others are being imposed upon them. It can be used with any age or ability group.

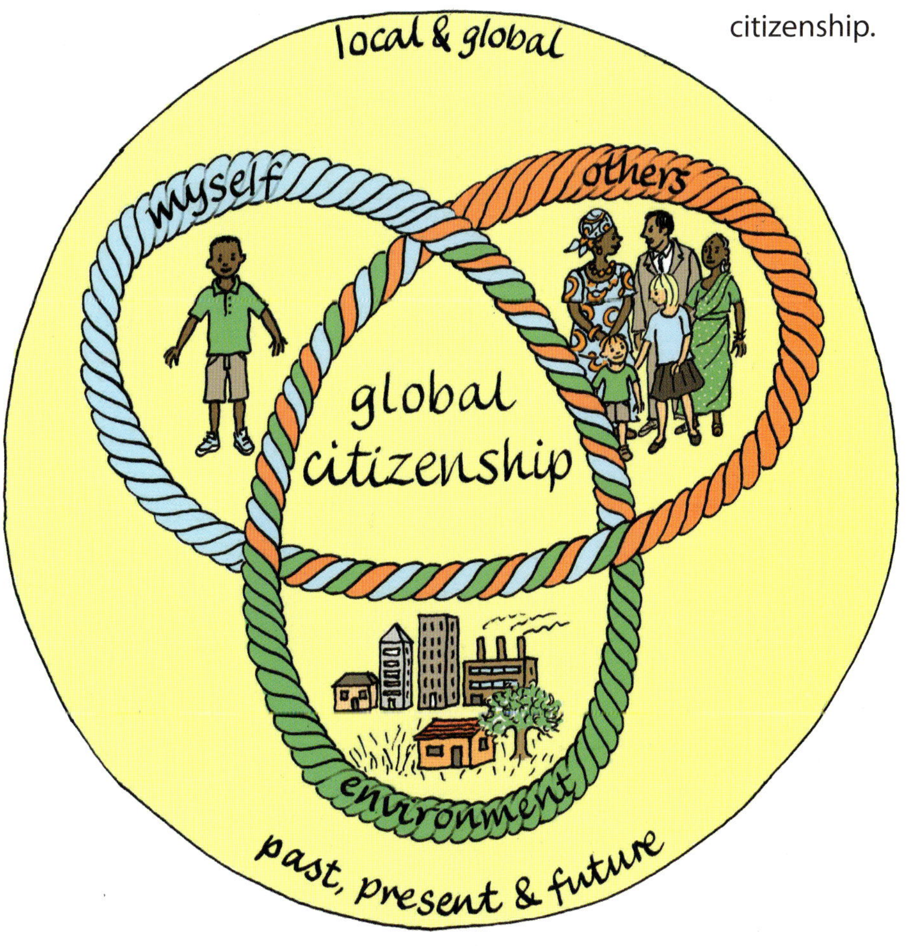

Fig 3.2: Diagram illustrating the concept of global citizenship as part of the new British Council framework.

An example of a Global Learning framework?

In May 2012 a new offer to schools was announced by the British Council in the United Kingdom. This included a revised Connecting Classrooms programme with funding in place for reciprocal visits. *'Connecting Classrooms is designed to help young people learn about international themes and become responsible global citizens. It facilitates partnerships between schools in the UK and other countries, providing educational benefits for young people around the world. Having a good grasp of global issues and of development is an important part of young people's education and supports them in becoming good global citizens for the future.'* [13]

This required the development of new online[1] and offline learning materials for teachers backed up by a new framework for global learning (known as education for global citizenship). To prepare for this, I worked with other writers and students of Cameroonian, Chinese Buddhist, Korean, Pakistani, Kazakh and Brazilian heritage to conceptualise global citizenship.

After rejecting an initial idea of placing the individual in the centre with concentric circles outside it, the discussions, backed up by, for example, the African concept of 'ubuntu' and the Buddhist idea of 'oneness', concluded that at the heart of global citizenship is the notion of interdependence between all peoples. Extending this to include the environment was seen to echo a strong current in indigenous spirituality, for example in the beliefs of the Kogi of Northern Colombia who presented their message to the Rio + 20 summit.[14]

We wanted to present a framework to colleagues worldwide that illustrated this idea in an accessible way. After much deliberation and many versions the illustrator, Teresa Robertson, produced the diagram shown in **Fig 3.2** (left).

The idea of 'interdependence' includes connections which are:

- about ourselves, others and the environment;
- immediate and locally relevant;
- global and also locally relevant;
- rooted in the past;
- present in our lives today;
- going to affect our lives in the future.

Fig 3.3: Diagram extended to include the global learning themes.

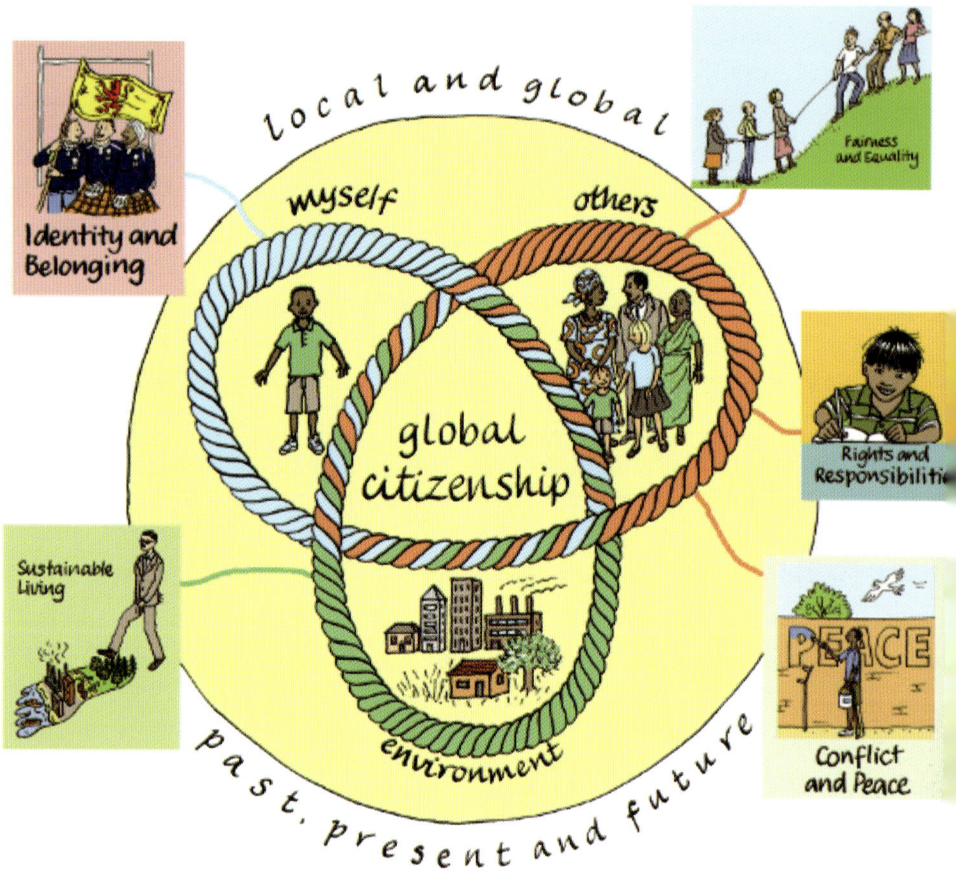

To develop the learning outcomes for the framework, we began with the existing global issues (themes), skills and outlooks cards from the British Council Global Education in Partnership materials which had been greatly influenced by Oxfam's 'Curriculum for Global Citizenship' framework.[15]

These were cut up and placed on sheets of flipchart paper. We then added outcomes from 'Auditing Citizenship'[16], which sought to provide a summary of education for global citizenship learning outcomes from a range of sources.

In selecting which skills to include we reflected on where the boundary lay between what constitutes a 'global skill' and what might be considered a 'key skill' or a 'higher order skill'. We found helpful guidance from Bourn who defined Global skills as those which *'...recognise the importance of globalisation, ... the relationship between the social and the environmental, and the recognition of cultural sensitivities.'*[17]

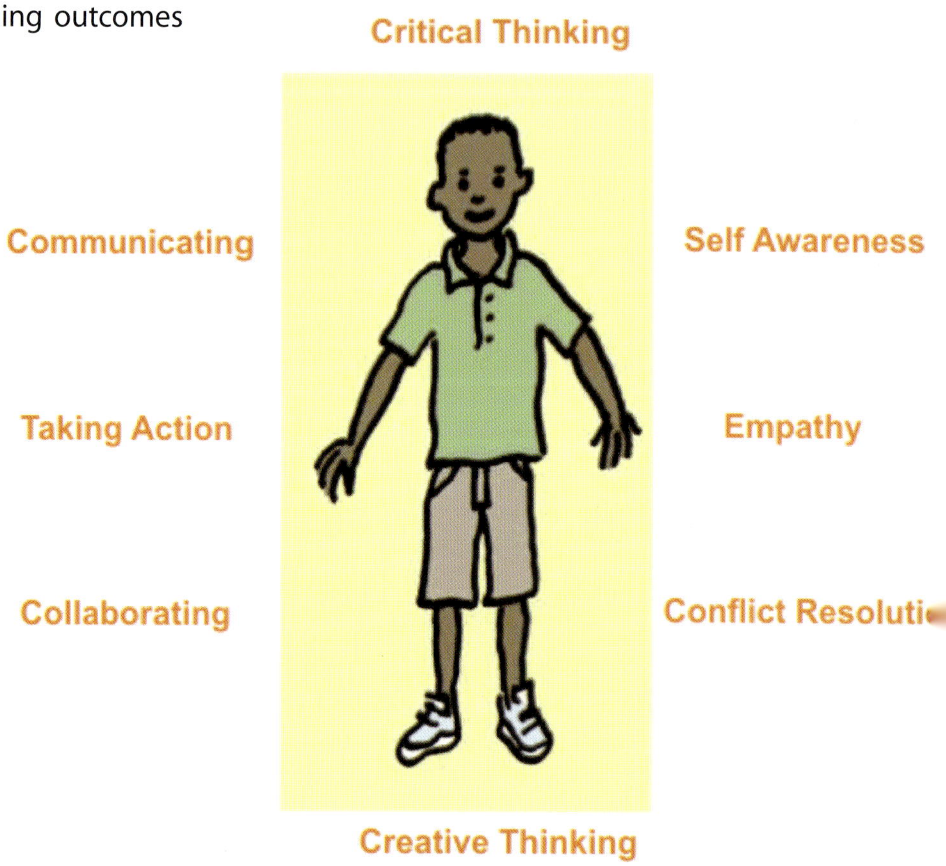

Fig 3.4: Diagram illustrating the categories of global skill in the framework.

It was a necessary but difficult challenge to halve the number of learning outcomes (from 156 to 78) to allow them to be incorporated into the final illustrated card format. The largest reduction took place in the global outlooks (values) which were reduced to just their titles (see **Fig 3.5** right), to keep the task of monitoring the learning outcomes more manageable.

We have advocated the development of global learning skills through classroom pedagogies that are active, inclusive and experiential. The free online course describes ten techniques that can be used to practise the skills in the classroom, including drama, critical use of images, ranking exercises, cooperative games and P4C. There are also individual reflection-based online activities for teachers with an opportunity to view the responses of other participants around the world.

Implementing Global Learning in the National Curriculum in England

The main approach towards building global learning in the school curriculum in England is summarised in the government guidance document 'Developing the Global Dimension in the School Curriculum' first issued in 2000 and in revised form in 2005.[18] The document lists eight key concepts: diversity, interdependence, citizenship, sustainable development, values and perspectives, social justice, conflict resolution and human rights. It aims to explore interconnections between the local and the global. The Secondary Curriculum from 2008 saw 'Global Dimension and Sustainable Development' as one of seven 'cross-curriculum dimensions' informing the whole taught curriculum and school life.

Whilst the National Curriculum for England has now been revised under a new administration, there remain opportunities for global learning through all subjects especially geography, history, citizenship and the creative arts as well outside the National Curriculum.

A new national 'Global Learning Programme' (GLP) aims to *'create a national network of like-minded schools, committed to equipping their students to succeed in a globalised world by helping them to deliver effective teaching and learning about international*

Fig 3.5: Diagram illustrating the global learning (citizenship) outlooks in the framework.

development and global issues.'[19] This idea is supported by 93 per cent of businesses who think that it is important for schools to help young people develop the ability to think globally and 80 per cent who believe that schools should do more.[20]

In terms of its effectiveness, a recent study of global learning in primary schools found that the large majority of the 217 schools responding thought that global learning had a positive impact in their school. Benefits to schools included enhanced community cohesion, school ethos and student voice. Involvement in global learning was thought to increase some students' attainment levels including knowledge and skill development. It also enhanced students' awareness and interactions with diversity tending to support mutual respect and responsibility towards others.[21]

Despite, however, the encouraging growth and interest in global learning the new draft National Curriculum orders for citizenship offer fewer opportunities for the development of global citizenship and its attendant skills. *'The current proposals ... largely strip out the active dimension of citizenship. What is left is a minimal model of citizenship in which the emphasis is on individual independence and volunteering.'* [22] Such an approach is thought to promote a *'narrow, individualistic and de-politicised model of the citizen'* [21] with little recognition of the importance of the local and global community and the value of thinking holistically and acting collectively.

Global Learning opportunities in the Chinese National Curriculum

The current Chinese National Curriculum is the result of the eighth round of curriculum reform which took place at the turn of the millennium and follows a trend dating back to 1985 which mirrors wider social and political changes in China.

Deng Xiaoping advocated the principle that *'education should be oriented to modernisation, to the outside world, and to the future'* and that it should *'enable the educatees to learn in active and lively ways and develop morally, intellectually and physically in an all-round way and to turn out a new generation who have high ideals, whose moral virtues are cultured/ educated and disciplined.'* [23]

Involved as I have been in a movement to lobby successfully for the inclusion of elements of world history in the revised National Curriculum for England, I find it encouraging to discover a strong emphasis on world history (alongside that of China) already present in the Chinese National Curriculum. The History Standards advocate *'Understanding of the diversity of the historical development of human society, understanding and respect for the world, all regions and all ethnic groups and cultural traditions.'* [24]

In history and social studies, students are required to gain an understanding of *'Today's population, resources and environmental issues, an active interest in the sustainable development of society'* and an understanding of globalisation and human rights. With regard to international development, it relates current global inequalities to the Western countries' colonial conquest of countries and regions in Asia, Africa and Latin America. There is also an emphasis on the value of 'inquiry-based learning' and *'making learning a positive, happy, successful experience'.*

These examples of content and intended pedagogy accord well with the concept of education for global citizenship developed by the British Council and other frameworks for global learning.

However a number of writers point out problems with both the content and the reality of the pedagogy in schools. The Deyu (moral, political and ideological education) curriculum, for example, *'extols harmony as a political aim for building a harmonious society. While students do give some weight to such traditional moral values as respect for parents, honesty, trustworthiness, personal loyalty, patriotism, justice, fairness and responsibility, they are less likely to identify with thrift, incorruptibility, public affairs, tolerance, collaboration, devotion to one's work and self- discipline.'* [25] This is seen to reflect the wider changes in social and economic policy and the pursuit of Western values by many young people.

In Beijing, new curriculum reform to introduce more discussion-based learning for citizenship has been frustrated by the *'deep-seated belief of teachers that controversial or sensitive issues, such as rights, should be kept out of the classroom.... Discussion, group work and role play strategies for learning are viewed as having a Western basis which does not fit with what people feel in their hearts.'* [26] This coincides with a more general challenge of promoting greater student autonomy and creativity in an educational culture where didactic approaches and exams tend to predominate. However my anecdotal experiences with both Xiehe and government schools indicate a strong interest in P4C amongst Chinese teachers.

How does Global Learning relate to Chinese philosophies?

There seems to be a clear interest in both England and China for embracing many of the outlooks, concepts and skills of global learning but how does it relate to underlying societal values?

Global learning in the West shares affinities especially with 'moral cosmopolitanism' and 'liberal multiculturalism', while other aspects of global citizenship education relate to elements of environmentalism and neo-liberalism, 'the dominant economic ideology in the current phase of globalization. These ideological constellations are commonly situated under the wide umbrella of liberalism, with its fundamental emphasis upon individual rights and liberties. Established ideologies such as liberalism are adapting in response to increasing public recognition of global interdependence.'[27] Can an approach that includes a Western focus on individual rights sit comfortably in the East?

Equating Confucian and Global Learning values.

In November 2012, I was fortunate enough to be invited to deliver P4C training with the Xiehe Kindergarten teachers in Shanghai and to run a British Council course for 60 teachers from six different cities across China in Chongqing. The course explored the new framework and in one exercise I asked participants to try and equate global learning and Confucian values. This stimulated broad consensus on four or five areas as highlighted in bold in the table in **Fig 3.6** which summarises the responses from eight different Chongqing course groups and from one Xiehe group who also tried out the activity.

It also provoked some interesting discussions around the areas of disagreement. The level of consensus was perhaps surprising given the potential for different understandings of particular words in two languages and from different traditions.

The links are likely to be approximations (for example 'Tiānmìng' is usually associated with the legitimacy of the power of a just emperor, though also with the right of people to 'make a difference' and overthrow an incompetent or despotic ruler). There are also important Confucian values that are not included, such as filial piety, but it may be significant to note that almost every global learning outlook is addressed.

Interestingly whilst Western education may be highly regarded by many Chinese students, British Education Ministers are busy trying to learn from Confucian values. In 2009 the UK Schools Minister Jim Knight noted that *'Confucius said that alongside knowledge you should have time to think. It is not just about acquisition of knowledge but about respect for the importance of education and the family and that is something I would love to see engendered in our culture as well as it is in China.'*[28] More recently the UK Secretary of State for Education, Michael Gove has expressed support for the Confucius Institute promoting Chinese language and culture across the world.[29] However it has been argued that the Confucian revival has only arisen recently, with support of the government, as the disruption to Chinese traditional culture in the Great Proletarian Cultural Revolution, and the reduction in the prominence of Marxism since, has led to an ideological vacuum.[30]

It is worthwhile also to consider how other significant philosophies might relate to conceptions of global citizenship and global learning. Certainly the global learning themes of fairness, equality and rights

Fig 3.6: Table showing the results of eight groups of Chinese teachers relating Confucian and Global Learning Values to each other (the numbers correspond to the numbers of paired cards)

Confucian Values	Global Learning Values: Positive sense of identity	Open to new ideas	Sense of Interdependence	Desire to make a difference	Rights and responsibilities	Peace	Justice	Sustainability
Tiānmìng (天命) *Mandate of Heaven*			1	**7**	1			1
rén (仁) *Humaneness & reciprocity*			2		**4**	**6**	1	
Lǐ (礼) *Propriety or Etiquette*	2		2		2	3	1	
Yì (义) *Righteousness*			1		2	1	**9**	
Xìn (信) *Integrity*	**5**	1	1		2	1	1	
Zhì (智) *Knowledge*	1	**7**		1				
Jiǎn (儉) *Frugal*								**9**

(particularly social and economic rights) may have been influenced by socialist and Marxist thinking; currents of thought and policy that have had influence in both the West and East. Taoism/Daoism, particular to the East, has been described as proposing that *'the best way to live is by modelling the forces of nature and living in harmony with it.'* [31] The Taoist principles of holism, non-individualism, mercy, frugality and 'going with the flow' accord well with the global learning value of a commitment to sustainability as well as the sense of interdependence.

As mentioned earlier in this chapter, aspects of Buddhist thought, particularly on interdependence, were brought to bear on how the British Council's framework on Education for Global Citizenship was conceived. Chan[32] tells us that in Buddhism, the world is *'as a massive flow of events that are linked together and participate in one another,'* an idea which he argues is backed up by recent discoveries in quantum physics. He sees both Taoism and Buddhism as emphasizing the idea of 'non-self', in contrast to the notion of the Western individualistic 'Cartesian-self' that seeks to strive for extraordinariness. Where Buddhism departs from Taoism is in the belief by the former in a 'real world' beyond the world of sensory perceptions. The sensory, or 'phenomenal world', and one's sense of self within it, is regarded as being socially constructed, full of different perspectives, meanings and languages conditioned by interactions with different people and environments. Such ideas are consistent with global citizenship skills such as critical thinking and self-awareness.

For Buddhists, the real world *'can only be understood through experience (for example through meditative practice) and a thorough understanding of important concepts like interdependence, impermanence/change and no-self.'*[32] The themes of self-transcendence and human connectedness run through the thinking of Lu Jie, the influential Chinese Professor of Moral Education who has led a team writing new text books. Lu criticizes utilitarian education to fit society as it is now and instead advocates a more authentic and meaningful education for a better future. She recognises the need for education to prepare students for globalisation, to give them an understanding of themselves in relation to world history and to promote an awareness of sustainable development. In terms of pedagogy, Lu is in favour of the curriculum relating closely to student's lives and allowing them to be freer to express themselves and to learn through dialogue.[33]

Such aspirations closely mirror those for global learning and point towards the need for real dialogue and the sharing of values and effective approaches and pedagogies in this area to continue between the East and West. Nisbett argues that the more holistic, relational systems of thought in the East and the more object-based thinking in the West could usefully blend to the benefit of each. In blending they may be themselves transformed but hopefully in a way that maintains for learners the best aspects of each tradition.[34] This would support the facing of the joint challenges of how to balance global learning *'with national developments and with the realities of life in modern society as experienced by young people'* [24] and in parallel with this, how to ensure that schools 'embody the very conception of social justice (and community) they are seeking young people to commit themselves to.' [23]

Fig 3.7: This table provides a summary of how understanding of global learning can be developed within the management model of the Xiehe Dual Stream School, as described in **Chapter 2**.

Global Learning Concepts	Developing the concepts within the Xiehe Dual Stream Global School
Interdependence: understanding how people, places, economies and environments are all inextricably inter-related and that choices and events have repercussions on a global scale. • Understanding the impact of globalisation. • Appreciating the links between the lives of others and children's and young people's own lives. • Understanding how the world is a global community and what it means to be a citizen.	• Experiential studies in the PYP and English National Curriculum of the students' own experiences in this respect. • Studies in the PYP of migrant schools in Shanghai, including school visits. • Studies of the United Nations, for example within local stream moral education.
Social change: change is a constant feature of our global society. • In every country individuals, groups and governments need to find ways of effecting change most successfully. • On occasions change is an inter-country phenomenon which needs to be tackled by global organisations.	• Studies, in both streams, of the recent very significant social and economic changes in China and how Local and National Governments are attempting to plan in consequence. • As above, studies of the United Nations.

Global Learning Concepts	Developing the concepts within the Xiehe Dual Stream Global School
Values and perceptions: developing a critical evaluation of representations of global issues and an appreciation of the effect these have on people's attitudes and values. • Understanding that people have different values, attitudes and perceptions. • Respecting each other. • Understanding that the values people hold shape their actions.	• A strong emphasis on both 'explicit' and 'implicit' values education. (See **Chapter 5.2**) • Students of different nationalities meeting both within and across streams.
Inequality in Income: both within and between countries there are very great differences in the personal incomes of individuals. • A very significant group of the total global population is extremely poor which subjects them to malnutrition and consequent disease. • In both economically developing and economically developed countries attempts are being made to offer greater support to people on low incomes. • Globally, such issues are being addressed by the United Nations and its agencies. Global NGOs also play a key role in this respect.	• For example, the International Geography Project 'Teaching Geography as if People and the Planet Matter'. Studies of inequality in China and worldwide and the role of migration in this context. (See **Chapter 7.1**). • Involvement in 'International Women's' Day. • Studies in both streams on the possibilities of taking informed action in response to inequality.
Co-operation: individuals, groups and countries often work together in order to tackle common problems. • Co-operation enables tasks to be performed which would not otherwise be possible. This is essential if conflicts are to be resolved. • Co-operation can be as stimulating and rewarding as many forms of competition, requiring as it does a high level of communication and sensitivity to others.	• Inter stream co-operation between staff and students. • Strong emphasis on the process of co-operative learning within the Pioneer Curriculum. (See **Chapter 5.5**) • Case studies of co-operation in PYP enquiry work. • Co-operation in inter-stream activities such as assemblies.
Global citizenship: gaining the knowledge, skills and understanding of concepts and institutions necessary to become informed, active and responsible citizens. • Learning about institutions, declarations and conventions and the role of groups, NGOs and governments in global issues. • Developing understanding of how and where key decisions are made.	• Studies in the local stream moral education programme. • International stream PYP studies.

Global Learning Concepts	Developing the concepts within the Xiehe Dual Stream Global School
Sustainable development: understanding the need to maintain and improve the quality of life now without damaging the planet for future generations.	
• Recognising that some of the earth's resources are finite and therefore must be used responsibly by us.	• Many studies in the Chinese and English National Curriculum, the PYP and Pioneer Curriculum.
• Understanding the interconnections between the social, economic and environmental spheres.	• Studies as part of English and Chinese language thematic work.
• Considering probable and preferable futures and how to achieve the latter.	• Studies of the Xiehe Global Schools' 'green' policies.

Conclusion

This chapter has attempted to define the aspirations of global learning and its potential for implementation in both the Chinese and English National Curricula.

The remainder of this book describes how global learning has been developed within Xiehe Dual Stream Schools: with respect to curriculum content and its development, school management, and school self evaluation.

Talkabout

- *How are you affected by globalisation? Sketch out a rough diagram based on the model in **Figure 3.1**.*
- *What do you think the major global issues are today?*
- *What sort of values, skills and understanding do you think the next generation should have to equip them to be effective and responsible global citizens in a world that faces the issues you listed above.*
- *How do your ideas compare to those in **Figures 3.3 - 3.5**?*

Rob Unwin is a National Leader in the Global Learning Programme for England and an Education Advisor and Coordinator at the Development Education Centre in South Yorkshire.

He is grateful to Chen Qiu for his advice and contributions towards this chapter and to illustrator Teresa Robertson (www.teresa-robertson.co.uk) and the British Council for kind permission to use the illustrations in **Figures 3.2 - 3.5**.

Acknowledgements

[1] British Council (2012). *Schools Online, Connecting Classrooms.* Available at https://schoolsonline.britishcouncil.org/connectingclassrooms-learning/

[2] Dobson, A. (2006). *'Thick Cosmopolitanism',* Political Studies, Vol.54, pp.165-184.

[3] Carvalho da Silva, M. (2010). *Global Education Guidelines.* Lisbon: North-South Centre. Available at http://www.coe.int/t/dg4/nscentre/GEguideline_presentation_en.asp [accessed 19 August 2013]

[4] DEEEP (2004). Online. Available at http://www.deeep.org/dear-definitions.html [accessed 19 August 2013]

[5] O'Loughlin, E. and Wegimont, L. (2002). *'Maastricht Global Education Declaration'* in *Global Education in Europe to 2015.* Lisbon: North-South Centre.

[6] Bourn, D. and Hunt, F. (2011). *'Global Dimension in Secondary Schools',* DERC Research Paper No. 1. London: Institute of Education.

[7] Parmentar, L. (2005). *'Linking national education and cosmopolitan citizenship beyond the school gates'.* Keynote speech, International Symposium on National Education, Hong Kong.

[8] Arnold, S. (1988). *'Constrained Crusaders- NGOs and development education in the UK',* Occasional Paper. London: Institute of Education.

[9] The terms 'Southern/South' and 'Northern/North' are used to denote countries of the historic 'Global South' - most of Asia, Africa and Latin America/Caribbean and the 'North' (or 'West') - broadly the OECD countries.

[10] Sen, A. (1999). *'The Ends and the Means of Development'* in *Development as Freedom.* Oxford: Oxford University.

[11] Lipman, M. (2003). *Thinking in Education.* Cambridge: Cambridge University Press.

[12] Griffin, H. (2009). Personal communication.

[13] British Council Connecting Classrooms team, www.britishcouncil.org/connectingclassrooms-pd.

[14] Zammit, J. and Unwin, R. (2012). TEESNET Conference Presentation. London: LSBU Available at http://teesnet.ning.com/page/resources [accessed 19 August 2013]

[15] Oxfam. (1997). *A Curriculum for Global Citizenship.* Oxford: Oxfam

[16] Unwin, R. and Harding, S. (2002). Auditing Citizenship. Sheffield: DECSY

[17] Bourn, D. (2008). *Global Skills.* London: Learning and Skills Improvement Service.

[18] Department for Education and Skills. (2005a). *Curriculum and Standards Guidance: Developing a global dimension in the school curriculum.* London: Department for Education and Skills.

[19] Global Learning Programme website. Available at http://globaldimension.org.uk/glp [accessed 19 August 2013]

[20] Think Global. (2011). *The Global Skills Gap.* Available at http://www.think-global.org.uk/news/item/?n=14183 [accessed 19 August 2013]

[21] Hunt, F. (2012). *'Global Learning in Primary Schools in England: Practices and Impacts',* DERC Research Paper No. 9, London: Institute of Education.

[22] Jerome, L. and Bhargava, M. (2013). *'Citizenship (3rd edition): Ideology and Citizenship in the National Curriculum for England'* in Inman, S. and Rogers, M. (Eds), TEESNet 2013 Conference Papers. London: LSBU

[23] Zhou, N. and Zhu, M. (2007). *'Educational Reform and Curriculum Change in China'* in International Bureau for Education. Available at http://www.ibe.unesco.org/fileadmin/user_upload/COPs/Pages_documents/Comparative_Research/EduReformChina.pdf [accessed 19 August 2013]

[24] Chinese Ministry of Education. (2003). National Curriculum Standards for History, Being Lab. Available at http://www.being.org.cn/ncs/his/his02.htm [accessed 19 August 2013]

[25] Zhang, J., Li, P., Zhing, M., and Lin, B. (2007). and Yang, S., and Wan, Z. (2007). quoted in Clark, J. (2008) *'Social Justice and Moral Education in China',* New Zealand Journal of Teachers' Work, Vol.5, Issue.1, pp.44-53. Available at http://www.teacherswork.ac.nz/journal/volume5_issue1/clark.pdf [accessed 19 August 2013]

[26] Kan, W. (2010). *Citizenship Education in China and the UK: Key features and contemporary challenges.* London: Institute of Education. Available at http://www.ioe.ac.uk/about/documents/About_Overview/Kan_W.pdf [accessed 19 August 2013]

[27] Schattle, H. (2008). *'Education for global citizenship: illustrations of ideological pluralism and adaptation',* Journal of Political Ideologies Vol.13:1, pp.73-94.

[28] Knapton (2009). *'Chinese culture to revive English education, says minister',* The Telegraph 22/02/2009.

[29] Hanban (2010). Available at http://english.hanban.org/article/2010-11/11/content_190750.htm [accessed 19

August 2013].
30 Lam, J. (2008). *China's Revival of Confucianism*. US-China Institute. Available at http://china.usc.edu [accessed 19 August 2013]
31 Sellman, J. (2010). *The Encyclopedia of Sustainability, Vol.1.* Massachusetts: Berkshire Publishing Group LLC.
32 Chan, H. K. (2012). *Engaging Buddhist Issues from a Global Perspective, (MA Thesis).* Oulu: University of Oulu. Available at http://oulu.academia.edu/huangkiatchan [accessed 19 August 2013].
33 Jianjun, F. (2004). *Chaoyue yu chuangxin* by Lu Jie. Book Review in Journal of Moral Education, Vol. 33, No. 4.
34 Nisbett, R. (2003). *The Geography of Thought.* London: Nicholas Brealey.

Students who will shape the future. Global learning is a key part of preparing them for this...

4. Combining Chinese and Western approaches in five curricula areas

In Chapter 2 the benefits of Chinese and Western teachers collaborating to develop the best practice in teaching and learning were highlighted. This chapter describes how this has happened in Xiehe with respect to five curriculum areas.

4.1 Chinese

Zhang Hong and Clara Li

In this section, the authors describe how the quality of Chinese teaching and learning within SUIS (Hong Qiao) has been significantly enhanced by inter-stream professional collaboration between teachers of Chinese. There is also very successful co-operation between students, across the two streams, in their Chinese language learning.

> *'There are twice as many people in the world who speak Chinese as their first or second language as English, with the great majority of them living in China.'*
>
> Martin Jacques

In the SUIS (Hong Qiao) Local Stream Chinese teaching and learning follows the Chinese National Curriculum, based on guidance from the Shanghai Municipal Government's Stage Two Curriculum Reform relating to the teaching of this language.

On the premise of consolidating basic language knowledge, the Local Stream has been implementing approaches focused on enhancing the students' listening, speaking, reading and writing in respect to Chinese. There is considerable emphasis on pre-set learning objectives. The students involved are almost all Chinese native speakers.

The Chinese programme at SUIS

The Chinese curriculum at SUIS (Hong Qiao)is divided into two sections: Chinese as a First Language (CFL) and Chinese as an Additional Language (CAL). Students are placed in different classes according to their language background, their particular needs and baseline test results. This ensures these individual needs are met.

Chinese as a First Language (CFL)

Students in this programme are those who have good Chinese language backgrounds. For primary and above, the students have usually already started to learn Chinese written language at other schools.

This curriculum meets the same level standards as those in China as a whole. We have different levels (CFL1-CFL5) for students from different grades.

Chinese as an Additional Language (CAL)

Students in this programme are those who have limited Chinese language backgrounds. Many of them have not studied any Chinese before they came to SUIS.

This is a five-year developmental course in listening, speaking, reading and writing. The course also provides a foundation for many international standardised examinations such as IGCSE and IB.

The general aims of the Chinese Programme at SUIS (Hong Qiao) are:

- To cultivate students' interest in learning Chinese.
- To develop students' ability in listening, speaking, reading and writing and to enable students to communicate accurately, appropriately and effectively.
- To teach students methods of learning and self-learning in the Chinese curriculum.
- To enhance students' ability in thinking, imaginative and creative skills and to complement the students' other areas of study.
- To enable students to learn the essence of Eastern culture and to have a better understanding of Chinese culture.

The number of characters students will learn from Grade 1 to Grade 5 for both the CAL and CFL programme's is shown in the tables below.

Chinese as an Additional Language (CAL)

Grade	to read	to write	to speak
CAL-1	130	60	400
CAL-2	200	100	600
CAL-3	250	150	800
CAL-4	250	150	1000
CAL-5	250	150	1000
Total	1080	610	4000

Chinese as a First Language (CFL)*

Grade	to read	to write
G 1-2	1600 - 1800	800 - 1000
G 3-4	2500	2000
G 5	3000	2500

* *The CFL numbers are accumulated; that means by the end of Grade 5, students need to be able to read about 3,000 characters, 2,500 of which they are required to write.*

In the school's International Stream, the Chinese teaching and learning is based on the approaches of international curricula, mainly the International Baccalaureate's Primary Years Programme (PYP). Here there is more emphasis on problem solving and different ways of learning relating to the students' individual abilities. Most of the students are foreigners but there are some native speakers who, eventually, will go abroad for further study.

Although Chinese teaching and learning has its own characteristics within each Stream, it is felt that great benefits result from co-operation between teachers and between students with respect to the acquisition of the language. These co-operative approaches are summarised in this chapter.

Staff (seated on left) involved in cross-stream lesson observation of Chinese language teaching.

Lesson observation and evaluation

There is rigorous cross-stream lesson observation and evaluation involving Chinese language teachers from both streams, using the type of proforma included on pages 228-229 in **Chapter 10**, which follows. It is felt that this is a key strategy for enabling colleagues to share their Chinese teaching and learning approaches.

In the Local Stream the Chinese lessons are shorter (35 minutes) and class sizes are larger. However, the International Stream teachers note that participation and concentration levels are, generally, extremely high. This results from very efficient teaching methods and good classroom behaviour. International Stream colleagues are usually impressed with the initiative shown by the Local Stream students.

When the Local Stream teachers observe the International Stream students they need to take account of the fact that many of the children are studying Chinese as an additional language. However, some of the very different teaching and learning strategies observed here are often adopted subsequently with Local Stream students.

A key issue considered by all teachers in the follow up to the inter-stream lesson observations is how differentiation in the teaching and learning can be most effectively undertaken.

Overall, there is an excellent professional spirit within the feedback sessions with many questions being raised and suggestions for improvement offered.

Teacher exchange

Teacher exchanges between the Chinese Departments across the two streams have taken place over the last five years. Colleagues from the Local Stream have taught Chinese as a Foreign Language in the International Stream in Grade 1, 3, 5 and 6 classes. This has been particularly helpful because many of the international CFL teachers' previous experience has been with adults. The Local Stream teachers bring with them new teaching ideas from the Shanghai Municipal Government's Stage Two Chinese Curriculum Reform Programme. Such ideas have also proved to be applicable to the Chinese teaching and learning in the International Stream. Additionally, the classroom management strategies used by the Local Stream teachers have greatly

Report on a lesson evaluated by an External Consultant and a SUIS (Hong Qiao) Senior Manager

Lesson 5, Grade 4, International Stream, Chinese as an additional language, IB PYP.

Number of students: 17

- There is an excellent pre-lesson planning document (a model of good practice).
- Extremely positive learning environment here: learner profile, Chinese additional language maths displays; 'How economics affects our everyday lives?'
- Some key questions are posed: 'Why do animals like to live in the forest?' 'What is the function of the forest?'
- Excellent brainstorming section (an extension would be to read about sustainability).
- Outstanding use of inquiry thematic work to promote Chinese language learning. Functions of the forest summarised.
- Outstanding paired work with pre-arranged partners. A girl with Attention Deficit Hyperactive Disorder (ADHD) is the only student slightly off the pace but she does well, overall, given her learning difficulty.
- Excellent use of PowerPoint. All language skills integrated. Reading (silently) in pairs, including evaluation by peers. Some useful/supportive praise. Pace extremely fast because of entirely appropriate change of tasks. Very much a 'Chinese classroom' within the International Stream. Water cycle explained carefully: very good global education (sustainable development concepts).
- Outstanding balance of pressure/support for students from the teacher. Affective dimension developed well from the reading text. Students applaud their peers after reading. Then IB reflection is incorporated very helpfully (personal review of lesson outcomes: Were we thinking? Did we take risks? etc.) Reflection on lesson content could have been more thorough.
- There has been excellence and enjoyment in education, combining the very best of Chinese and Western teaching and learning pedagogy.

Students' responses to one of the evaluators were as follows.

- *'I enjoyed the lesson greatly'*
- *'This is teaching us to save the planet'*
- *'Very interesting'*

The language content of the lesson has been excellent also.

Teachers from the International and Local Streams exchange their experiences.

influenced their International Stream colleagues, for example: the use of a wide range of instructions to improve the classroom behaviour of the lower grade students; instructing students to read aloud; emphasizing the importance of pre-review of learning targets; promoting the reading skills of the upper grade students.

Similarly the Local Stream exchange teachers gain enormously from working in the International Stream. Many of them have stated, for example, that they have learnt a great deal about the ways in which the International Stream teachers focus more strongly on developing the students' abilities to question, collaborate, create and reflect, instead of concentrating exclusively on knowledge acquisition.

Reflections on teacher exchange

The Head of the Chinese Teaching and Learning Department in the SUIS (Hong Qiao) Local Stream reflects on the impact of her work as an exchange teacher in both the International and Local Streams

- I find that the Chinese traditional teaching and the 'freer' Western methods both have advantages.
- I try to capture these advantages in my own teaching and to encourage my peers in both the local and International Stream departments to do so as well.
- I have noticed that the International Stream teachers pay more attention to linking the language acquisition process to real life situations and to fostering student creativity.
- The Local Stream teachers are particularly effective in creating a positive 'behavioural' classroom climate for the learning to prosper.
- In my International Stream teaching I have introduced more group competitive approaches. If one group listens carefully and actively raise their hands to answer questions and show good discipline and concentration levels they receive a 'praise band' with a 'big thumb'. By using such strategies, I hope that the students develop good behavioural habits.
- I also instruct the International Stream students in the training commands I use in my own Local Stream classes, such as 'Eyes on the whiteboard, ears listen to me carefully'; 'One, two, three, sit up straight'.
- In terms of teaching content, I find that the International Stream students respond well to such traditional methods as word repetition, reviewing and the use of a variety of questions to practise what they have learnt. Such strategies help to consolidate the students' learning.
- The International Stream's differentiated and team teaching approaches are now adopted in the Local Stream, including tasks related more to individual students' learning abilities and interests. This has had a significant impact on attainment.
- I now focus more on inter-group co-operation in the Local Stream and ask my students to work interactively and inquire together. I also encourage them to express their own ideas when they encounter problems. Common points are sought when differences arise.
- More and more in the Local Stream, we encourage students to extend their use of in-class textbooks to a wide range of reading materials, out of school.
- We now encourage students to display feedback from their wider reading experiences. For example, after finishing an interesting book they can create a tabloid or prepare a verbal presentation on 'An introduction to my good book'.
- There is now more emphasis in both streams on textbook-based drama and role play.
- We have found that all these methods are helpful in stimulating students' interest and good habits in reading.
- Where Chinese and Western approaches are combined effectively, the teaching and learning is more effective, relaxed and enjoyable for the students. They show more interest in learning and are much more willing to express themselves in both written and verbal forms.
- I find that across the two departments (Local and International) we share a common bond because we are all language teachers. We greatly value the opportunities to share our differing professional perspectives. *'East meets West'* co-operation stimulates us to strive harder towards exploring new methods and to adopting new educational ideologies.

Xue Bei-Li (Lily)

There is much evidence to suggest that, on their return from the International Stream, these teachers have had a significant influence on teaching and learning approaches within the Chinese Local Stream Department.

Cross-stream Chinese drama performance.

Student activities

There are countless student activities relating to Chinese language acquisition. Each semester in the Local Stream, for example, Chinese writing competitions, speech contests, textbook-based dramas and famous writers' lectures have been held.

In the International Stream there have been grade-level Chinese academic competitions, story telling and speech contests and Chinese cultural exhibitions and celebrations.

Some activities are cross stream, for example the Chinese New Year celebrations (above right) and Grade 5 debating competitions. In some activities teachers from both streams are invited to be judges. Students observe activities cross stream and learn from one another. The school's principles of 'co-operation, sharing and harmony' between the streams is well reflected in all these aspects of learning. This has helped to establish many firm inter-stream student friendships.

Overall, these activities help to create a much broader and 'freer' learning environment beyond the classroom and provide the students with opportunities to use and demonstrate what they have learnt.

Involvement in the Xiehe Stars Project

Both Chinese and Western teachers participate in this ambitious whole Xiehe professional development initiative. Many Chinese language teachers from SUIS (Hong Qiao) have been involved over the last four years.

All have been given an opportunity to feed back on their invaluable experiences to teachers within the school's two stream Chinese departments. In terms of the dissemination of ideas on teaching and learning, there is evidence to suggest that *'a single spark has started a Prairie fire'.*

The Stars Project is dealt with in detail in **Chapter 9.1** which follows.

In-house professional development

Considerable emphasis is placed on school-based professional development:

- The Co-Principals and Stream Chinese Language Co-ordinators work together to ensure that newly recruited teachers quickly become familiar with the school's Chinese teaching and learning philosophy, teaching standards, student characteristics and technology.
- There are inter-stream meetings which enable teachers to share their 'golden Ideas' on Chinese teaching pedagogy and their related research.
- Videos of the school's agreed good practice in Chinese teaching and learning are analysed collectively. Copies of these are made available for individual teachers to borrow and reflect on in their own time.

Teachers participating in an In-House Professional Development session.

- Inter-stream seminars are organised on specific topics. Recent themes have included: 'Differentiation in CAL Teaching and Learning'; 'Assessing students Chinese Language Ability Levels'; 'CAL Reading and Writing'; 'Stimulating Classroom Instructions'; and 'Inquiry Based Teaching in Chinese Lessons'.
- In some cases a number of the above activities have taken place at the inter-school level.

Conclusion

Undoubtedly, the *'East meets West',* inter-stream collaborative approach to Chinese language teaching has had very significant benefits.

- The merits of both traditional and contemporary methods have been acknowledged. Recently, the latter have included, for example, recognition of the importance of multiple intelligences in student language acquisition, inquiry based thematic approaches and the need to focus more on individual student achievement. The learning targets framework has been broadened to include values education.
- The differences between Chinese as first language learning and Chinese as additional language learning have been fully recognised and thoroughly investigated.

- Considerable emphasis has been placed on the importance of teacher-student relationships. Enjoyment in language learning and the pursuit of linguistic excellence are recognised as key aims.
- There has been a very significant extension in the range of teaching and learning methods used within both streams, including experiential learning and the use of ICT.
- The quality of Chinese language learning environments throughout the school has been significantly enhanced.
- Outstanding student work has been published and celebrated in various Shanghai newspapers and magazines.

Chinese is the oldest and one of the most difficult languages to learn in the world. Nowadays, it is one that many people outside China wish to acquire. The challenge for us at SUIS (Hong Qiao) is to maintain all the strengths of traditional/National teaching and learning of Chinese and, at the same time, to adopt new international/advanced concepts of language acquisition.

Undoubtedly, our Dual Stream *'East meets West'* co-operation, with its spirit of mutual co-operation and support between both students and teachers, gives us a firm foundation for taking on this challenge. Already, the evidence from the test results our students achieve is very encouraging.

Talkabout

- *If you have a Chinese Department in your school, compare and contrast the curriculum development strategies it adopts with those outlined in this chapter.*
- *Consider whether any of the curriculum development strategies summarised in this chapter could be employed by other departments in your school.*

Zhang Hong is the Superintendent, Executive Director and Co-Principal of the International Stream, SUIS (Hong Qiao).

Clara Li is the Assistant Head of the International Stream, SUIS (Hong Qiao).

4.2 English

Trevor Higginbottom, Qing Yao Xu and Jia Xu

In this section consideration is given to the ways in which Chinese and Western teachers have collaborated, in Xiehe Global Schools, to decide on the best teaching and learning practice in English.

> ***'Tell me and I will forget.***
> ***Show me and I may remember.***
> ***Involve me and I will learn.'***
>
> L. S. Vygotsky

Over the last decade, the teaching and learning of English in the Local Stream at SUIS (Hong Qiao) has been profoundly influenced by the school's International Stream English Department. From the outset, the English teachers in the Local Stream observed English lessons in the International Stream and, subsequently, there have been many teacher exchanges between the two Departments.

Additionally, there has been collaborative production of teaching and learning materials, particularly with respect to thematic studies in English by Western and Chinese English teachers in the Local Stream.

English in SUIS Local Stream School

In March 2012, Trevor Higginbottom produced the following discussion paper with regard to the teaching and learning of English in co-operation with colleagues from the school's Local Stream English Department. This was based very largely on evaluative evidence gathered from lesson observation in both Streams over a number of years.

In our English Department:

- Equal emphasis is placed on the four skills of **listening, speaking, reading** and **writing**. These skills are integrated within the English curriculum. We recognise that reading is a key skill for promoting the other three skills as is confirmed by much educational research.
- All our students are made aware of the English language targets for each lesson. These are explained by the teacher at the outset and reviewed in a concluding plenary.
- We aim to create a non-threatening, language-rich classroom environment supportive to teaching and learning. Lessons are planned thoroughly but also demonstrate flexibility in exploiting learning opportunities as they occur in lessons. We encourage students to take risks in their language learning.
- There is not an over-reliance on the textbook. We supplement textbooks with the production of school produced resources which are more relevant and experiential for the students (for example, materials on the layout of the school, or toys familiar to the students).
- Every lesson is carefully differentiated to meet the learning needs of individual students. In this way it is acknowledged, for example, that our classes may include some students who already have high English linguistic skills and others who are, currently, very unsuccessful in this respect.

- Differentiation of students' learning needs is undertaken through, for example:
  - *grouping students of the same or similar ability;*
  - *differentiation of language activities by task or outcome;*
  - *differentiation of learning materials such as worksheets (for example, by means of an incline of difficulty);*
  - *differentiation of assessment;*
  - *incorporating different teaching strategies such as questioning; and*
  - *accepting answers from students which are different from standard answers.*
- Occasionally, to promote differentiation by outcome, we give our students open-ended, short inquiry-based projects for homework over a period of, for example, two weeks (e.g. recently, as a follow up to a local shopping centre study devised by one of our teachers).
- We teach phonics:
  - *in context;*
  - *explicitly in a systematic and structured way in the early years of schooling;*
  - *integrated into everyday English lessons; and*
  - *with a focus on an accumulative structure (ie under a theme or a topic);*
- Our teachers aim to strike a balance, across lessons, between the four strategies of teaching and learning (whole class, paired and group work, and individualised learning).
- We recognise that, although whole class teaching is useful for introducing learning targets and reinforcing their acquisition, it is the least effective, overall, in terms of differentiation.
- Our paired and group work is very carefully structured using co-operative learning techniques. This ensures that all our students, whatever their ability, participate in this work.
- We find paired work, in particular, a very useful teaching and learning strategy because, at any stage, half the students are using English. Semi-permanent 'shoulder' partners are often paired together so that the more successful students support those who are less successful.
- Increasingly, we are using individualised learning strategies during lessons as, clearly, this is the most effective means of differentiating the teaching and learning.
- We use communicative tasks to promote English language learning. A communicative task involves two or more participants in the language classroom interacting in an authentic manner using the appropriate language for that context. Such a task refers to both oral and written English; in the primary years, however, there is more emphasis on oral language.

  Our most effective and appropriate communicative tasks:
  - *emphasise fluency and meaning;*
  - *provide students with sufficient and appropriate input including language input, conceptual knowledge input and skills input;*
  - *are relevant to students' real life experience, age and cultural background;*
  - *maximize students' use of English language;*
  - *provide students with a context for communicating/interacting in English;*
  - *minimise unnecessary and meaningless drilling;*
  - *motivate students to learn;*
  - *keep students on task;*
  - *allow students to have fun and enjoyment; and*
  - *are creative, interesting and meaningful.*
- We recognise that one of the most effective ways of promoting English language acquisition is by means of creative learning activities. These engender students' interest in the language and arouse their motivation and desire to both learn and use English. Some of the creative approaches we have used of late are as follows:
  - *open-ended language tasks;*
  - *drama/role-play experiences;*
  - *songs;*
  - *poems;*
  - *thematic learning;*
  - *experiential learning.*
  - *big book shared reading and related activities;*
  - *pair work/group work;*
  - *collaborative learning opportunities;*
  - *children's literature;*
  - *field trips/outside school visits;*
  - *comic strips;*
  - *problem-solving tasks; and*
  - *students' use of their own language store in addition to the target language being introduced.*

- We have recognised, increasingly, that lack of confidence and self esteem is a significant cause of under-achievement with regard to our students' language acquisition. With this in mind, we have reviewed lessons with a view to promoting the confidence and self esteem of individual students.
- We take account of the fact that our students may be learning English in other curriculum contexts (for example in thematic bilingual team teaching, in other bilingual lessons and in subject lessons taught in the English medium). As far as possible, we plan co-operatively with the teachers of these curricular areas: for example, (i) we let the teachers have brief summaries of our students' learning targets for a specific period of time, so that they can reinforce them in their lessons; (ii) we receive English vocabulary lists on specific themes or topics which are being studied so that we can, on occasions, reinforce the learning of these in our lessons. In doing this, both English subject teaching and bilingual learning is taking place collaboratively in the interests of the students' learning needs.

The content of this discussion paper was significantly influenced by the *'East meets West'* professional dialogue between teachers across SUIS (Hong Qiao). Subsequently, it has greatly informed the day to day work of the Local Stream English Department.

The development of the local stream's school based English curriculum

Six years ago, SUIS (Hong Qiao) introduced a standard phonetics course *'Sing, Spell, Read and Write'* (SSRW) from the USA. All SSRW teachers are trained and certified with respect to the course. The textbook is divided into 36 steps. In two academic years, children remember the word pronunciation rules by singing, thus capturing the skill of natural word-spelling and laying a good foundation of reading and writing for the future.

Compared to the commonly used English textbooks in Shanghai where the English alphabet and pronunciation are taught independently, the Grade One students learn just the English alphabet. Not until Grade Three will they start to learn the pronunciation of English letters, individually and combined. SSRW, as a subsidiary English curriculum for lower grade students, helps students in their first exposure to the 26 English letters, to understand their pronunciation and to master pronunciation rules. The whole set of 17 storybooks, which are integral with the textbooks, also provide students with practice opportunities step by step. This also links well with higher grade students' reading and writing.

'Longman - Welcome to English' is the main school-based curriculum for the more successful classes in the Local Stream. The textbook is characterised by a large vocabulary and rich daily dialogues which help to quickly improve the students' communicative competence. Short stories in each unit also play an important role in improving their English reading ability. This contrasts with the more traditional Shanghai textbooks which start from teaching words and grammar, then gradually move to an understanding of the meaning of words and grammar in real contexts.

Our own approach is supported by the Shanghai English Teaching and Learning Researcher, Mr Zhu. Using the *'Longman - Welcome to English'* textbooks, we do not abandon Shanghai English teaching materials but instead integrate the good points from both into daily teaching practices. As to the school-based teaching materials, there is no corresponding reference book available, so our English teachers refer to the Oxford English examination draft papers based on the key points listed in the teaching outlines and prepare school based exercise books which include content from both textbooks. In addition, all students have their own weekend exercise paper and review tips to enable them to consolidate the learning content.

As a result of this approach and the adoption of teaching and learning approaches summarised in the discussion paper (see pages 39-41 above), our students have performed exceptionally well in the Shanghai Municipal and District Level English examinations.

The Local Stream English Department also makes good use of foreign teaching resources. Each week we arrange two to three classes on reading and writing instruction. The mastery of SSRW phonics helps to remove many of the obstacles for students reading English in the higher grades. In addition to 6000 bilingual books in the school's Learning Resource Centre, we also provide each class with different levels of reading books in English aimed at stimulating students' interest. In the reading ability tests organised by the Shanghai Xiehe Education Group, our students have also achieved very highly. With respect to writing, the Shanghai curriculum standards only require students to complete a short essay of five sentences: our students have a rich vocabulary and, with their reading as a firm foundation, are able to create stories by themselves from Grade Two upwards. In the school's creative writing competitions, our Grade Two and Grade Three students are able to write extensive prose. These original stories are often very accurate in content but also extraordinarily creative. Our standards in this respect are much higher than those required by the written tests administered by the Shanghai Municipal Education Department.

Whole school English activities

Our students are given maximum opportunities to practise their spoken English. The first three minutes of each English lesson is always allocated to individual student's English speech time. During each semester, every student has the opportunity to participate twice. They can select a theme for their speech. Before presentation, the teacher gives them individual counselling on both speech content and gestures, ensuring that each student can stand in front of the class and confidently speak English. Many students also create impressive PowerPoint presentations to illustrate their speech. This combines the development of ICT with English language acquisition. The annual English Speech Contest is always very competitive and exciting, with standards rising every year. The winners represent the school in National and city-level oral English competitions. Our school's annual English Festival is also very popular amongst our students. Their experiences in these language cultural activities stimulates their interest in English learning. Spelling Bee Competitions, which have been held in the past two years, are also an excellent stimulus. By creating word cards and learning vocabulary beyond textbooks, the students become very enthusiastic regarding spelling. In the 2013 Spelling Bee Competition in the Shanghai Minhang District, our school gained notable success in all grades. Subsequently, two of our students participated in the finals of the Municipal level competition representing the Minhang District.

One of the key innovations in Local Stream English teaching and learning has been the use of thematic studies as a vehicle for language learning. Teachers use the textbook content as a starting point and then develop related themes, maximising the use of experiential learning. The example which follows is a theme devised by a SUIS (Hong Qiao) Local Stream teacher based on the Primary Longman Express Chapter ***'What does it taste like'.***

Module: *Using my Five Senses*

Chapter 4: *'Taste it!', 'What does it taste like?'*

Teaching aims and language focus:

- Read an article about the food pyramid and try to understand its main meaning.
- Discuss healthy food with your teacher and decide how best to have a balanced diet.
- Learn to use why- questions to ask about the taste of the food.
- Learn how to describe the taste of the food.
- Read a simple recipe and find out how to make the dish.
- Try to use imperative sentences to write a simple recipe.

Other learning targets:

- To know about healthy food, nice tastes and how to enjoy your life.
- Work in a group and learn from each other.

Useful words and key sentences:

Words: food pyramid, carbohydrate, vitamin, mineral, protein, fat, sweet, balanced diet, nice taste, sour, bitter, salty, spicy, soy sauce, mustard, vinegar, chillies, tablespoon, pinch, salad dressing, put into, mix, stir,

Sentences:

What does/do … taste like?
It's/They're …

Preparing the salad - the lesson in images

1. Lesson introduction: teaching new words in the 'classroom kitchen'.

2. Clarifying the instructions.

3. Group work to prepare the salad.

4. Supporting the group work.

5. Enjoying the outcomes.

6. Some students prepared another salad at home.

Teaching Plan			
Procedures	Content	Teacher's activities	Student's activities
Warming up	Daily talk	1. Little speech	Answer the teacher's questions
Four mins:		2. Daily talk: Ask some questions about food.	
Pre-task preparation Six mins:	Revision	1.Teacher helps the students to read an article about food pyramids and to know what the food pyramid tells us. Part 1. Our bodies need carbohydrates, vitamins, minerals, proteins and fat. Part 2 .What kinds of foods contain carbohydrates? Part 3. What do we need to eat to get more vitamins and minerals? Part 4. Why do we need protein? Part 5. Suggest why we should not eat a lot of oil, sweets or butter? 2. Conclusion: We should keep a balanced diet	1. Read and answer the teacher's questions. 2. We should …
Main-task procedure Eighteen mins:	Ask and answer Do a taste test Read the recipe and make some salad	1. The tastes of foods. Shows some pictures and asks the students: What does it taste like? (Help the students to answer). It's/They're … We test with our tongues. We can taste four main flavours: bitter, salty, sour and sweet. 2. Do a taste test of different sauces: mustard, vinegar, sugar, bitter melon, chillies, pepper To teach : spicy 3. Make a super healthy salad 1) Ask students to discuss in groups: What kinds of food will you put into your salad? Why? 2) Read the recipe for making salad. Make salad with the students, teaching some verbs such as put into, mix, stir …	1. To learn the tastes of foods. Ask and answer: What does/do … taste like? (Help the students to answer). 2. Do a taste test. To learn different sauces: mustard, vinegar, sugar, bitter melon, chillies, pepper To learn : spicy 3. Make a super healthy salad with the teacher. 1) Discuss in groups. I will put… into my salad, because… 2) Read the recipe and help the teacher to make the salad. To learn some new verbs and use imperative sentences.
Post-task activity Five mins:		1. Ask the students to read a recipe on making a salad dressing by themselves. 3 tablespoons olive oil 1 tablespoon vinegar 1 pinch of salt 1 pinch of pepper Half tablespoon of mustard 2. Ask the students to make salad dressing in the group. 3. Ask the students to give their salad to the teachers to taste if it is nice or not.	1. Read a recipe on making salad dressing. 2. Make salad dressing in the group with all members working as a team. 3. Give the salad to the teachers to taste. What does/do… taste like? It's/They're…
Assignment Two mins:	* Select the ingredients for making a salad. ** Finish the recipe for making the salad *** Help your mum to make super healthy salad for dinner today. (Speak in English)		
Post lesson reflection/evaluation			
Good ideas			

See a sample worksheet for this lesson on the following pages

CH4 What does it taste like?

Food Pyramid

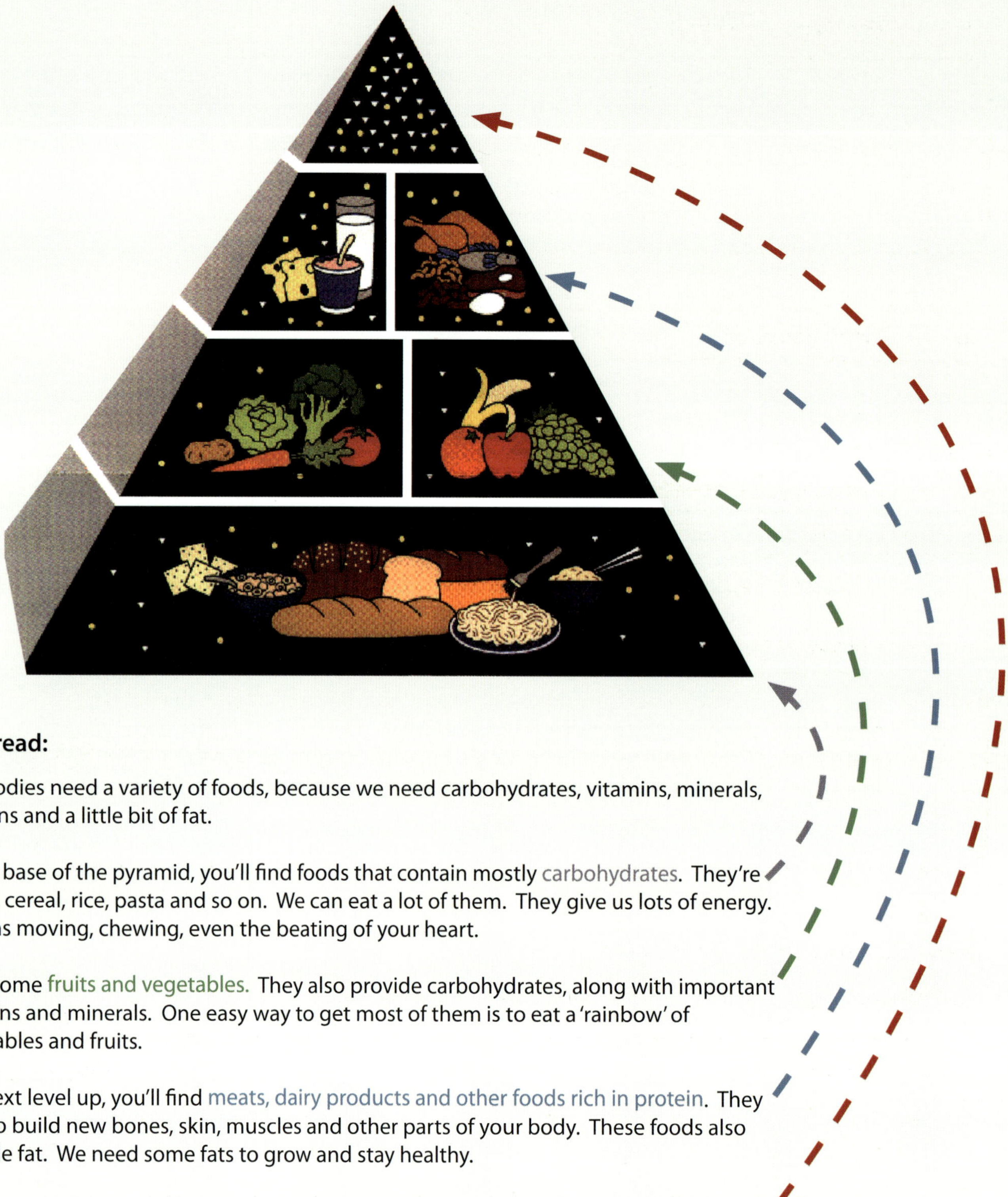

Let's read:

Our bodies need a variety of foods, because we need carbohydrates, vitamins, minerals, proteins and a little bit of fat.

At the base of the pyramid, you'll find foods that contain mostly carbohydrates. They're bread, cereal, rice, pasta and so on. We can eat a lot of them. They give us lots of energy. Such as moving, chewing, even the beating of your heart.

Next come fruits and vegetables. They also provide carbohydrates, along with important vitamins and minerals. One easy way to get most of them is to eat a 'rainbow' of vegetables and fruits.

The next level up, you'll find meats, dairy products and other foods rich in protein. They help to build new bones, skin, muscles and other parts of your body. These foods also provide fat. We need some fats to grow and stay healthy.

At the top of the pyramid you will see oil, sweets and butter. There is a lot of fat in these foods. Our bodies need some fats to keep warm. Fats give us even more energy than carbohydrates. But our bodies need only small amounts of fat. Remember don't eat too much. You may become fat.

The food pyramid shows us how much of each different kind of food we should eat. Try to eat mostly the kinds of food at the bottom. We should eat some of the foods shown in the middle every day. But only eat a little of the kinds of food shown at the top.

Salad Recipe

According to the Food Pyramid write the things we need:

1. Vegetables and fruit

2. Meat, fish or eggs

3. Cheese or nuts

Describe how to make super healthy salad

(useful words: **get, wash, break, rub, dry, add, chop, mix, stir**)

1. ______________________________

2. ______________________________

3. ______________________________

4. ______________________________

5. ______________________________

As with other areas of the English curriculum, the thematic work is assessed both formatively and summatively through tests which incorporate benchmarks relating to English language acquisition.

The benchmarks are designed to determine:

- student progress starting from when the students arrive in Grade One; and
- their ability to meet targets that would generally be considered 'average' for students studying EAL in a non-immersion environment.

They also show teachers where their students stand in relation to first language English speakers.

Grade 3 Pioneer Class: English

Teacher: **Ms Joanna (English Longman Express)**

Vocabulary

- Can listen to sounds and is able to apply these in written form.
- Can understand and use the 180 words in Longman Express 3B.
- Can use adjectives to describe the objects and people.
- Can use simple connective words to link sentences.
- Can use simple adverbs to describe actions

Listening

- Identifies basic sounds and can discriminate between a small range of sounds in words.
- Can locate or provide specific information in response to simple questions.
- Recognises the connections between ideas supported by appropriate cohesive devices, including connectives and pronouns.

Speaking

- Can use simple sentences to communicate with others with the help of clues.
- Opens an interaction by eliciting a response.
- Maintains an interaction by providing information in response to yes/no questions.
- Has a greater understanding of past tense and can use it in conversation.
- Shows willingness to speak English outside of the classroom.

Reading

- Is able to locate specific information in a short text.
- Can scan a text to locate specific information by using strategies such as looking at repeated words, words in bold, italics or capital letters.
- Is able to guess the meaning of unfamiliar words by using contextual or pictorial clues.

Writing

- Uses appropriate formats and conventions of short written texts.
- Can draft, revise and edit short written texts with teacher's support.
- Gathers and shares information, ideas and language by using strategies such as brainstorming, building concept maps, listing and observing.

Grammar

- Uses personal pronouns as objects to identify people.
- Use prepositions or prepositional phrases to indicate positions, times or festivals.
- Uses '-ing' nouns or noun phrases to refer to activities.
- Uses general determiners to show quantities.
- Use adverbs to express similar opinions.
- Uses the simple past tense to talk about past states, activities or events.

Teacher: **Mr Ben (English Longman Express)**

Overall

- Can work well in a variety of classroom situations; independently, paired and in groups.
- Listens attentively during the class.
- Exhibits behaviour expected in the classroom environment, is courteous and polite to both fellow students and teachers.

Writing

- Has shown progression in ability to write in narrative form.
- Can identify and is able to use instructional language to complete a related task.
- Is able to write a simple piece of poetry in couplet form.
- Can identify key facts and is able to summarise these.
- Knows what persuasive writing is and can write a reasonably concise argument.

Reading

- Is making progress in both the Oxford Reading Tree Programme and related assessment criteria.
- Is able to predict in both spoken and written language what will happen in a book.
- Can summarise key points in a book.
- Exhibits the ability to read independently outside of the school environment.

Speaking

- Is involved in classroom discussions.
- Can hold a conversation in English at length.
- Is willing to converse in English outside of the classroom environment.

Topic

- Shows an understanding of the topic and the related issues.
- Is able to write a story related to the topic.
- Shows the ability to conduct research independently.
- Can work together in a group to produce a diorama exhibiting key features of the different zones in the sea.

The benchmarks have been devised from a variety of sources, including the English National Curriculum.

Work is still in progress in this respect.

Conclusion

These Western approaches to the English curriculum in the local stream of this Xiehe Dual Stream School have resulted mainly from the inter-stream professional dialogue between Western and Chinese English teachers. Combined with the Chinese classroom culture described in **Chapter 10** which follows, this has enabled the students to attain remarkably high English language standards in all the four skills of listening, speaking, reading and writing.

Talkabout

- *Review your school's English curriculum using the criteria contained in the discussion paper included in* ***pages 39-41*** *in this chapter. Highlight areas for potential improvement in this curriculum area. How might this improvement be most successfully achieved?*
- *Consider the advantages and disadvantages of thematic approaches to primary English as an additional language (EAL) learning. Devise a new thematic EAL study using the approaches outlined in this chapter.*

Qing Yao Xu is Grade Four Co-ordinator for the Pioneer Curriculum classes and a Grade Four Pioneer Curriculum English teacher at SUIS (Hong Qiao).

Jia Xu is the English Co-ordinator, Local Stream, SUIS (Hong Qiao).

4.3 Bilingual Education across the curriculum in the local stream at SUIS (Pudong)

Trevor Higginbottom and Vivia Xu

In Xiehe Global Schools, children in the local streams learn English as a discrete subject (see ***Chapter 4.2****) and its learning is reinforced through its use as the medium of instruction in other selected subjects. This chapter describes the latter context and illustrates, here again, how the 'East meets West' philosophy has influenced teaching and learning pedagogy.*

> *'For many schools worldwide, English as an additional language (EAL) is a key curriculum challenge. Meeting it successfully greatly empowers students in their future lives.'*
>
> Zoltán Dörnyei

In the Local Stream at SUIS (Pudong) the bilingual curriculum is as summarised in the table in **Figure 1**, below. Bilingual Education is co-ordinated by Vivia Xu, Head of Bilingual Education, who works closely with the Head of English in this respect.

Grade	Bilingual Curriculum	Lessons per week
Primary department Grades 1-5	Music	2
	Art	2
	PE	3
	Science	2
	Inter-disciplinary thematic studies	2
	ICT	2
	Virtues/Values Education	1
Secondary department Grades 6-8	Music	1
	Art	1
	PE	3
	Science	2
	Physics	1
	Chemistry	1

Fig 1: Bilingual curriculum in the Local Stream, SUIS (Pudong)

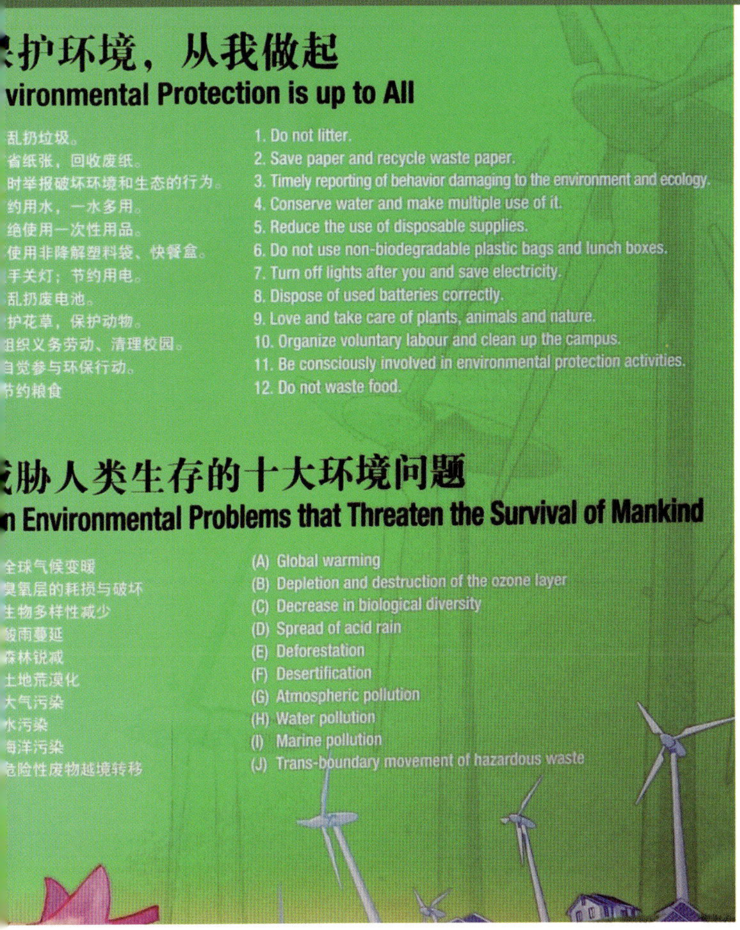

ABOVE LEFT: Bilingual environmental education.
ABOVE RIGHT: Classroom rules have been negotiated bilingually.

Aims of bilingual education

The main aims with regard to the bilingual dimensions of all these lessons are:

- to integrate the current English subject learning targets into the lessons;
- to practice the English the students are learning day-to-day in the subject lessons; and
- to extend the students' vocabulary through the identification of specific subject vocabulary (e.g. for science: microscope, habitat, atmosphere, solar system, gravity, species).

Collaboration between the Head of Bilingual Education, the Head of English and the bilingual teachers is regarded as crucial. Regular meetings support this process. The Head of English provides the bilingual teachers with the English learning targets.

Significantly, in this Dual Stream School, the Western English teachers provide language training to enhance the English language proficiency of their bilingual teaching colleagues. Also, there is dialogue between them on the most effective form of English medium teaching and learning in the bilingual lessons.

A Xiehe policy on bilingual education: the Shanghai United International School.

A group of Western and Chinese teachers have devised the following policy (see pages 51-52) on Bilingual Education within Xiehe, which has influenced classroom practice across the Group's schools.

In all their lessons, the bilingual education teacher should implement the following agreed good practice in their teaching in English and Chinese (with the former as the main language medium).

1.0 Indicator of Excellence

The teacher understands that he/she is teaching: (i) a subject (science, art, music, pottery, physical education and moral education) and (ii) at least some English, depending upon the teacher's own English language ability.

Some examples of observable features:

- Is the teacher teaching as much English as possible, according to his or her English language ability?
- In science and moral education, across the lessons, there is reading, writing, speaking and listening in English. In art, music, pottery and physical education there is (usually) only speaking and listening in English.

2.0 Indicator of Excellence

If the teacher is confident in using English he/ she should use the language as much as possible during the lesson. This might be 'immersion' English: insisting the pupils speak almost entirely in English and discouraging the use of Chinese; or 'contrastive' English: the teacher and the students repeat the Chinese version of the English used initially in words, phrases and sentences.

Some examples of observable features:

- Is the teacher using as much English as possible, throughout all the lesson?
- Is the teacher clear as to whether he or she is using the immersion or contrastive approach?

3.0 Indicator of Excellence

If the teacher is confident in using English, he or she recognises that some Chinese will need to be used (e.g. to make certain that the students who are less successful in English understand the instructions for tasks undertaken during the lesson, for homework details or for disciplinary or safety issues).

Some examples of observable features:

- Is Chinese being used only where appropriate in the lesson?

4.0 Indicator of Excellence

If the teacher is less confident in using English, at least he or she uses words from his or her subject language list. The number of words will obviously depend upon the English language proficiency of the class. (Grade level).

Some examples of observable features:

- Is the teacher using as many English words as possible from his or her subject language list?

5.0 Indicator of Excellence

The teacher creates a bilingual environment for the students, for example (i) in displaying the lesson's learning targets in Chinese and English; (ii) planning worksheets, as far as possible, in both languages; (iii) ensuring classroom displays are bilingual.

Some examples of observable features:

- What evidence is there in the content of the lesson (e.g. DVDs, worksheets) and the classroom itself, of a bilingual atmosphere?

6.0 Indicator of Excellence

The teacher tries to be as clear as possible in using English words, phrases and sentences. He/she insists the students do the same.

Some examples of observable features:

- Does the teacher correct the students' use of English at any stage during the lesson?
- Does the teacher drill (repeat) specific English words or phrases to try to make sure the students have learnt these successfully?

7.0 Indicator of Excellence

During parts of the lesson the teacher creates a task during which he or she tries to involve all the students in using English (e.g. singing a song in music, describing a picture in art, describing

an exercise in physical education). In some cases the teacher uses a student with good English to help with this task (the 'little teacher' approach). In classroom lessons the visualiser is used, for example to enable a student with good English to describe his or her work.

Some examples of observable features:

- Is there a part of the lesson when a specific task has been planned to enable the students to use English, either using the immersion or the contrastive approach?
- How successful has this part of the lesson been?
- Has the visualiser been used successfully?

8.0 Indicator of Excellence

The teacher uses paired and/or group work for at least part of the lesson, during which time he or she insists that students try to use English in their discussion. To help this process, the teacher pairs or groups together students who are successful in English with those who are not so that they help one another to learn the language.

Some examples of observable features:

- Has the paired and/or group work been successful in helping the students to learn English? (See **Chapter 5.5**).

9.0 Indicator of Excellence

The teacher realises that learning English depends very much on the confidence of the student. He or she therefore promotes the self esteem and confidence of individual students and encourages them to take risks in using English. The teacher uses 'wait time' if an individual student is slow to answer in English (e.g. due to lack of ability or confidence).

Some examples of observable features:

- Does the teacher praise the students enough for using English successfully?
- Does he or she use 'wait time'?

10.0 Indicator of Excellence

In terms of management, the Bilingual Education teacher plans the lesson appropriately, with clear learning targets (for the subject (eg science) and for the English language dimension).

Some examples of observable features:

- Is the teacher clear about the lesson's learning targets?
- Are these learning targets realistic in view of the timing of the lesson?
- Are the students clear about the main learning targets of the lesson?
- Are the learning targets displayed during the lesson by the teacher?
- Does the teacher (i) refer to these learning targets in the introduction to the new content of the lesson; (ii) refer to them during the main part of the lesson; and (iii) at the conclusion of the lesson, review the learning targets to try to determine whether or not they have been achieved by the students?
- Overall, do the learning targets provide a structure to the lesson?

Bilingual virtues display.

(The second half of the policy is concerned with the generic processes of teaching and learning including good practice in whole class teaching, individualised learning, paired and group work. See **Chapter 5.5**).

Two school improvement strategies are used in SUIS (Pudong) with regard to bilingual education.

- School self evaluation, on occasions involving an external adviser.
- Appraisal of bilingual teachers by the Head of Bilingual Education and between the participating teachers. The form in **Figure 2** (below), is used during the appraisal process.

Professional development priorities for bilingual teachers are identified as a result of these strategies.

Fig 2: Bilingual Appraisal Form

Shanghai United International School (Pudong)
Bilingual Teacher's Appraisal Form

Subject: ______________________ Teacher: ______________________

Evaluator: ______________________ Date: ______________________

Item	Evaluation Criteria	Marks
Planning	• Meets standards of agreed bilingual teaching plans.	5
English language targets	• Clear targets related to English Department policies. • With differentiated language focus or not?	10
Subject focus	• With clear subject, subject vocabulary and other English language targets. • With differentiated subject focus or not?	15
Teaching aids	• Aids used effectively.	5
Teaching methods	• Good range of four approaches. • Challenging questions. • Focus on inquiry.	20
Students' understanding	• Based on pre-set targets. • Meeting individual needs.	15
Practice/exercise	• Well designed and differentiated.	10
Teacher's English language proficieny	• Accurate use of English.	10
Self-reflection	• Positive thinking about teaching. • Suggestions for self improvement.	10
Evaluation	Suggestions	

A number of future growth points in the development of bilingual education in the SUIS (Pudong) Local Stream have been agreed.

- More attention will be given to assessing the English language component of the bilingual subject work, both formatively and summatively.
- English language professional development workshops will be established for each grade in each bilingual subject (i) to enhance the subject bilingual teachers' own English language ability; and (ii) to further develop the bilingual dimension of the curriculum. The school's Western English teachers will continue to play a key role in this work, see page 50 above.

Conclusion

Bilingual Education in the manner described in this chapter can significantly enhance students' English language acquisition. The process has been strongly supported in this Dual Stream School as a result of professional collaboration between the Western English teachers in the International Stream and the Local Stream Chinese bilingual teachers, within the spirit of the *'East meets West'* philosophy.

Talkabout

- *Imagine that you were a bilingual science teacher at SUIS (Pudong). Plan a lesson on global warming for Grade Six students, also aimed at reinforcing their understanding of adjectives.*
- *Evaluate, overall, the three main approaches which Xiehe Global Schools adopt to develop English language learning (Subject English:* **Chapter 4.2***; bilingual team taught thematic learning:* **Chapter 5.1***; and those outlined in this chapter). Suggest areas for improvement.*

Vivia Xu is Head of Bilingual Education, Assistant Principal and Head of the Premier Curriculum at SUIS (Pudong).

4.4 Mathematics

Pan Guangbo and Zhang Cui-Ye

The Shanghai Xiehe Education Group's Dual Stream school management model provides a unique context for combining Chinese and Western approaches to mathematical education. In this way maths can become part of our global culture.

> ***'Mathematical knowledge is timeless. It can be easily segmented into topics. It can be clearly explained. Graded exercises can be constructed to guide practice. The steps of reasoning can be set out so errors are easily spotted. There are unambiguously right answers, which make for rigorous and objective assessment.'***
>
> Professor Guy Claxton

The complementary advantages of Chinese and Western maths

Zhang Cui-Ye formerly worked in a government primary school in China as a maths teacher for seven years, before joining Xiehe in 2004. Subsequently, she has taught maths in two Shanghai United International Schools (SUIS's) and been a maths research group leader for nine years.

Her view is that **Chinese maths teaching and learning** have three key advantages.

The introduction of new knowledge after review of previous knowledge. Also, the learning of new knowledge through reasoning from formerly acquired information.

It is acknowledged that learners have beliefs about how the world works based on their experiences and prior learning. The Russian Lev Vygotsky defined learning as *'the creation of meaning that occurs when an individual links new knowledge with existing knowledge.'* A constructivist approach is used in the teaching of maths. Consequently, when planning to teach it is important to ascertain students' prior knowledge and provide experiences through the curriculum and through the environment that give them opportunities to test and revise their models, make connections between their previous and current perceptions, and construct their own meaning.

For Chinese maths teaching, most of the new knowledge is introduced by reasoning from old information. When an individual student links new knowledge with existing knowledge, this will allow the meaning and content of the new knowledge to be acquired gradually, as a natural process. For example, when teaching multiplication in Grade 2, we must allow a student to understand the concept behind multiplication before he/she learns how to multiply, ie multiplication is the easier way to figure out addition with repeating numbers. We can use the example of apples to demonstrate this: show 2 apples once and repeat this process 5 times, then how many apples in total? Because students have not learned multiplication, students will use the equation: $2 + 2 + 2 + 2 + 2 = 10$. The teacher affirms it and then asks: how about six times, seven times, eight times and nine times …100 times? Students feel uncomfortable, if 2 apples in each for 100 times, do we need to add two evenly for 100 times too? Is

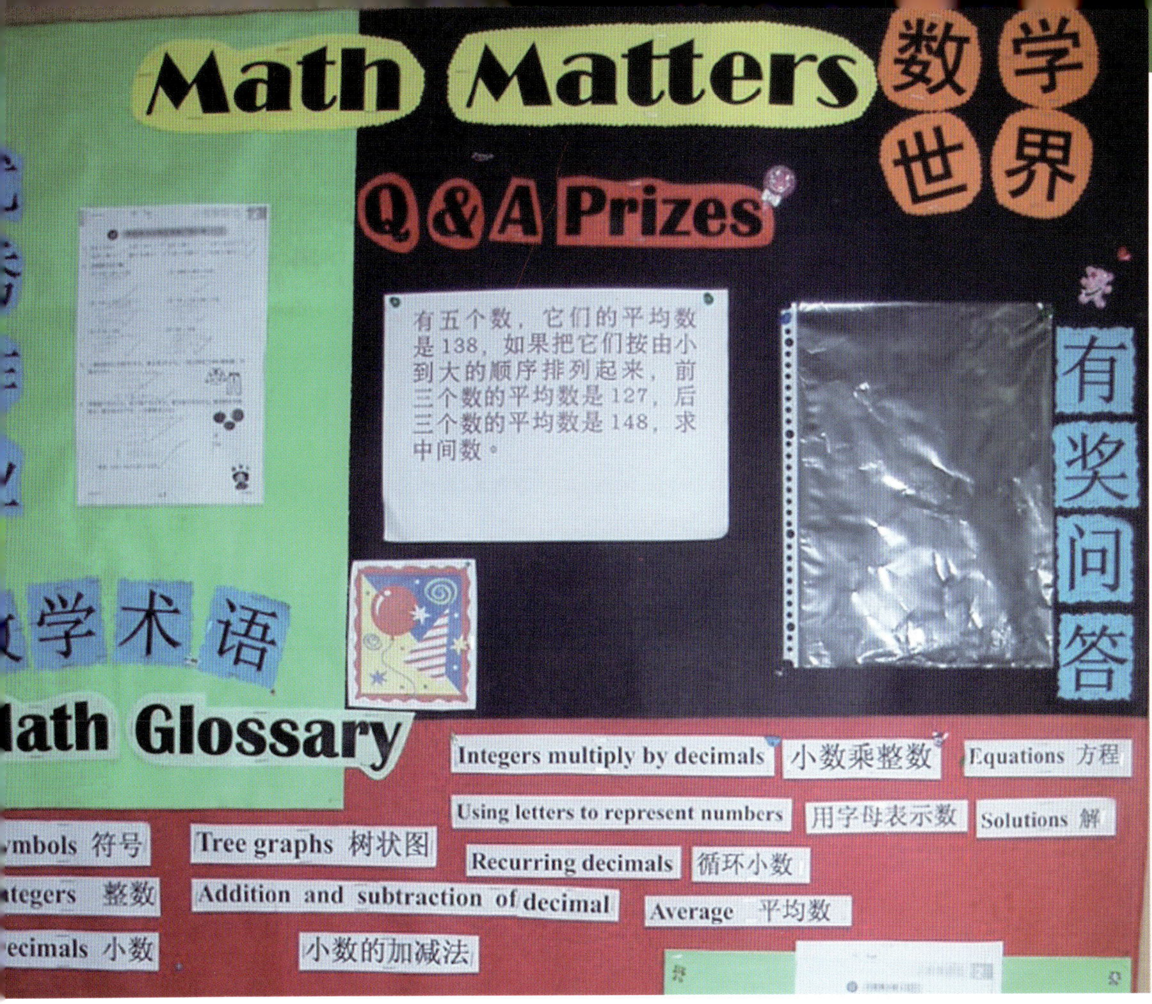

LEFT: Bilingual classroom display of maths terminology

there no better way to do this? The teacher capitalises on the trend to introduce multiplication and the times symbols (x or a dot). The students all show great interest in the new knowledge 'multiplication'; hence, they are motivated to learn effectively about what multiplication is and when multiplication is used. This shows that multiplication teaching is based on the students' prior knowledge of addition of repeating numbers more than 2 times, e.g. 120 + 120 can change to 120 × 2, or 16 + 16 + 16 + 16 can change to 16 × 4.

An emphasis on problem solving skills and methods.

Maths education in China focuses strongly on problem solving. It is therefore essential for students to master the basic skills and methodology of this approach in order to establish a good foundation for further study. In the problem solving process, teachers place particular emphasis on structure/design of the problem, such as: one problem with more solutions and more problems with one solution, i.e. the pedagogy of variation, which is typical of Chinese maths. Chinese maths places emphasis on establishing the knowledge system which allows students to actively participate in the class and engage in meaningful learning. This allows students to systematically and effectively understand and master the subject knowledge. Besides, the use of pedagogy of variation can also prevent mechanical exercises, e.g. A + B = B + A, 205 + 390 = 595, so 390 + 205 = 595. The law of children's cognitive development is 'proceed from easy to difficult' and 'step by step'. Therefore problem solving exercises with a clear structure and various forms help students to understand cognitive law. This requires teachers to effectively design lively and interesting exercises for students, both to consolidate new knowledge and develop students' intelligence. For example, with respect to teaching 'the area of a rectangle', the following are examples of problems that show this development.

- ***Basic exercises:*** Xiao Ming places a piece of 'glass' on his desk. Please find the area of the 'glass' using the measurement grid the teacher has given you (count the squares).
- ***Comprehension exercises:*** (i) Xiao Ming hangs a rectangular painting on the wall with a known width of 8 centimetres. What is the area of this rectangle? (Instruction: add another measurement so that you can calculate the

area in one or more steps); (ii) Xiao Ming installs a curtain in the window, which is a rectangle with width of 12 decimetres and height (i.e. length) of 18 decimetres, what is the area of the curtain? (Allow students to create/design this).

- ***Practice:*** find out the rectangles around us and measure their length and width, find their areas and then discuss the findings in groups.
- ***Challenges:*** give students an irregular figure and allow students to think how to calculate its area. The problem solving concept is to divide the irregular figure into rectangles and then find the area.

This kind of lesson makes use of progressive problem solving approaches and develops students' thinking skills. Basic exercises aim to check whether the students master the formula for calculating the area of a rectangle; comprehension exercises aim to understand whether students can utilize their knowledge to solve problems; challenging activities are designed to extend the students' knowledge. Such a hierarchical problem solving design with a gradient of difficulty both differentiates the learning and stimulates students' interest.

An emphasis on review, memory and reflection.

Traditional Chinese maths teaching is based on a multiplicity of exercises, tests and examinations which indicate students' current level and enable them to see their mistakes. Memory driven basic exercises in China involve an emphasis on the memorisation of maths knowledge such as multiplication tables, number bonds and relevant maths facts. This enables students to consolidate and grasp knowledge very effectively. For example, in teaching addition less than 20 for Grade 1, ask the students to find numbers to make up 10. Each time before starting the class, leave three to five minutes for practising: the teacher says "I have one" and the students say "we have 9"; and then students and teachers say "1 and 9 is 10" together, and so on. Higher grade students in the primary school undertake mental calculation practice before each maths class. This learning method of review, memorisation and reflection establishes a solid foundation for students' mathematical computations.

Through the evaluation and teaching of Western maths lessons in two of Xiehe's international streams, Zhang Cui-Ye has found that **Western maths** has the following advantages.

There is a stronger focus on individual learning needs.

Western maths teaching and learning activities are based much more on personalised education, teacher/student equality and interactive learning. The classroom atmosphere is more relaxed, the students have more freedom and learning is more active. Teachers encourage students to express themselves and find answers in their own ways, unlike Chinese primary and secondary teaching where the atmosphere often remains strict. This more relaxed mode of maths education can both stimulate students' initiative and cultivate their creative thinking.

Greater emphasis on group activities.

Western maths teachers are more adept at managing group learning activities and in promoting cooperative learning. Based on relationships which emphasise greater teacher-student equality than in the Chinese system, group learning is also seen as promoting social skills. This frequently encourages a harmonious classroom culture for maths teaching and learning to take place.

BELOW: We are happy shopkeepers

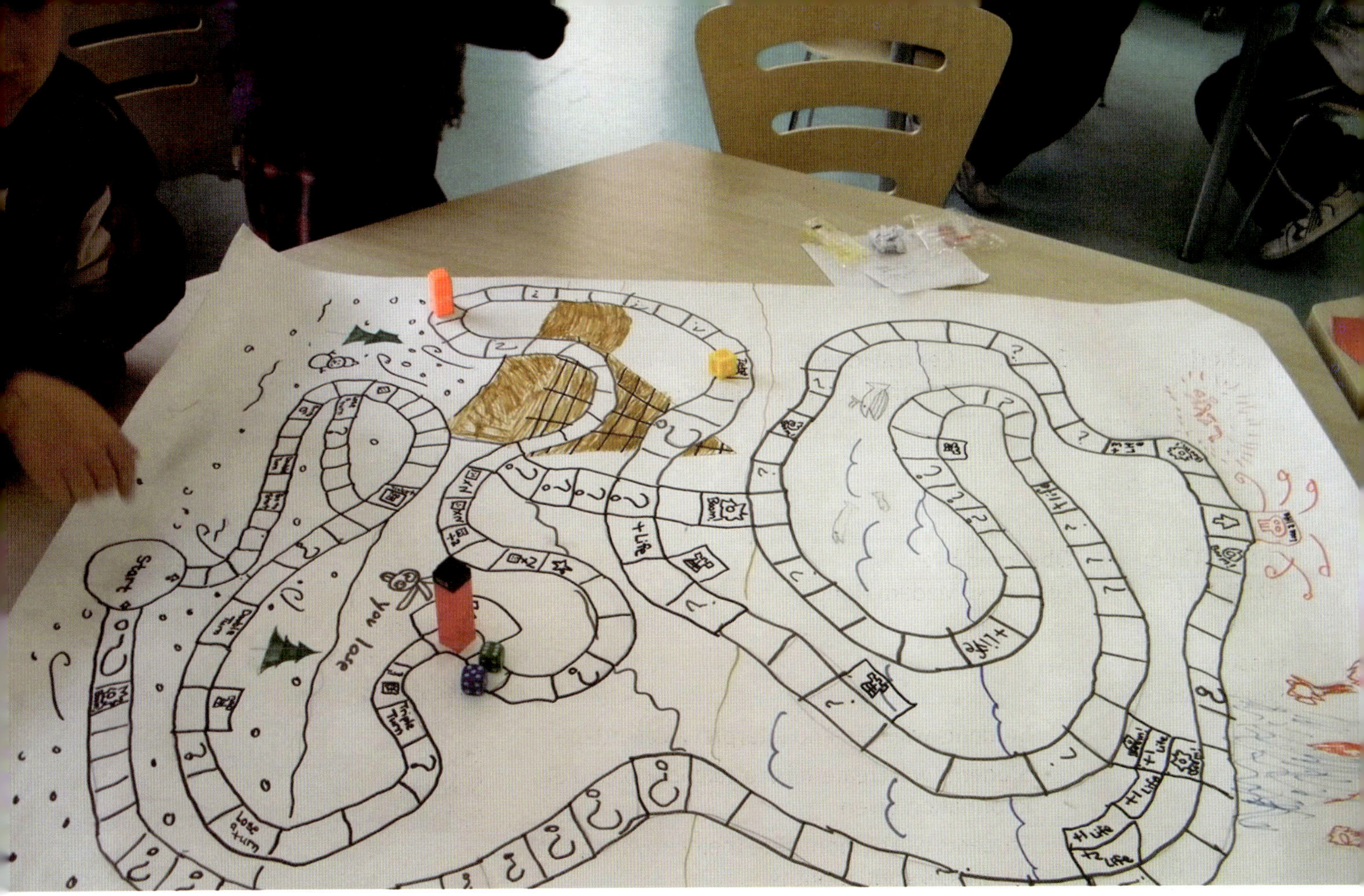

ABOVE: We are playing a game we made ourselves during the maths Shopping Day

More varied learning styles

Normally there are two basic learning approaches developed in maths teaching and learning. First, teacher-led, receptive learning; secondly inquiry-based learning. Traditional basic maths education is provided more through the former, modern applied maths is a feature of the latter. Both authors feel that these two approaches are complementary and well-balanced within Xiehe's students' overall teaching programme.

In summary, in Xiehe Global Schools local stream maths teaching and learning focuses more on knowledge and skills acquisition and on the teachers' professional abilities to ensure that this succeeds. Here, the overall teaching model is one of the construction, mastery and application of mathematical knowledge. In international stream maths there is more emphasis on the teacher allowing the students to discuss their answers between themselves, focusing on the student's individual ability. Our aim as Xiehe mathematicians is to make the best of both these 'maths worlds' and to establish a 'global maths' approach with very distinctive Xiehe characteristics.

It can be seen from **Figure 1**, Lesson Plan 1 which follows, that our English maths adopts the International Baccalaureate (IB) Primary Years Programme (PYP) teaching and learning philosophy.

The IB advocates integrating maths within the curriculum with the aim of establishing links between different subjects. The teaching of maths also contributes to the curriculum's transdisciplinary themes, focusing on the practical and problem solving skills of students. The IB Learner Profile used by teachers in maths classes requires the student to be a thinker and to be courageous. The inquiry focus section of this lesson plan is weather. The two maths teachers (one Chinese, the other English) combine the calendar with weather in dealing with this subject, so that students can comprehend by analogy and consolidate what they have learnt in the inquiry focus section. After a short review, the students work in groups and complete class calendars to be used throughout the year with birthdays, holidays, weather, etc. Each group then presents their calendar and answers their peers' questions. In activities, teachers design the questions to encourage students to constantly focus on self-reflection. The two teachers prepare the lesson plan together which ensures that Chinese maths is incorporated into new knowledge step by step, using an inquiry, activity based approach and group work methods.

Fig 1: International Baccalaureate Primary Years Programme [PYP Lesson Plan 1: English Maths (measurement of time: days, weeks and months) for Grade 2] PYP Lesson Planner:

<table>
<tr><td>Teacher(s):
Siobhan Haizlip and Apple Zhang

Date: 1 Nov 2011</td><td>Grade:
2C</td><td>Central idea:
Weather patterns impact our lives</td><td>Subject Focus:
Maths (measurement of time)</td></tr>
<tr><td>Lesson Time:
10.50-12.10</td><td colspan="2">Observed by:
Leaf, Jane, Madam Hong</td><td rowspan="2">Resources:
What resources will be used?
Maths journals
Large blank calendars
Task sheets
Pencils
Glue
Scissors
PPT (Who wants to be a maths master?)</td></tr>
<tr><td>Lesson Objectives</td><td colspan="2">What do you want the students to know, understand at the end of this session?
• Students will read and interpret a calendar
• Students will create/fill in a calendar based on information given
• Students will demonstrate their knowledge of days, weeks and months</td></tr>
<tr><td>Inquiry Focus</td><td colspan="2">What is/are the main question(s) or lines of inquiry driving this lesson? How does this relate to the central idea?
• Stand alone measurement - Why are calendars useful to us?
• How do you use a calendar?
• What information can you find on a calendar?</td><td>Grouping strategies:
How will students be encouraged to work together?
Students will work in their regular classroom groups (grouped according to gender, mother tongue, academic ability and behaviour).
They will have to work co-operatively to complete the calendar for their month.</td></tr>
<tr><td>Prior Knowledge</td><td colspan="2">Activities:
How will the students discover or demonstrate what they know?
• Problem of the Day (review): How many months are in a year? How many days are in March? June? October?
• Students will then work in pairs to review how many days are in a month using the knuckle method.</td><td>Differentiation:
Each task will be levelled by difficulty.
Each group will start with the easiest task and work towards the hardest task.</td></tr>
<tr><td>Skills and Concepts:</td><td colspan="3">What skills will the students be using/developing? How?
Interpreting Data - Students read a calendar in order to find information and answer questions
Questioning - Students will use information from their calendar to create questions for others.

What are the main concepts of the Unit of Inquiry?
How is this lesson using or developing these concepts?
Change - Students can compare the calendars and observe changes/trends.</td></tr>
</table>

Activities:	***What activities will engage the students and achieve the desired outcomes?*** • Have students complete their daily problem in their Maths journal (check as a whole class). • Discuss what they learned the previous day (days of the week, number of days in a week/ month/year/leap year) using the PPT. • Ask the questions from the inquiry focus section (Why are calendars useful to us? How do you use a calendar? What information can you find on a calendar?) • Introduce the activity for the day (working in groups and using information to complete class calendars to be used throughout the year). • Show an example of a calendar with birthdays, holidays, weather, etc. • Show an example of how to fill in certain information (Eg it is snowy on the third Wednesday. Where would you put that? Ms Apple's birthday is September 11. On which day would you write that?) • Explain the different tasks that each group will be doing and that once they are finished with one task, they will get the next one. • Pass out one calendar and the first task sheet to each group and have them start working. • Once each group has written at least two questions and answers, conclude the activity. • Have each group go to the front of the class to present their calendars and ask the class two questions about their work. • When all have presented, discuss once again how calendars are useful and how they will use them in the future.
Student reflection:	***How will the students be guided to assess what they have done?*** • Students can check the days of the week using the classroom calendar. • Ask what improvements or changes they would make to their calendars. • Ask what kind of information people could get from their calendar.
Action/ application:	***How will they use what they have learned?*** • Students will be constantly tracking the daily weather throughout the UOI and recording it on a calendar, bar graph and line graph.
Follow up:	***What will happen next?*** • Students will help create a weather calendar for the months of November and December where the daily weather will be recorded. • This information will also be transferred into a bar graph. • The student created calendars will be displayed in the classroom during the appropriate month.
Teacher Self Reflection:	***How do the teachers feel about the lesson?*** ***What would they change? Why? How?*** ***What do they feel good about? Why?***

Lesson Plan 2 which follows relates to Chinese maths lesson on "Days, months and years" taught by an experienced maths teacher with sound English language skills. The teacher focuses on student acquisition of systematic knowledge. She designs the activities to ensure that the students grasp the basic concepts of day, month and year, such as the days per month and the memory aid "knuckle method". These concepts then correlate so that students establish a solid foundation for cognition. Inquiry based learning in groups provides the lesson framework.

Fig 2: Lesson Plan 2 - Chinese Maths (measurement of time: days, weeks and months for Grade 2) Maths book for first semester Grade 3

Learning Objectives:

1. Students will demonstrate their knowledge of days, months and the year and remember the days of each month.
2. Students will develop a sense of the length (time) of a day, month and year, and observation and thinking skills.
3. Students will learn cooperative, inquiry based methods in groups.

Subject Focus : measurement of time - day, month and year.

Difficult Points: guide students to understand the difference in the number of days in February in a leap year and a normal year.

Resources: PPT, computer, calendar sheets, paper.

Lesson Plan

Teacher: *let's guess what this is?*

1. Course work presentation:

I am riddle: it is special. I wear 365 sets of clothes. I take off one set of clothes each day. At the end of a year there will only be the cover left. What am I?
The teacher shows the calendars.

2. Subject plan

(a) We learn and live for a day, then tear off a page from the calendar. Twenty four hours can also be called what? Then the teacher writes "日" (Ri, a Chinese character, meaning a day) on the whiteboard.
(b) What do we call the period of time from January 1 to 31? Then the teacher writes "月" (Yue, the Chinese character, meaning a month) on the whiteboard.
(c) How much time has past when we tear the last page off the calendar? Then the teacher writes "年" (Nian, the Chinese character, meaning a year) on the whiteboard.

3. Review and pose a new question.

Today, let's learn the days and months in a year. Before we start, I would like to ask you: what do you know about the days and months? Please write this down.

4. Group work

Provide calendars (2004-2009) for each group of four students.

Teacher: *What can you learn from the calendar sheets?*

(i) Ask students to read by themselves.

(ii) Show discussion results.

(iii) Use your calendars to answer these questions:

- How many months in a year?
- Which months have 31 days? Which months have 30 days?
- How many days in February?
- How many days in a year?

Whiteboard summary: solar month of 31 days : January, March, May, July, August, October, December (7 months)
solar month of 30 days : April, June, September and November (4 months)
February (28 or 29 days) (1 month)

5. New knowledge: solar month of 31 days and 30 days

Teacher: *We have learnt that there are 12 months in a year, including 7 solar months of 31 days and 4 solar months of 30 days, as well as special February.*

How do you remember which is a solar month of 31 days and that of 30 days?

Do you have any ideas about how to remember this ?

Let me give you some tips.

First the memory method: make a fist and count the knuckles and sunken parts, the knuckles represent solar months of 31 days, the sunken areas between the knuckles represent solar months of 30 days and February.

Let's try: start counting from the knuckle of the forefinger(January), then dip(February), then index finger(March), then dip(April), then ring finger(May), then dip(June), then little finger(July), forefinger knuckle again (so that you get two 31s in order) and so on.

6. Exercise (PPT):

- When is it your birthday? Is it in a solar month of 31 days or 30 days?
- I was born in May; is it a solar month of 31 days or 30 days?
- Those who were born in solar months of 31 days, please stand up; those who were born in solar months of 30 days, please stand up.

7. How to identify a typical year or leap year.

(i) Teacher : which February has 28 days and which February has 29 days?

Display calendar sheets showing years and days in February

E.g. 28 days in February 1981
28 days in February 1982
28 days in February 1983
29 days in February 1984

Continue the cycle up to the year 2000. ***What do you discover?***

Summary: February has 29 days every four years; this year is called a leap year; if February has 28 days, this year is called a common year.

(Whiteboard summary): Leap year February 29 days, common year February 28 days

Please name each leap year. Look at the last two digits. What do you notice? E.g. 19**92**, 19**96**, 20**00**. The last two digits of the years are 92, 96 and 00.

Summary: if the last two digits are multiples of 4, then the year is a leap year; otherwise it is a common year. The Olympic Games are generally held in a leap year.

Teacher : *do you know the origin of "Every four years is a leap year?"*

Knowledge: do you know that the Earth orbits the sun once a year, in precisely 365 days 5 hours 48 minutes and 46 seconds. If we calculate a year with 365 days, we lose 6 hours each year, i.e. 24 hours in 4 years (nearly a day). So every four years, we add one day to February; this year is called a leap year.

(ii) Exercises : how do you identify a common year or leap year? E.g. 1984, 2003, 2008

(iii) Calculate the days in a common year or a leap year? How many days are there in a common year? What equation do you use? How about a leap year? How do you work this out?

8. Summary.

(i) What have you learned from this lesson?

(ii) Use a riddle to conclude

Teacher: *I would like to ask you to solve one more riddle? Here is the riddle:*

What am I? I am the longest and shortest, the most and the least, the slowest and fastest, the cheapest and most valuable. What am I? (Time)

Teacher: *'Since time is so precious, what should we do about it?'* (Cherish the time)

The integration of Chinese maths and English maths

SUIS (Hong Qiao) is an IB PYP school integrating the best of Chinese and Western educational philosophy and management. We have to satisfy the demands of (i) IB maths, and (ii) students from many different countries.

The IB does not provide set textbooks. Such an approach is not felt to be appropriate in a time of rapid technological change. This means that teaching is more demanding. We spend a lot of time and effort in developing our own "SUIS Maths Scope and Sequence", which is a textual procedure with operating instructions that offers strong support for teachers. **Figure 3** (right) is the abstract of "data handling" in the SUIS Maths Scope and Sequence for Grade 1.

As summarised in **Figure 3**, IB PYP maths emphasises integration and links with the Units of Inquiry, across six transdisciplinary themes: 'Who we are'; 'Where we are in place and time'; 'How we express ourselves'; 'How the world works'; 'How we organise ourselves'; and 'Sharing the planet'.

Each theme is six weeks in duration. Every theme contains a central idea which relates to all the students' learning activities and to assessment. For example, the Grade 4 theme is 'Young Entrepreneurs'. In this unit the teaching and learning focuses on exchange rates, estimation, cost and profit calculation, etc. The PYP maths teaching and learning emphasises a theme based approach, the application of ideas and problem solving. Chinese maths focuses on knowledge, logicality between differing areas of knowledge and students' reasoning ability.

The PYP Maths Scope and Sequence divides maths into five strands: data handling, measurement, shape and space, pattern and function and number. Except for number teaching which is generally taught as 'stand-alone' lessons, the other four are related to the Units of Inquiry. Each strand defines the learning objectives of knowledge, skills and concepts and suggests appropriate resources, activities, assessment items and evaluation strategies, together with links to inquiry. Additionally, we have our own teachers' guide which provides advice on identifying and unifying the links between Chinese and Western maths. The guide also defines the strengths of each approach.

Two examples of our approach to maths teaching are summarised below.

Example 1 : Multiplication tables

Multiplication tables are taught in both Chinese and Western maths. Chinese teachers find that their students' mental calculation ability is almost as fast as the calculator. In the Programme for International Student Assessment (PISA), conducted in 2009, Shanghai students ranked first in maths amongst 65 countries and regions. Chinese students begin to recite their multiplication tables from Grade 1 onwards. This ancestral wisdom makes our multiplication algorithm easier. Our Western teachers and students have begun to recite their multiplication tables in English but in the Chinese way, e.g. 1 x 1 = 1 (one one one), 1 x 2 = 2(one two two) 1 x 3 = 3 (one three three) and, as a result, their computing capacity has been greatly enhanced.

Multiplication tables allow students to grasp and learn maths confidently. They also enable students to not only design their own games, but also to play maths games, such as '24 points'. This game involves the use of playing cards. Randomly choose four playing cards, e.g. 5, 6, 8, 3. The idea then is to make the number 24 using each number once only and any of the four operations to calculate 24. The solution could be $8 \times 3 \div (6 - 5) = 24$; $6 \times 8 \div (5 - 3) = 24$.

In group work students discuss the patterns in the multiplication tables in order to reinforce their understanding of multiplication. The students have roles in the group and record the outcomes of their work. This stimulates students' interest in learning maths and demonstrates the advantages of 'learning by doing'.

Example 2 : Smart calculation.

A Grade 5 class was asked to practise mental calculation: $7 \div 2.5$. After a while the Chinese students had completed the task and put their hands up quickly. The Western students, however, looked anxious and asked: *"Can I use a calculator?"* Later, when explaining the problem to them, the teacher realised that the Western students could not undertake smart

Fig 3: Data Handling in the SUIS Maths Scope and Sequence for Grade 1

Data Handling: Learners will understand how information can be expressed as organised and structured data, and that this can occur in a range of ways. They will collect and represent data in different types of graphs, interpreting the resulting information for the purpose of answering questions. The learners will develop an understanding that some events in daily life are more likely to happen than others and they will identify and describe likelihood using appropriate vocabulary.				
Learning Outcomes will include development of strand specific knowledge, concepts and skills	**Sample activities linked to the Units of Inquiry**	**Resources**	**Sample Assessment**	**Identified links to Units of Inquiry** *(please explain how and give transdisciplinary theme, unit title and central idea).*
Conceptual understandings • Information can be expressed as organised and structured data using tallies. • Objects and events can be organised in different ways. • Some events in daily life are more likely to happen than others. **Constructing meaning** • Understand that information about themselves and their surroundings can be collected and recorded using tally, bar graphs and word form. • Understand the concept of chance in daily events (impossible, less likely, maybe, most likely, certain). **Transferring meaning into symbols** • Collect and represent data in different types of graphs, for example, tally marks, bar graphs and pictographs. **Applying with understanding** • Collect, display and interpret data for the purpose of answering questions. • Create a pictograph and sample bar graph of real objects and interpret data by comparing quantities (for example, more, fewer, fewer than, more than).	• Conduct a survey (e.g. favourite fruit) • Construct a pictograph of favourite living things according to classification • Construct a bar graph of jobs in the school community • Predict common shapes/favourite activities etc • Share results of findings	• Clip boards • Graphs • Posters • Picture cards • Unifix cubes	• Students could work in groups to create a survey and carry it out • Give students data and ask them to represent it in a bar graph and/or pictograph	• Countries: learning about countries, statistics, surveys. • Senses: pictograms, posing questions. • Recycling: classifying rubbish, predicting. • Living things: classifying, surveys. • Telling Stories: classification of, stories, Venn diagram.

calculations and did not understand the concept of 'rounding'. The process was then written on the whiteboard:

$$7 \div 2.5 = (7 \times 4) \div (2.5 \times 4) = 2.8$$

This was followed by related questions, such as, if the divisor is 12.5, it is necessary to multiply by 8 to make 100. One Western student sighed deeply: *'No wonder Chinese students finish so fast!'* It is not difficult to see from this example that the Chinese approach has its advantages in terms of simple mental calculation. It helps students to avoid the tedium of written calculation when doing exercises and provides a faster way of undertaking such a task. Once students have mastered the rules, challenging puzzles become simpler. This enhances students' interest and paves the way for more effective maths learning.

A review of our progress in combining Chinese and Western maths

In February 2010 the SUIS (Hong Qiao) International Stream received the International Baccalaureate Organisation (IBO) accreditation to become an IB PYP school. We then began our own school-based research on the development of Chinese and Western approaches within the SUIS Maths Scope and Sequence. The lessons of two International Stream maths teachers, one Chinese and the other Western, were evaluated by a Research Group consisting of school colleagues and an external maths expert. There was also detailed analysis of the views of both the students and the two teachers in the follow up.

The Group's conclusions were that our PYP students greatly enjoy their maths and that this *'East meets West'* approach enables both Chinese and Western teachers to unify the Units of Inquiry and to develop the problem solving approach rigorously. There was also evidence that effective use was being made of the students' multiple intelligences. Our team teaching, with a Chinese and a Western teacher involved, was found to be particularly effective. Chinese parents

BELOW: Pan Guangbo evaluates a maths lesson

LEFT: Our maths Olympics

BELOW: A mental maths contest

concerned about their child's progress can ask the Chinese teacher to set more homework tasks for them. Individualised/differentiated learning in maths has been greatly enhanced as a result of the team teaching process. Another (indirect) advantage highlighted in the research was that the students' Chinese and English language levels had improved significantly as a result of this bilingual maths approach. It was found to be advantageous to have a Chinese and an English speaking teacher in the class when maths students wished to clarify a problem/ difficulty in their own language.

The Research Group also concluded that it was extremely helpful for the Chinese and Western maths teachers to combine their different teaching and learning pedagogies through both collaborative pre-planning and teaching together in the classroom. Whole class teaching was found to be a particular strength of the Chinese teacher, group work of the Western teacher. The Research Group stated that the post lesson activities of joint teacher reflection/ self evaluation, sometimes involving the head of maths and senior managers, were particularly helpful in enhancing the combined *'East meets West'* pedagogical approach. In such discussions general problems relating to maths education within the Stream as a whole were often tackled, as was the overall issue of 'what constitutes excellence in our maths teaching and learning?'

Each semester the International Stream Maths Department invites the school's Local Stream maths colleagues to observe and evaluate their lessons in the company of external maths consultants. It is felt that the post lesson discussions are an excellent catalyst in terms of ongoing improvement in the quality of the teaching and learning. Parents are regularly invited to observe maths lessons. The annual Maths Olympics and Mental Calculation contests (see above) are major events for both students and staff. They help to both enhance student attainment and to stimulate their interest in maths. Parents volunteer to support the activities.

Supportive teaching and learning materials are exchanged within the International Stream Maths Department: for example Western teachers use Chinese maths 'Mental arithmetic and multiplication table activities books'; Chinese teachers use Western 'Fun-maths' games such as 'My favourite number' and 'Maths project activities'.

A student's response to '*East meets West*' maths

Melissa Hu studied maths in the SUIS (Hong Qiao) International Stream and the SUIS (Pudong) Local Stream before leaving for a private school in England. She has therefore had experience of two contrasting types of maths education.

'Ever since the day when, at two and a half years of age, I agreed to learn the arabic numbers from one to ten in return for a visit to a fair in a local Shanghai park, maths has been both an amazing experience and sometimes a nightmare for me. Up to Grade 8, in Shanghai, I studied Chinese maths intensively as a subject in at least five hours of lessons per week. It was very knowledge based. In these early years the Chinese teachers continuously emphasised that maths would play a very important part in my future life. I was made to appreciate that, even if it was not my favourite subject, it was certainly one that I should take very seriously. I took this advice and now feel that Chinese maths gave me a very firm foundation for my future studies.

In my first year in Grade 9 in the UK studying English National Curriculum maths I won gold medals in National maths competitions and achieved 'A' grades throughout. Here maths was a compulsory GCSE subject but it was treated no differently to my other subjects.

I found there was much greater freedom in my maths education. For example, we were allowed to choose which topics we wished to review in preparation for the GCSE exam. There were three maths lessons per week. It was good to have the opportunity to choose whether or not I wished to continue with the subject at GCE Advanced (A) Level, in Grades 11 and 12. I feel that the greater freedom in the choice of both lesson topics in maths and in the choice of options for A Level encouraged me to choose the subject for further study.

I feel that the combination of Chinese and Western maths I have studied since I started school has given me many advantages over my present classmates. The Chinese methods gave me a firm foundation for my future studies, the English approach taught me how to apply my maths, to problem solve and to control the pace of my work in the subject. The latter is important because in the end I shall be responsible for what I want to achieve'.

Conclusion

Nowadays, the *'East meets West'* approach to maths education at SUIS (Hong Qiao) is a combination of the two approaches Melissa has encountered during her schooling. We feel that our students are fortunate in having these experiences at the same time within their maths curriculum. We fully appreciate, however, the need to continually focus on ongoing improvement in our maths curriculum. The Maths Research Group, referred to above, will continue to play a key role in this process.

Talkabout

- *Consider whether any aspects of the 'East meets West' approach to maths education, as described in this chapter, would enhance student achievement in the subject in your school and/or organisation.*
- *What quality assurance strategies do you use with respect to maths? Would the type of Research Group mentioned in this chapter be a useful addition to these processes?*

Pan Guangbo was formerly Maths Inspector for the Xiehe Education Organisation.

Zhang Cui-Ye is Head of the SUIS (Pudong) Secondary International Stream.

Acknowledgements

The authors are grateful to Fran Bruce for her support at the editing stage for this chapter.

4.5 Combining Chinese and Western approaches to Art Education in Xiehe Global Schools

Cecile Girard

Art has proved to be a particularly interesting subject in terms of Chinese and Western teacher collaboration. Here Cecile Girard, a French artist and art teacher, writes about how her team teaching with two Chinese art teachers has meant that both Chinese and Western approaches to art have been adopted by their global students.

> ***'Art enables children to see, explore, record and interpret their world and communicate thoughts and feelings through a common visual language which transcends national boundaries and develops understanding of the creativity of all peoples. It is a powerful tool for global learning.'***
>
> Ann McGough

I have team taught with Xu Wen Yan and Wang Bing in two Xiehe Global Schools, SUIS (Hong Qiao) and SUIS (Wan Yuan). This has meant that we have been able to share our Chinese and Western perspectives on art education.

From Yan and Bing I feel that I have learnt, in particular, how to more effectively integrate traditional Chinese art painting into my Western teaching, the specificities of Chinese calligraphy and how to combine Chinese teaching and learning pedagogy with my Western classroom approaches. I also think I am now much more effective in working with Chinese students.

In turn, Yan and Bing have suggested that, in particular, they have learnt from me Western artistic skills and cultural influences, the importance of art history, thematic approaches, the value of museum visits and strategies for exhibiting students' work.

Working together

Together we have developed a range of approaches across the primary/secondary age range to include drawing, painting, collage, print, sculpture, assemblage and construction.

With older students, we have also introduced photography and video work. In a logical progression our students explore the elements of line, shape, form, colour, value, texture and principles such as movement, harmony, unity, contrast, variety, proportion, pattern, emphasis and rhythm.

LEFT: Grade 1 student - Shanghai buildings, Delaunay, oil pastels.

Our key aim is to provide both our Chinese and Western students with artistic knowledge and techniques based on the work of artists and masters from the past and present and from different cultures. Across the grades, the students build on and improve their knowledge and experience of materials, processes and practices. Examples of their work, included in this chapter, illustrate the progression in the students' artistic development.

BELOW: Grade 2 student - Morandi, still-life, mixed techniques. Well balanced and atmospheric still-life combining Western and Chinese techniques in a series of three art works. Pencil, water colour and Chinese ink on rice paper.

Together, as teachers from differing professional backgrounds and cultures, we search for harmonious teaching and learning approaches. Crucially, we attempt to both build on and combine the strengths of our Chinese and Western students, some of which are summarised in the table below.

Fig 1: Combining the best of Chinese and Western approaches

Artistic strengths of our Chinese students	Artistic strengths of our Western students
- Line (calligraphy) - Bright palettes (aesthetic) - Space relationships (Liubai) - A sense of design (cartoon approaches) - Their cultural heritage	- Colour research - Experimentation (mixed techniques) - Study of techniques (drawing, painting and 3D) - Art appreciation (Western students are more exposed to a diversity of artistic approaches) - Their cultural heritage

Overall, we find that our Chinese students have very high levels of drawing skills, as a result of their national tradition in calligraphy and arts (referred to in Chinese as 'Guohua'); our Western students are more used to experimenting with a variety of techniques and styles.

With all our students we attempt to develop their:

- artistic techniques (drawing, painting and 3D);
- colour research;
- creativity through experimentation; and
- art appreciation.

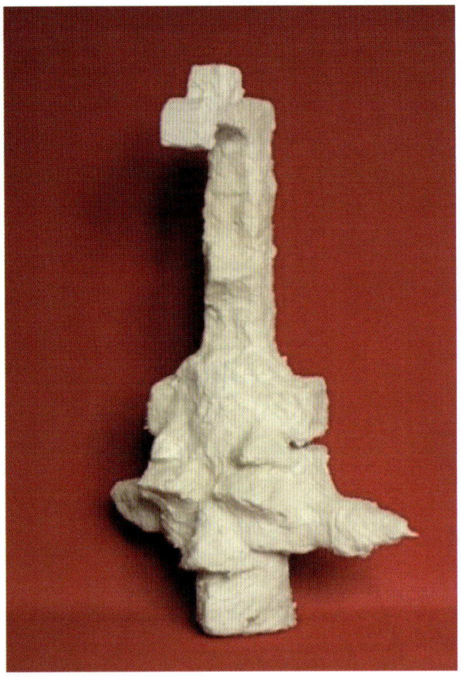

LEFT: Grade 3 student - Chinese bronze, ancient mask, Sichuan, mixed techniques.

Construction with recycled material and plaster of Paris.

There is solidity in the structure and a sense of design.

RIGHT: Grade 6 student - series, still-life, Le Brun, Bruegel, Cezanne, mixed techniques.

This is an interpretation of a traditional still life with pencil and gouache.

The sketches are processed with western brushes.

Here there is the influence of Chinese Art into a Western topic:

- space relationship - the work reflects the "Liubai" concept in traditional painting (Guohua).
- The brushstrokes are powerful and are a combination of the use of "maobi" Chinese traditional calligraphy brush and western brushstroke techniques.

LEFT: Grade 7 student - gouache and Chinese ink.

This is an interpretation of traditional Chinese characters (Jiaguwen) from the work of the artist Zao Woo Ki, into a modern piece of gouache and Chinese ink painting.

- Chinese characters are "designed" and no longer written in a traditional way. They become a symbol rather than a character.
- Colours researched are a combination of Chinese and Western style. Students have a different approach to the "aesthetic".

The Chinese student will use a full palette of colours (acid colours with a decorative effect). The foreign student will select a limited palette.

RIGHT: Grade 7 student - landscape, Nicolas de Stael, mixed techniques.

The photography becomes designed scenery. Strong graphics (calligraphic line) and space relationship (Liubai) with pastels.

The students are creating a geometrical style through a methodic analysis approach.

RIGHT: Grade 8 student - German Expressionism, woodcut print.

In order to appreciate this subject, the students will start by developing a traditional sketch study and progressively will express a contemporary style by the use of a more analytical approach rather than a creative and imaginative one.

The Chinese students will emphasise the woodcut technique. The Western students will concentrate on the expressivity of the portrait.

ABOVE: Grade 8 student - Boccioni, oil painting on canvas.

The students will use a calligraphic style with a Western brush to sketch the main composition. They will develop various and balanced lines within their work.

The outcome will be a harmonious Chinese and Western expressive landscape influenced by mastering the Chinese calligraphic brush.

BELOW: Grade 8 student - Picasso, collage, oil painting on wood board and recycling material.

Students need to search for an object to be analyzed and decomposed. Western students will tend to look for a familiar object.

According to the Cubist process, Chinese students will break the object into recognizable shapes. Western students will break the object into unrecognizable shapes and forms.

RIGHT: Grade 9 student - Naum Gabo, construction with cardboard.

Here the students are building their construction with a strong space relationship effect according to the figure they are designing. Western students wlll focus on the expressivity in the face with a more emotional emphasis.

ABOVE and LEFT: Grade 10 student - installation (photography), land art, new technologies.

Conceptual realizations. This is a combination of Chinese and Western Art. There is a harmonious balance between the past and the present China.

BELOW and RIGHT: Grade 10 student - Robert Motherwell, ink and acrylic on canvas.

Chinese students will have a natural ability in composing the main structure with ink. Western students will not have this direct, emotional and spontaneous impact on the canvas.

RIGHT: Grade 10 student - Millet, pastels.

Here there are advanced techniques, with a deep sense of design and space relationships.

Conclusion

Working collaboratively as fellow professionals, in terms of pre-planning, classroom team teaching and follow up review/self evaluation we constantly attempt to improve our:

- knowledge of Western and Chinese art, both traditional and contemporary;
- art appreciation approaches; and
- mutual advice/criticism strategies.

Our professional 'international' collaboration in two Xiehe Global Schools has been a hugely rewarding experience for us. We believe that, as a result, students of all nationalities in our classes have received a significantly enhanced quality of art education. We are encouraging students to make an artistic choice and believe strongly that this will help them to grow as individuals and to confront their responsibilities.

Talkabout

- *Consider what benefits the appointment of teachers from very different international backgrounds could bring to your school's art department.*
- *How would you attempt to ensure that such appointments would extend and enrich your students' experience*

Cecile Girard is Head of the SUIS (Wan Yuan) Art Department, both Local and International Streams, and a painter.

She is grateful to Xu Wen Yan and Wang Bing for their advice and contributions towards this chapter.

Acknowledgements

The artwork in this chapter was undertaken by students at SUIS (Hong Qiao) and SUIS (Wan Yuan)

5. Curriculum development initiatives within Xiehe Global Schools

This chapter includes five very significant examples of school based and centrally supported curriculum development within Xiehe over the last decade. In each case, both the content of the innovation and the processes of curriculum change which ensured its success are described.

5.1 A bilingual team teaching approach to thematic education: the SUIS (Pudong) model

Mark Renie, Charlaine Reid and Sarah Zhang

This section deals with one of the key features of the Xiehe Global School curriculum: bilingual team teaching in a thematic context. This approach was introduced at the outset when the first Global School opened in 2003, partly because it was a feature of the Fortune Kindergarten Curriculum (see **Chapter 6.1***) but also because the school's co-founder had found it to be very successful in a Hong Kong Education Department Primary Project with which he had previously been associated.*

> *'Teachers of differing cultures/nationalities working in the classroom can exemplify many of the aspirations of global education to their students.'*
>
> David Hicks

SUIS (Pudong) serves a large and diverse population of students in Shanghai. At present the students in the school's International Stream represent more than 35 different nations and speak more than double that many languages. This diversity is also clearly reflected in the cultures of the students, the parental perceptions of education and, on a macro level, in the histories and issues that their countries face in the present and will face in the future. However, there are three clear unifying facts that resonate amongst all the students of this Stream: all of their parents share a desire for an education that is globally recognised, bilingual in nature and able to prepare their children to be successful in the global village of the future.

We, as educators and administrators have recognised these three unifying facts and have striven to meet these educational expectations. One way that this has been done is to implement and utilise the English National Curriculum as the core curriculum of the school. Yet this world recognised curriculum still falls short of addressing all the needs of our students. As a primary school curriculum, it offers clear support for teaching and assessing numeracy and literacy whilst developing key historical, geographical, scientific and artistic skills. However its contextual relevance to such a diverse group of students is minimal.

The history of England means little to an Indian child being raised in China, who might eventually end up working in Russia. Knowledge of the geography of the British Isles will do little to prepare some Chinese children for the challenges they may face in their lifetime in addressing the impact of rising sea levels on the coastal city of Shanghai. Most importantly, how can a curriculum written mainly for a culturally and linguistically homogenous student body ever prepare these students to be future global citizens who will interact with each other daily to do business, socialise and solve the world's problems in spite of cultural and linguistic barriers?

It is with this in mind that the staff of SUIS (Pudong) decided three years ago to develop and implement a curriculum that would address the shared desires of all of our parents for their children to truly be successful global citizens of the 21st century.

The curriculum

The thematic curriculum was developed to act as a vehicle by which students can explore topics that are relevant to them as global citizens. Its goal is to provide an opportunity for the exploration of these topics through the use of a transdisciplinary approach. Its focus is on the learning and mastery of key skills rather than being knowledge centric. Students learn and apply a diverse set of skills that come from a variety of subject fields such as history, geography, maths, English, Chinese, science, art, music and ICT. Although knowledge based learning is still very important, the world that our students are growing up in is one where knowledge is easily accessible if you have the effective skills to find that knowledge. Workplaces of the future will require them to not only have knowledge but to have the necessary skills to find and/or develop and apply new dynamic ideas.

The curriculum's explorations also foster critical thinking amongst our students whilst nurturing an appreciation for our diverse global community and the issues that we face now and will face in the future. They are encouraged to view these issues through a multiple of cultural lenses, always remembering that their impact should be seen in a global rather than a local context. To properly explore these issues, the students utilise relevant technological tools and develop analytical and critical approaches that provide the with necessary skills, whose mastery will be a requirement in their future careers.

Furthermore, through the use of small group discussions and projects, the students learn to discuss and develop solutions to issues cooperatively and collaboratively.

The Chinese curriculum at SUIS (Pudong) is divided into two sections: Chinese as a First Language (CFL) and Chinese as an Additional Language (CAL). Students are placed in different classes according to their language background, their particular needs and baseline test results. This ensures these individual needs are met.

Key highlights of the SUIS (Pudong) thematic curriculum

Topic centred

Each unit's exploration is driven by a central idea and question that relates to a key topic about the unit's theme.

International in scope

Topics cover global issues and encourage students to view their explorations from a global perspective.

Critical in analysis

Students are actively encouraged to utilise, within the English National Curriculum, effective questioning strategies in Key Stage 1 and critical research skills in Key Stage 2 during their explorations.

Transdisciplinary in nature

Various skills and other aspects of the curriculum's attainment targets for geography, history, citizenship and PSHE are met during theme explorations. The use of technology is embedded in most of the units of exploration.

Cross stream in application

The thematic curriculum was developed through collaboration between International Stream, Pioneer Programme (see **Chapter 5.5**) and Local Stream teachers across the school.

Curriculum structure

The curriculum is based around an exploration cycle (see **Figure 1**, right) that provides students with various opportunities to gain an in-depth understanding of the topic of study. Students are first provided with a central idea and question. They then follow an exploration cycle as described below.

Central idea

This is an overall idea that provides a focus for the exploration and lays out clear grade specific learning objectives adapted from the attainment targets of the English National Curriculum for history, geography and science for the theme unit.

Ask

These lessons in the cycle utilise a variety of open-ended small and large group discussions and activities to introduce the students to the theme and to gauge their existing knowledge of the topic.

Investigate

These lessons are for gathering information about the theme. Researching, studying, crafting an experiment, observing, planning and utilising surveys are a few examples of activities that are utilised in this part of the exploration.

Create

These lessons utilise the information gathered from the investigation section to shape new ideas and theories outside of the students' prior experiences and knowledge. They can represent this new insight by participating in an activity or creating a piece of work that represents their new knowledge of the central idea and puts forward solutions to pertinent issues raised during their exploration.

Discuss

These lessons are for students to share new knowledge with each other. Comparing notes, discussing conclusions and sharing experiences are examples of this process in action.

Reflect/evaluate/assess

These lessons are for students to look back on the central idea, the exploration and the discussions

Fig 1: The theme exploration cycle

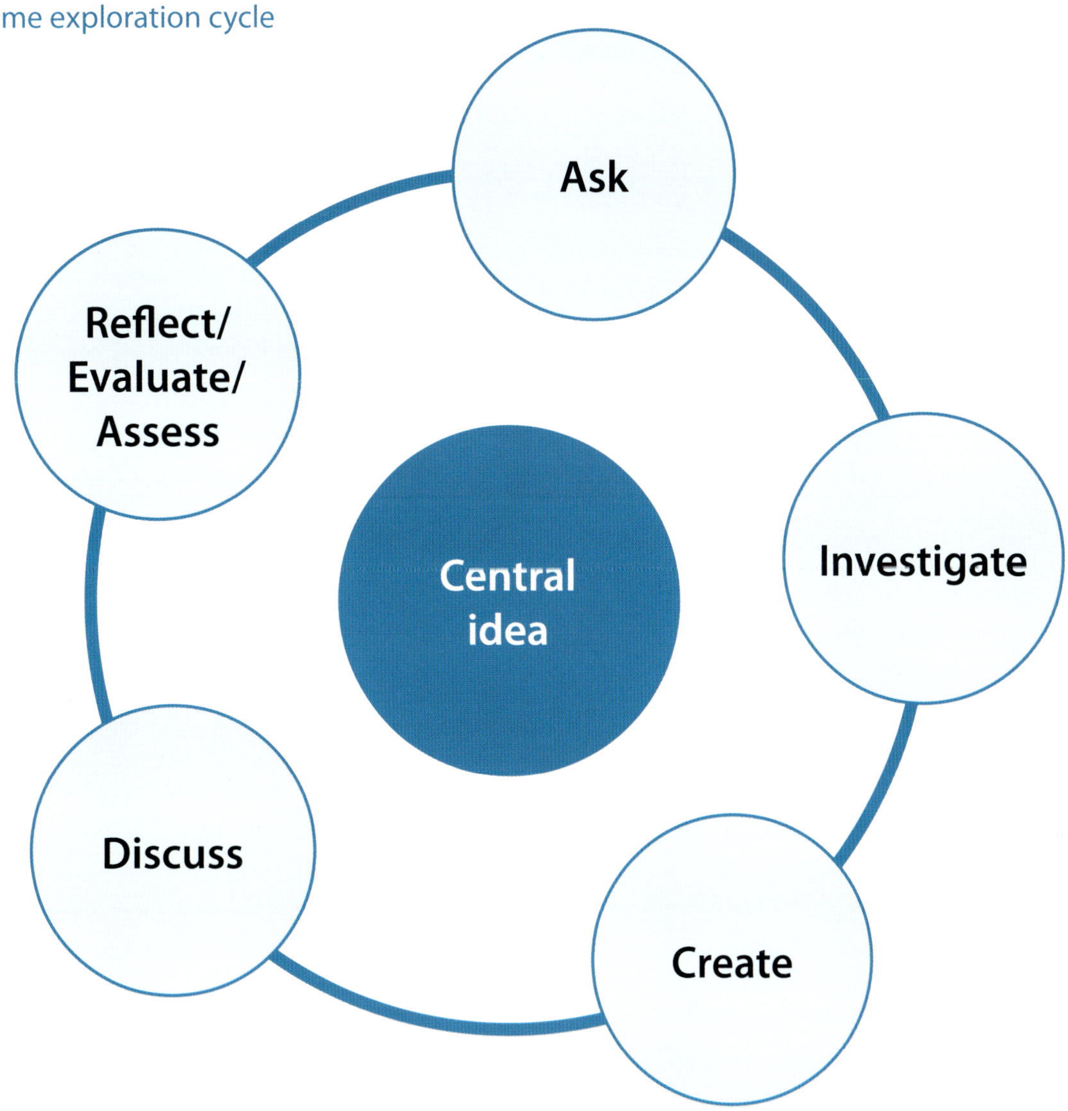

and draw conclusions about the theme. They are also an opportunity for students to reflect on new ideas that can build on their new knowledge and be used as a springboard for the following year's study of the theme. It is also an opportunity for teachers to assess students by utilising the adapted English National Curriculum attainment targets as indicators of progress.

Teaching methodology

As one of the underlying desires of our parents for their children is the need for them to become bilingual, the methodology that is utilised to teach lessons is as critical as the curriculum itself. As the world has become more integrated and globalised, the need for bilingual education has become more pertinent to students around the world. At SUIS (Pudong) primary students are expected to become biliterate before they move on to the secondary school. The school supports students to achieve this goal by providing them with 270 minutes a week of levelled Chinese language instruction and 300 minutes of English language instruction. All other classes are bilingually team taught to ensure that students are provided with multiple opportunities to apply the language skills they learn in their Chinese and English classes.

The team teaching methods that we utilise encompass a variety of different approaches based on the needs of the lesson being taught and the students' understanding of the topics and their own language ability in the target languages. Four examples are summarised below

The 'lead and support teacher' model.

This approach is used when the majority of students understand the concepts being taught. One teacher will teach the lesson in their own language whilst the other provides support in their language throughout the lesson. This ensures that students will be given an opportunity to reinforce the concept they are learning in both languages.

The 'differentiated co-teaching' model.

Here, more individual attention is provided to the less successful students. In this approach, one teacher will take the lead whilst the other works with a group of students less successful in the language with which they are most comfortable. Obviously, this approach can also be used to support the most successful students in any language.

The 'teach and observe' model.

This is used when the students need to be observed for assessment purposes. In this approach one teacher will lead the entire lesson while the other will observe students' participation in class to assess their understanding of the key concepts and their progress. This is ideal for the assessment of students while also allowing the teachers to identify students in need of further support or more challenging material.

The 'lead and drifter teacher' model.

This approach has one teacher leading the lesson in their language while the other will move around the classroom providing support to students in need of help with the concept being taught.

The three key hallmarks of all of these approaches are:

- students are continually given opportunities to learn and apply new concepts in a fully bilingual environment;
- translation is not relied on to teach as this does not effectively allow students to synthesize the language and concepts they are learning; and
- students are continually provided with differentiated instruction which ensures that the needs of all students are being consistently met.

These bilingual team teaching models are used in our theme classes to ensure that students are given both a variety of opportunities to learn complex concepts within the language and the learning support necessary to be successful. Furthermore, the teachers themselves model multicultural and multilingual cooperation and collaboration for the students. This is one of the key aspects of the theme curriculum. By utilising this diversity of teaching methodologies, our teachers are practicing what they teach to our students.

Bilingual team teaching

The development process

The curriculum was developed over a period of three months. It was planned in six stages (see below) and involved the collaboration of seventeen teachers from three different departments of the school.

The Co-Principal of the school, Dr Roger Morgan, served in an advisory role by providing the curriculum team with direction, insight and feedback. A team of three individuals formed the Coordinating Committee. This Committee was responsible for the planning and scheduling of meetings. It was also responsible for any overall decisions regarding the curriculum.

Stage 1: Survey (Feedback)

A survey, requiring feedback about the previous curriculum and asking for ideas about the future curriculum, was developed by the Coordinating Committee and issued to staff over a week-long period. The staff were informed about the purpose of the survey and were encouraged to be honest and open in their responses.

Stage 2: Directional meeting

Staff reflected on and summarised the data gathered from the survey at the directional meeting. The data provided direction for discussions about the new curriculum. These discussions provided a framework for the curriculum planning process. The staff members were placed into Theme Planning Groups of their choice and were tasked with collaboratively planning the teaching methodology and the learning opportunities for the group's theme.

The purpose of utilising this approach was to ensure that the theme curriculum eventually developed was born out of a collaborative and co-operative approach. It was expected that issues regarding language and culture would be effectively addressed by teachers during the development process.

Stage 3: Presentation of themes

Each Theme Planning Group presented their teaching methodologies and learning opportunities for their corresponding theme unit. Staff members were given the opportunity to provide feedback on the curriculum plan's ability to effectively meet the needs of their students. Changes were made based on this feedback. This approach ensured that there was an effective feedback loop whereby every teacher would be given an opportunity to participate in the development and modification of each theme and the overall curriculum. It also ensured that any concerns that were raised were immediately and effectively addressed.

Stage 4: Finalisation meeting

At this meeting, the first draft of the curriculum document was presented to the staff. Any modifications that staff required were made and the document content and structure were finalised. Initial discussions about the implementation of the curriculum were held with the focus placed on the timeline for implementation and the type of material and administrative support needed for the effective implementation of the curriculum.

Stage 5: Editing

The Co-ordinator of the Curriculum Committee added necessary explanatory elements to the document and edited the final document.

Stage 6: Implementation

The Co-ordinator presented the final document to the staff. The implementation process was explained in detail to the teachers. Clear forms of material and administrative support were outlined to the teachers based on previous discussions and avenues for feedback were provided in the form of weekly meetings during the first few months of implementation. These weekly meetings have now become pre-theme unit meetings where teachers meet in their grade groups before the start of a new theme to collaboratively plan for the upcoming unit and also to document feedback about the previously taught unit. This feedback is presented when the staff start the process of modifying the curriculum for the upcoming school year.

The thematic curriculum is reviewed and updated annually. A diagramatic representation of the six stages can be seen on the next page in **Figure 2**.

Fig 2: The curriculum development process

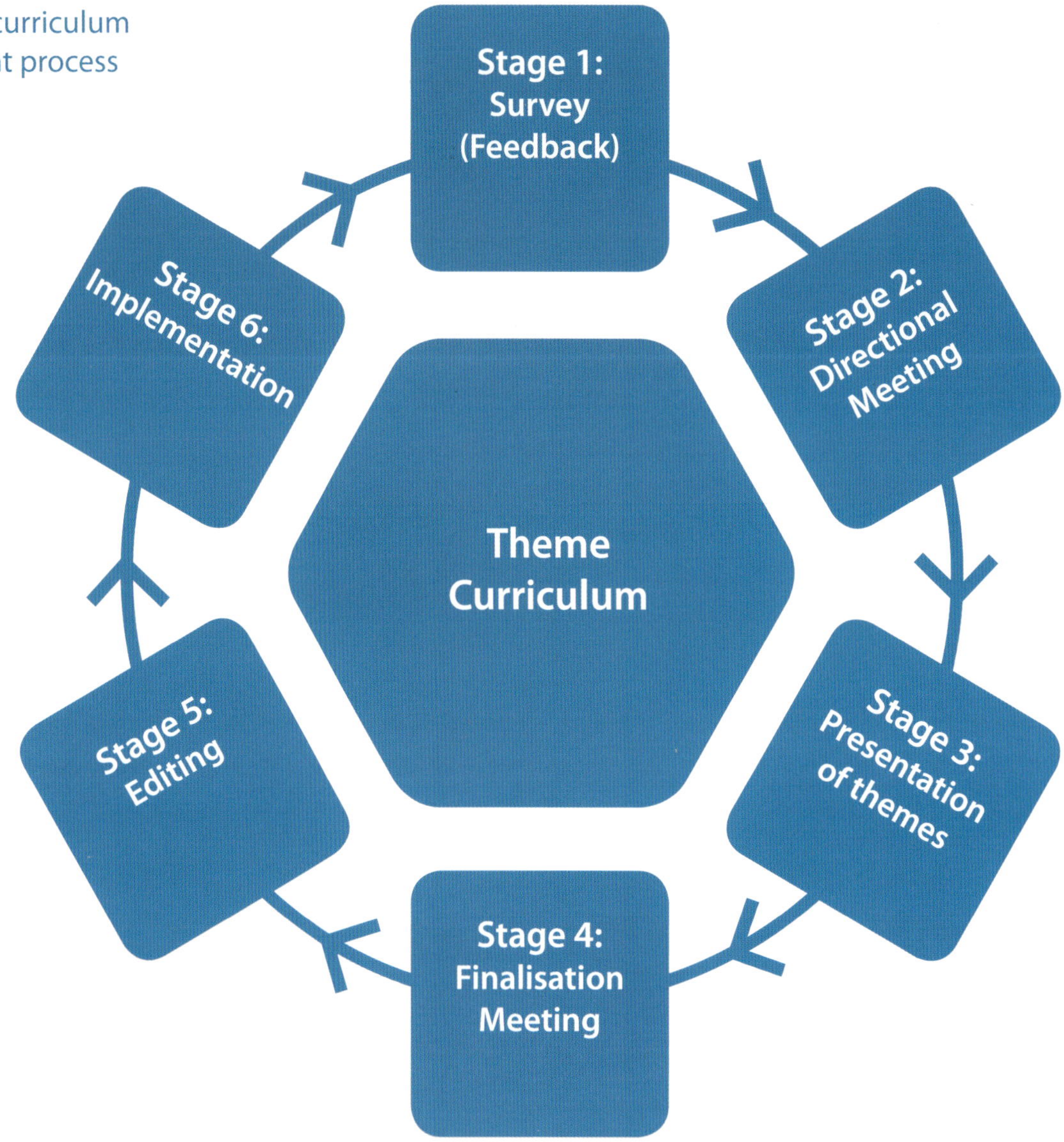

Evaluating bilingualism

The following indicators of excellence devised by Trevor Higginbottom[1] are used for evaluating the bilingual dimension of our thematic curriculum.

- Was a specific bilingual strategy used during the lesson? (e.g. 'total immersion' or 'mixed code')
- What language medium was used during the lesson (Chinese or English)? Did the language medium restrict subject development?
- To what extent was the language content appropriate to the language needs of the majority of the students?
- Did the teachers make any attempt to focus specifically on particular language issues (e.g. repeating words bilingually)?
- How did the two students who were identified as being the least proficient in the language medium being used cope with this language?
- Did the teachers make any attempt to give individual support to these students? If so, how?
- Did the teacher not leading the lesson at a particular time(s) make any attempt to support the language needs of individual students, other than the two students identified?
- Was there any evidence of bilingualism in any other aspects of the lesson (e.g. teaching and learning worksheets; displays of students work)?

Reflections on bilingual team teaching

A Canadian teacher's perspective: Charlaine Reid

One of the biggest challenges of team teaching is finding the time to plan and collaborate effectively with your teaching partner. Many struggles with co-teaching can be linked back to lack of co-planning. If one teacher is unclear about the elements of the lesson, they are not able to participate as well as they could and become more of a teacher's assistant rather than a co-teacher. It is much easier to come up with a great lesson when you have someone to brainstorm ideas with to develop concepts further. Once both teachers have a full understanding of the lesson, they can work together to deliver the lesson cooperatively.

I find that one of the biggest benefits of co-teaching is the simple fact that there are two teachers who can do two things at once. How many times have teachers wished they could be in two places at once? The class can easily be divided into two groups depending on their needs, interests or abilities and can be led by each teacher. This is often useful to give students extra help with certain concepts or additional coverage for more successful students. Having two teachers also makes supervising group work easier since you can circulate between groups more effectively. Again, this only works when both teachers are very clear about the lesson's objectives and the overall plan.

A key to successful team teaching is not only the increased communication and support during the planning of the lesson, but also during the teaching. Teachers can talk to each other during the lesson and both are always involved: this models co-operation for the students. Teachers can take turns in leading the lesson in either language while the other teacher can be circulating to assist and manage the students. Once a positive relationship between teachers has been established, teachers can smoothly interject into each other's explanations or discussions so students can have the benefit of hearing two points of view. It can give the lessons a more conversational feel which can be engaging for the students and encourages them to take part as well.

Overall, I find co-teaching to be a more rewarding experience than teaching on my own. By creating and delivering lessons collaboratively and having someone to share your successes and good times with, teaching becomes a more enjoyable and effective experience.

A Chinese teacher's perspective: Sarah Zhang

I feel that team teaching is a creative way to teach in a Global School setting, one that utilises the strengths of both teachers to serve the needs of all students in the class. In my opinion, thematic study is the most important subject in our curriculum because it provides the perfect *'East meets West'* balance that Xiehe schools are known for.

The most Important goal of a thematic lesson Is that students are able to orally express the key points in both Chinese and English, and all activities are based around this goal. My co-teacher and I plan for these lessons one week in advance, and during this time we write down what we need to implement a successful class (materials, resources and activities) whilst taking into consideration the unique interests and needs of the students. It is crucial to have open communication with your co-teacher in order to ensure the class runs smoothly and effectively. We discuss our lesson plan before each lesson to ensure we are both clear on every aspect of the class. While these discussions are not long, the planning process never stops and we are continually teaching, assessing, reflecting and planning. It is an ongoing and efficient cycle.

We divide the work accordingly to guarantee appropriate use of Chinese and English instruction. For example, one teacher can do a warm-up activity with the class to activate prior knowledge on the topic, while the other teacher can lead a mini-lesson or a role play exercise. Each teacher seamlessly picks up where the other teacher leaves off which creates an interesting and dynamic educational experience for the students.

With regard to language, I feel the Chinese teacher should give special attention to individual students using Chinese. All students have unique needs, such as requiring a deeper explanation or positive encouragement to complete the task. Chinese teachers can ensure that students understand the lesson content.

Team teaching is successful and enjoyable because of teacher compatibility. I strongly believe that two teachers cannot just be put together and told to team teach. I am very lucky to have had very considerate, friendly and open-minded co-teachers. We might not have the same personality or similar views, but I believe when you have the same goal of making the lesson enjoyable and educationally rewarding for students, everyone can benefit.

Exemplar bilingual lesson

An exemplar lesson taught by Charlaine Reid and Sarah Zhang: the bilingual and team teaching dimensions.

For this lesson the team teachers had two regular planning meetings followed by a few short conversations to discuss modifications to the overall plan. The first meeting was held during their regular weekly grade level planning meeting where grade level teachers get together to discuss the learning objectives for the following week's lessons. At this meeting teachers discussed and standardised the general learning objectives for all classes for the coming week. Later that week, the co-teachers met again for their own weekly meeting and agreed the methods they would utilise to teach and assess the lesson, such as the use of an introductory video and the modelling of the learning objectives.

At this time, there was no discussion about which co-teaching methods would be used at various times since the teachers had been teaching together for a while and understood how the flow of a co-taught lesson usually progresses. They spoke a few more times during day to day interactions to sort out issues such as preparing resources and deciding who would be taking a record of the assessment. Once they decided who would be the lead teacher for the lesson, that teacher prepared most of the resources in advance and discussed the materials she found with her co-teacher.

Lesson Evaluation

Ongoing evaluation of our lessons is a crucial element within our bilingual team teaching. Teachers' lessons are observed twice a semester for evaluation purposes and form a large part of their overall yearly appraisal. When observing bilingually team taught lessons, some of the core indicators of excellence as formulated by Trevor Higginbottom[1] are used as follows.

- Teachers take on equally shared roles throughout the lesson.
- Lessons are conducted seamlessly.
- Teachers are comfortable and confident in their interactions with each other and the students.
- Teachers model co-operative and collaborative strategies to students.
- Teachers work as a team to meet the individual needs of students.
- Teachers' roles are changed from lesson to lesson.
- Overall, teaching team works effectively.

Observable features relating to each indicator are devised as the basis for detailed evaluation. In this exemplar lesson we used the 'Lead and Support Teacher Model' to deliver their lesson (see page 80). The lesson was taught to a Grade 1 class and the theme being explored was 'Community: our globalised village'. In this lesson the teachers were evaluated using the above criteria. Some examples of the evaluator's comments of how the indicators listed above were met are listed in the table (right).

Overall, Charlaine and Sarah felt that the lesson was successful, although some of the higher order concepts being taught were challenging for some students.

Charlaine (left) and Sarah (right) reflect on their co-teaching.

Indicator	Examples in the lesson
Sharing roles	- Support given by teachers by one taking the lead in discussion whilst the other is writing down students' ideas and reinforcing the idea in the second language. - Tasks are equally shared and the lesson is obviously collaboratively planned. - Both teachers provide support during student centred activities. - Teachers undertake their question and answer sessions together which shares the teaching and also reinforces classroom management.
Seamless teaching	- Great classroom management in place and clear understanding of the system by students and consistency of implementation by teachers. This ensures a seamless and effective lesson. - Lesson is successfully bilingual throughout the duration of the class. - Teachers seamlessly take the lead and are well aware of their roles for each part of the lesson.
Teacher interaction	- The support teacher monitors on-task responses and prompts students when necessary. - Teachers are comfortable with intervention by their colleagues and in many cases build on these interruptions to support their colleague and reinforce what they have said.
Co-operation/ collaboration	- Story told at the beginning of lesson is undertaken cooperatively and is an excellent model for students. - There is a consistent focus on group learning activities. Teacher modelling is used effectively as a method to introduce students to these activities.
Team working	- During group work teachers provide support to groups based on language needs meaning that the Chinese teacher is with the less successful Chinese students and the Western teacher is with the less successful English students. - Differentiation is collaboratively planned using a diversity of approaches.
Roles	- Teachers seemed comfortable in and familiar with their roles throughout the lesson.
Summary	- The teachers were well prepared and respectful to each other. - The teachers demonstrated a high professional standard which was reflected in the content and layout of their classroom displays, the behaviour of their students and the overall achievement of their lesson objectives.

Conclusion

Our bilingual team teaching approach to thematic education has, generally, been very successful but there is still work to be done to ensure consistency in excellent practice in this respect across the school. Bilingualism remains a particularly challenging curriculum dimension.

Mark Renie is Head of Primary, SUIS (Pudong).

Charlaine Reid is Key Stage 1 Co-ordinator, SUIS (Pudong).

Sarah Zhang is a Grade 1 Homeroom Teacher, SUIS (Pudong).

Talkabout

- *What strategies would you advise SUIS (Pudong) to adopt to ensure excellence across the curriculum in their thematic bilingual team teaching?*
- *Why might team teaching be a worthwhile teaching and learning strategy to adopt despite its high staff costs?*

Acknowledgements

[1] Higginbottom, T. (2011). *Evaluation Report on 'Thematic Bilingual Team Teaching', SUIS (Pudong)* - unpublished

5.2 Contrasting approaches to Values Education in a Xiehe Global School.

Rob Bowden, Trevor Higginbottom, Jayanthi Nayak, Xu Wei (Julia) and Zhou Li-Ping (Julia)

Arguably, education with respect to both the 'development' and 'clarification' of values is a key dimension of the Global School curriculum. In this chapter, the authors describe how this is being tackled in very different ways in the Local and International Streams of SUIS (Hong Qiao) and in an exciting new Curriculum Development Project in England. Here again, 'East meets West' dialogue between both students and teachers during the last decade has greatly enhanced the quality of the innovation in this Xiehe Global School. In a concluding section, the authors summarise the future ways in which they hope to further develop this complex area of the curriculum.

> *'Values education can build more resilient and capable young people, enrich the curriculum and contribute to school improvement. Evidence from the UK and internationally clearly signals that values-based approaches to learning consistently help schools to raise standards, improve behaviour and develop a stronger sense of being and belonging for the school and its community. What this work also demonstrates is the pivotal role of leadership in achieving this and the significance of leaders giving themselves the time and space to engage in the debates and the learning, for themselves.'*
>
> Rob Bowden

Explicit values education in the SUIS (Hong Qiao) Local Stream: The Virtues Project

In order to strengthen the values dimension of its curriculum, the Local Stream adopted the Virtues Project from the International Stream in 2005.

This is a Canadian curriculum development initiative aimed at teaching children virtues in order to build character. [1]

In this case values education is developed **explicitly** in the curriculum. There are 52 virtues incorporated within the Project, each of which is taught thematically over a period of two weeks in 'homeroom' (class) lessons by the class teacher. Additionally, the fortnightly virtue is referred to in subject lessons across the curriculum. At the end of each two-week thematic study of a virtue, individual students are nominated as 'stars' with respect to the virtue in question. Student voting on the 'top star' follows after the nominees have appeared in the SUIS (Hong Qiao) closed circuit TV show.

RIGHT: Virtues learning in action

LEFT: Inter-stream semester activity

Monthly, virtues are considered in inter-stream assemblies. Other activities have included whole school events which review aspects of the Virtues Project. Inter-stream sister classes, on occasions, come together to discuss and share the outcomes of their work with respect to specific virtues (see page 12).

Each student is given a 'Virtues Practice Journal' which is the outcome of school based curriculum development. The Journal aims to promote student understanding of each virtue through a wide range of oracy and literacy skills. It is hoped that this will motivate and inspire the student to practise each of the virtues. Pages 89 and 90 contain an extract from the Student's Journal relating to the virtue 'Peace'.

The outcomes of student work relating to the Virtues Project are widely displayed throughout the Local Stream in an attempt to ensure that these values help to promote the school's mission and influence day to day working practices.

The true test of this approach to values education is for parents and others visiting the Local Stream to ascertain whether or not they feel there is significant evidence, from both students and staff, to suggest that the 52 virtues (see picture left) are permeating the culture of the school (school culture being defined as 'the way we do things around here'). Do we practice what we preach? Also, do our parents see this impacting on their own child's value system?

• Virtue proverb

When there is no peace in the family, there will be no peace in society.

Daisaku Ikeda

• What is peace?

Peace is a feeling of inner calm, a way of dealing with conflicts so that nobody suffers. When you give up violence, prejudice and not regarding others as enemies, peace will happen.

• How to practice peace

Maintain peace of mind and let your heart feel completely quiet, then you will be able to think over and self-reflect.

To create peace, the language of peace should be used. Do not say 'I hate ...' or anything like it. Do not curse, talk nor criticize behind another person's back. Even when you are very angry, use moderate words to express your emotion: 'Do you know that entering my room without knocking first makes me feel very angry.' Speak softly and gently; do not hurt others. Avoid any acts of violence.

If you do not agree with the opinions of others, find a way to talk about things peacefully with them.

Learn to appreciate difference; do not let them become reasons of bias or battles.

• Discussion on the virtue

In the following cases, how will you practice the virtue of 'peace'?

- Your brother or sister comes into your room, and steps on a painting or model which you have just completed...

- There is a new student in your class, some students always make fun of him...

- Some children begin to provoke you, looking for a fight with you...

• My virtue actions

'Once my friend accidentally tore my exercise book in class when we were doing some work together in maths. She then left it on her desk and I couldn't find it. This meant that I fell behind the rest of the class in finishing my subtraction exercises. At the end of the lesson I found the book. I just spoke to my friend calmly and did not blame her in any way. I asked her politely to be more considerate in future.'

Fang Yi-An, Class 5D

Reproduced extract from the Virtues Project Journal relating to the virtue 'Peace'.

- **Self evaluation**

Do you have the virtue of peace?

Please colour in stars which describe your situation.

☆ I can think over or self-reflect, creating inner peace of mind.

☆ Even when I am angry, I am able to use the language of peace, speaking softly and gently.

☆ I try to avoid hurting anyone.

☆ When I disagree, I am able to find a peaceful way to solve the problem.

☆ I learn to appreciate differences.

- **Comments from parents/ teachers/classmates**

'Ann is a peace ambassador at home. Sometimes when adults are in a bad mood she tries hard to improve the atmosphere and to calm everyone down. This creates a much more peaceful family'

Mother of Fang Yi-An, Class 5D

Virtue Story: The dove of peace

The origin of regarding a pigeon as the symbol of peace started with Picasso. In 1940, Hitler conquered Paris, the capital of France. Picasso was depressed when sitting in his painting studio. Somebody knocked on the door, it was his neighbour Mr Mish who was carrying an injured pigeon with blood on his hands. He told a sad story to Picasso: his grandson raised a flock of pigeons and he usually put a white cloth on a bamboo pole to attract pigeons. When he knew that his father died in battle with the German army, his heart was filled with hatred. He knew that the white cloth was an indicator of surrendering to one's enemies, so he used a red cloth to attract pigeons. The eye-catching colour drew the attention of the German army. Inhuman Fascist gangsters threw him onto to the ground and stabbed all the pigeons dead. Mr Mish spoke to Picasso, 'Sir, I'd like you to draw a pigeon for me to help me remember my grandson who was killed by the Fascists.' After that, Picasso drew a sad looking flying pigeon, this is the origin of today's 'Peace Dove'. In November 1950 Picasso drew a flying pigeon with an olive branch in its mouth in memory of the World Peace Conference held in Warsaw. At that time the famous Chilean poet Neruda named it as the 'Dove of Peace'. Since then the pigeon has been recognised officially as the symbol of 'Peace'.

Implicit values education in the SUIS (Hong Qiao) International Stream

The need for values education was recognised by the International Stream when the school opened in 2003. As a result, the Virtues Project was established at that stage as an important dimension of the International Primary Curriculum (IPC).

Later in the decade two significant developments took place: first, the International Stream adopted the International Baccalaureate (IB) Primary Years Programme (PYP). Secondly, as summarised above, the Local Stream adopted the Virtues Project. This led to much purposeful professional discussion on values education between the two streams.

Subsequently, the International Stream reduced the content of the Virtues Project and combined this with the 'attributes' within the PYP Learner Profile, see the table below.

These attributes were combined, within the PYP, with a consideration of twelve 'attitudes' which it is felt support the development of these attributes:

Attributes within the PYP Learner Profile [2]	
'The aim of all IB programmes is to develop internationally minded people who, recognising their common humanity and shared guardianship of the planet, help to create a better and more peaceful world. As IB learners we strive to be:	
Inquirers	We nurture our curiosity, developing skills for inquiry and research. We know how to learn independently and with others. We learn with enthusiasm and sustain our love of learning throughout life.
Knowledgeable	We develop and use conceptual understanding, exploring knowledge across a range of disciplines. We engage with issues and ideas that have local and global significance.
Thinkers	We use critical and creative thinking skills to analyse and take responsible action on complex problems. We exercise initiative in making reasoned, ethical decisions.
Communicators	We express ourselves confidently and creatively in more than one language and in many ways. We collaborate effectively, listening carefully to the perspectives of other individuals and groups.
Principled	We act with integrity and honesty, with a strong sense of fairness and justice, and with respect for the dignity and rights of people everywhere. We take responsibility for our actions and their consequences.
Open-minded	We critically appreciate our own cultures and personal histories, as well as the values and traditions of others. We seek and evaluate a range of points of view, and we are willing to grow from the experience.
Caring	We show empathy, compassion and respect. We have a commitment to service, and we act to make a positive difference in the lives of others and in the world around us.
Risk-takers (Courageous)	We approach uncertainty with forethought and determination; we work independently and cooperatively to explore new ideas and innovative strategies. We are resourceful and resilient in the face of challenges and change.
Balanced	We understand the importance of balancing different aspects of our lives – intellectual, physical and emotional – to achieve well-being for ourselves and others. We recognise our interdependence with other people and with the world in which we live.
Reflective	We thoughtfully consider the world and our own ideas and experience. We work to understand our strengths and weaknesses in order to support our learning and personal development'.

'appreciation', 'co-operation', 'commitment', 'confidence', 'creativity', 'curiosity', 'empathy', 'enthusiasm', 'independence', 'integrity', 'respect', 'tolerance'. The language of the Virtues Project was used to support the development of the learner profile among students, as necessary. An example is given below with reference to the IB Learner Profile attribute 'principled', where integrity, tolerance, respect and commitment are attitudes advocated by the IB PYP and the rest are virtues which connect to the Learner Profile.

After the International Stream was accredited as an IB World School the main content 'vehicles' for values education within the PYP became the Units of Inquiry which are used to develop an integrated approach to subject areas such as language, maths, science and social studies. The teaching of values in the school then evolved from **being explicit to being implicit within the curriculum.**

To make the teaching of values an integral part of the curriculum, every grade group has mapped the Learner Profile attributes and attitudes that link to a specific Unit of Inquiry. These are taught during the Homeroom periods and promoted through the Unit, for learners to understand the attributes contextually. The learner profile attributes and attitudes are selected based on their relevance and connection to the Unit. For example, during Grade Two's Unit of Inquiry into 'People work together to help each other', students are taught about and expected to develop the Learner Profile's attributes 'Caring' 'Reflective' and 'Communicators' and the attitudes of 'empathy', 'cooperation' and 'integrity'. As demanded within the PYP, the grade group teachers collaboratively plan activities to engage children about the Learner Profile attributes and attitudes. These are explored, explained and taught during Homeroom periods through stories, role plays, poster making and activities.

Additionally, through self-assessment, the students are expected to reflect on the progress of their own learning based on the learner profile, and to identify or provide evidence of having displayed a learner profile attribute or one of the attitudes (see worksheet and student's work on pages 93-94). Students also reflect on their behaviour and goals every week and record it in their PYP Journal.

Further, to encourage their practice, the learner profile attributes and attitudes are presented or highlighted during class assemblies. The language of the virtues is not forgotten and is used during Flag Raising, a monthly inter-stream event for the International Stream, which is attended by all the school's students (see photo on page 100).

During assemblies, the students are awarded certificates for displaying the learner profile attributes and attitudes. They also receive green cards or reward cards in class for demonstrating their adoption of these qualities.

Name:______________________________ **Date:**______________________________

Individual Reflection

Use the circle to show your participation in group work. You can make a pie chart or use a percentage.

Group work

What did you do to help your group this week?	What can be done better for next week?

Attitudes

Choose two attitudes you displayed this week that were helpful to your group. Explain.	Choose two attitudes that will be helpful to your group next week. Explain.

Transdisciplinary skills

Choose two skills you used this week that were useful to your group. Explain.	Choose two skills that will be helpful to your group next week. Explain.

Learner Profile

The learner profile attribute(s) I displayed this week.	The learner profile attribute(s) I want to display next week.

Reproduced from original student work by Ji Min, Grade 4.

Field Trip Reflection (Blind School)

We went to the blind school (Shanghai School for the Blind) for the Unit 2 field trip to learn about how do blind children learn.

When we were going past the playgrounds and grassy fields, I saw that the floor has some red and yellow pop-up things that helps them to walk. I also saw some blind childrens that seems to be second or first grader were using the adults' help to walk and seemed like they are not used to it.
In the classroom, I saw about twelve blind childrens that is working very fine. How come they needed help?

I think because that blind school that we went is the only blind school in Shanghai, many blind students are there. And I think that they sometimes feel more happier than us. They're well-trained, and now I think that they are very happy!

I hope that the class that we taught songs and interviewed would never forget about us and be super happy to meet us again someday and tour in our school! I hope next time they can come to our school and we can have them sit beside us and listen to our classes and study with us for a day and tour with us in break times. I think that would be a good experience for them and us, too! I hope that I can study Braille someday and teach the blind students how to read when I grow up and doesn't have a job because we need warm hearts to survive and I liked being with blind children, after all.

Excellent reflection! I also hope blind children can come to our school one day.

Mapping the development of Values Education within the curriculum

Care is taken to ensure that each of the learner profile attributes and the related attitudes within the PYP are being fully developed. This is undertaken by the monitoring of their implementation within the curriculum. For example, 'co-operation' is one of the attitudes that the PYP suggests that schools should encourage. This attitude requires students to demonstrate cooperation, collaboration and taking on the roles of leader or follower, as the situation demands, during various paired and group work activities.

All students in the International Stream are familiar with collaborative learning strategies. However, this might not necessarily mean that they know how to work cooperatively. At the beginning of Grade 5, some students encountered unhappy moments when working with other students. For example, one student who speaks limited English was excluded in group work; students who were quite articulate usually dominated the group discussion and students were more likely to talk to people they liked in a group.

In order to change this situation, Xu Wei (Julia) and her co-teacher Annie Lopez led a lesson on 'Co-operation'. Students were asked to discuss in groups about what cooperation looks, sounds and feels like. At first, students found it quite difficult to respond. Teachers then guided them to think in the opposite direction: 'what does non cooperation look, sound and feel like?' This triggered a heated discussion. Some of the responses were: 'students do not look at each other to discuss what they should do next. Each student is busy doing what he/she likes doing; people do not take turns to talk so that there is more than one voice at a time; we feel uncomfortable and even angry; how can we change this to something positive called co-operation then?' After group discussion, ideas were shared with the entire class. Students volunteered to write on the co-operation poster.

Taking action

Since 'taking action' is emphasised in the PYP, students are encouraged to demonstrate attributes of the learner profile during their Unit of Inquiry.

In Grade 5, the Unit on 'Children's Rights' provided them with real life examples of caring and an opportunity to demonstrate this attribute. They learnt about Children's Rights through their inquiry into 'Children's rights are established to protect children'. Students studied the UN Convention on the Rights of the Child and understood that Child Rights can easily be neglected and violated and individuals and organisations need to take action to remedy the problem.

One of the learning activities was listening to a talk given by a guest speaker, John Paul McCarthy, the Stream's PE teacher who, together with several other SUIS teachers, ran for 24 hours to raise funds for the 'Pass Love Charity Foundation' which focuses on building quality village libraries in impoverished areas of China. Children in these communities only have textbooks to read. The libraries open up the world for these deprived rural children by providing a wide range of books and activity materials.

Inspired by John Paul's speech, the Grade 5 students decided to take a very active part in the 'Giving Tree Project'. This was established in China to provide migrant children with basic stationery, toys and clothes during Christmas.

Taking action: students prepare the 'Giving Tree' bags.

While in previous years Grade 5 students had filled gift bags, this year they went further and chose to take action by playing an active part in the gift bag preparation work. They helped to put information letters in the bags, stapled receivers' personal information cards to them and sorted out gift bags so that the bags were ready to be sent to people who wanted to donate gifts. Students acted upon what they knew about Children's Rights and also demonstrated how caring they were.

Likewise, in Grade 2, the Unit of Inquiry into 'People work together to help others' enabled students to develop an understanding of how people can work in co-operation to be caring and help people or animals in need. For their assessment, students created an organisation (a group) and tried to raise funds to help a cause of their choice. Despite their young age, the seven and eight-year-old students came up with different ideas to raise money and demonstrated different ways to show caring.

Integrating values within the learning context as detailed above has thus served the purpose of showing children that values are a part of life.

Assessment

Assessing values development has proved to be a rather difficult process. For a while, the learner profile attributes and attitudes linked to each unit were assessed as part of the Unit of Inquiry and included in student reports. This was, however, subsequently dropped on the advice of the IB evaluation team.

At present, our assessment approaches in this context include, for example, student self-assessment and reflections in portfolios. Every Friday, students set goals for the following week and then reflect on these before new ones are set. This process is taught to the students initially by teacher modeling. As students continue to reflect and share their goals and reflections each week they are also encouraged to think about how they will achieve their goals. Paired work review is a powerful assessment instrument. This process encourages introspection and focuses students inwards rather than outwards. The International Stream is also trying to encourage student reflection (intrinsic motivation) and reduce student motivation through rewards (extrinsic motivation). Student goals are also discussed and reviewed during student-led conferences and parent-teacher-student conferences.

The future of Values Education at SUIS (Hong Qiao)

The development of values education is an ongoing process. Whilst the International Stream has integrated the teaching and learning of values within the curriculum, there continues to be a need to further strengthen the programme by enhancing the overall content in this respect and the experiences of students.

Bearing in mind that skill-building is a necessary part of values development, an attempt is being made to link the personal and social health curriculum (known as 'Personal, Social and Physical Education' in the PYP) with the learner profile and the attitudes so that the development of individual identity and the development of values are contiguous. This is still in the exploratory stage.

In the International Stream, with its wide and varied student profile, a significant challenge is that of extending values beyond the school walls. An initial effort to involve parents through the sharing of stories from different countries met with a disappointing response, in part because this requires considerable follow up. Parent involvement, while welcome, requires substantial investment in time by the school because of the need for careful planning and preparation.

How parents can be helped to better understand the values promoted in a multi-cultural school is not an easy question to answer, given that the interpretation of values is contextual and actionable. An incident will help illustrate this conundrum: students learn about the learner profile 'principled' and the attitude of 'respect' and are taught that the latter involves using polite language. A student in lower primary was found using inappropriate language and when it was pointed out that he was not showing respect, he said that his older brother used it when interacting with him.

Fig 1: An annotated version of the 'leadership engagement model' used in Leading Through Values (see page 99)

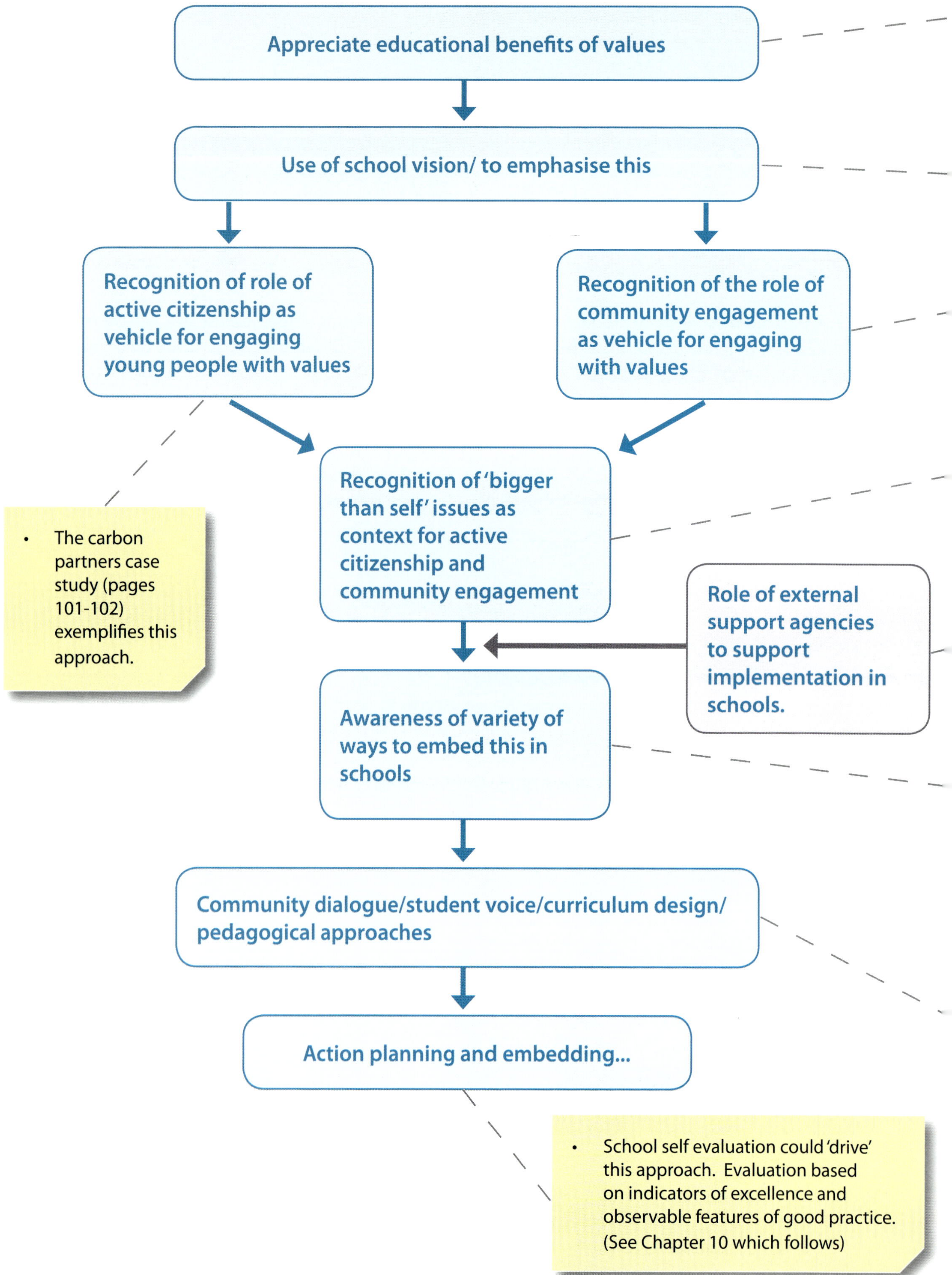

- Leadership has a key role in ensuring that the school develops such a philosophy. (See Chapter 8.1 which follows).
- This must be 'owned' by the staff, students and governors.
- Clearly articulated (and explicit) aims and objectives are essential.

- It would be helpful to undertake an initial audit of the school's culture ('the ways we do things around here'). Are changes necessary?
- The school mission should reflect this overall framework.

- 'Community' studied at the family school, local, city/town, national and international levels.

- Support given by the school for students to engage actively in the issues.

- External agencies could support the policy development process (see Chapter 1 above), the production of relevant teaching and learning approaches and school self evaluation strategies.

- Cross curriculum auditing is essential.
- The process of policy development as advocated in Chapter 8.2 which follows would be helpful in this context.
- A person with responsibility for cross curriculum co-ordination would be key here.

- A review of the aims and objectives of global learning would be a useful starting point. (See Chapter 3 above).
- The student council has a key role to play.
- Philosophy for Children would be a key pedagogical approach (See Chapter 5.3 which follows)
- Global linking would support international community dialogue (See Chapters 7.1, 7.2 and 7.3 which follow).
- Cross phase continuity and progression in terms of the aims and objectives would be essential. (See Chapter 6.2 above)
- All these activities must reflect the school's explicitly defined culture and ensure implementation of the aspirations of the school's mission.

The young child thought it was acceptable because his mother had told him that the older brother was allowed to use such language to his younger brother. How should the school then encourage parents to create a family environment that enhances the development of these values? Both Streams will continue to tackle this difficult issue in the future.

Assessment in values education will be subject to ongoing review throughout the school. Should the development of student values be assessed? If yes, what assessment strategies and tools are effective in this respect? How can values taught in school be internalised by each student? Are tools such as self-assessment and reflection adequate?

International collaboration in Values Education: Learning Through Values

Students completing values 'self-world' to be part of Leading Through Values pilot project, 2012-13

In Autumn 2013 Xiehe Global Schools and Kindergartens began to collaborate with a particularly interesting and innovative values education project based in England: 'Leading through Values'. The initiative is co-ordinated by Lifeworlds Learning in partnership with other UK National Organisations, including Oxfam Education, Think Global and British Red Cross.

'Leading through Values' is particularly relevant to Xiehe Global Schools and Kindergartens because it takes a whole school approach to values education within the context of global learning. **Figure 1** on pages 97-98 is an annotated summary of the Project's aims and objectives within what is defined as its 'school leader engagement model'. The key dimensions are shown in the flow diagram with explanatory notes linked to each of the dimensions.

The pilot phase of the Project was undertaken from September 2012 to March 2013, in nine primary schools. Research during this period relating to its key objectives suggested the following preliminary outcomes.

- A shift in the ethos of the school towards the promotion of intrinsic values.
- Increased curriculum time spent on values and 'bigger than self' (BTS) learning.
- The development of skills and dispositions necessary to support values and BTS learning.
- Greater awareness of the support that external agencies can offer to schools.
- Increased recognition of the value of these approaches for learning.

In late Autumn 2013 the main phase of 'Leading Through Values' was being planned and developed by Lifeworlds Learning with the anticipation that some Xiehe Global Schools and Kindergartens could be involved in this ongoing action research project.

Conclusion

Any society (for example, as a family, a school, a nation or a global community) must define its aspirational values and attempt to achieve them if it is to be healthy, caring, equitable, sustainable and progressive. Schools have a vital role to play in this respect. Values education is a key curriculum dimension of any school. If neglected within a country's educational system this has the potential to create a rootless, drifting and incoherent nation. A key challenge for individual schools pursuing some of the strategies recommended in this chapter is to ensure that they 'practice what they preach'.

Talkabout

- *Review the place of values education within your school and/or educational organisation. What values do you feel you currently aspire to? How do you discover whether or not this is happening? Are you 'practicing what you preach'?*
- *Discuss the advantages and disadvantages of each of the three approaches to values education (explicit, implicit and leading through values)summarised in this chapter.*
- *If you feel one of these is worthy of adoption at the school level, plan a programme for its implementation.*

Jayanthi Nayak is a Homeroom Teacher and Co-ordinator of the Values Education Programme in the International Stream at SUIS (Hong Qiao)

Xu Wei (Julia) is a Homeroom Teacher and Grade 4 Co-ordinator in the International Stream at SUIS (Hong Qiao).

Zhou Li-Ping (Julia) is Head of Primary in the Local Stream, SUIS (Hong Qiao).

They are grateful to Derek Lee for devising the student reflection worksheet included on page 93.

Acknowledgements

[1] www.virtuseproject.com
[2] International Baccalaureate Review Report and Recommendations. (April 2013)

Inter-stream flag raising ceremony

Global Learning in Action:

Studying the issue of sustainability, Carbon Partners: a case study

Clive Belgeonne

'We have to learn how to adapt to climate change and to oil supplies peaking and then finally running out. Taken together these two issues mean we have to move as quickly as possible to a zero-carbon economy or, more broadly, a sustainable future. What a challenge for education!' [1]

The challenges of adapting our lifestyles to deal with the implications of climate change and the need to overcome our reliance on fossil fuels can seem daunting and are often avoided by educators.

The Carbon Partners Project has tried to bring the issues to life and enable schools to engage in practical action. The Project uses the idea of carbon footprints (see box) to get schools to measure their carbon impacts, compare them with other schools and develop action learning to adapt to climate change.

The concept of climate change can seem quite abstract and, for young people, only a threat to be worried about some time in the future. The notion of carbon footprints makes the issues measurable and personally pertinent.

Carbon Footprint

A Carbon Footprint is used as shorthand to mean the best estimate that we can get of the full climate change impact of something. [2]

A carbon footprint is a measure of how much greenhouse gas you produce, measured in tonnes of carbon dioxide equivalent.

The two biggest contributors to a school's carbon footprint are usually energy usage and purchasing of equipment and resources. Schools also need to look at travel to school and the waste created, as well as the type of food served in their dining room.

Carbon Partners in action - Meadow View Primary School

Meadow View Primary School in Rotherham, England, is part of the Rotherham Global Schools Network. The network has looked at different global themes and decided to focus on energy and carbon footprints. Meadow View liked the Carbon Partners model as they have a partner school in Zambia.

They started with an Energy Week: every class did something slightly different, with younger children looking at their energy usage and recycling and the older classes learning about sustainability and deforestation.

Pupils in a Key Stage 1 assembly on carbon footprints hold up balloons representing 1 tonne of CO_2 each (99 representing Meadow View emissions; 1 representing their Zambian link school emissions)

The students helped to calculate their carbon footprint by carrying out an Energy Audit around school. It helped to raise understanding of the students' roles as global citizens and that we can only make a difference by working together.

ABOVE: *A Y2 student measures the school perimeter with teacher.*

LEFT: *Y6 students calculate their carbon footprints.*

On a visit to the Zambian school, the teachers shared their work on carbon footprints; that has led to a joint project between the two schools and discussion about energy usage, as there is a huge difference between the two (carbon footprint of UK school 529kg per student; Zambian school 5kg per student).

The Rotherham teachers have been amazed by the impact of the Energy Week, with the students now monitoring the teachers' energy usage and also taking ideas home. The students suggested setting up a Global School Council with representatives from Foundation to Grade Six to steer this work. They are now investigating the issues of food waste and composting. There are, also, plans for the students to grow food on the school site.

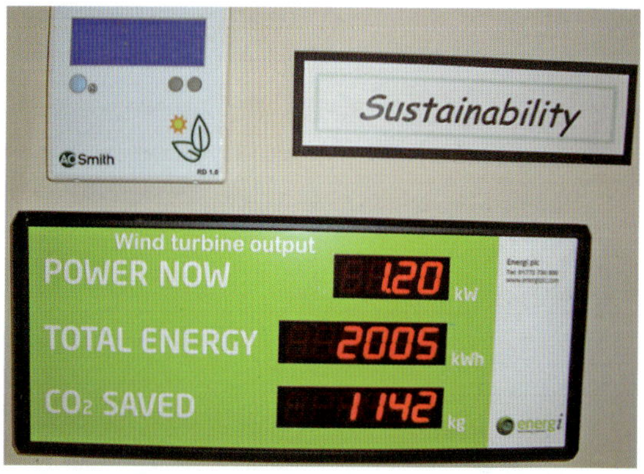

Part of a Sustainability display board at Canklow Woods Primary School (another school in the Rotherham network) shows energy from school wind turbine and CO_2 savings.

For more information visit www.carbonpartners.org.uk

(the Meadow View case study is in the 'Participating Schools' section.)

Further useful resources:

- Action Aid. *Power Down,* available at http://powerdown.actionaid.org.uk/
- British Council. *Climate 4 Classrooms*, available at http://schoolsonline.britishcouncil.org/climate-4-classrooms
- Marshall, G. (2007). *Carbon Detox: Your step-by-step guide to getting real about climate change.* London: Gaia

Notes:

1. Hicks, D. (2012). *Sustainable Schools, Sustainable Futures.* WWF, available at http://teaching4abetterworld.co.uk/downloads.html (Accessed 7/8/13)

2. Berners Lee, M. (2010). *How bad are bananas? The Carbon Footprint of everything.* Profile Books

5.3 Philosophy for Children (P4C) within the Xiehe Education Organisation

Helen Griffin

Philosophy for Children (P4C) is a teaching pedagogy which has proved, worldwide, to have been very supportive in developing global learning in schools. Here the author describes the P4C approach and the process of its successful implementation into Xiehe.

> ***'P4C touches the children's soul'***
>
> Guo Ying Zheng
> Xiehe Bilingual Kindergarten Principal

Philosophy for Children (P4C) has been developing in the Shanghai Xiehe Education Group since 2011 through a partnership with a professional development centre (Development Education Centre South Yorkshire: DECSY) with expertise in P4C and schools in Sheffield, England. This has represented, arguably, a unique curriculum and professional development model.

Background to P4C

P4C originated in the USA in the late 1960s and versions of it have since spread to around 60 countries across the world. It came to the UK in the 1990s following the televising of a BBC programme called 'Socrates for Six Year Olds' where Professor Matthew Lipman and his associates at Montclair State University, New Jersey, USA explained the aims and methodology of P4C and showed its successes with children as young as six.

Many educators in the UK were impressed with the eloquence and thinking capability shown by such young children as well as its impact on 16 year-old students. A few of the former went to the States to meet Lipman and receive training in the methods. P4C was brought back to the UK and adapted to the local situation.

Since 1992, when it was founded, SAPERE[1] (Society for Advancing Philosophical Inquiry and Reflection in Education) has overseen the development of P4C in the UK. This has included setting up a rigorous 'training the trainers' programme to ensure the quality of its Level 1, 2 and 3 courses.

P4C has been internationally evaluated and found to improve both cognitive and affective skills. Professor Keith Topping's (University of Dundee Faculty of Education and Social Work) in his review of P4C evaluation studies writes *'Some educators argue that improvement in thinking is impossible to measure. However, this review identified ten rigorous controlled experimental studies of P4C. These studies measured outcomes by norm-referenced tests of reading, reasoning, cognitive ability and other curriculum-related abilities, by measures of self-esteem and child behaviour, and by child and teacher questionnaires. All studies showed some positive outcomes and a consistent moderate positive effect size (0.43) for P4C on a wide range of outcome measures. This suggests a gain in IQ of 6.5 points for an average child.'*[2]

Whenever children are given the opportunity to say

what they think about P4C some common themes emerge. Children say they feel 'relaxed'; they value each other's contributions and want to hear from everyone: *'I like listening to what everyone else thinks'* (child aged 6), *'I especially like it when we discuss the question chosen because you find out how many different opinions there are'* (child aged 9). In fact teachers report that children who are normally quiet in other lessons find their voice in P4C. They like thinking deeply: *'I like it when people challenge me because it gets my brain thinking'* (child aged 9); they find P4C 'fun' and motivational and their confidence developed: *'I've become more confident at speaking to the class'.* Children can see the usefulness of it in the rest of their lives: *'P4C helps because when you have a problem you can think about it and sort it by asking questions of yourself'* (child aged 10).[3]

Passing the string as the dialogue develops, keeps P4C interactive and fun.

Community of Philosophical Inquiry

Lipman was influenced by the philosopher John Dewey (1859-1952) who said *'an education that emphasises community, communication, intelligent inquiry, and a reconstructive attitude can best serve the citizens of an ever-changing world.'*[4]

The purpose of P4C is to attempt to answer the questions *What kind of person do I want to be?* and *What kind of world do I want to live in?* and so its aims fit closely with the aims of global education.

The pedagogy of P4C is strongly influenced by the Russian psychologist Lev Vygotsky (1896-1934) who has come to the fore in the study of child development in the UK since his work was translated into English in the 1970s. Vygotsky said *'What the child can do in co-operation today, he can do alone tomorrow.'*[5] We learn both to speak and think by internalising the patterns of thought and speech around us.

Hence P4C aims to develop a community of philosophical inquiry where children and young people engage in communal dialogue to find answers to questions about life that they find compelling. These questions are philosophical in nature but not confined to any one curriculum or subject area; they easily arise from the study of literature and the humanities but may also relate to mathematics or any other subject area. With children these questions may be described as 'big' or 'chewy' and they explore central concepts such as right and wrong, rights and responsibilities, how we know about things and what we appreciate and value as human beings. These correspond with some of the traditional branches of philosophy: ethics, politics, epistemology and aesthetics.

A community of philosophical inquiry operates well when four kinds of thinking are engaged: critical thinking, creative thinking, caring thinking and collaborative thinking. These have come to be known in P4C as the '4 Cs of thinking' and all four are seen to have equal importance. This is one of the characteristics of P4C that makes it a unique pedagogy: it recognises that for good thinking the intellectual and affective need to work together.

Central to P4C is the idea of 'reasonableness'. A 'reasonable' person is someone who is able to think logically, question ideas and make distinctions and connections (intellectual skills) but is also willing to listen to the perspectives of others and modify their own thinking in the light of these. A 'reasonable' person also has the skill to recognise the consequences of their thinking on their own lives and the disposition to change their behaviour accordingly. Thus the '4 Cs of thinking' which are used and developed in P4C relate closely to Global Education.

Critical Thinking

'Critical Thinking' is a key requirement of global 'reflective citizenry'. In an information-rich society children need to develop the skills to critically engage with the information and viewpoints that they encounter in their lives, being able to recognise and challenge bias, indoctrination and propaganda. Thinking about the likely consequences of actions and making judgements and decisions based on good reasons are essential skills in being able to behave in ways which are not damaging to themselves, others or the environment.

P4C involves a process of opening out or problematising an issue or concept. Through critical inquiry, understanding about the global web of political, economic, social and environmental relationships can be clarified and deepened. This process can lead to the kind of deeply reflective last thoughts expressed by a nine year-old pupil following a dialogue about world peace: *'supposing you stopped all the fighting in the world and made it illegal to even touch someone there might be still hatred in the world among other people, and people hating each other inside, and that's not really peace.'*

Alongside this critical engagement, P4C encourages openness to other people's ideas and perspectives and a willingness to change opinions in the face of new evidence and rational arguments. These are all crucial skills for citizens to enable them to engage actively in their communities locally and globally.

Creative Thinking

Understanding and critically engaging with complex global issues can be overwhelming and lead to a feeling of disempowerment unless we also nurture the ability to think creatively and imagine different futures: *'hopes and anticipations of the future are not a transfiguring glow superimposed upon a darkened existence, but are realistic ways of perceiving the scope of our real possibilities, and as such they set everything in motion and keep it in a state of change. Hope and the kind of thinking that goes with it consequently cannot submit to the reproach of being utopian, for they do not strive after things that have 'no place', but after things that have 'no place as yet' but can acquire one.'* [6]

Through philosophical inquiry children have the chance to wonder, speculate and try out their tentative ideas. They are encouraged to problem solve and imagine alternative possibilities.

Caring Thinking

Research on P4C carried out with young children by a clinical psychologist, Elizabeth Doherr[7], uncovered the success of P4C in helping children to make links between thought and feelings. P4C has never merely been about intellectual inquiry, divorced from feelings and values. This bringing together of the affective and the intellectual is also essential to global education.

The opportunity, within a community of inquiry, to deeply listen allows children to put themselves in another's shoes, to empathise and potentially understand. Empathy is a core skill for global citizens for without it there can be no desire for the alleviation of suffering of other people.

The notion of 'Caring Thinking', originated by Lipman and further developed by his colleague Ann Sharpe, encapsulates this bringing together of the emotions and intellect. 'Caring Thinking' is not just the procedural aspects of respect and listening to others required for a community of inquiry to function, caring about ***someone***, but also crucially encompasses caring about ***something***.

In P4C children make up their own questions and choose the one that they think is most important. They then engage in a discussion about that important matter and even learn *'that there are some things that you can think deeply about.'* [8] Sharpe breaks down this aspect of caring thinking into four areas as shown in the table below.

Aspect of caring	Key characteristics of a caring thinker
Valuational thinking: to value is to highly appreciate or prize.	Commitment to giving reasons to oneself for ones values.
Affecting thinking: to experience strong emotional and cognitive response to an offence.	A strong sense of justice coupled with a commitment to non-violence and an intense sensitivity to the feelings of others.
Active thinking: to passionately care about and be involved with a cause.	Highly conscious of the other; passionate commitment/inner locus of control; disposition to act to improve a situation; compassionate thinker.
Normative thinking: to compare the actual with what could be.	Sensitive to inconsistency between ideals and behaviour; ability to conceptualize and offer solutions to society's problems; deep concern for humanity and global issues.[9]

Collaborative Thinking

A community of inquiry is by its very nature collaborative. Without the collaboration there would be no community. Children work together to seek answers to a question and grapple with ideas. Learning to co-operate and to work together for change have always been a core requirement of global education, and co-operative activities are included in programmes of work. P4C provides a real context for collaboration. It is only through listening and working together that the goal of trying to find answers to a question or deeper understanding of a concept can be achieved.

The ability to listen to other people, see their point of view and perhaps change your own mind is another skill essential to living peacefully in a plural society. Peaceful dialogue between people with potentially opposing points of view and even value systems can contribute to a world where the possibility exists of tensions being resolved without the use of force or violence. At its best, P4C gives young people an experience of how it is possible to engage with people with differing viewpoints and disagree with them in a non-confrontational way. 'I think that no matter how old you are you can benefit from other people's opinions.' [10]

Steps in an Inquiry

P4C provides a ten-step framework within which the community of philosophical inquiry can develop. This framework is designed to take up a traditional lesson length of about an hour but can be adapted to take up a shorter time for very young children or spread over two or more lessons for older children. As a group of students and the teacher become familiar with the process then the steps can be used more flexibly according to the needs of a particular inquiry, group of students or the curriculum. For example, the stimulus for an inquiry may arise out of some work in a particular curriculum area or an inquiry may start where a previous inquiry left off with a summary of key ideas discussed and a decision making process to choose what to focus on.

1. Getting set

- Students seated in a circle or horseshoe shape to enable dialogue between them.
- Rules for P4C developed with students (relating to listening, respect etc).
- Game or activity which either develops inquiry skills or relates to the content of the stimulus.

2. Presentation of stimulus

- Stimulus could be a picture book or story; other text fiction or non-fiction; other narrative such as film or animation; music, pictures or objects or a combination of different media.
- Needs to be something which is thought provoking for the group; something which will make them want to ask questions.

10. Review

- Chance for students to reflect on the process of inquiry using, e.g. two stars and a wish, plus, minus, interesting or www.ebi (what went well, even better if …) or a quick visual feedback, e.g. thumbs up if you enjoyed the discussion / learned something new / changed your mind.
- More in depth review could be done once a term in separate lesson.
- Important that review does not become an opportunity to assess 'performance' of the group. Evaluation needs to be formative and focused on having better discussions.
- Review could look at whether there are any themes/issues that the group would like to follow up? (Either in private research, in another lesson or in a future inquiry).

10 step of a P4 inquir

9. Last thoughts

- Chance for final words uncontested (often students who haven't spoken in a large group before use this opportunity to contribute).
- Back to pair discussion or go round with 'talking object' (can only speak when holding object). One turn each.
- Could ask : 'how far have we got with trying to find answers to the question?' or 'What are the implications of what we have been talking about for your lives?'

8. Building

- Consider how students will take turns speaking e.g. hand out when person who is talking has finished then teacher chooses next person or last speaker chooses (but teacher has right to intervene at any time to facilitate inquiry) or 'speak into the space' (an important skill for anyone to learn in group discussion).
- Consider your role as facilitator (page 109).

An inquiry may throw up some questions suitable for research and this could be conducted by the students between inquiries. There may be specific skills-focused work that it would be fruitful to concentrate on (for example work on developing questioning skills) or time might usefully be spent on exercises to explore concepts that have arisen during an inquiry or appear in a question prior to its discussion.[11]

In fact it is hard for the processes and skills developed in P4C not to permeate other teaching and learning. Teachers commonly report that their own listening and questioning has improved through facilitating P4C and that even their normally quieter students are more willing to speak, question and give reasons in other lessons.

3. Thinking time *(about the stimulus)*

- Time to reflect on the stimulus.
- Thinking time is essential and should be built into the inquiry whenever it is appropriate.
- Could be timed (e.g. with a minute timer) individual thinking.
- Ask students : 'What are you wondering?' 'What interests you about the stimulus?'
- Students could talk in pairs and feed back a summary or one word to capture their ideas.
- Students could write in their 'Philosophy Jotters' (individual notebooks for children to use during and after P4C).

4. Question formulation

- It is important that students develop their own questions rather than being given a question by the teacher so that the children feel engaged and have ownership of the inquiry. Asking questions is a critical and creative process important to learning.
- With a group new to P4C or younger children this could be done as a whole group: gather thoughts and questions and write them down on a flipchart or whiteboard, point out when a question is given but don't show bias towards any one idea or question.
- Questions could be developed by the students in pairs or small groups, you could say: 'think of a question which you are really interested in talking about and one which we can find some answers together by talking and thinking without needing to look things up on the internet or ask the author'.
- Teachers describe such questions as 'big', 'chewy', 'about life', 'deep and meaningful', 'philosophical'.
- Write questions on a whiteboard, flipchart, individual pieces of paper (but large enough for everyone to see).

5. Question airing

- So that all questions are understood and valued.
- Students could ask for clarification or elaboration of others' questions.
- They can make connections/ distinctions between questions.
- With a more experienced community, can sort questions into 'research' or 'reflection' and then choose from the 'reflection' questions and use the 'research' questions in other lessons.

6. Question selecting

- Omni-votes (can vote for all) or multi-vote (e.g. 2 or 3 votes) or preferential voting or random selection?
- Secret (e.g. backs to group with thumbs up behind back to vote) or open ballot? (E.g. put counters on questions or stand near question).

7. First thoughts *(about selected question)*

- Could go round to find out everyone's initial ideas (could restrict to 2 or 3 words). Anyone can pass.
- Could share first thoughts in pairs or ask students who made up the question chosen to start the discussion off.

Facilitating P4C - the role of the teacher

Facilitating P4C is both hugely enjoyable and challenging for most teachers. It is thus duly accorded a substantial amount of time on the SAPERE Levels 1 and 2 training courses and therefore can only briefly be touched upon here.

Even teachers accustomed to inquiry-based learning often find it challenging to let go of the reins in P4C and give over control of the learning to the students, especially during the 'building' part of the inquiry. It is important that the group is engaged in genuine dialogue with each other rather than with the teacher; that the students are, in fact, thinking for themselves rather than second guessing what is in the teacher's head.

To enable this to happen it is recommended that the facilitator refrains from offering her own point of view and only makes substantive interventions in the form of open questions that support the students' thinking in response to what they have said, for example:

> *'how are you using the word 'true'?'*
>
> (Possible response: *'True means the way things really are.'*)
>
> *'So are you assuming that the truth of what is said is independent of those who say it?'* [12]

Other interventions will be procedural and concerned with supporting the '4 Cs' of thinking (see pages 105-106). The facilitator might ask for a reason or an example, a summary or a different point; they may support the students' in their turn-taking or listening or respect for each other; always in response to what the students are saying or doing.

Facilitation requires curiosity and deep and attentive listening to what the students are actually saying and concentration to follow the threads of the children's thinking. The facilitator will be continually evaluating when and how to make an intervention to support the progress of the inquiry and when to hold back.

It is recommended that, fairly early on in a teacher's journey of developing effective facilitation, an audio or video recording is done or the teacher is observed by someone else to give an opportunity for reflection on the frequency and quality of interventions. One teacher was recently surprised after having led around five inquiries to be given the feedback that he was responding to every single contribution by his students so their talk was always directed at him (he had been wondering why they were always looking at him instead of each other). He genuinely felt that he had been keeping his interventions to a minimum.

Quite often teachers need to be reminded initially to relax and just listen to what the children are saying, the skills of making interventions which challenge the group's thinking and support a forward direction in the inquiry will develop over time.

P4C within the Xiehe Kindergartens

Implementation of P4C, as with any major curriculum development initiative, has to be well planned. Otherwise, there is a danger of 'innovation without change' at the classroom level. The process of introducing and developing P4C within the Xiehe Kindergartens has taken place through an impressively well thought out series of stages.

Stage 1: November 2011

Helen Griffin leads a P4C training course for Xiehe school and kindergarten teachers (below). She introduces P4C to the principals of the International/Bilingual Xiehe Kindergartens by means of a P4C inquiry. A number of representatives of kindergartens also take part in two days of P4C demonstration lessons followed by evaluation feedback.

Stage 2: November 2012

- Rob Unwin leads an introductory, five days P4C training course for 28 kindergarten practitioners. [*1 below]
- They have an opportunity to evaluate his teaching of P4C with a kindergarten class (right).
- In turn, six kindergarten trainees teach a P4C class themselves and all the lessons are carefully evaluated. Feedback from this evaluation informs the latter sessions of the course.
- Feedback from the course as a whole is very positive.
- A two hour session is held to plan the follow-up to the training course. This is attended by kindergarten principals, trainees and Xiehe Kindergarten Inspectors.

Stage 3: June 2013

- Guo Ying Zheng and Stephen Walshe, Xiehe Kindergarten Principals, are nominated as 'Xiehe Kindergarten P4C Trainers' and attend the full Level 1 and Level 2 courses at DECSY in the UK. [*2 below]
- They also have the opportunity, over the period of the month, to observe P4C in the classrooms of five English primary schools and to attend various other P4C meetings and the third annual P4C Regional Conference (right) organised by DECSY and Sheffield Hallam University, on the theme of 'Critical and Creative Thinking'. [*3 below]

Stage 4: September 2013

Guo Ying Zheng and Stephen Walshe commence their leadership of a series of whole Xiehe Kindergarten and inter Xiehe Kindergarten P4C courses.

Notes for stages 2 and 3 above:

[*1] Feedback from trainees was 100% positive with comments in response to the question *'Please tell us your gains, ideas about P4C after training?'*

'It is exciting for us to know how to teach for global citizenry.' 'Through the training I realised the importance of encouraging children to ask questions… I need to think how to improve students skills …. critical skills, thinking skills, care for others.' 'P4C will enrich teaching methods and guide children to enjoy their learning.' 'It is very important for children to ask and think, let students lead their classes.' 'P4C training changed my view of teaching.' 'P4C gave us a new way to think and to stimulate children to express ideas.' 'Picked up the enthusiasm for interaction with the students. Education/ being a teacher can be a very interesting job.'

[*2] The SAPERE Level 2 qualification requires each teacher to complete a further 12 enquiries and write a reflective 3000 word essay on the children's progress and their own progress as facilitators including a detailed analysis of a transcript of one of the inquiries. This then qualifies the teachers to coach others in their institutions.

[*3] Evaluations from the P4C Regional Conference: 94% *'good'* or *'excellent'* for all aspects of the conference. Most common words circled to sum up the overall view of the conference were: *'inspiring, 'thought provoking'* and *'valuable'.*
Comments included : *'The maths workshop was without doubt the best workshop I have ever attended – I was moved to tears'. 'Many of the activities introduced here will completely change the way we approach our teaching and learning'.*

Reflections on P4C

Guo Ying Zheng and Stephen Walshe were invited to 'brainstorm' about their responses to the Level 2 'Philosophy for Children' (P4C) training and the various P4C meetings and conferences they attended during their one month stay in South Yorkshire. Their responses were as follows:

- Overall, yet more convincing evidence, after our initial training course, of the relevance of P4C for early years students.
- The importance of developing the P4C inquiry in a number of parts with students in the three to five years age range and then introducing the whole process from (approximately) six years onwards.*1 below
- Very simple student questions in the earliest years (eg asked of a teddy bear) and then increasing levels of sophistication in this respect.
- The positive influence of P4C in the context of teaching and learning pedagogies in a wide range of curriculum areas.
- P4C's influence in promoting a wide range of skills (e.g. speaking, listening, thinking (deeply), collaboration).
- The potential for extending dialogic learning.
- The pedagogy encourages children to use logical sentences.
- P4C as the springboard for purposeful writing.
- P4C's potential for e.g. questioning students' values and raising ethical issues.
- The importance of not over-structuring children's talk, which did happen within a small number of the classes observed. Questions must come from the students, in a natural manner (the teachers may have over-structured some inquiries because they were being observed).
- Observing children with seemingly major learning difficulties, both asking and answering questions so confidently.
- The paired activities during inquiries could have been more tightly structured. Children sometimes worked individually or in groups of three or four when asked to work in pairs. In one school the learning buddy system worked extremely well within the inquiry process.
- Overall, the way in which P4C promotes the cognitive as well as the affective dimensions of the curriculum.
- P4C is, obviously, very successful with students from a remarkably wide range of social and ethnic/cultural backgrounds (as was revealed in the visits to the five schools).
- Seeing the considerable potential of P4C within schools that had not, thus far, adopted the Project.
- Easily the best professional development we have ever had.
- We particularly valued the active/participatory style of all the training.
- Training which was modelled on P4C principles (e.g. collaborative, caring, listening).
- The P4C training took account of where individual colleagues were at professionally.
- It developed teachers as reflective practitioners.
- There was a clear agenda throughout all the training days but also much flexibility in the overall programme.
- We appreciated the fact that the trainees had to lead their own inquiry, in a mutually supportive professional context. It made us think deeply about, for example, the questioning process, language levels and the concepts involved.
- It was great to experience the theory of P4C (within the training courses) and its practical application (in five schools).
- We found P4C to be very challenging for both teachers and students.

Notes for reflections on P4C above:

*1 Although, in fact, many teachers successfully use a modified 10-step process with children as young as three. In the EYFS at Wharncliffeside Primary School, Sheffield the children do 'Tummy Talk' where for first thoughts/building and last thoughts they all lie on their tummies facing inward. This helps them concentrate, hear each other better and gives them a sense of intimacy and security.

Conclusion

This chapter has provided a brief outline of the rich pedagogy of P4C. It has pointed towards its value, when carefully implemented, for all children and young people growing up in a complex and increasingly interconnected world.

As the Institute for Advancement of Philosophy for Children at Montclair University, USA, where the work begun by Matthew Lipman and Anne Sharp is being continued, states *'Rather than dictate a set of prescribed values to children, Philosophy for Children seeks to help them strengthen their own capacity to appraise and respond to these beckoning alternatives; to self-correct their habits of thought, feeling and action through sustained ethical inquiry. Moreover, Philosophy for Children's egalitarian nature, commitment to varying viewpoints and insistence on the inherent value of all participants helps foster empathy and pro-social behaviour as an essential basis for values education'.* [13]

Talkabout

- *Discuss the advantages of introducing P4C into your school and/or educational organisation.*
- *Plan a detailed programme which you feel would ensure the successful implementation of the initiative.*
- *Devise a set of criteria to evaluate the success, or otherwise, of P4C at the classroom level.*

Helen Griffin is the P4C Advisor at DECSY.

Acknowledgements

[1] www.sapere.org.uk
[2] SAPERE Handbook Level 1, 2010, pp.69
[3] Quotes from children attending the Philosophy for Children conference organised by DECSY and Sheffield Hallam University in June 2013.
[4] Blackwell Guide to Philosophy of Education quoted in SAPERE Handbook Level 1, 2010, pp.11
[5] Vygotsky, L. (1978). *Mind in Society: The Development of Higher Psychological Processes*
[6] Moltmann, 1967, quoted p.71 in Hicks, D.W. (2006). *Lessons for the Future.* Trafford Publishing
[7] Doherr, E. (2000). *The demonstration of cognitive abilities central to cognitive behavioural therapy in young people: examining the influence of age and teaching method on degree of ability.* Unpublished clinical psychology doctoral dissertation, University of East Anglia.
[8] One of the things that a 10-year-old child said she had learnt from participating in P4C for several years.
[9] Sharp, A. (2007). *'Education of the Emotions in the Classroom Community of Inquiry'* in Gifted Education International, Vol.22, Issues 2 and 3.
[10] Child, aged 9 at Philosophy for Children conference, Sheffield 2013 when asked whether teachers can learn anything from facilitating P4C.
[11] Many examples of these kinds of skill and concept development activities can be found at www.p4c.com
[12] Splitter, L. and Sharp A. (1995). *Teaching for Better Thinking*, pp.59
[13] http://www.montclair.edu/cehs/academics/centers-and-institutes/iapc/what-is/why-philosophy/ accessed.

5.4 Differentiation in teaching and learning within the Xiehe Global School classroom

Dr Zhang Lu and Qiu Chen

It is recognised that 'differentiation' is the planned process of intervention in the classroom in order to maximise the potential of each child according to his / her needs. Also, that this is one of the most discussed but least well implemented activities in education. In this chapter, the authors describe a major Xiehe curriculum development initiative which has attempted to tackle the challenges involved in differentiating effectively in the Group's classrooms.

> *'There is nothing so unequal as to treat unequal children equally.'*
>
> Thomas Jefferson

Background to the process of differentiation

Stratification, individualisation and differentiation

With the changes in Chinese education theory and practice, awareness of the concept of differentiation continues to develop. Although Chinese educationalists have always advocated this traditional concept of 'individualised teaching', the reality of China's demography has meant that the whole class teaching model has been dominant.

From the beginning of the 1980s, the Chinese system has implemented 'stratification': students are broadly categorised according to their cognitive ability and taught accordingly, but still mainly through whole class teaching. Although, this is better than the 'one size fits all' approach, 'stratification' does not take account of student diversity in terms of emotional attitudes, learning methods and styles. Additionally, there has been concern that 'stratifying' students is particularly damaging to the self esteem of the least successful students.

'Individualisation' has been suggested by Western educators as an alternative. Although this does not rigidly imply one-to-one teaching it does demand individualised learning programmes for students. This is not a realistic aim within China's current education system. Carol Ann Tomlinson[1] has suggested that 'individualisation' has two shortcomings: first it is difficult to design a separate teaching programme for each student; secondly, the overall teaching process becomes disjointed with a resultant lack of systematic learning.

'Differentiation', as defined above in the introduction, is very gradually becoming more of a reality in the Chinese classroom.

The advantages of differentiation

The approach is valuable not only because it acknowledges the differences between students but also recognises that all have the potential for development. Differentiation also aims to ensure that each student recognises his / her own strengths and accepts their differences when compared with others, in order to reach their full potential. Each student should have equal rights and freedom within the classroom, as well as access to strategies which allow appropriate development.

Differentiation incorporates the concepts of individualisation and stratification. Overall, the process is an holistic teaching and learning pedagogy. It involves the creation of a democratic classroom culture. The students' family, cultural, cognitive and affective backgrounds are taken into account. Students are viewed as a resource in the learning process.

Differentiation in Shanghai United International Global Schools (SUIS)

From December 2012 the Shanghai Municipal Government has been supporting what it feels are high quality schools with appropriate three-year development plans and practical support with respect to policy, funding and professional guidance. SUIS were amongst the first schools to be selected to join this new initiative and chose differentiation as their topic for study.

Students in SUIS have very diverse socio-economic backgrounds, abilities and aptitudes, far more than many other private and local government schools in Shanghai.

In **Figure 1**, below, IN (individual needs) refers to the children who fall outside the 'average' range within the class. These children may find learning significantly more difficult than the average in one or more areas or may find learning much easier than the average.

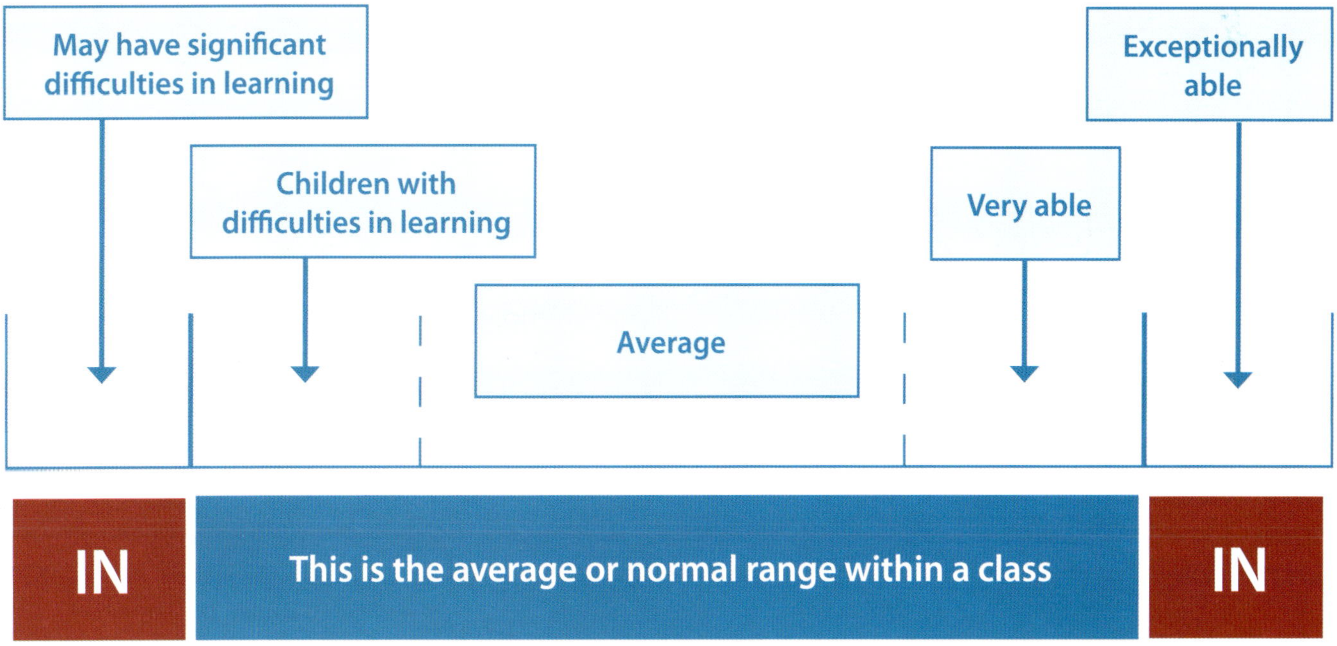

Fig 1: The possible range of ability within your class

Teacher professional development with respect to differentiation

From the outset, it was felt that teacher development by means of inquiry, reflection and repeated practice would be the key strategy to the successful introduction of differentiation as a major curriculum innovation. With this in mind, a three-year teacher training programme was organised by Xiehe in collaboration with the Shanghai Academy of Educational Sciences, summarised as follows.

Stage 1 (2010-2011)

The 'foundation period': the creation of a study team of nine outstanding Chinese, English, maths and thematic inquiry teachers. Six of the team's teachers were from primary schools, three were from secondary schools. The Team's Co-ordinator was

Dr Zhang Lu from the Shanghai Academy of Private Education Institute. She provided both professional and research support for these colleagues. The study team undertook their work through classroom activities, individual projects and seminars. The workshops had three key features: first, all participants were viewed as equals, there was a genuine sharing of experiences and ideas; secondly, the group size never exceeded fifteen; thirdly, all participants were required to contribute in very practical ways. All the workshop participants had more than five years classroom experience. The principle of 'positive, active self development' was felt to be the essence of workshop activity as well as the soul of the differentiation process in the classroom.

Workshop duration was one and a half hours. In each one there was a balance of theory, practical classroom experience and policy development. Team members fed back on a classroom programme they had planned and implemented with regard to differentiation.

Special project studies were undertaken by all study team members. These involved the formulation of differentiated teaching and learning programmes incorporating the three categories of 'planning and design', 'strategy and method' and 'assessment' (see **Figure 2** below).

Stage 2 (2011-12)

During this period the study team shared their individual classroom experiences with respect to differentiated teaching and learning. The outstanding teachers brought what they had learnt into their departments. There was also further consolidation and practice through team seminars and reciprocal lesson observation.

Stage 3 (2012-13)

Dissemination of the outcomes of the study team's work and experiences to teachers across Xiehe: 'a hundred flowers bloom'. This involved the exchange, sharing and extension of teaching and learning experiences between the teachers after the previous year's study. This was mainly through workshop activities, an example is given right.

Fig 2: Planning and implementing a differentiated teaching and learning programme

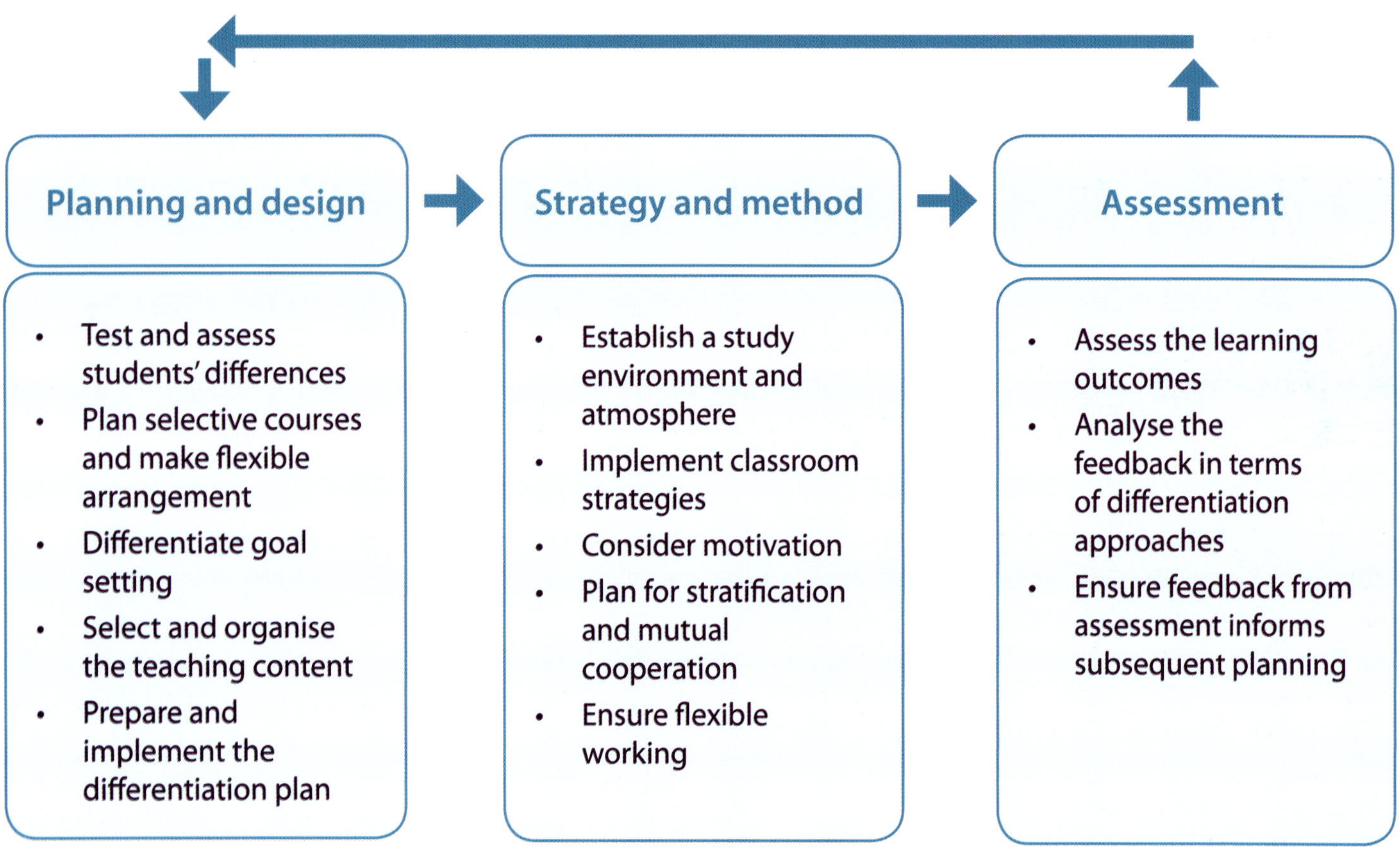

Example of workshop study

Topic: differing approaches to differentiated group work activities.

Host: Song Liang

Participants: all members of the workshop

Key questions:

- What is effective and efficient group teaching?
- What is the core?
- What is the interdependence relationship of group teaching?
- Grouping methods?
- What is role assignment?
- What is the role of the student recorder, supervisor and spokesperson?
- Which group work strategies should we use?
- Specific content of a strategy? How to use it?

Study mode: a class exemplar inquiry.

Source of class example: video an of English lesson taught by Song Liang. Theme: buying a new house

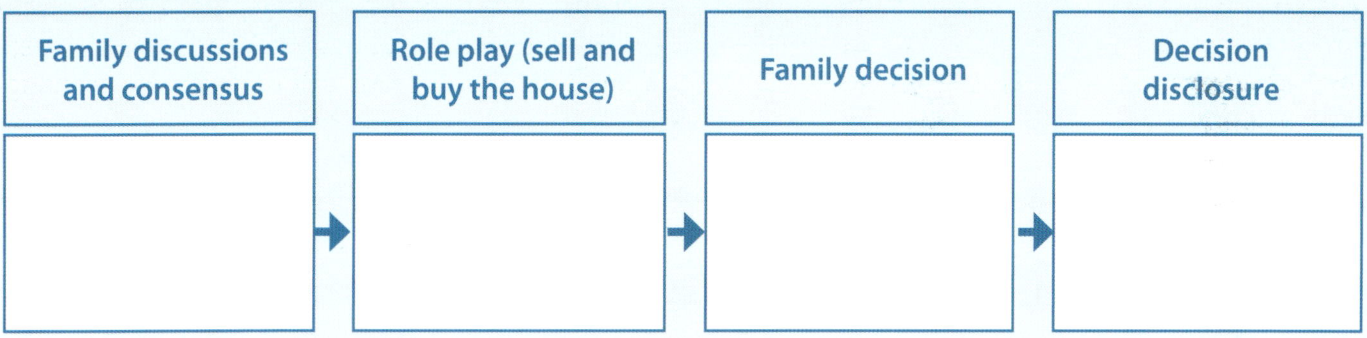

Differentiation in the workshop was achieved through a variety of group work activities involving trios. There was systematic feedback.

The video was analysed by the workshop members. This type of lesson analysis proved to be an excellent professional development strategy.

Overall the three-stage approach was regarded as a concentric circles approach to professional development.

Differentiation approaches in the SUIS classroom

The main task with respect to differentiation is to design and offer a variety of differentiated learning materials which include tasks and activities which take account of students' preparedness levels, multiple intelligences and differences in learning style. Overall, this involves the preparation of a 'differentiated course'. The study team decided on five main approaches, as follows.

Differentiation according to students' levels of preparedness

This is when a minority of students lack the pre-requisite knowledge and understanding to begin a new lesson. In this case they can be given a 'remediation' lesson before the new lesson starts.

Differentiation according to differences in students' interests

In this case the students select a topic they are interested in from a common class theme, for either independent study or group co-operative learning. For example a member of the study group developed the 'Jigsaw' approach with respect to Chinese language learning. In an inquiry theme, students

Differentiation by means of 'interest' groups.

formed 'temporary' groups based on their interests to work on a related topic, and then later joined the 'permanent' class group to present their learning outcomes. The 'Jigsaw' was completed. With this approach the students can learn different aspects of a common theme co-operatively.

Differentiation according to students' cognitive ability levels.

Teachers differentiate by task with more challenging and complex activities for the most successful students. The study team defined these as 'stratified' tasks.

For example, a teacher in a Grade 4 lesson left the final 20 minutes for the students to do their homework, which was divided into two parts; one task for the majority of students and a second one for the most successful. The teacher informed the class that they must complete their respective tasks before the lesson ended. Students who did not complete the more difficult task successfully were not allowed to undertake such tasks in the next lesson. The teacher's role in this latter part of the lesson was to support individual students. Those who completed the most difficult tasks quickly and successfully were designated as 'teacher inspectors' whose role was to assist the teacher in checking their fellow students' work. In differentiating by task the teacher needs to recognise that there is progression in students' learning as defined by Bloom.[2] See **Figure 3** right.

Differentiation according to students' multiple intelligences

In this case the teacher recognises that students learn in different ways, defined by Gardner as 'Multiple Intelligences'.[3] He/she then attempts to differentiate the work in order to meet individual student's learning styles. The eight 'Intelligences' are defined in **Figure 4** on page 119. **Figure 5** is an example of the implementation of the use of the multiple intelligences approach in English language thematic work.

Fig 3: Suggested progression in cognitive learning

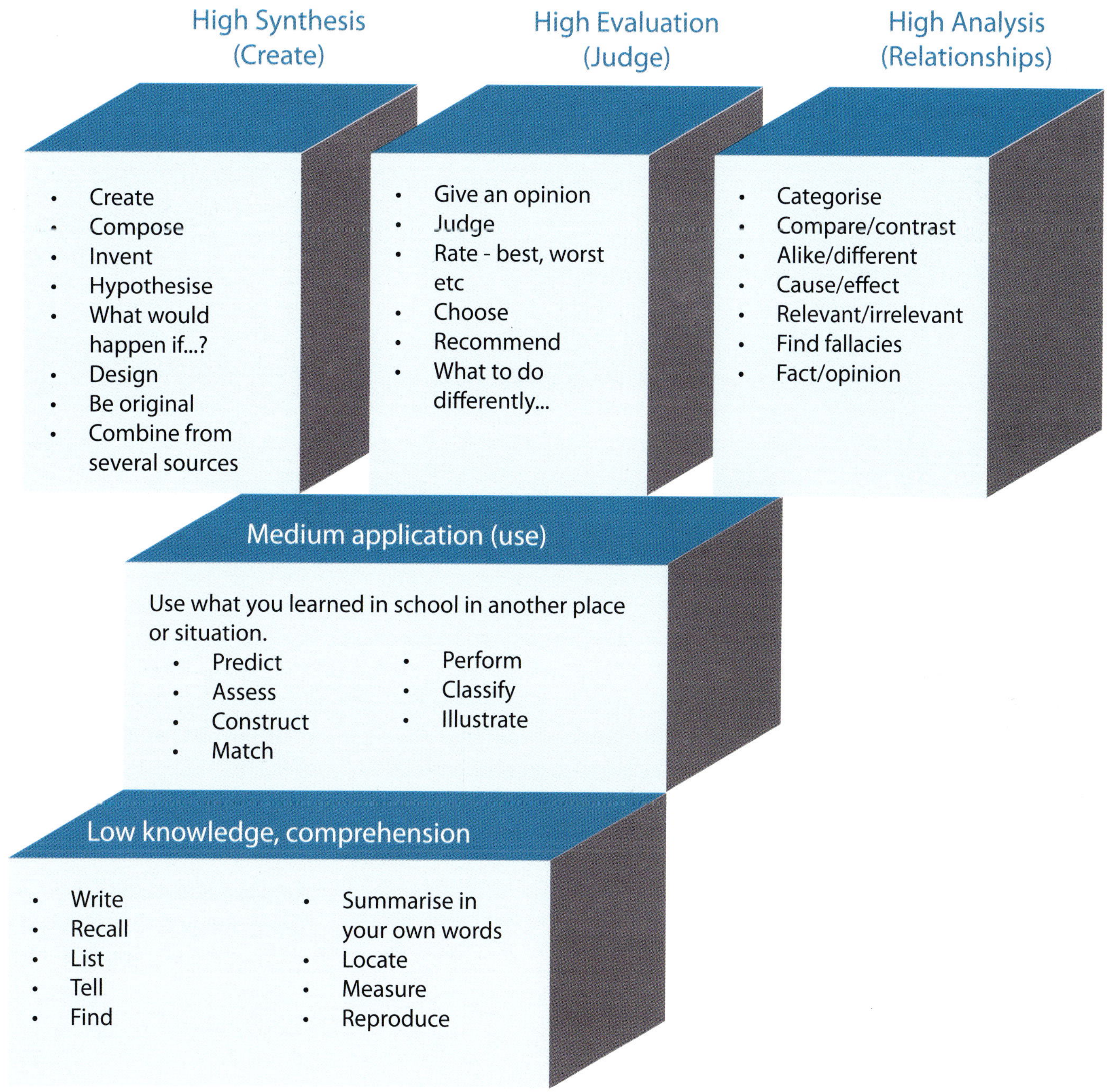

Fig 4: Gardener's eight 'multiple intelligences'

Multiple Intelligences	What is it about?	Suggested activities
verbal/linguistic	Children favouring this intelligence have the ability to use words and language and perform well in activities that involve speaking and listening. They also like writing and use words to recall and learn (e.g. a poet).	• reading • playing cards and games • conversation and discussions
logical/ mathematical	Children favouring this intelligence think conceptually and perform well in activities involving numbers, classifying and problem solving. They recall and learn by making connections (e.g. a scientist).	• classifying and sequencing activities • playing number and logic games • solving puzzles • computer activities
visual/spatial	Children favouring this intelligence have the ability to visualise. They perform well in activities that involve creating and picturisation. They recall and learn by creating images (e.g. a sculptor/an aeroplane pilot).	• graphic and plastic arts • solving mazes • Treasure Hunt
bodily/kinaesthetic	Children favouring this intelligence move in well-co-ordinated movements. They perform well in activities that involve movement and physical activity. They recall and learn by physically interacting (e.g. an athlete /a dancer).	• dancing • miming • playing active sports and games • role-play / drama activities
musical	Children favouring this intelligence think in sounds, rhythms and patterns. They perform well in activities that involve singing and tapping. They learn and recall best through sing along.	• rhythmic games and activities, e.g. tapping • singing • dancing
interpersonal	Children favouring this intelligence have the ability to relate and understand others.	• co-operative games • group projects and discussions • drama and role-play
intrapersonal	Children favouring this intelligence have the ability to self-reflect. They perform well in individual activities. They learn by reflecting and working along (e.g. exhibited by individuals with accurate views of themselves).	• independent projects • journal-writing • finding quiet places for reflection
naturalist	Children favouring this intelligence have the ability to be involved with nature.	• identifying flora and fauna • learning about natural events.

Fig 5: Multiple intelligences in the classroom: an example

"Shopping"

Textbook - 1B-New Welcome To English

Objectives:

1. Use modals to make requests
2. Use adjectives to show quantity
3. To express 'thanks'
4. To reply to requests

Activity 1 - Whole class teaching

Verbal/Linguistic Intelligence

Introducing new vocabulary:- Picture cards, Sentence strips.
Objectives:- 1,2,3,4
Skills:- Listening.
Extension:- *Big Book reading.*

Activity 2 - Pair work

Logical-Mathematical Intelligence

To learn numbers in English:- Matching games, Ping-Pong
Objectives:- Use adjectives to show quantity
Skills:- Reading, speaking, listening.
Extension:- *Students can make a simple graph to show number of students liking different fruits.*

Activity 3 - Group work

Visual/Spatial Intelligence

Reinforcing previously learned vocabulary:- Making a shopping list
Objectives:- To review previously learned vocabulary, use numbers learned
Skills:- Reading and writing
Extension:- *Making a menu.*

Activity 4 - Pair work

Interpersonal Intelligence

Role play:- Going shopping
Objectives:- Use of modals to make requests, use of adjectives to show quantity, to express thanks, to reply to requests.
Skills:- Speaking and listening
Extension:- *Students can be taken to a real market to use a language learned.*

Activity 5 - Pair/Group work

Bodily/Kinaesthetic Intelligence

Cooking:- Making fruit salad in the classroom
Objectives:- Use of modals to make requests, use of adjectives to show quantity, to express thanks and reply to requests.
Skills:- Speaking and listening
Extension:- *Groups cook a recipe they have made up.*

Activity 6 - Individual work

Intrapersonal Intelligence

Creative writing:- Journal writing, writing about 'making fruit salad in the classroom'
Objectives:- Use of adjectives to show quantity, use of previously learned vocabulary.
Skills:- Reading and writing
Extension:- *Writing about cooking experiences at home.*

Activity 7 - Whole class or Group work

Musical Intelligence

Reviewing numbers:- Number songs, 10 little apples.
Objectives:- Use of adjectives to show quantity.
Skills:- Speaking and listening.
Extension:- *Make up songs or chants using the vocabulary learned.*

The study team prepared the following guidelines for classroom management relating to differentiation with respect to multiple intelligence.

- Pay attention to the overall teaching plan.
- Ensure the eight kinds of intelligences are integrated into the teaching in some form as much as possible.
- Identify which parts can be arranged with individual, group or whole class activities.
- Pay attention to proper role assignment for co-operative group learning.
- Set deadlines for each part of the lesson.
- Consider fully how to use the classroom space and AVA.

Differentiation through the use of a classroom learning centre

Another approach is to establish a learning centre in the classroom setting for expanding and enriching the content of learning. Thematic activities can then be planned incorporating more challenging tasks for the more successful students. These might usefully be extended over several weeks.

Figure 6 below is a summary of differentiation strategies provided for participating workshop teachers.

Fig 6: A summary of differentiation strategies

Strategy	Examples
By task	• open-ended activities • extension activities • challenge corner • differentiated homework
By support	• use of additional support for the teacher • teacher's intervention (one of a teaching team pair) • different targets from the same task
By interest/negotiation	• students select from menu • students involved in planning e.g. type of work, format of outcomes • devising own challenges • research
By resource	• bank of materials to which students have access • varied text / prompts but different levels of complexity • varied picture / artefacts • different resources from others
By organisation	• layout of classroom (grouped by ability) • location of resources • pair / group; friends/ability • learning styles (e.g. use of ICT)
By student expertise	• groupings: reading/writing partners • group composition... the thinker, the ideas person, the writer, the artist, the presenter
By outcome	• different amounts of work • more complex for more successful • different products from the same task • different targets from the same task

Some outcomes of the study team's action research on the implementation of various differentiation strategies.

- It is vital to match the strategies to the students' particular needs, for example in terms of cognitive ability, interests and multiple intelligences.
- The key issue is the design of specific teaching and learning materials to enable this to happen.
- It is essential to constantly build on and refer to the 'strengths' of individual students rather than their 'weaknesses'. As always, student self esteem is a key dimension within the differentiation process.
- The study team emphasis on differentiation within groups in a class has proved to be successful. Within these groups any differences between students, in terms of ability/characteristics/interests and/or attitude, can be used to advantage through cooperative learning and self and mutual understanding.

Assessment within the differentiation process

Appropriate and rigorous assessment is particularly important in order to ascertain the outcomes of planned differentiation approaches. This needs to take into account the following.

- Affective as well as cognitive learning objectives need to be assessed. For example, students' effort and attitudes to learning.
- Both formative and summative approaches should be used.
- Assessment strategies need to be wide ranging. For example, oral, research orientated and group approaches.
- Feedback from assessment is essential in order to maximise opportunities for student self evaluation.

Conclusion

The study team's work is ongoing and much has yet to be achieved. To date, however, there have been two key outcomes: first, action research evidence suggests that students of all abilities have benefitted from a more rigorously planned differentiated approach to their teaching and learning, both in academic and social terms. Secondly, this process of curriculum development, with its emphasis on 'expert', trained teachers working with their peers, has led to genuine and meaningful curriculum innovation at the classroom level.

Talkabout

- *Review the school self-evaluation/ external inspection evidence you have with respect to the success, or otherwise, of differentiation regarding particular year groups. Suggest areas for improvement.*
- *Plan a new differentiation strategy for a specific class of students, using one of the strategies developed by the study team.*

Acknowledgements

[1] Tomlinson, C. A. (2001). *How to Differentiate Instruction in Mixed Ability Classrooms. Second Edition.* ASCD

[2] Adapted from Eyre, D. (1997). *Research Centre for Able Pupils.* Westminster Institute of Education, Oxford Brookes University.

[3] Gardner, H. (1993). *Multiple Intelligences: The Theory in Practice.* New York: Basic Books

Dr Zhang Lu is a school based research counsellor and teacher trainer.

Qiu Chen is an English and Science teacher , Co-ordinator of Bilingual Teaching Subjects and Director of the Educational Science Research Office at SUIS (Hong Qiao)

5.5 The hybrid *'East meets West'* Pioneer Curriculum.

Maxine Lu Hui Wen and Cathy Wang Yi

This chapter is concerned with the Pioneer Curriculum, a key and highly innovatory outcome of curriculum development within Xiehe's Global Schools over the last decade. In many respects this initiative has been 'the jewel in the crown' in terms of the Group's 'East meets West' educational practice.

> ***'When devising any international, national or local curriculum we must decide on the very best educational practice worldwide and develop it in the interests of our children'.***
>
> Professor Peter Mortimore

The Xiehe Global Schools have developed a 'hybrid' Pioneer Curriculum which attempts to combine the best of educational practice in their local (Chinese National Curriculum) and international (Eg International Baccalaureate, Primary Years Programme; English National Curriculum) streams. What is particularly exciting is the potential for change in the Chinese National Curriculum as a result of these curriculum experiments.

With the fundamental changes in China's economy and society, more Chinese parents wish their children to have a globalised education. However, many parents cannot afford the higher costs of international schools or, in the case of Xiehe, international streams. Additionally, they are forbidden, under Chinese law, to send their children to international schools which have a totally foreign curriculum. Many parents are still attracted to the basic subject courses which are provided within the Chinese National Curriculum.

The Pioneer Curriculum with both its basic subject and global/inquiry dimensions is therefore a very attractive option for them.

The Pioneer Curriculum Programme

The Xiehe Pioneer Programme is a transcultural international experimental course within the Shanghai Municipal Government's second period of curriculum reform for Chinese national students.

Those students achieving good results in the high school entrance examination at the end of Grade 8 have two future course options: they may either enter the local Chinese high school or progress to international schools at home or abroad, or in the case of Xiehe, international streams.

The Pioneer Curriculum has four key objectives:

- To ensure the overall academic quality incorporated within the Shanghai Municipal Government's second period of curriculum reform.
- To ensure excellent achievement in terms of their students' Chinese and English language acquisition.

- To develop a significant global inquiry dimension within the curriculum.
- To ensure that the students receive high quality moral/values education.

Students

The students involved are those who appear to have the potential to succeed in this very competitive local curriculum and a willingness to challenge themselves both in the subject and thematic work.

Teachers

The teachers involved in the Pioneer Curriculum Programme, both Chinese and foreign, are expected to have considerable vision in terms of global education and high level professional understanding, skills and motivation.

无锡协和双语学校小学部课程表
WUXI UNITED INTERNATIONAL SCHOOL
PRIMARY SCHOOL GRADE 1 TIMETABLE

Class　　　　Homeroom Teacher

	WEEK / TIME	MONDAY	TUESDAY	WEDNESDAY	THURSDAY	FRIDAY
	7:50 8:10	REGISTRATION				
	8:10 8:30	MORNING READING & EXERCISE				
1	8:30 9:10	Virtue	English	Math	Chinese	English
2	9:20 10:00	Chinese	Math	English	Chinese	Chinese
	10:00 10:15	BREAK				
	10:15 10:20	EYE EXERCISE & SNACK				
3	10:20 11:00	Math	Inquiry (team-teaching)	Chinese	English	(Math)
4	11:10 11:50	English		English (team-teaching)	Art (team-teaching)	English (team-teaching)
	11:50 12:30	LUNCH				
	12:30 12:50	HOMEROOM				
5	12:50 13:30	SSRW (team-teaching)	Chinese	Chinese	SSRW (team-teaching)	(Chinese)
6	13:40 14:20	Art (team-teaching)	Swimming / LEGO	PE (team-teaching)	English	PE (team-teaching)
7	14:30 15:15	PE		Music (team-teaching)	Music (team-teaching)	14:30 14:45 PACK UP
	15:20 15:30	SNACK				
	15:30 16:30	HOMEROOM				
	16:30 16:45	PACK UP				

Fig 1: A sample timetable of the Hybrid Pioneer Curriculum for Grade 1 students.

Notes on timetable above:

- *Maths, art, physical education, music, inquiry and SSRW (phonics) are team taught bilingually, in English and Chinese, with the former being the main language medium.*
- *All the team teaching is by pairs of Chinese and Western teachers.*
- *The Lego lesson is experiential science motor and mechanical skills.*
- *'Virtue' is values education. (See* ***Chapter 5.2****).*
- *Pastoral support for the students is provided by a Chinese teacher in the 'homeroom' sessions. She also frequently visits other lessons to work with the students and their subject teacher(s).*

Teaching materials

The teaching materials in use within the Pioneer Curriculum Programme are a combination of Chinese (eg basic subject materials relating to the Shanghai Municipal Government's second period of reform) and international (eg Longman Express English, Oxford Reading Tree, integrated subject) texts.

Classes

In September 2013 thirty eight Pioneer classes were established in three Xiehe Global Schools (Grades 1 to 8).

Extra Curricular Courses

A full range of extra curricular courses are provided. (e.g. craft, fencing, golf, judo, Beijing Opera, drama and gardening). Students choose two options per week. Additionally the students are involved in experiential project work once a month (e.g. museum visits, nature observation, society investigations).

Moral Education

The Shanghai Municipal Government has some basic requirements for moral education: there is compulsory curriculum content for primary and junior high students to follow in the Pioneer Curriculum (for example relating to moral and values education at the primary level and sociology at the junior high level).

The Xiehe Global Schools adopting the Pioneer Curriculum also develop the Virtues Project and selected values recommended by the United Nations (see **Chapter 5.2**).

Moral education is further extended through activities designed to enhance the students' sense of responsibility and service to the community (e.g. through the school's house system, Shanghai City voluntary work and outdoor activities).

Assessing the Pioneer Curriculum

There is both formative and summative assessment of student responses to the Pioneer Curriculum. Students are also assessed through peer, group and individual demonstration/oral approaches.

Five subjects (Chinese, English, maths, physics and chemistry) are assessed at the junior high school level by the Shanghai Municipal Government's Education Department using the same standardised test papers used by other such schools in Shanghai. For English assessment the Xiehe Global Schools have adopted the English National Curriculum Key Stages 1 to 3 English tests, in addition to the Shanghai Municipal Test.

Course Evaluation

Considerable emphasis is placed on school self evaluation of the Pioneer Curriculum Programme, which incorporates different models, including external adviser led evaluation exercises (see **Chapter 10**). Chinese and international education experts have been invited to monitor Pioneer classes and to suggest improvements to the Programme. Student satisfaction surveys are an important part of the evaluation process.

Teacher Appraisal

Pioneer Curriculum teachers are set professional development goals and are provided with related in-service training (e.g. with respect to lesson planning, inquiry based work, the use of cross curricular teaching and learning materials). Teachers are appraised on a regular basis through both 'planned' and 'random' lesson observation.

Creating a Pioneer Curriculum programme ethos

The overall Programme has a strong *'East meets West'* flavour for example with respect to:

- The learning environment: this presents the course characteristics and the students' learning levels; displays are interactive, instructive and reflect enjoyment in student learning.
- There are Programme related student activities in each semester (e.g. English spelling bees, cross stream events and moral education presentations).
- The partnership between the parents and the school is seen as crucial and many activities are planned to ensure that this is effective (e.g. parents' meetings, parents' lesson observations, family day activities, course information sessions, a parent volunteer organisation).
- Information computer technology is used extensively to ensure a strong 'parents as partners' relationship (e.g. a class blog; the Weixin Group: a Chinese social platform on the Internet).

Teaching and Learning in the Pioneer Curriculum Classroom

Considerable thought has been given, over the last decade, to the processes of teaching and learning within the Pioneer Curriculum. During this period Chinese teachers have learnt to combine the strengths of their own teaching and learning pedagogy (particularly with respect to whole class teaching and a classroom culture which exhibits competitive learning and extremely high concentration levels) with the strengths of the teaching and learning they have observed in their school's international stream. For example, co-operative learning and inquiry based work.

In recent years evaluation of Pioneer classroom teaching and learning has frequently focussed on the following indicators of excellence and observable features.

Whole Class Teaching
Indicator of excellence: *the whole class teaching is enhancing the educational attainment of students of all abilities.*

Some examples of observable features.

- Is the teacher asking different types of questions, for different purposes and students' abilities?
- Is the teacher asking open-ended questions which encourage risk taking within the learning?
- Are there also higher order, probing questions?
- Are the students talking/learning as well as the teacher talking?
- Does the teacher build on unexpected outcomes during the whole class teaching?
- Are the most and least successful students making progress in the lesson, as well as the average ability students?

Paired Work
Indicator of excellence: *the paired work is enhancing the educational attainment of students of all abilities.*

Some examples of observable features.

- Are the students already in pre-determined pairs, as 'shoulder partners', to ensure effective classroom management?
- Has the teacher thought carefully about the criteria for choosing the pairs throughout the class? (For example: mixed ability pairs to encourage co-operative learning; similar ability pairs to enable students to work on differentiated tasks).
- Is there pre-task modelling (either between the teacher and a student or between two students) to ensure that the students understand the task they are about to undertake?

LEFT: Students undertaking paired work.

Paired Work *(continued).*

- If a single student has been left on his or her own (because of an odd number in the total class size) has the teacher taken account of this in the classroom management?
- Is the task long enough for the pairs to undertake purposeful work?
- Is the task structured so that both students are contributing (approximately) equally in the paired discussion?
- What is the teacher doing whilst the paired work is being undertaken? (For example: monitoring and extending individual students; supporting individual students, ensuring that students of differing abilities are remaining on task; ensuring that the appropriate language is being spoken as much as possible).
- Is there any evidence that the teacher is intervening too much in the paired work?
- After the paired work has been completed, is there effective feedback and review of the work which has been undertaken? (For example: by one or two pairs modelling what they have been doing in the paired work).
- Is the length of this feedback and review appropriate?
- Has the teacher thought carefully about why specific pairs have been chosen to undertake this feedback and review modelling? (For example: a pair who have worked particularly successfully; a pair who have done unusually well, in order to promote self confidence).

Group Work (more than two students)
Indicator of excellence: *the group work is enhancing the educational attainment of students of all abilities.*

Some examples of observable features.

- Are the students already in pre-determined groups (perhaps with pre-determined names such as 'Tiger Group', 'Snake Group' etc) to ensure effective classroom management?
- Is the group work task sufficiently well structured in order to ensure that all students contribute equally to the task and that individual students are not seen to be dominating the task?

(other examples as for Paired Work above)

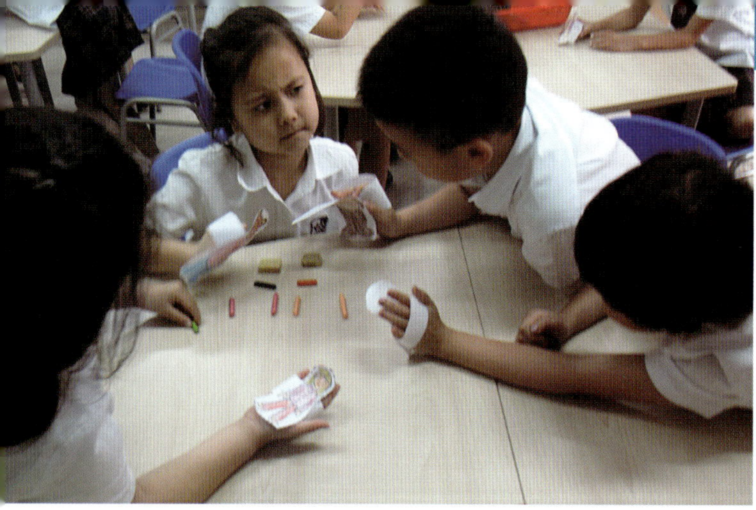

Students working in a group of four.

Individualised Learning

Indicator of excellence: *the individualised learning is enhancing the educational attainment of students of all abilities.*

Some examples of observable features.

- Is the work set by the teacher meeting the individual needs of each student, either by means of a worksheet(s) with an 'incline' of difficulty or by differentiated tasks designed to meet specific ability levels?
- Is the teacher being appropriately supportive to each student?

Crucially, considerable attention has been paid, over the last two years, to enhancing the differentiation of Pioneer Curriculum teaching and learning, particularly in order to meet the needs of the most and least successful students. Ensuring that all students are challenged in their learning is now seen as a key priority. There is, increasingly, more emphasis on individualised learning within the classroom, hitherto the most neglected of the four processes of teaching and learning. (See **Chapter 5.4** for an account of how differentiation has been planned and implemented within Pioneer classrooms).

School self evaluation has revealed in the past that paired and group work, overall, were often weaknesses within the Pioneer teaching and learning.

The following extracts from a school self evaluation report in a Xiehe Global School written in 2008 summarise the problem:

'Paired work is again far too short'.

'When the pairs feedback, approximately half the class is disinterested'.

'Group work follows which is somewhat chaotic'.

'There is a need to introduce more structured co-operative learning strategies, given that the students were seen to be learning least effectively during the paired and group work across the curriculum as a whole'.

Developing co-operative learning

Structured co-operative learning has, therefore, been an important in-service training priority for Pioneer Programme teachers. Considerable use has been made of DVDs showing excellent classroom practice in this respect. The following are extracts from the training materials.

Co-operative learning within a whole class context is:

The use of small groups so that students work together to maximise their own and each other's learning.

Advantages of collaborative group work.

- Quantity of learner speech can increase.
- Individualisation can increase.
- There is increased time on task.
- Thinking can increase.
- Motivation can increase.
- Enjoyment can increase.
- Independence can increase.
- Friendships can increase.
- Students can learn to co-operate and work in a team.
- Enhanced learning can be achieved.

The teachers role in collaborative group work

In undertaking co-operative group work the teacher undertakes the following.

- Provides a clear purpose and desired outcomes.
- Gives a clear role for each group member.
- Demonstrates that they value the performance of group work.
- Identifies the group skills they are looking for in a session.
- Provides a clear structure to the task.
- Designs tasks so that they have a low risk of failure in terms of social progress.
- Supports the group work process but learns how much to intervene.
- Provides tasks which are cognitively at the edge of students' understanding so that they need to collaborate to achieve their aims.
- Encourages students to take responsibility for organising their groups.
- Facilitates students talking about and evaluating how well the group worked.
- Provides opportunities for group members to talk about their feelings about working as a group.

Stages in managing group work

Modelling the group activities at the beginning of the lesson (have pre-arranged groups)

↓

Supporting the group activities

↓

Arranging feedback after the group work e.g. students model good practice (ensuring that the class, as observers, are well focussed on this modelling as peer evaluators).[1]

Features of effective group work:

Positive interdependence:
the group depends on all its members to get its task done. All have a role to fulfil and a task to achieve.

Individual accountability:
all members have a responsibility to work for and with the group and have to account for what they do.

Face-to-face interaction:
students must discuss with others.

Social development:
students acquire the skills of listening, encouraging, explaining, organizing.

Reflection:
students are encouraged to think about what they have done and understand the process of their learning.

Some of the social and collaborative skills that students need to learn effectively in co-operative group work include the following.

- Getting into groups effectively.
- Saying and responding to thanks.
- Giving and responding to praise.
- Attentive listening.
- Eyes focused on the speaker.
- Asking for and giving help.
- Giving and following instructions.
- Interrupting appropriately and accepting appropriate interruptions.
- Getting the group back on task.
- Disagreeing politely and responding to disagreement.

Some criteria for forming groups in co-operative group work might include:

- what you think the students can achieve (e.g. pairing/grouping of students of differing ability; or differentiated pairs/groups, by ability, with appropriate teacher support);

- levels of present achievement (e.g. differentiated tasks set to differing ability pairs/groups);
- work attitude;
- personality (e.g. introvert/extrovert);
- friendship groups;
- gender (mixing boys and girls); and
- Special Educational Needs.

There has also been considerable emphasis on the development of structured paired and group work techniques, as exemplified in the diagrams below. and right. These were first introduced into Xiehe by George M. Jacobs in 2005.[2]

Shoulder Partner Group Work

Hello, how are you?

I'm fine thank you

It's your turn

What is the opposite of quiet?

Loud

It's your turn

What is the opposite of ugly?

Beautiful

It's your turn

What is the opposite of fat?

Thin

It's your turn (Questions go on, in turn)

(At some point one student may say: 'I don't know')

When teacher says: *'stop, please',* both students say *'thank you for working with me.'*

Numbered Heads Together

STEP 1:
Students numbered off

STEP 2:
Teacher asks questions

STEP 3:
Heads together

STEP 4:
Teacher calls number

These techniques have been developed very successfully in Pioneer Curriculum classrooms and have greatly enhanced the quality of both the paired and group work. (Particularly with respect to ensuring that all students are on task, there are higher levels of collaborative learning and differentiation is more rigorous).

Conclusion

In all its aspects (including content, learning materials, teaching and learning processes, assessment and evaluation) the Pioneer Curriculum has proved to be both a challenging and an exciting school based curriculum initiative. One significant outcome has been its value as a catalyst for teacher professional creativity in the *'East meets West'* context of Xiehe Global Schools.

There is still much 'work in progress' but classroom evaluative evidence already suggests that the Pioneer Curriculum, thus far, has been a highly successful educational innovation.

Talkabout

- *Discuss the advantages of a locally/ school based curriculum development initiative of this type.*
- *Highlight a feature of the teaching and learning in your own school and/or organisation which needs improvement.*

  How do you know this?

  Suggest improvement strategies

Maxine Lu Hui Wen is Principal of SUIS (Wan Yuan), (Hong Qiao) and (Pudong).

Wang Yi is a researcher at the non-government Education Institute, Shanghai Academy of Educational Sciences and Principal Assistant of Shanghai United International School.

Acknowledgements

[1] Centre for Teacher and School Development. (1998). *Improving the Quality of Education for All.* (IQEA) University of Nottingham.

[2] Jacobs, G. M., Power, M. A. and Loh, W. I. (2002). *The Teacher's Sourcebook for Co-operative Learning: Practical Techniques, Basic Principles and Frequently Asked Questions.* Corwin Press.

6. Establishing curriculum continuity and progression in the Xiehe curriculum

This chapter is concerned with the ways in which Xiehe is attempting to ensure that children progressing through the Group, from the early years to high school, receive an education which always builds on previous learning, with respect to both the cognitive and affective dimensions.

6.1 The Xiehe Fortune Kindergarten(s)

Vivian Chen

Xiehe has 28 Kindergartens (19 Local, 7 Bilingual and 2 International). This means that children can experience a 2 to 6 years education within the Group. Approximately 80 per cent of the kindergarten students do so. The challenge is to ensure that these children, and others as they enter Xiehe schools, experience cross phase continuity and progression in their teaching and learning. In this chapter the author describes the early years curriculum foundation established for international students in the Xiehe Fortune Kindergarten(s).

> *'An excellent and enjoyable early years education provides the vital foundation for every child's future in life.'*
>
> Mary Kitchin

One of the most important educational developments throughout the world in recent years has been recognition of the importance of a child's early years learning in determining his or her later educational achievement. Fortune Kindergarten(s) offer bilingual international education funded and managed by Shanghai Xiehe Education Group. They carry the dream of a group of educators who believe a true international education is to prepare young children with healthy bodies, sound personalities and international vision.

Mission and goals

The Fortune Kindergarten(s) Mission Statement is:

- to provide a highly recognized international education that prepares young children for the future, supporting their development into good global citizens and proud representatives of their national cultures;
- to merge Chinese and Western teaching and learning approaches, practicing bilingualism and ensuring that children are confident in English as well as in Chinese.; and
- to emphasise the personal as well as the academic development of the students, so the children become open minded, reflective, caring, moral, and cooperative.

Fortune's curriculum goals are to help children understand and accept social rules, develop their own personalities, begin to understand communication between people belonging to different cultures and develop every aspect of their personality, life, language and perceptive skills. We attempt to achieve this by providing an active, relaxed and homely learning environment and adopting a bilingual and multicultural approach to education.

It is recognised that the children have a right to participate in high-quality education programmes that encourage active learning, problem solving, effective communication, creativity, social adjustment and participation. We believe that all children, irrespective of nationality and cultural background, must find the school a welcoming, nurturing, open and tolerant environment in which to grow and develop.

Situated at the confluence between Eastern and Western educational approaches, the Fortune Kindergarten curriculum focuses on the following.

- Ensuring that the students have equal exposure to the most valuable characteristics of both Eastern and Western cultures, including a school based curriculum that includes and coordinates elements coming from different systems and education theories: for example thematic, project teaching, self discovery, whole class and group teaching approaches.
- Accomplishing truly bilingual learning, both Chinese and English are used during school hours in a balanced way by Chinese and English speaking homeroom teachers.
- Two particularly key Fortune curriculum dimensions, thematic bilingual team teaching and Philosophy for Children (P4C), are considered in more detail in **Chapters 5.1** and **5.3**.

Key components of the Fortune Kindergarten curriculum.

Core curriculum	
Academic	Life Skills
• Language & Literacy • Science • Music • Maths • Art	• Self-Help • Personal Values • Social Values • Health and Safety
Physical	Play
• Sports (with/without equipment) • Exercise • Games	• Sports (with/without equipment) • Exercise • Games
Support curriculum	
Circle time	Field trips
Learning diary	Family brainstorming research
Drawing diary	Resource rooms
A story a day	Whole school events
Friday activities	Optional courses

Teddy Bear Family
FIRE

Teaching and learning processes

In a caring and positive atmosphere, teachers and support staff create a warm and happy place for the pre-school students to learn, such as a bright smile to a child and a hug when they come to school in the morning. We always encourage the children to try everything, for example when they are offered a new snack or introduced to a new game. As the kindergarten bridges the gap from home, staff guide the children towards having a continued good self-image whilst building social skills in the Fortune setting.

Sensory, motor, perceptual and language skills are introduced through materials and activities, which are child-centred and teacher-facilitated. Work is planned which emphasises the process rather than the product, fostering a sense of accomplishment and pride for our young children.

Based on the theory that children learn through play, classroom routines encourage active involvement, meaningful experimentation and reinforcement through repetition. Schedules are designed which balance structure and free choice, as well as active and quiet times (see the daily schedule for children aged 4-6 and guidance for teachers below and on the following page).

Recognising that children grow in predictable stages, teachers treat each child as an individual, working from the level they have attained and moving forward a step at a time. Fortune Kindergarten(s) teach a love of learning by allowing the children to experience their own stage of development and helping them to feel success without pressure.

We also value the active involvement of parents in the daily programme, through their involvement in both classroom activities and outside visits. Parents are encouraged to join exploring and discussion programmes such as how a car was produced and what a manager does during his day. Parents are invited for all the kindergarten events such as the Winter Concert, the Multi-Cultural Month, the Language Art Festival and the Children's Day Fair.

Daily schedule for Kindergarten 1 and Kindergarten 2 (children aged 4-6 yrs)

Time	Regular Day		Rainy Day	
	Activity	Place	Activity	Place
8.15 - 9.20	PE *(10.30 in winter)*	Outdoor	PE	Outdoor
9.20 -10.00	Life Skills Free Play	Classroom	Life Skills Free Play	Classroom
10.00 - 10.30	Teaching and Learning	Classroom/Resource rooms	Teaching and Learning	Classroom/Resource rooms
10.30 - 11.15	Life Skills Role Play *(8.15 in winter)*	Classroom	Role Play	Classroom
11.15 - 14.30	Free Play *(15 mins)* Life Skills Lunch Nap or Optional Courses	Classroom/Outdoor/ Resource rooms	Free Play *(15 mins)* Life Skills Lunch Nap or Optional Courses	Classroom/Outdoor/ Resource rooms
14.30 - 15.00	Snack	Classroom	Snack	Classroom
15.00 - 15.30	Activity Areas	Classroom	Activity Areas	Classroom
15.30 - 16.00	Outdoor play	Outdoor	Indoor PE games	Outdoor
16.15 -	Free Play and wait for parents	Classroom	Free Play and wait for parents	Classroom

Daily schedule guide for teachers

Time	Activities	Methods	Guide
8.15 - 9.20	PE	Prepared by teachers Whole class/individual	• Remind children to prepare themselves for PE time, such as changing shoes, checking shoe laces, suitable clothes, etc. • Include one whole class game and free choice facilities, such as balls, jump rope, etc. Remind children to follow the rules and take turns. • Observe and remind children to drink water during the activity.
9.20 -10.00	Life Skills	Child-centred Class/group discussion	• Children wipe their sweat, wash hands, drink water, take morning snack. • Topic of discussion should be related to the theme, or children's recent interests. Teachers facilitate and help gather the ideas from the discussions.
10.00 - 10.30	Teaching and Learning	Teacher-directed Class/Group/ Individual	• Teacher prepares the activity based on the age development goals, no longer than 30 minutes for K2, 20 minutes for K1.
10.30 - 11.15	Role Play	Child-centred Individual	• Teachers observe and try not to interrupt the game.
11.15 - 14.30	Free Play Nap Optional Courses	Child-centred Class/Individual	• Allow children to arrange their time based on their individual needs, talk to peers or read by themselves, or record their personal interests by drawing, writing, etc.
14.30 - 15.00	Snack	Prepared by kindergarten Class	• Encourage children to try different food, cultivate table manners.
15.00 - 15.30	Activity Areas	Child-centred Individual	• Teachers prepare the materials in the activity areas to meet children's needs and add/change the materials based on their observation. • A class discussion may be held to encourage children to share their experiences whilst playing in the areas.
15.30 - 16.00	Outdoor Play Facilities	Child-centred Individual	• Teachers stand at different outdoor areas to make sure children are safely playing. • Children are allowed to play freely with other classes.
16.15 -	Free Play	Child-centred Individual	• Teachers remind children to prepare their bags and personal items, goodbye song, free play whilst waiting for the parents.

Benchmarking of students' development

In order to ensure students have a solid foundation of basic knowledge, understanding and skills, Fortune establishes benchmarks for each age group over two semesters. The benchmarks are used during daily teaching and learning assessment. Individual students are observed and their progress is reported. The Benchmarks for the Kindergarten 2 curriculum areas are as follows.

English *(speaking and listening, literacy – reading and literacy – writing)*

- Demonstrates understanding of increasingly complex age appropriate concepts and ideas.
- Expresses increasingly complex age appropriate concepts and ideas clearly and confidently.
- Speaks in logically sequenced sentences expressing complex meaning .
- Tells a story in own words without prompting or can make up story line .
- Scans and reads age-appropriate sentences in story books, with some support, using different word decoding techniques.
- Sounds out CVC words and other sound blends.
- Writes several names of people, places and things, usually as labels.
- Begins copying or independently writing simple sentences with some punctuation.

Chinese *(listening skills and understanding of the language, speaking and oral expression ability and Chinese character recognition and reading ability)*

- Demonstrates understanding of increasingly complex age appropriate concepts and ideas.
- Joins confidently every activity conducted in Chinese and is ready to interact with others.
- Understands multiple instructions and game rules and is able to act according to teacher's requirements.
- Expresses increasingly complex age appropriate concepts and ideas clearly and confidently.
- Uses short sentences in Chinese, is careful about the correct choice of vocabulary and can simply describe different things.
- Uses complex sentences in speech and can use correctly connective words.
- Arranges two to four pictures in correct story order and can tell story based on pictures.
- Answers questions confidently and correctly, using full sentences.
- Recognises and can read previously learnt Chinese characters and words without picture support.
- Demonstrates well-developed, correct reading habits and skills.
- Understands the meaning of Chinese books with coordinated single pictures and complex sentences.

Mathematics *(number concepts, sorting and classification, shape/time/space, handling data and mathematical reasoning)*

- Counts well from 1–100; can count by 2-s, by 5-s or by 10-s.
- Demonstrates operations with numbers 1-20 (addition, subtraction operations and addition, subtraction stories).
- Sorts well by three or more characteristics.
- Establishes some relationship between 2D and 3D shapes.
- Demonstrates good understanding of spatial orientation in relation to self or other reference.
- Tells time by whole hours and halves.
- Demonstrates use of simple strategies for keeping personal, small group or whole class records.
- Infers data from tables, statistics, etc (e.g.- weather and calendar statistics, etc).
- Establishes correspondence between objects, signs and symbols (one apple – one circle – number one).
- Composes word problems based on pictures or operations with some support.
- Solves addition and subtraction word problems.
- Uses objects and body parts to make simple measurements.

Science *(attitudes, skills, knowledge and understanding)*

- Shows deeper knowledge and understanding of certain aspects of the natural world (likes dinosaurs and knows a lot about them, etc).
- Follows own inquiry with some independent or guided research (looks at books, collects pictures, organises small collection of objects, etc).
- Develops skills for using specific tools, instruments and methods for scientific inquiry (use of scales, thermometer, meter, clock, etc).
- Understands the difference between solid, fluid, gas and begins to grasp related concepts like dilution, solidification, crystallization, evaporation, condensation, etc.
- Understands and can operate with simple concepts related to geography, the Earth and the Universe.

Art and music *(attitudes, skills, using materials)*

- Shows confidence in performing individually or as a group using a variety of expression styles (song, instruments, song and dance, choir, etc).
- Recognises and expresses the emotions generated by different music styles as well as different types of visual artistic expression.
- Takes pride in own performances and art work and in collective performances and art projects, being able to express personal opinions or interests related to such work.
- Draws a person with complex details and complex contextual landscape.
- Chooses materials appropriately and creatively, uses them to achieve artistic outcomes

PE *(participation and enjoyment, motor skills, fitness and strength, sportsmanship and using equipment)*

- Enjoys team games and takes pride in personal and team accomplishments.
- Uses own physical skills to accomplish competitive (football game, obstacle course) and cooperative (three legged race) goals.
- Sustains 20-30 minutes of moderate to high intensity physical activity requiring complex coordination of physical skills (obstacle courses, jump rope, ball games, etc).
- Demonstrates basic game playing skills and understands sporting concepts like team and fair play.
- Shows familiarity with age relevant equipment and can cooperatively use it paying attention to own and others' safety during play.

Life skills *(personal needs, social behaviour, overall motivation and participation)*

- Eats well independently with spoon or chopsticks, keeps space clean and can independently help set up and clean up.
- Respects a quiet play or nap routine independently.
- Demonstrates independent self help skills and is careful about personal hygiene and appearance.
- Anticipates or initiates relevant school tasks based on familiar school routines.
- Anticipates and avoids conflicts by using appropriate language and behaviour in interactions with peers and adults.
- Demonstrates confidence in social interactions and readily offers support when relevant.
- Approaches school tasks diligently and is well motivated by personal, group and peer success.

Experiential learning in the kindergarten garden.

Cross phase continuity and progression strategies within the Xiehe Global Schools

Fortune Kindergarten(s) work closely to ensure Kindergarten 2/Primary School Grade 1 continuity, for example in the following ways:

- Holding annual family marathons with Kindergarten 2 and Grade 1 students' parents.
- Developing professional links between Kindergarten 2 teachers and Grade 1 teachers. At the beginning of the 2012 academic year, Kindergarten 2 teachers from Fortune Kindergarten (Pudong) and teachers from SUIS (Pudong) had an initial meeting to set up the benchmarks for Kindergarten 2 students. Teachers from the two campuses worked for the whole year to develop the benchmarks for literacy and several joint professional development sessions were held.
- Grade 1 teachers were invited to the Kindergarten 2 classes to observe lessons and to answer questions from the students about life in the primary school.
- In 2012 a one day visit was organised with the theme 'I am a Grade 1 student' for Kindergarten 2 students to experience daily life as a Grade 1 student in the primary school.
- The Kindergarten 2 programme in the second semester is changed so that it reflects the Grade 1 curriculum content more. Also aspects of the teaching and learning are modified to reflect the Grade 1 approaches in this respect. (For example, fewer activity areas and less role play).
- Optional courses are introduced during Kindergarten 2 'nap time' to prepare students for the Grade 1 timetable.
- There is close collaboration with parents to prepare the students for the transition period, both psychologically and physically.

Conclusion

The children we are working with are pure and innocent, filled with a thirst for knowledge and great expectations. They are future citizens of the world, who will take responsibility for our future. No matter where they will live and work, their present early years education will leave a deep impression on their future. As educators, we must try to both keep in mind and strive to carry out our mission: preparing our students for their long journey in global education.

Talkabout

- *Consider how early years students can be prepared most effectively as young global citizens, using examples from this chapter.*
- *Compare the strategies the Fortune Kindergartens use for attempting to ensure cross phase continuity (kindergarten to primary) with those used by your own kindergarten/school/organisation.*

Vivian Xiaoyun Chen is the General Principal of Fortune Kindergarten(s), Shanghai.

6.2 Creating curriculum continuity and progression in Xiehe's cross phase Global Schools

Clive Belgeonne and Trevor Higginbottom

The most recently opened Xiehe Global Schools are cross phase, based on the same campus. (SUIS (Wan Yuan) 6-19 years; SUIS (Wuxi) 2-19 years). As with all cross phase schools, the challenge is to ensure that students benefit educationally from this school management model as they progress through the age range. Worldwide, good practice in this respect appears to be very limited.

> *'We must view the curriculum as a spiral, with students constantly building on their understanding as they progress through the phases of their schooling.'*
>
> Jerome Bruner

Cross phase curriculum

The framework of a cross phase school curriculum provides a tremendous opportunity for continuity and coherence in education, something that has been lacking in the educational context in England in recent decades, with successive governments producing a constant stream of short-term directives and the types of school becoming ever more varied in the name of 'choice' and the 'free market'.

The only area where a notion of 2-19 years or 6-19 years age-range schooling exists in the UK is in some elements of the independent sector, which has tended to adhere to an essentially 19th century notion of schooling exemplified by academic and sporting achievement along with character building.

A cross phase curriculum also provides the possibility of overcoming the difficult bridge of the transition between primary and secondary school. This is a key stage when children can lose interest in education:

> *'Children starting secondary school, even those lucky ones entering the school of their choice, find that far from being launched into a brave new adventure, they are reassessed, their previous work and achievements are undervalued and they are forced to mark time going over old ground. A series of studies over the past 20 years shows students regressing between the last year of primary and the end of the first year of secondary school. Primary-secondary transition is now regarded as the crucial time, when learners drop out or are made for life.'* [1]

So what are the cornerstones of a cross phase curriculum? The starting point is to think about what learners will need to survive and thrive through the challenges and opportunities of the 21st century.

Those starting school at the age of two in the next few years can reasonably expect to live into the 22nd century, but humanity will have to have overcome a number of hurdles if there is to be a meaningful existence for the majority of humans and other species on the planet. Issues such as climate change, energy production, food production and distribution, migration, ageing populations, youth unemployment, inequality, sustainable development and a global economy that allows these, will need to be addressed. John Beddington,[2] the former UK Chief Scientific Adviser has warned that a 'perfect storm' of food shortages, scarce water and insufficient energy resources threaten to unleash public unrest, cross-border conflicts and mass migration as people flee from the worst-affected regions by as soon as 2030. Endnote *1

A useful beginning is to ask teachers to think about the knowledge, understanding, skills, values attitudes and behaviours young people will need to live meaningful lives in the 21st century. Endnote *2

Clive Belgeonne has undertaken this activity with hundreds of teachers of all age groups, trainee teachers and teacher trainers and there is an extraordinary amount of similarity in what they feel is needed. **Figure 1** below includes an amalgamation of the responses from two groups of primary teachers who claimed they had no knowledge of global learning.

An activity such as this could be the starting point for deciding what a cross phase curriculum should entail. Teachers can then decide how to develop a spiral curriculum that enables learners to be introduced to key elements at the appropriate stage in their development and revisit and build on them as they get older.

Fig 1: Core knowledge, understanding, skills and attributes for 21st century learners as defined by a group of primary teachers in the UK.

Knowledge and understanding	Skills	Attributes (values and attitudes)
• Self-awareness • Diversity/Recognise similarities and differences • Action impacts change (and future) • Social justice • Equalities/inequalities • Cultural awareness • Economic awareness • Interdependence • Self to local, community to global: where one is, how one affects others, what one can do to make a difference • Access information to make informed judgements • Understanding of fairness • Circle of life • Different types of community • Knowledge of current events (locally and worldwide) • Issues that face the planet • Limits of resources • Sustainability	• Communication • Language • Ability to step outside comfort zone • Conflict resolution • Research/ICT: ability to discriminate sources and their purpose • Debate/listen, articulate and justify a view • Discussion • Ability to challenge • Inquiring mind • Listen to opinion of others	• Active citizens • Empowering/feeling empowered • Sense of fairness • Understanding • Empathy • Moral dimension • Appreciation of others and where things come from • Tolerance for others • Open mindedness • Receptive to change • Value other opinions, appreciate a different point of view • Respecting difference • Wanting to find out about others

The table in **Figure 1** suggests 'social justice' under knowledge and understanding, and 'sense of fairness' under values and attitudes. Children can develop a sense of fairness from a very young age and this can be built on to introduce the concept of 'social justice' when they are older. What time and when such concepts should be introduced will depend on the teacher's understanding of a particular group of students.

Children's thinking ability

Many teachers are still influenced by Piaget's cognitive development theory that suggests that children can only manage certain types of thinking (e.g. logically or abstractly) at certain ages. This has been challenged by recent research outlined in the Cambridge Primary Review:

> *'Children, even babies, are able to think and learn in the same way as adults, albeit in rudimentary forms…infants possess the same neurological structures as adults, and it is experience rather than neurophysiological change that accounts for the greater sophistication of adult thinking.'* [3]

Clive Belgeonne experienced this when teaching Philosophy for Children (see **Chapter 5.3**). Children as young as five or six are capable of raising philosophical questions and can demonstrate imaginative reasoning. Some would argue that small children are regularly asking themselves open-ended questions about the nature of the world as they try to make sense of it but that it is formal schooling, with an emphasis on closed questions and 'one right answer', that closes down their thinking and limits their potential.

Professor Tanya Byron has raised concerns[4] that too much subject teaching in schools is only addressing the Lower Order Thinking Skills of Bloom's Taxonomy (see **Figure 2** below), those of 'remembering, understanding and applying'.

If we want young people to have the skills to deal with the challenges of a complex and uncertain future, they need to develop the higher order thinking skills, of 'analysing, evaluating and creating'.

Fig 2: Bloom's Taxonomy of thinking skills

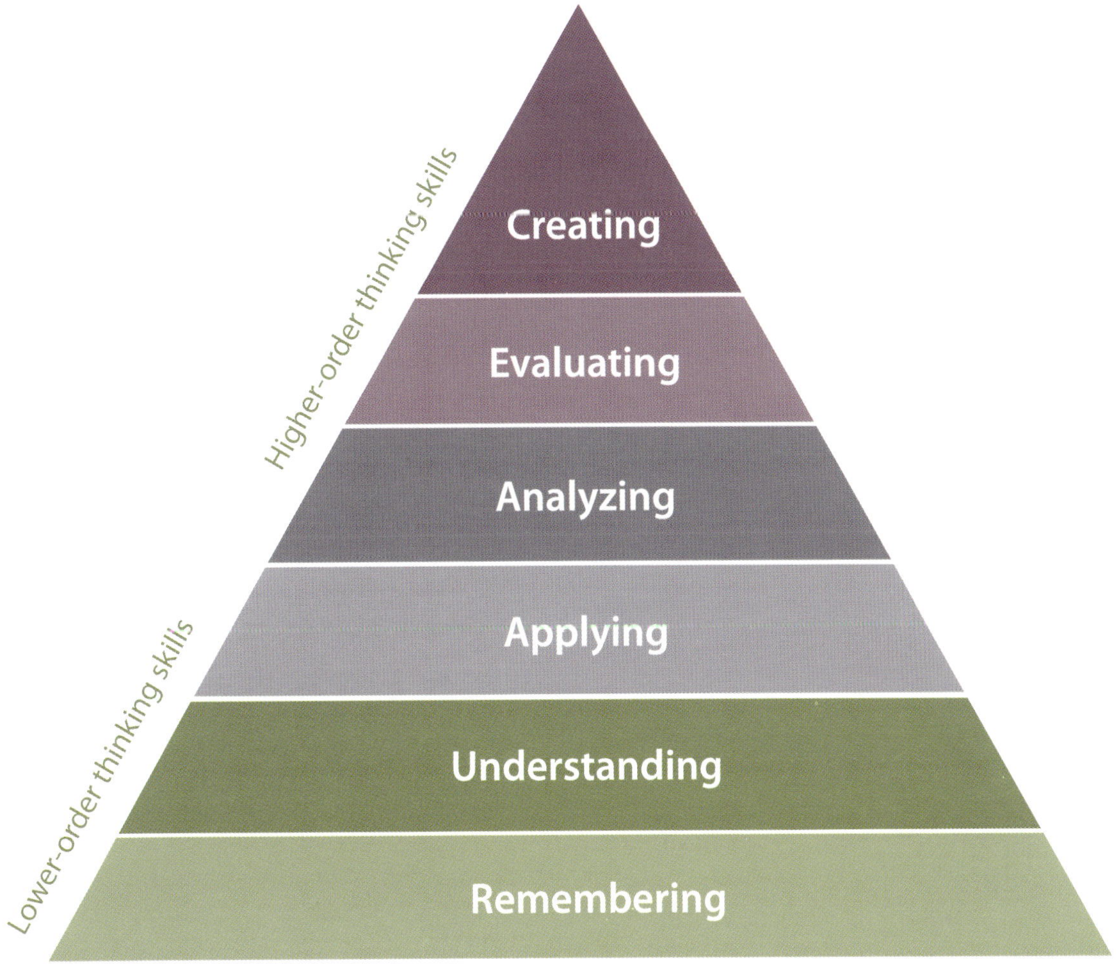

This emphasis on the importance of key skills is endorsed by Professor Guy Claxton in his work on 'Building Learning Power',[5] developed as a response to his belief that schools are failing to prepare young people to be lifelong learners in a more uncertain and complex future. He proposes a focus on 4Rs, as shown in **Figure 3** below.

Fig 3: The 4 R's from Building Learning Power

Resourcefulness	Resilience
• Curious and questioning • Imaginative • Taking responsibility	• Persevering, improving • Concentrating • Taking feedback
Relating	**Reflecting**
• Learning alone and with others • Empathising • Being a team player	• Self-evaluating • Planning • Transferring

Schools that have adopted the 'Building Learning Power' approach have improved attainment, whatever their context, though Claxton says this should not be their motivation, but because it is the right thing to develop their students as flexible, adaptable lifelong learners. His key message is that *"...schools need to get better at helping young people learn how to flourish in demanding times."*

Given the current and growing challenges facing humanity, skills such as 'Resourcefulness' and 'Resilience' will be key to giving people realistic hope that we can make things better for all.

Emotional aspects of learning

Such skills are also endorsed by the SEAL (Social and Emotional Aspects of Learning) curriculum that was introduced in England in 2006. This was based on the work of Daniel Goleman on 'Emotional Intelligence',[6] which he sees as probably more important than traditional measures of intelligence such as I.Q. He identifies five key domains: the intra-personal – self-awareness, managing feelings, motivation and the inter-personal – social skills and empathy. Schools that have embraced the SEAL curriculum in a whole-school manner have found positive results. Research[7] into 53 primary and secondary schools found that the schools that were perceived by both their students and staff to have a more positive social and emotional ethos were also found to have:

- more positive student experiences of peer interaction;
- better Ofsted ratings for behaviour;
- lower levels of persistent absence; and
- higher attainment in Key Stage 2 SATs and GCSEs.

A key skill for our times is that of empathy. A report for Oxfam[8] suggests that it is crucial for young people to develop empathy for those beyond their social group, extending to those in different cultures and parts of the world, and also for generations yet to come (if we are to properly consider what sort of world we are passing on).[Endnote *3] Recent research[9] has shown that empathy is innate in all humans but that it can be lost through neglectful upbringing. It can, however, be reactivated by a supportive environment. It is very important therefore that the curriculum actively seeks to engage and develop empathy in learners. Rifkin suggests we are in a race between attaining a level of global empathic consciousness to be able to act together as a species and impending environmental destruction.

The affective dimension of learning is crucial, as research is also showing the link between learning and emotions:

> *'Learning requires emotional engagement. Only then do certain chemicals, such as dopamine and adrenaline, get released in our brains, and initiate chemical processes that lead to the modification of synapses. Without modification of synapses, no learning takes place, hence there is no learning without emotional engagement'.* [10]

Traditional 'Western' education has promoted mental and physical activity ('mens sana, in corpore sano'), and only recently has begun to actively address the emotional sphere. Many indigenous cultures see the need for a balance between the mental, physical, emotional and spiritual spheres.[Endnote *4]

This also brings us to the issue of knowledge. Many commentators and politicians in the UK and USA have recently criticised what they see as too much focus on skills in education and not enough emphasis on knowledge, with debates about what constitutes 'core knowledge' in the contemporary world and debate over which subject areas are more important or which should be prescribed in a 'national curriculum'. The classical Western idea of a 'body of knowledge,' the knowing of which makes you an 'educated' person, is questionable in a more pluralist local and global society. There is also confusion between the rapidly increasing volume of, and access to, information via modern technologies and what constitutes knowledge. The Cambridge Primary Review is helpful here:

> *'If the various domains of knowledge are viewed not as collections of inert or obsolete information but as distinct ways of knowing, understanding, inquiring and making sense which include processes of inquiry, modes of explanation and criteria for verification which are generic to all content in the domain, then far from being redundant or irrelevant, knowledge provides the means to tackle future problems and needs as well as windows of unparalleled richness on the past and present. Knowledge in this sense also provides the student with essential tools for testing the truth and value of all that information which pours from the internet, television, radio and newspapers, and the teacher's task becomes one of initiation into this critically-armed frame of mind rather than the mere transmission that is the stock-in-trade of the teacher 'barking out facts'.* [3]

In addition Lawton (1983),[3] notes that as *'the curriculum is necessarily a selection from culture, and Britain is anything but a monoculture, there are two questions.*

- *Which knowledge?*
- *Which culture? '*

If one accepts notions of a curriculum that is relevant to a local context within an increasingly global society, the need to balance issues of tradition with modernity, identity with diversity and what we may need to know for a future we cannot predict, the question of what knowledge to include can be seen as highly contestable. The solution suggested in the Cambridge Primary Review quote above is to see knowledge *'...as distinct ways of knowing, understanding, inquiring and making sense which include processes of inquiry, modes of explanation and criteria for verification...'* The teacher will bring certain expertise to areas of study, but in many cases may become a co-learner and inquirer with the student.

Values

A crucial part of the development of a holistic curriculum is to recognise the importance of values education. There is a need for the school community (in as broad a sense as possible) to agree a set of core values[Endnote *5] (ideally working towards 'bigger than self values' – see **Chapter 5.2**) and try to put them into practice.

> *'My research, undertaken at Oxford University indicates that the most effective teachers of values are those who work to be more self-aware and take time to reflect on the deeper meaning of the values being emphasised in the school. Self-reflective work by teachers is seen to have a powerful impact on students, who appear to make a connection between what the teacher says and what she does'.*
>
> *'Such teachers are authentic, meaning that they seek to achieve congruence between their thoughts, feelings and actions. They are aware that they have the potential (as we all do) to be consumed by negative emotion (e.g. anger) and for this to be inappropriately translated into action. Developing reflection as a tool to aid self-control enables both student and adult to behave in ways that reflect positive human values such as compassion and respect'.* [11]

Many schools have 'Mission Statements' that often propose a set of values that the school will promote. However, they are not held accountable to these and the mismatch between espoused values and their enactment can be a source of disaffection for young people.

Being explicit about these values, reflecting on how they are put into practice and reviewing their continued relevance or need for adaptation, is key to becoming an authentic learning community and preparation for engagement in a deliberative democracy. Dialogic teaching and learning methodologies such as P4C can enable such reflection.

The challenge is to ensure that the student experience is a holistic one, joining what the Sustainable Schools Strategy (England) called the 'Curriculum, Campus and Community' (see **Figure 4**, below).

The 'Curriculum' is the formal, taught curriculum, but also the informal curriculum and learning outside the classroom.

The 'Campus' is the ethos of the school and the way it is administered and run.

The 'Community' encompasses the local community and its wider, global connections (it has been argued that there is a 4th C: 'Culture' the culture in which that community operates).

Very often the values espoused in the ethos may not be reflected in student-teacher relationships or relations with the wider community; or something may be taught in the classroom (e.g. the importance of waste reduction) but this may not be reflected in the way the school is run or in the behaviour of the wider community. This leads young people to question the integrity of the adult world and can lead to disaffection if there are not opportunities to reflect on and enact the values espoused.

This approach is endorsed by Hicks[12] who talks about the need to engage young people in real life sustainability issues in their school community, to learn from trying to come up with practical solutions. Such real-life learning is highly motivating and aids social skills as well as cognitive development.

The values the school espouses will also reflect ideologies about the purpose of education. This book is about global schools. It can be argued that we are all now global learners as we are learning in an increasingly globalised context. Yet there are different perceptions about what this global aspect entails and schools generally reflect the tensions exemplified in governmental policies. As Alexander notes:

Fig 4: Curriculum, Campus, Community

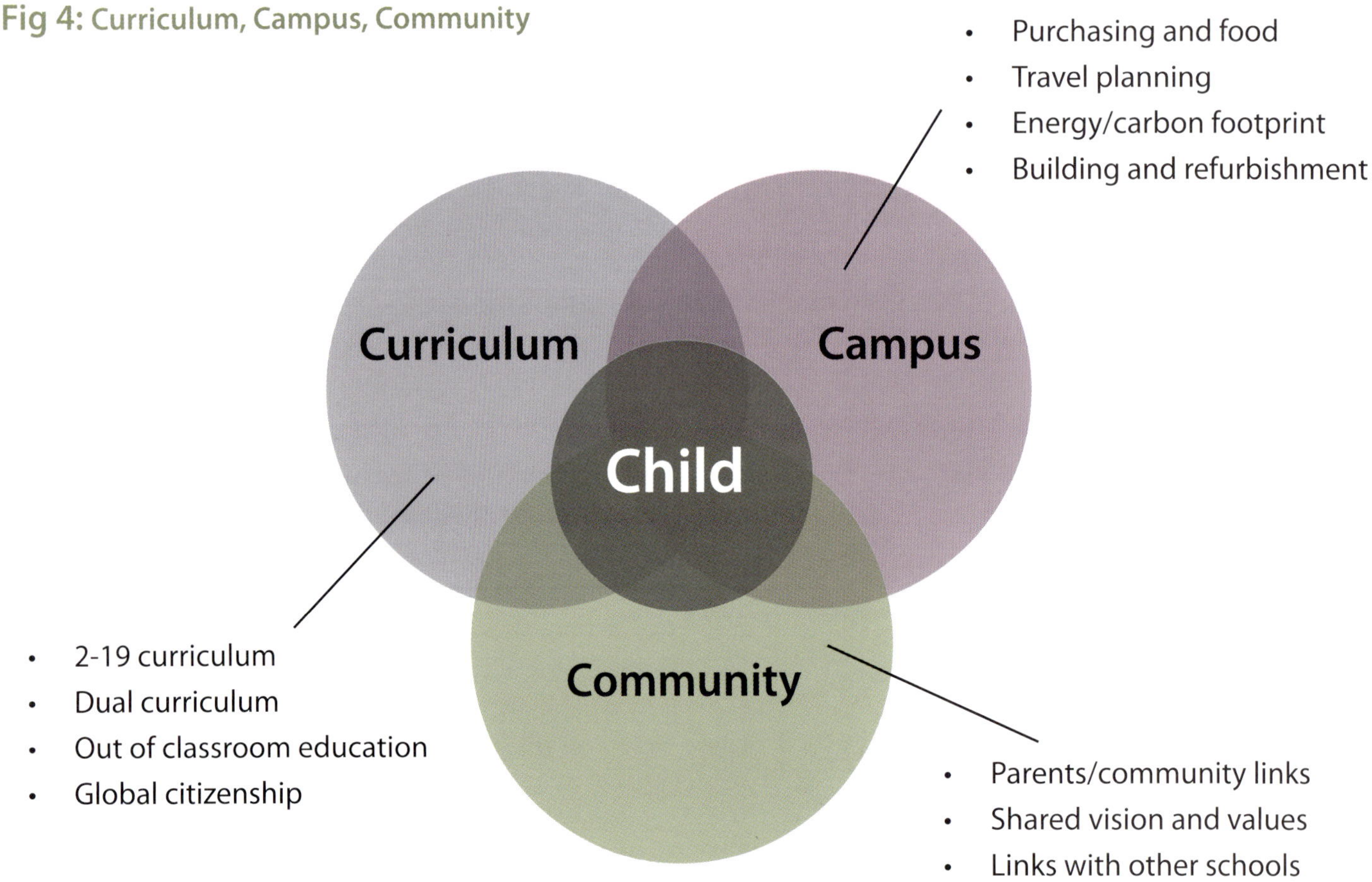

Adapted from Sustainable Schools Strategy (England)

'There are two broad senses in which the architects of a national education system can think internationally. They can view the world as an essentially competitive arena of trade and influence and use education in order to maximise national advantage – economic, scientific, technological, ideological, military – over other countries. Alternatively they can apply a more genuinely international outlook (international rather than contra-national) acknowledging that global interdependence carries moral obligations, from which no country is immune and that education can serve to unite rather than divide'. [13]

As the Common Cause research (see **Chapter 5.2**) indicates, we all hold competitive as well as collaborative values within us and clearly elements of competition can be motivating, but it is becoming increasingly clear that many of the core challenges facing our global society will only be solved by increased co-operation.

Learning together

In summary, a cross phase curriculum particularly for the 2-19 years or 6-19 years age range, offers tremendous opportunities for more consistent, coherent and holistic learning, with the school staff and students able to develop as a mutually supportive learning community. It offers the opportunity to agree a set of knowledge and understanding, skills, values and attitudes that will equip learners to survive and thrive in the 21st century.

The Cambridge Primary Review was the most comprehensive inquiry into English education for 40 years, built on 31 independent research reports. It outlined an ambitious set of proposals for a new primary curriculum, two of which are particularly relevant to our present discussion. It proposes a curriculum that:

'Is planned and implemented with clear regard to principles of procedure which highlight and safeguard, for example, entitlement, quality, breadth, balance of attention to present and future needs, rights, equity, guidance not prescription, local responsiveness and the pursuit of explicit aims and values.

Starts from an account of the aims of primary education which is grounded in the analysis of the needs, capabilities and circumstances of children now, of their likely future needs as adults and lifelong learners, and of the condition of the society in which they are growing up. These aims are fundamental and inform not only the curriculum but also wider aspects of pedagogy and the life of the school'. [3]

Curriculum development processes helpful to establishing cross phase continuity and progresssion in the curriculum

Any school with more than one phase (kindergarten, primary, secondary, high school) needs to consider the processes of curriculum development with respect to curriculum continuity quite separately from the curriculum content issues covered so far in this chapter.

Xiehe's Global Schools try to answer the following questions in this regard.

Is there an overall commitment to the curriculum continuity issue within the school?

This is key: unless there is vision which ensures that the issue is embedded into a school's culture, little is likely to happen. Clearly, the senior managers have a critical role here. Curriculum continuity should be highlighted in both the school's mission statement and its aims.

Are there individual colleagues responsible for this?

There is a strong case for appointing a cross curriculum co-ordinator and/or a cross phase working party, with senior manager representatives from each phase, to both monitor and develop curriculum continuity.

What are our policies in this respect?

Schools should have clearly articulated policies on curriculum continuity but it is critical that these influence their day-by-day working practices: they should not be merely rhetoric. **Chapter 8.2**, which follows, deals with the process of policy development within schools.

A whole school policy on the generic processes of teaching and learning, highlighted in this chapter, would be helpful. For example, students can build on and develop their co-operative learning and 'Philosophy for Children' (P4C) work as they progress through the school (see **Chapters 5.3** and **5.5**).

Interesting work has been done on progression in the students' use of vocabulary in P4C as they progress from 5 to 14 years[14] (see **Figure 5**, below).

Fig 5: Progression in students' P4C discourse vocabulary

Ages 5-7	Ages 7-11	Ages 11-14
• Listening – speaking • Talking – discussing • Thinking – thoughts – ideas • Brain – mind • Knowing – believing • Imagine – imagination • Questions – answers • Reason • Rule • Agree – disagree • Example • Decision • View – opinion • Problem – solution • Similar – different (same – not the same) • Rights – wrong • Fair – unfair • True – untrue • Real – not real • Wondering	• Accept – reject • Compare – contrast • Argument – quarrel • Version – statement • Reasons – supporting arguments • Predict – assess • Clarify – confuse • Respond – reply • Rule – exceptions • Example – counter example • Prove – disprove • Evidence – example • Explain – justify • Relevant – irrelevant • Meaning – definition • Argue – persuade • Fact – opinion • Data – information • Possible – probable – certain • Cause - effect	• Assumption • Logic/logical – illogical • Implications – consequences • Analysis – classification • Concepts • Identical – contradictory • Cause/effect relationships • Definition – distinction (between words, ideas) • Criteria (criterion) – judgement • Assumption (implicit) – assertion • Clear – ambiguous (vague/ imprecise) • Analogy – metaphor • Empathy • Objective/subjective • Principle • Dilemma – compromise • Authority - evidence • Prejudice (bias) – balanced view • Observation – interpretation • Paraphrase – summarise

What can we do to support policy development?

Schools should be prepared to undertake specific curriculum development initiatives which support continuity. Two examples might be as follows.

- The University of Nottingham's 'Improving the Quality of Education for All' (IQEA)[15] approach could be adopted: a 'cadre' (group) of staff from across the school (drawn from all phases, representing a cross section of management roles and experience) could undertake a school-based curriculum project on, for example, 'continuity in global learning' or 'whole curriculum ICT' across the phases. The support of an external adviser might be helpful.
- Linking with the English 'Leading Through Values' Project, co-ordinated by Rob Bowden.[16] This exciting innovation supports schools in developing cross phase progression in values education (see **Chapter 5.2**).

What generic processes of curriculum development do we need to be aware of?

When undertaking this type of curriculum development schools should:

- ensure that staff have genuine quality time to determine purposeful outcomes;
- effectively pace the initiative (through rigorous/realistic school development planning);
- plan the initiative with clear formulation, implementation, evaluation and review phases;
- ensure that all staff feel a 'sense of ownership' throughout;
- make certain that senior management is totally supportive; and
- possibly, link some staff participants' work to (in the case of Xiehe) the Stars Project initiative (see **Chapter 9.1** which follows); and/or their external degree studies (see **Chapter 9.2** which follows).

How will we know if students and staff have benefitted?

School self evaluation can be a useful strategy both for reviewing and developing cross phase continuity. It might be helpful, for example, to use the type of external adviser led evaluation exercise described in **Chapter 10** which follows.

Conclusion

This chapter has provided a summary of the theoretical background to cross phase curriculum continuity and progression and of the practical ways of ensuring that this happens successfully. These two dimensions are of equal importance, given that ineffective curriculum development and management appear to be the reason why a significant number of cross phase schools all too often operate as separate phases. If this happens, critically, many opportunities for enhancing the students' attainment are missed.

Talkabout

- *Consider how some of the knowledge/ understanding components of global learning included in* **Figure 1** *on page 141 might be developed across the age range in your school.*
- *Plan a school based curriculum development initiative relating to continuity, taking account of the theoretical and practical issues raised in this chapter. Decide how you would evaluate the outcomes.*
- *If your school is not cross phase, review the strategies you use for preparing students in the transition period (e.g. From Kindergarten to primary, from primary to secondary). Suggest areas for improvement.*

Clive Belgeonne is an education advisor at the Development Education Centre, South Yorkshire (DEC(SY)), England and is currently seconded as one of the National Leaders of the Global Learning Programme (England).

Acknowledgements

Endnotes:

*1 Many leading scientists are quite pessimistic about our chances. Sir Martin Rees, the Astronomer Royal in his 2004 book 'Our Final Hour' estimates that the probability of human extinction before 2100 CE is around 50 per cent, based on the possibility of malign or accidental release of destructive technology. 'The Revenge of Gaia: Why the Earth is Fighting Back - and How we Can Still Save Humanity' (2006) by James Lovelock (author of the Gaia theory) says lethal heat waves and rising sea levels will increasingly threaten civilisations.

*2 There is a useful activity in the booklet 'The Global Dimension in Action' (QCA 2007) 'Visualising our global learners' http://clients.squareeye.net/uploads/global/documents/qcda_global_dimension_in_action.pdf (activity done with primary teachers about to work with trainee teachers an Active Citizenship / Community Engagement project at Liverpool Hope University, 2009-10)

*3 This is echoed and amplified in the Framework for Sustainable Schools in England, which suggests it begins with a vision of care: care for oneself, care for each other (across cultures, distances and time), care for the environment (both far and near).

*4 See for example the Native American concept of the Medicine Wheel, which sees the 'Learning Self' trying always to find a balance between these four areas. This is explored in the SEAL and the Global Dimension training materials www.sealgd.org.uk. The teaching materials on this site try to put the SEAL Learning Outcomes in a more global context.

*5 As part of an activity such as that suggested in Figure 1.

References:

[1] Williams, E. (2010). *Primary/secondary transition* in Times Educational Supplement 2003 (updated 2010). http://www.tes.co.uk/article.aspx?storycode=380390 [accessed 7/8/13]

[2] Beddington, J. (2009). *World faces 'perfect storm' of problems by 2030, chief scientist to warn* on Guardian online. http://www.theguardian.com/science/2009/mar/18/perfect-storm-john-beddington-energy-food-climate [accessed 7/8/13]

[3] Alexander, R. (Ed.) (2010). *Children, their World, their Education: Final report and recommendations of the Cambridge Primary Review.* London: Routledge.

[4] Byron, T. (2013). Keynote address North of England Education Conference, 18/1/2013 Sheffield Hallam University.

[5] Claxton, G., Chambers, M., Powell, G., and Lucas, B. (2011). *The Learning Powered School: Pioneering 21st Century Education.* TLO Limited

[6] Goleman, D, (1996). *Emotional Intelligence: Why It Can Matter More Than IQ.* Bantam Books

[7] Banerjee, R. (2010). *Social and emotional aspects of learning in schools: contributions to improving attainment, behaviour, and attendance.* University of Sussex.

[8] Krznaric, R. (2008). *You Are Therefore I Am: How Empathy Education Can Create Social Change.* Oxfam

[9] Rifkin, J. (2009). *The Empathic Civilization: The Race to Global Consciousness in a World in Crisis.* Penguin

[10] Egan (1990) cited in Puchta, H. (2011). *Teachers need to join the teenage fan club* on Guardian online http://www.theguardian.com/education/2011/jan/11/tefl1 [accessed 7/8/13]

[11] Hawkes, N. (2008). *A Quiet Revolution: placing positive values at the heart of the curriculum.* National Education Trust http://www.nationaleducationtrust.net/ShapingIdeasShapingLives017.php [accessed 7/8/13]

[12] Hicks, D. (2012). *Sustainable Schools, Sustainable Futures.* WWF http://teaching4abetterworld.co.uk/downloads.html [accessed 7/8/13]

[13] Alexander, R. (2008). *Essays on pedagogy.* London: Routledge.

[14] Fisher, R. (2007). *Teaching Thinking* in Sapere Level 1 Handbook

[15] School of Teacher Development. University of Nottingham 1998.

[16] Bowden, R. (2013). *Leading Through Values.* www.learningthroughvalues.org/leading.html [accessed 26/09/13]

RIGHT: The Social and Emotional Aspects of Learning are vital to successful cross phase progression.

7. Three case studies of Xiehe Global Linking

Global linking is a key dimension of global learning for both students and their teachers. This chapter includes three examples of how Xiehe has developed such initiatives.

7.1 The International Geography Project (IGP)

Timothy Booth, Trevor Higginbottom and Peter Round

This major global curriculum initiative has already provided invaluable opportunities for Xiehe geography teachers to establish close professional dialogue with their peers in Yorkshire, England. It has the potential, in future, to make a major contribution to geographical education both in China and the United Kingdom.

> ***'Geography as a subject can bridge the gap between 'cultural exchange' and 'global citizenship' approaches and can be usefully developed as the key organising principle underpinning school linking projects'.***
>
> Alan Disney

The International Geography Project (IGP) is entitled 'Teaching Geography as if People and the Planet Matter'. It is another form of *'East meets West'* collaboration involving Xiehe Global Schools.

The Project is a collaborative venture between the UK Geographical Association (GA), the Development Education Centre - South Yorkshire (DECSY), the Shanghai Xiehe Education Group, and the UK Yorkshire Partnership of Schools.

Additionally, the British Council is funding the teacher exchange dimension of the Project through its 'Connecting Classrooms' initiative.

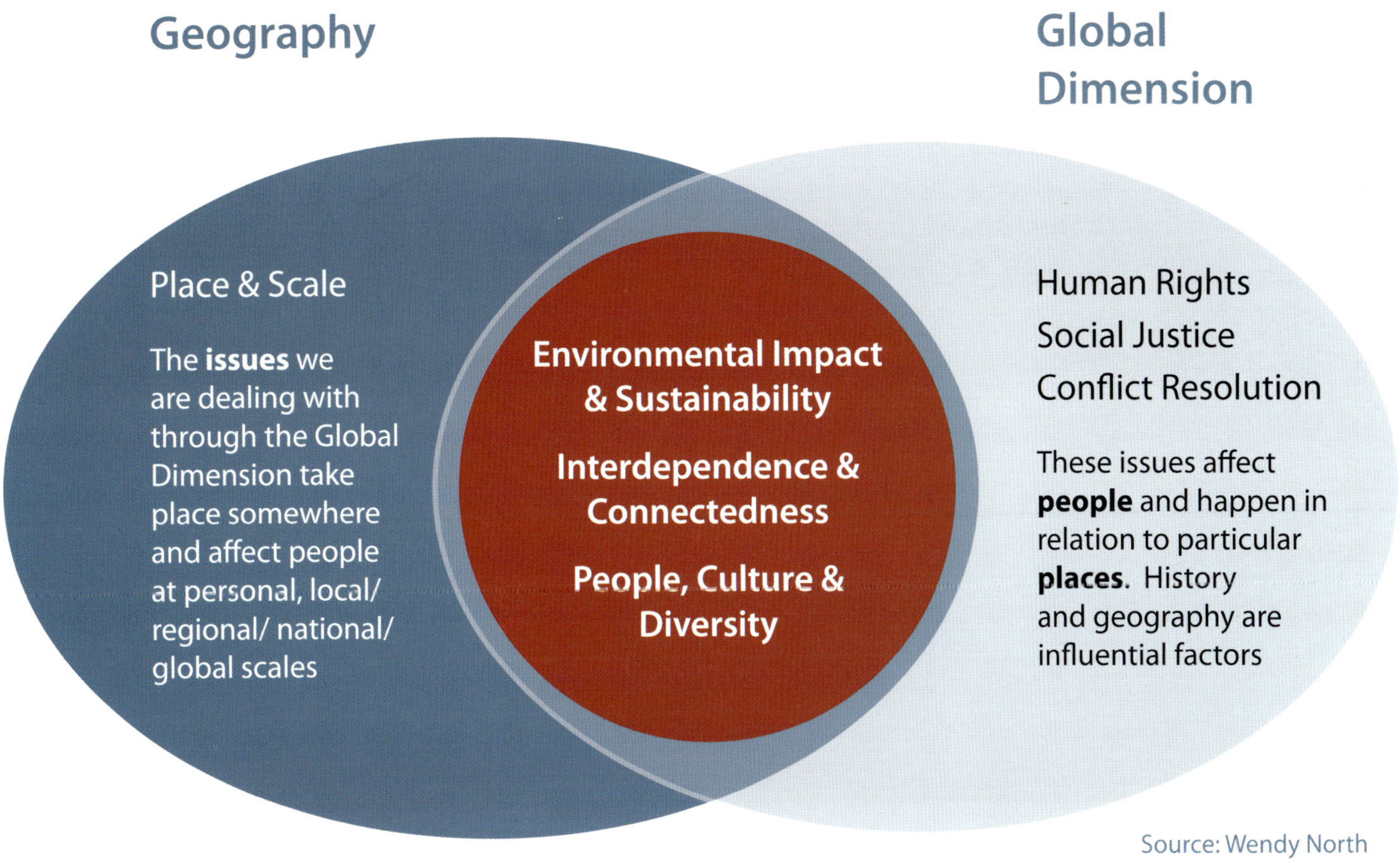

Fig 1: Paradigms which have informed the International Geography Project

The aims of IGP

The International Geography Project aims to determine geography's contribution to students' global learning and sustainable development studies, and to show how this can be achieved through the publication of exemplar teaching and learning materials.

It aims to involve teachers creatively in the process of curriculum development. The Project recognises that teachers:

- are the key players in the curriculum development process;
- need to feel a sense of 'ownership' for this process;
- can develop the curriculum most effectively by working collaboratively with other teachers: (i) within individual schools; (ii) from local schools; and (iii) nationally and internationally;
- are extremely busy professionals and given this they can often benefit from external support from fellow educators who are not teachers; and
- are likely to succeed as curriculum developers if they are engaged creatively in the process.

The IGP also aims to conduct research, both in terms of its curriculum content (geography/global learning/sustainable development) and as a process of curriculum change.

A final aim is to ensure that ongoing self-evaluation is a key dimension of all the Project's activities.

Project structure and management

Two clusters (groups) of schools are involved in the IGP initiative.

The Yorkshire Partnership, England

- Southdale CE Junior School
- Hall Cross Academy
- Ossett Academy
- Watercliffe Meadow, Sheffield (associate basis)

Within the Xiehe Education Organisation, Shanghai, China

- SUIS (Hong Qiao)
- SUIS (Shang Yin)
- SUIS (Wan Yuan)

In Xingyi, Guizhou Province, China.

- Middle School Number 8

Cluster co-ordination is managed as follows:

- Martin Shevill, Head Teacher, Ossett Academy and Peter Round are the Yorkshire Partnership Cluster Co-ordinators;
- Timothy Booth, International Stream, is the Xiehe Schools' Cluster Co-ordinator.
- Trevor Higginbottom is the Inter-Cluster Co-ordinator.
- Consultancy support for the Project is provided by Rob Unwin, DECSY.

The teachers within each cluster meet on average, six times per academic year during the three year duration of the Project (three times per semester in Shanghai, twice per term in the Yorkshire Partnership).

Some existing curriculum development initiatives are supporting the Project's work: for example, 'Philosophy for Children' (DECSY); the Carbon Partners Project (DECSY); the Geographical Association/ DECSY, 'Geography and the Global Dimension Primary Project'.

An International Pilot Project Consultative Committee is offering additional advice on the initiative during its duration.

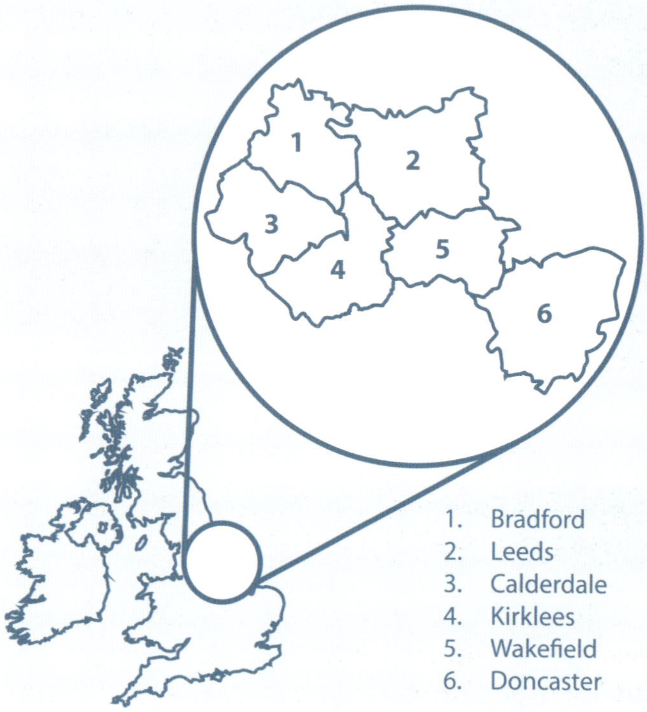

ABOVE: The UK cluster is based in the Yorkshire area, in the North of England, UK.

BELOW: The IGP partners in China are located in Shanghai and Xingyi, Guizhou.

Maps are representative illustrations only.

Research and evaluation

The research and self evaluation dimensions of the Project are receiving support and guidance from: the Institute of Education, University of London; East China Normal University, Shanghai; the Xiehe Research Institute.

The self evaluation dimension of the Project mirrors a key dimension of Xiehe curriculum philosophy. (**See Chapter 10**).

Higher degree opportunities

If individual participating teachers wish there are opportunities for their Project continuous professional development work to be accredited as part of their studies for an MA in Geography and Education, Institute of Education, University of London. Professor David Lambert will co-ordinate this dimension of the Project.

Student involvement in the IGP

It is hoped that students in the schools will be 'twinned' in 'sister' classes between the Shanghai and Yorkshire Partnership clusters. The concept of 'learning buddies', internationally, is being developed. The students in both clusters will be involved in the classroom trialling of the Project materials. At a later stage it is anticipated that there will be student exchanges between Shanghai and the Yorkshire Partnership.

Inter-cluster teacher exchanges

In 2012 the Project was awarded a £9,000 grant from the British Council's 'Connecting Classrooms' initiative. Four of the Yorkshire Partnership cluster teachers visited Shanghai in May 2013.

David Scholey teaches an American High School class at SUIS (Wan Yuan)

ABOVE: IGP cluster colleagues at the British Council in Shanghai.

BELOW: Peter Round presents his school's emblem to Professro Zhang Qi

During their visit to Shanghai the United Kingdom teachers visited Xiehe Global School local and international stream classrooms. They also participated in several inter-cluster IGP meetings and attended meetings at the British Council and East China Normal University, the latter with Professor Zhang Qi (see photo above) and some of her trainee geography teachers.

A reciprocal visit by Xiehe Cluster teachers to the UK took place in November 2013.

UK teachers' responses to their visit to China

Peter Round, on behalf of the UK Yorkshire Partnership cluster, described the recent visit to China as *'an eye opener' and the whole team have come back with an incredible experience and a very large number of ideas'.*

(Extract from the minutes of a Yorkshire Partnership Cluster meeting,19 June 2013)

Richard Upton:

'Having brainstormed our own students about China, we were more than curious to find out what Chinese students thought about the UK. To our delight we were given such an opportunity with a group of older students. The ensuing discussion demonstrated that they had as limited awareness and understanding of the UK as their English counterparts had about China. During the visit the aims and benefits of IGP became much clearer to us. We were very pleased and surprised that the press release of our meeting at the British Council was circulated to teachers throughout China'.

David Scholey:

'The impeccable attitude and infectious enthusiasm of the students was awe inspiring: all the students enjoyed and were engaged with all the lessons that I observed, no matter what the content. I had expected strictly regimented lessons but all the teaching and learning was both impressive and thought provoking, including the collaborative learning and the students' presentation skills. To cap it all most presentations were given bilingually, in Chinese and English, with great ease by most students. Both the local and international teachers showed great imagination and commitment to teaching'.

Peter Round:

'We learned a lot from our observations of both local and international stream lessons which provided us with unique insights into Chinese education and these served as an excellent springboard for the IGP meetings that followed. These meetings were something special: they were a melting pot of ideas contributed by colleagues from all over the world. However, one common aim that united us all was the further development of IGP and its materials production dimension in particular. Without face-to-face discussion and this sharing of ideas I doubt whether it would have been possible to move forward as quickly as we did.

An exciting outcome of our University meeting with the trainee geography teachers was the possibility of linking them with their peers in the UK. I think what excited us most was the prospect of developing materials and ideas that could benefit children (and teachers) in both countries and perhaps we could begin the process of breaking down the barriers and 'Connecting Classrooms' for real'.

Collaboration between IGP clusters

An example of initial collaboration between the IGP clusters in the UK and China has been an inter-cluster student perception study.

The geography teachers in Shanghai and Yorkshire asked their students what they first thought of when they heard the name of their exchange classes' countries. Their responses are summarised in the table in **Figure 2**, on the opposite page.

Fig 2: Results on an inter-cluster student perception study within the IGP.

Thoughts about China *Responses of students in Southdale Primary School, Ossett, Yorkshire, UK*		**Thoughts about the UK** *Responses of students in Shanghai United International School (Shang Yin) ,Shanghai, China*	
Dragons	*Lanterns*	*Pigeons*	*David Beckham*
Chopsticks	*Olympics*	*Poems*	*One Direction*
Eat insects	*Selfridges*	*Fish and chips*	*Mr Bean*
Great Wall of China	*Takeaway*	*London Eye*	*King Arthur*
Sushi	*Rice*	*Olympics*	*The Queen*
Bruce Lee	*Noodles*	*Fog*	*Old Castles*
Jackie Chan	*Japan*	*Rain*	*Knights*
Eyes	*Busy*	*Sherlock Holmes*	*Powerful*
Manufacturing	*Huge*	*Harry Potter*	*J K Rowling*
Fireworks	*Pollution*		

The following were agreed by the teachers, on an inter-cluster basis, as follow up points/questions arising from the student perception study.

- Most teachers will recognise this as a starter activity for a new topic. The information provided by the students could be used or presented in many different ways.
- How many of these ideas would you want to challenge or do some follow up work on?
- Is this what you expected? More importantly, how many lesson ideas do these words create?
- How many of these ideas match your first thoughts?
- Our children live in a world that is getting smaller each day and where information is at our fingertips, yet stereotyping is common place, conflict is common and empathy is not always apparent in the classroom. Children and adults frequently make assumptions about people and places with very little knowledge and understanding of them. Consider using some of the students' responses as a P4C stimulus. (See **Chapter 5.5**).

Project timetable

The Project is being implemented, currently, as a three year initiative.

Year One: 2012-13

At the time of writing exemplar teaching and learning materials were being prepared for use with students in the 5-14 years age range, relating to the 14 themes summarised in **Figure 3** on page 157.

Each theme will include teaching and learning materials for use at differing ages, in the 5-14 years age range (Key Stages 1-3). This is an approach suggested by Jerome Bruner: *'Ideas can be developed at different ages with our students, at differing levels of sophistication'.* For example, the idea of 'conservation' can be studied by very young children, perhaps with a simple experiential focus and later with upper secondary students in a very complex manner. The approach is interesting because it will help teachers to consider the issue of progression in understanding

Fig 3: Examples of thematic teaching and learning materials.

Theme	By Xiehe cluster teachers	By Yorkshire cluster teachers
People on the move *	*Moving from Guizhou Province (Chinese internal migration)*	*Moving to England (English immigration)*
Caring for our planet	*The Chinese SmartTech revolution*	*How SmartTech is changing England*
Changing World (a focus on physical geography)	*Changing landscape of a changing China*	*Changing landscape of a changing England*
Sustainable Development (a focus on human geography)	*Green Shanghai*	*Growing up green in Yorkshire*

in the geography curriculum. The teaching materials will have a strong information computer technology dimension: students will be able to access the individual learning resources, with their central core of knowledge and understanding, at whatever level they need.

Year Two: 2013-14

- The exemplar teaching and learning materials will be trialled in the Project schools (see **Figure 4,** pages 159-160)
- Towards the end of this period work will begin on the final versions of the teaching and learning materials, which will be published internationally.
- The self evaluation, research and higher degree dimensions of the Project will continue.

Year Three: 2014-15

This will be the dissemination phase of the Project: locally, regionally, nationally and internationally.

The final outcomes of the IGP will be the following.

- A set of exemplar teaching and learning materials on geography/global learning for use in both subject and thematic curriculum contexts for students in the 5-14 age range, to be published internationally (format to be agreed).
- Publication, internationally, of practical guidelines for schools and educational organisations on, for example, schools global linking, the school self evaluation process (relating to curriculum development in geography) and the Project's research outcomes.

Conclusion

If extra funding became available and with the co-operation and support of other educational organisations/projects, IGP could obviously be extended into an initiative involving schools throughout the UK and China, using the cluster model of curriculum development.

The Project has already demonstrated admirably the benefits of global linking with regard to a specific curriculum area.

Talkabout

- *Consider whether you might find it worthwhile to plan a schools global linking initiative using the same curriculum development model as the IGP.*

  Which curriculum area would you choose and why?
- *Review the funding sources which might be able to support your proposed new project.*
- *Prepare a draft project development plan to support your bid(s).*

S. Timothy Booth is Head of Humanities in the International Stream, SUIS (Hong Qiao).

Peter Round is Associate Assistant Headteacher at Hall Cross Academy, Yorkshire, England.

*** See following pages for an exemplar of a student worksheet on the 'People on the move' theme.**

Fig 4: *IGP trial teaching and learning materials - Wu Lin and family, Anlong, Guizhou Province.*

Wu Lin
Anlong,
Guizhou Province,
China.

Wu Lin lives with his wife, son, daughter, mother and father in Yulan, a small village in the mountains 100 kilometers from the city of Anlong in Guizhou Province, China. His son is 16 years old, his daughter is one year old.

Wu Lin's family income each year is RMB 4,160 (£462). He makes some money by managing to sell a little rice, after his family have eaten the rest. His farm is only half an acre in size. He grows two crops of rice each year. Wu Lin owns half a cow.

The family store their rice in their house, along with their hand carts. The farming is done by the five adults in the family. They have no machinery to help them.

Wu Lin's family are not able to cook because they cannot afford cooking oil. They live on rice, vegetables and milk. When they are sick they are cared for by a nurse who lives in the village.

It costs Wu Lin RMB 1,040 (£115) each year to send his son to a high school in Anlong, where he is a boarder.

Wu Lin is thinking about moving to Shanghai to work. He is 'pushed' by some ideas and 'pulled' by others. In Shanghai he would hope to earn about RMB 12, 500 (£1389) each year. He would probably be able to come home once each year, for the Chinese New Year holiday.

Fig 4: *IGP trial teaching and learning materials - Wu Lin and family, Anlong, Guizhou Province.*

Will Wu Lin be a migrant?

Wu Lin is thinking about leaving Anlong in Guizhou Province: What would **PUSH** him?

1. ______________________________

____

2. ______________________________

____

3. ______________________________

____

Wu Lin is thinking about going to Shanghai: What would **PULL** him?

1. ______________________________

____

2. ______________________________

____

3. ______________________________

____

A. All students must answer these questions.

1. Draw a sketch map showing the journey Wu Lin would take if he decided to migrate from Anlong to Shanghai. Name Anlong and Shanghai on your map, as well as any **three** other places.
2. Using the scale on the map in your atlas, calculate the approximate distance of Wu Lin's journey from Anlong to Shanghai (in kilometres).
3. What fraction of Wu Lin's annual family income is spent on his son's high school fees?
4. What would be the approximate percentage increase in Wu Lin's family income each year if he decided to migrate to Shanghai to work?
5. Pretend you are Wu Lin. Decide whether or not to migrate to Shanghai. Try to think of **six reasons** for your answer.

B. The following questions are optional. Answer them if you can.

6. Explain how Shanghai's location has helped it to become a large, prosperous city.
7. Suggest **three ways** in which the Chinese Government might try to help Guizhou to become a more prosperous province.
8. Why do you think Wu Lin's family is prepared to spend so much on the son's high school fees each year?

7.2 Developing global school partnerships: theory and practice

Jen Delaney, Gemma Eden, David Edwards and Rob Unwin

This chapter aims to review the principles of good practice with regard to establishing successful school global links, and to provide a practical case study of such a link, involving a Xiehe Global School and an English primary school.

> *'My visit to Xiehe in Shanghai was, professionally, a life changing experience for me'*
>
> Gemma Eden, Watercliffe Meadow, Sheffield, UK

In January 2012 there were 4,130 partnerships between the UK, defined in this context as a 'Northern' country, and 62 'Southern' countries. (The terms 'Northern' and 'Southern' are used to denote, the 'North' (or 'West'), countries (OECD); and those of the broadly historic 'Global South: most of Asia, Africa and Latin America and the Caribbean).[1]

The British Council 'Connecting Classrooms' school partnerships programme has so far been promoted in more than 40 cities or districts in China with more than 600 Chinese schools establishing partnerships with UK schools;[2] clearly these figures are a fraction of the total number of school links across the world. In the context of so many competing pressures faced by schools today, why is it that school global partnerships are so attractive?

Why set up a school global partnership?

Some of the main reasons why 'Northern' schools engage in a link with 'Southern' schools are 'because of an interest in learning about global issues; the wish to build relationships and friendships and an interest in developing support, either one-way (North to South) or mutual between schools'.[3] These would seem to relate to school vision and ethos and possibly to the influence of parents and others in the local community more than governmental pressure.

The benefits of school partnerships are primarily seen in:

- bringing a particular subject to life;
- being fun and making learning more efficient;
- being immediate by 'learning about the real lives of real people in a real place'.[4]

This certainly rings true in a number of school partnerships in which Rob Unwin has been involved where off-timetable days have been planned to take advantage of multi-disciplinary learning opportunities applied to an engaging real-world context, sometimes with direct input from international partner schools. 'Global school partnerships can actually provide 'life-changing experiences' for teachers who bring back their learning and transformation into their classrooms, reflecting on their role as a teacher and learning new knowledge, skills and understanding'.[3]

Such partnerships have been shown to have a wide impact on schools. Over 90 per cent of respondents in a recent survey involving 17 countries of the 'South' indicated that the Global School Partnership programme had an impact on improving the quality of education in their schools, staff professional development and motivation, substantial improvements in ICT and English, a general increase in student's attainment and in student willingness to engage in initiatives which support positive change locally and globally.[5]

A programme impact evaluation also found that involvement by UK schools in the Global School Partnerships programme led to *'a significant positive effect on the awareness, attitudes and response of students about global issues at both primary and secondary school level'.*[6] This includes the challenging of stereotypes.[4]

The benefits to both sides may be different but can be of equal value, providing that there is plenty of opportunity for dialogue and reflection to ensure partnerships are truly mutual and reciprocal.

The three main impetuses for UK schools entering into North-South relationships have been described as:

- the educational context (for example citizenship education in the UK);
- the political context (for example the availability of funding for teacher visits); and
- teacher disposition (personal motivation that might stem from a visit).[7]

Some of these impetuses can become problematic when 'Northern' perspectives may be influenced by unconscious attitudes of superiority, resulting from unexamined cultural baggage from colonial times and possibly triggered by differences between partners in terms of material resources.

These point to the need for professional development for staff and curriculum opportunities for students to help develop a more balanced world view based on a wide range of global perspectives.

What does a successful global school partnership look like?

A typology of UK school linking in relation to possible educational consequences has been sequentially described as follows.

Starts with an 'incidental link', often a charity or tourist's approach led by one teacher. The latter is the most common type of link.

↓

Progresses to a 'basic link'.

↓

Then to a 'developing partnership', often underpinned by inter cultural understanding.

↓

Then to a 'sustained partnership' which has the greatest educational and whole school impact.

This sequencing is supported by the Global School Partnership evaluation which found that positive impact was *'more pronounced in schools where the partnerships were well established and the principles and values (of the programme) had had time to become embedded in whole school policy, partly because more staff and students had become involved'.*[6]

Another key characteristic is a recognition that *'students, above all else, benefit from and enjoy direct contact (and the development of a personal connection) with teachers and students from their partner school ... and that exchange opportunities should be shared among teachers and leaders'*[4]

This last point is another strategy for involving more of the school community which Rob Unwin has witnessed being successfully deployed in a school with a well-established partnership.

The development of strong personal connections between partners through the building of good communication, understanding and trust can greatly benefit from each person involved developing *'a keen understanding of his or her own cultural norms and expectations .... to understand his or her own cultural box before stepping into someone else's'*[8], as well as having mutual perspectives and practice, shared reflection and review and planning time.

The following summarises the characteristics of an effective school partnership and suggests ten key partnership principles.

An effective educational partnership is a dynamic collaborative process between educational institutions that brings mutual, though not necessarily symmetrical, benefits to the parties engaged in the partnership.

Partners share ownership of the projects. Their relationship is built on respect, trust, transparency and reciprocity. They understand each other's cultural and working environment.

Decisions are taken jointly after real negotiations take place between the partners. Each partner is open and clear about what they are bringing to the partnership and what their expectations are. Successful partnerships tend to change and evolve over time.

Finally, an effective educational partnership should go beyond the concept of 'borrowing' or 'replication' policies to that of 'knowledge sharing', and constructing a relationship of 'mutual learning'.

Ten Key Partnership Principles

1. Shared Ownership.
2. Trust and Transparency.
3. Mutual Understanding of different Cultural and Working Environments.
4. Clear Division of Roles and Responsibilities.
5. Effective and Regular Communication.
6. Joint Strategic Planning and Implementation.
7. Strong Commitment across the board from Staff and Management.
8. Supportive Institutional Infrastructure.
9. Monitoring and Evaluation.
10. Sustainability.[9]

Getting started

Schools interested in commencing a school global partnership have been encouraged to copy and enlarge the illustrations **(Figure 1)** opposite and to cut out and sort/prioritise the cards with colleagues to aid decision-making.

Fig 1 (right): Illustration from British Council Connecting Classrooms materials.

headteacher support

ensure the support of the headteacher and senior management team

staff involvement

involve as many members of staff as possible

realistic expectations

start small and build

learners' perceptions

find out what perceptions learners have of potential partner countries

start-up costs

identify any essential start-up costs

aims

What sort of international collaboration is right for our school?

external support

seek sources of advice, funding and training, including e-learning (eg http://schoolsonline.britishcouncil.org)

curricular audit

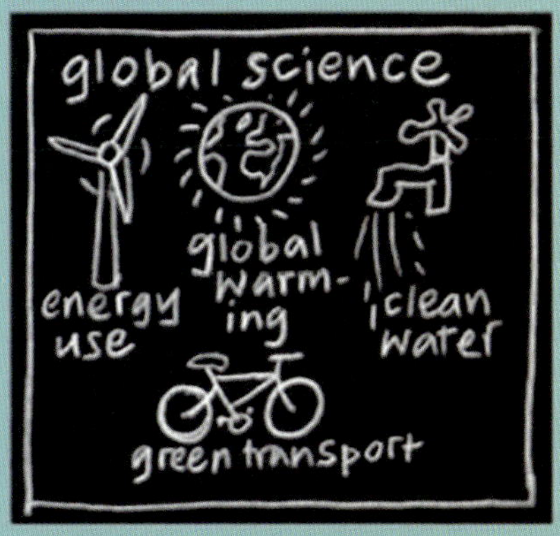

identify what's already happening your school

international committee

set up an international committee and consider appointing an international coordinator

Developing a global schools partnership in practice

Teacher Linking

In September 2010 SUIS (Pudong) began a global school partnership with Watercliffe Meadow School (WCM) in Shirecliffe, Sheffield, located in a deprived area towards the outskirts of the city. During the first two years of the partnership the links were largely professional, between the teachers in the respective schools, through the Internet and school visits. Between December 2010 and June 2011 a steady stream of SUIS (Pudong) colleagues visited WCM.

In the academic year 2011-12 James Waldron, now Secondary Vice Principal at SUIS (Wuxi), was a placement 'Trainee Head teacher' at WCM as part of his studies for the National (English) Professional Qualification for Headship (which he completed successfully). Linda Kingdon, then Head teacher at WCM, undertook the role as his 'Placement Head teacher'. Two of James' key leadership tasks were:

- to expand and deepen the global linking partnership between SUIS and WCM; and
- to share his Xiehe Global Schools' English as a second language (EAL) experiences with the WCM 'Reading Recovery Experts'.

James is currently using his professional experiences at WCM to inform his work in his new role at SUIS (Wuxi):

'WCM's leadership model and culture identified for me what an outstanding English school looks like in this respect. This has very much influenced my thinking day-to-day at Wuxi: as a result of the school global linking process WCM's ideas in these key areas have gone global!'

In May 2013 Gemma Eden and Jen Delaney visited SUIS (Pudong). Their responses to the visit are described below.

Jen Delaney

- *'I observed high levels of concentration in all the classes I visited across the three schools from the youngest to the oldest. The children were allowed more freedom to share ideas and answers than I had expected and I have begun to use some of the features of teaching I observed in my own lessons. The Chinese approach of using the children as 'little teachers' during guided reading and lesson plenaries has been particularly successful. After a few times of trying it, the children became a lot more confident and the vast majority in the class wanted to give it a try.*
- *Lessons were faster paced than my own lessons had been and I observed more 'mini-plenaries', particularly during maths lessons which seemed very beneficial to the children's learning and I am now doing more of this in my own lessons.*
- *There was very high quality English teaching in SUIS (Pudong). It was beneficial to see how values education was being developed through the Virtues Project, also in English, and this is something I can think about incorporating into RE celebration days. The Chinese children's level of English was incredibly impressive across the schools. The children in the primary reception classes used their excellent English skills to help me learn Chinese during the Chinese lesson. Their ability to translate for me so I could understand was truly amazing.*
- *It was reasonably easy for me to understand what was being taught during the maths lessons in the Chinese medium because the teachers used very visual approaches throughout the lessons. I can see huge benefits in using the whiteboard more effectively and body language in my own lessons, particularly for EAL children and those with speech and language needs.*
- *Since coming back from Shanghai and talking about my visit to my class, they have become significantly more interested in the wider world, not just Shanghai, and they have been asking lots of questions about life in other countries and where they would like to visit. They have very much enjoyed writing their letters to their Chinese pen pals and I am going to pass this information on to the next teacher they have.*
- *As a result of the visit I feel that I have raised my expectations of what the children can achieve in a lesson and what they should be doing at home. I would not expect the children to be completing the same amount of homework as the Chinese children were, but I believe now that there needs to be an expectation that they will complete some home learning or, if their home circumstances mean*

they cannot undertake work there, to support them in doing it during school time. I showed my class videos of the Chinese children learning and they could pick out and explain the difference in their behaviour. Subsequently, the children have become far more focused in their own learning.

- *Having observed 'Philosophy for Children' at SUIS (Pudong) I now feel a lot more confident delivering P4C sessions with my class. David taught it in such a way that the teaching and learning processes became a lot clearer for me and the discussions my class have had following the new methods I have incorporated are much improved. He gave me a great insight into how to generate philosophical questions with the children and how to model/ facilitate their discussions.*
- *Finally, through working with Gemma and maintaining the links with SUIS (Pudong) we aim to make much more of the international nature of our own school and do more work on the different languages/cultures children have in school'.*

Gemma Eden agreed with many of Jen's comments but added these of her own.

- *One thing that struck me was that the children in both schools face similar issues and have many common interests.*
- *The teachers also face similar challenges such as parental collaboration and concentration levels (in the international stream).*
- *It was good to share our professional ideas. For example, one lesson we observed on the valuable skills of scale with a Grade 2 class was exemplary and I have adopted this approach with my own students. In turn, we were able to offer ideas to SUIS (Pudong) colleagues on how the Community's of Inquiry strategy can be developed.*
- *The visit made me reflect on the global dimensions of our history and geography curriculum and I have now updated our planning document for these subjects.*
- *I was impressed with the ways in which the learning environment in Xiehe's Global Schools reflected the global dimension. We plan to emulate this approach.*
- *Watching the Chinese and maths lessons demonstrated to me that outstanding teaching can be identified across the globe without language as a barrier. I was able to fully understand the objectives of the lesson and pick up on such teaching nuances as behaviour management and praise. This enabled me to reflect on my own teaching style.*
- *I was inspired by the Chinese children's maths attainment: at least two years ahead of our own children's. This has led me to raise my expectations of my class even higher!*
- *With this link our children can learn, first hand, the importance of interdependence and their place in the world.*

David Edwards provides the global partner's perspective.

'One of the difficulties of curriculum development in international schools is the distance (both figuratively and physically) between the country in which the curriculum is operating and its parent country. Often the teaching staff implementing the curriculum may have little experience of the founding country, or in many cases be familiar with a very different curriculum from their home nation. While diversity of methods and structure can bring strength to a school, there is also the real danger that the common vision of the school can become muddled.

Creating links with Watercliffe Meadow has allowed SUIS (Pudong) the opportunity to learn from the experiences of a school operating within the clear guidelines of the English Department for Education and with a wealth of teaching and managerial experience within its walls. These links allow us to remove the element of trial and error involved in implementing new policy. A common question that arises now during curriculum development meetings is 'how is this done at Watercliffe Meadow?'

Whilst it is true that the needs of our students differ from those of students growing up in outer-city Sheffield, we have found that, remarkably, the same challenges that we face in educating students are shared by Watercliffe Meadow (WCM). In many respects the links forged between the two schools has seen the gap between our two curricula narrow. SUIS has moved towards clearer target setting based on detailed assessment for learning in English literacy, whilst at the same time WCM has implemented a much greater global perspective into their geography and history curriculum.

We have also greatly valued WCM's ideas on, for example, teacher appraisal procedures, other than lesson observation, record keeping and working with other colleagues. This narrowing of the gap is only to be expected: as the world continues to become smaller factors affecting the lives of the citizens of one nation will become common to all. The challenges and opportunities facing students at SUIS and WCM will become increasingly homogenous. I am confident that the links and partnership formed by the two schools will continue to develop the mutual benefit for both our teaching staff and, more importantly, our students'.

Student Linking

During the course of 2012-13 attention began to focus, also, on student linking within the partnership. The table below provides a summary of some dimensions of the action plan in this respect for the academic year.

Item	Issue	Action plan 2012-13	Remarks
1	How to easily share materials/information	• Set up a cross-school Drop Box account.	• Drop Box is an online, cloud based, file sharing system.
2	Grade 1 and 5 links	• Relevant staff in both schools to send student self-introduction and questions. • Agree on a template for the students to fill in for their self-introduction and questions.	• Students write, teachers scan and place in the Drop Box folder. Students read and reply.
3	Grade 6 links	• Gemma to share Watercliffe Meadow Year 6 writing blog.	
4	Grade 5/Year 2 Links	• Grade 5 (SUIS)/Year 2 (WCM) to present their linking activities at assemblies in the respective schools	
5	Developing global citizenship links	• WCM/SUIS to identify opportunities for student linking or cross-school global issues. • The SUIS Project Themes Booklet to be sent to Gemma.	• David will compile a list of possible opportunities and send to Gemma to review. Once common links are found, David will present to the SUIS SMT for approval.

Conclusion

This chapter illustrates the value of global school partnerships for teachers and students and the ways in which such collaboration can significantly enhance global learning for both. The WCM /SUIS case study also illustrates that such linking is a long term process: both schools would acknowledge that there is still much to be done, particularly with regard to their student exchanges.

Talkabout

- *If you are already involved in a school global partnership(s) compare your collaborative processes with those developed by WCM/SUIS.*
- *If these schools decided to establish a third partner school, in which country do you feel this should be located and why?*
- *If you are not yet involved in a school global partnership and wish to develop one, list 10 key principles you feel would be important in developing a successful link.*

Jen Delaney is Modern Foreign Languages Co-ordinator

Gemma Eden is a Class Teacher and Global Learning Co-ordinator, both at Watercliffe Meadow.

David Edwards is Key Stage 2 Leader at SUIS (Pudong).

Acknowledgements

[1] Najda, R. and Thakwalakwa, G. (2012). *Global School partnerships and development goals : Equity and Participation in African Schools*, PowerPoint presentation at DERC conference, Institute of Education.

[2] British Council China. (2013). *What is Connecting Classrooms* (available at http://www.britishcouncil.org/china-education-connecting classroom-intro.htm)

[3] Fricke, H-J. (2006). *North-South School Linking: A Review of Approaches.* Unpublished report commissioned by Plan International.

[4] Edge, K., Fayman, J., and Lawrie, J. (2009). *The influence of North South School Partnerships: Examining the evidence from schools in the UK, Africa and Asia.* London: IOE, UKOWLA and Cambridge Education. (available at http://www.ioe.ac.uk/IOE NSSP IntSchoolPartnerships FullReport.pdf)

[5] British Council/DFID. (2010). *Global School Partnerships Southern Impact Survey* (Unpublished)

[6] Sizmur, J., Brzyska, B., Cooper, L., Morrison, J., Wilkinson, K., and Kerr, D. (2011) *Global School Partnerships Programme-Impact Evaluation Report for DFID.* London: NFER. (available at: http://www.nfer.ac.uk/nfer/publications/GSPP01/GSPP01.pdf)

[7] Martin, F. (2007). *'School linking: a controversial issue'* in Claire, H. and Holden, C. (eds) The Challenge of Teaching Controversial Issues, pp. 147-160. London : Trentham Books

[8] Hunter, B., White, G., and Godby, G. (2006). *What Does It Mean to Be Globally Competent?* in Journal of Studies in International Education 10, p267-285

[9] Wanni, N., Hinz, S., and Day, R. (2010). *Good Practices in Educational Partnerships Guide: UK-Africa Higher & Further Education Partnerships.* London: ACU (available at: https://www.acu.ac.uk/publications/?pageID-14)

[10] Zammit, J., Unwin, R. and Najda, R. (2012). *International learning – get started.* British Council, accessible when enrolled and registered on Connecting Classrooms e-platform. (available at https://connecting classrooms-learning.britishcoucil.org)

Students from Birley School in Rotherham, UK discussing carbon footprints with students from their link school, Pwani Mchangani in Zanzibar, Tanzania.

7.3 Xiehe kindergarten principal's visit to England (June, 2013)

Trevor Higginbottom, Stephen Walshe and Guo Ying Zheng

International visits by educational professionals are another type of global partnership. These can provide opportunities for student global learning and professional study in comparative education. This chapter is a short case study of an international visit describing the benefits of such an initiative.

> *'The experience of participating in P4C training, attending conferences and visiting schools where P4C is being implemented in Yorkshire, England, has highlighted for me the richness and educational value of such professional exchanges. I was also very impressed by how well children in Yorkshire schools responded to cultural classes in Chinese language, history and geography. I believe that there exists here a goldmine of opportunities for cultural and educational exchange between Xiehe and Yorkshire.'*
>
> Stephen Walshe

An important aim of the visit of Guo Ying Zheng and Stephen Walshe, two Fortune Kindergarten Principals, to South Yorkshire, England in June/July 2013 (as well as their P4C training described in **Chapter 5.3**) was to first visit primary schools to observe good practice in early years education; and secondly to team-teach 'China Awareness' sessions with selected classes.

A total of seven visits were undertaken to schools in Sheffield and Barnsley with very varied social and ethnic intakes. In all the schools Guo Ying and Stephen met the Headteacher and or a senior manager(s). They frequently had student escorted tours of the school, observed lessons, discussed the outcomes with the teachers and met the children socially.

One interesting outcome of the visits was that they became studies in individual school 'culture' and the impact of leadership and management on the quality of educational practice. This led to very interesting dialogues between them and with Trevor Higginbottom who also participated in five of the visits. One strategy afterwards was for each person to list ten to twelve 'key words' which appeared to sum up their views on the culture of the schools. This provided the basis for a stimulating follow-up discussion on each occasion.

Professional responses to the visits

At the conclusion of the visits Guo Ying and Stephen 'brainstormed' their overall responses to what they had experienced.

- 'Very clear lesson objectives, in most cases, with target descriptors often displayed. Very focussed learning in all the schools visited. Constant reminders of learning targets from the teacher. (Regarded as a key issue)'.
- 'Using ICT to capture and feedback into the computer instant 'golden moments' in children's learning as a contribution to individual, ongoing assessment profiles. (Regarded as a key issue)'.
- 'Making older children, in particular, aware of their individual learning targets. (Regarded as a controversial issue)'.
- 'Assessing students much more holistically against bench marks'.
- 'Close observation of individual children within

classes e.g. in team teaching. Use of software to build up their assessment profile'.

- 'Differentiation by task, with the teacher and the teaching assistant working with students at differing levels in groups, worked very effectively'.
- 'In one school its values were made extremely explicit through very wide ranging displays. These included student work which strongly reflected the school's values'.
- 'The UNESCO values framework was seen to be very effective in helping schools to articulate (and hopefully achieve) their agreed values'.
- 'Our Xiehe Kindergarten children need many more opportunities to engage in purposeful talk as happened frequently in these schools'.
- 'Valuable to have puppets as both positive and negative role models for the children, particularly with regard to values'.
- 'Film making extremely creative in one school'.
- 'Love' was a marked characteristic of one school's culture. (A word we should not be afraid of using in educational contexts(?))'
- 'We should listen (even) more to students' views of their school'.
- 'Our Xiehe Kindergartens must consider the use of UK style 'teaching assistants'. Chinese 'class helpers' need to be re-named and to be considered as equal partners in the teaching process'.
- 'Flat screen video screens in most school lobbies, with very varied regularly updated school information, were felt to be extremely helpful'.
- 'Class names often used imaginatively. (e.g. named after animals, with their positive characteristics being used as a stimulus)'.
- 'Schools with hugely challenging student intakes, in social terms, were seen to be extremely successful largely because of the very high staff aspirations for the students. Also as a result of considerable emphasis on individual student self esteem'.
- 'Observation of leadership across the seven schools was invaluable. The most effective appeared to be those who were both calm and pleasant but, clearly, very determined that the school should succeed'.
- 'It was felt that schools at different stages of development needed leaders with differing styles'.
- 'Hugely positive impact of leadership and management on school 'culture'.'
- 'Inter-school visits should concentrate more on analysing/reviewing school 'culture'.'

China - awareness sessions

Ten lessons were taught across the seven schools visited. The lesson duration averaged one hour. The ages of the children involved ranged from 5 to 11 years.

Guo Ying and Stephen played a 'Cultural Mentor' role here, with the aim of introducing the students to aspects of China's geography, history, art, music, language and cultural traditions. Their aim was to make the lesson as experiential as possible.

Stephen and Guo Ying team teaching at Carrfield Academy, Barnsley, in the UK.

Trevor Higginbottom evaluated a lesson in one of the schools and produced the following report.

Class: Year 2

Number of students: 28

Student backgrounds: vast majority socially deprived, many with special educational needs, wide ability range.

'Stephen leads the lesson. The class teacher and a teaching assistant are also present. A PowerPoint presentation displays a world map: comparisons are made between Britain as islands and the more land locked China. There is reference to parts of China being far hotter than Britain and why. One student formerly lived in Hong Kong and Stephen exploits this skilfully.

Comparisons between the populations of Britain and China are made but the students have some difficulties with the large numbers shown on the screen.

Guo Ying then introduces a discussion on the origin of four Chinese characters. The children are intrigued by the various shapes which they excitingly see as various animals (e.g. cows, roosters, birds).

The class teacher interrupts in a very supportive manner, reminding the class that they have many Chinese characters on a calendar they had talked about at Chinese New Year, which is incorporated into an excellent display. This builds usefully on their previous knowledge of China.

Guo Ying encourages the students to speak as much Chinese as possible and this proves to be one of the highlights of the lesson. Their pronunciations are remarkably accurate. Guo Ying encourages the class to speak to the Headteacher and other staff in Chinese, later.

There is first class team teaching with the two visiting teachers asking questions of one another and the class joining in the dialogue.

Stephen then introduces a very creative exercise: the students decorate Chinese fans, which have been brought from Shanghai, with dragons and their own names written in Chinese characters. Towards the end of the session individual students proudly display their fans on stands provided for this purpose.

The students are particularly pleased to help with displaying a larger red paper cut which the two teachers have also brought with them. Impressively, several children remember the importance of red as a colour from their previous studies of Chinese New Year and why this is important within Chinese culture.

Encouragingly, the class teacher tells the class that they will be invited to talk about their work in the session and to display their fans at a whole school assembly which is to be held later in the week.

One student tells the class that his Grandma has recently visited China and speaks confidently about several aspects of the country and its people. He is familiar with several websites relating to Chinese history and geography.

This session, with a challenging class of students, has been outstandingly successful with learning objectives relating to Chinese language, culture and geography having been achieved across a wide ability range. At no point, in seventy minutes, have student concentration levels dropped below 95 per cent'.

Some key overall outcomes of the lessons were:

- The children's responses in all the lessons observed were extremely positive.
- They showed particular enthusiasm for the language dimension, which is interesting for those who believe that all primary students should learn a second language.
- The team-teaching proved to be a very useful strategy. When Guo Ying and Stephen conducted their own bilingual dialogue the students responded enthusiastically.
- The creative dimension, with respect to the fans, was a highlight in all the lessons.
- The older students' basic knowledge and understanding of China was worryingly patchy.

Conclusion

The professional and student learning dimensions of the school visits both proved to be very successful.

The Cultural Mentor role (where a teacher promotes knowledge/understanding of a country's culture), particularly when it involves a strong language component, is a very useful curriculum model worthy of further development through exchange/ secondment visits.

Talkabout

- *Discuss the benefits of the 'Cultural Mentor' role in primary schools.*
- *Consider the most effective way of undertaking a school visit of the type outlined in this section: in terms of pre planning, the visit itself and follow up.*

Stephen Walshe is Co-Principal, Fortune Kindergarten, International Dongfang Campus.

Guo Ying Zheng is Principal, Fortune Bilingual Kindergarten, Shanghai.

8. Leadership and policy development issues in Xiehe Global Schools

This chapter is concerned with two key issues that fundamentally affect the development of all schools: leadership and how policies can be used to ensure overall consistency in the quality of educational practice.

8.1 Chinese and Western perspectives on school leadership

Leadership has been the biggest single influence on the quality of Xiehe Global Schools. In this chapter Chinese and Western dimensions of this key concept are considered through three different perspectives.

(a) Leading a Chinese school

Tan You Kang

First, a very experienced Chinese colleague gives his views on leadership, having been involved with the role in many contexts in China.

> ***'The leader can act as a warrior or as a healer. As a warrior, the leader acts with power and decision. That is the Yang or masculine aspect of leadership. Most of the time, however, the leader acts as a healer and is in an open, receptive and nourishing state. That is the feminine or Yin aspect of leadership. This mixture of doing and being, of warrior and healer, is both productive and potent.'***
>
> Lao Tzu

I am an old educator. I started my career as a subject teacher and then was given pastoral responsibility for a class. Subsequently I was Dean of a teaching research group, Dean of a grade and a school Vice Principal and Principal, the latter in two schools. Most recently, I worked in a local government education department where I had many contacts with principals.

A good principal means a good school

The quote 'a good principal means a good school' is very familiar to many educationalists. When expressed to a new principal by an educational director, it is a kind of expectation; when suggested by an educational adviser/inspector it is a kind of evaluation; when told to parents it is a kind of encouragement. To a principal, it is a personal and professional target.

The starting point for any principal is to recognise his/her legal responsibilities and obligations. Clearly, the principal is in charge of human, financial and material resources. He/she has to deal with both the internal affairs of the school and also be its main representative externally. Obligations such as school safety, students' progress, maintaining a harmonious school society, enhancing quality and serving society need to be considered. In summary, a school can be viewed like a small community or a family. A principal has both privileges and obligations in a highly pressurised management situation.

Trust is a fundamental dimension of school leadership. This has to be established step by step through interaction with staff, at all levels, for example through home visits and seminars with various school groups. The traditional Chinese concept of management was to ensure obedience. Nowadays, achieving mutual trust is regarded as being a key aspect of management. Confidence is another important factor. To establish this with staff, the principal must make decisions very carefully and, on occasions, take decisive action.

Arguably, it is easy to lead a traditional Chinese local government school but this does not necessarily make the person a 'good principal'. In a Chinese public school the staff tend to require the principal to be 'a good teacher first, then a superior officer', no matter what his or her academic background and educational experience. Most local government school leaders are talented in respect to some teaching area. They write papers, tirelessly, promoting this aspect of their role.

Clearly, there is not one model of the 'good principal, good school' concept. The strengths of the school might well be very varied, for example relating to aspects such as management, school features (culture, scientific research and management), and subject areas (the sciences, arts and humanities). What a principal needs to do is to establish overall quality by having a clear vision and recognition of his or her own strengths and weaknesses.

Whatever kind of school you lead, you must be prepared to take account of the school you inherit before making innovations. A principal needs to have his/her own ideas on running a school and have the necessary determination to make it successful. Persistence is a key attribute needed to ensure that the principal and the staff have common goals. The principal must recognise and understand his/her management style. The school must develop its own distinctive features or 'brand'.

The 'two triangles' perception of the principal's role

1. *The Survival Triangle* *(right)*

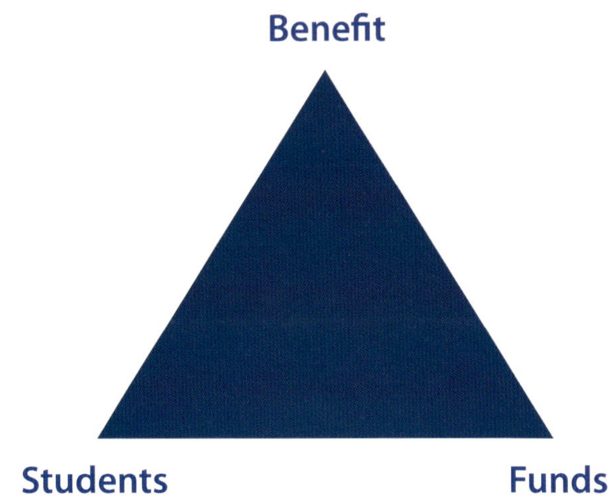

Every principal wishes his/her school to be successful in both social and academic terms. If the good students achieve highly and gain prizes in competitions, this will lead to significant benefits in terms of funding: the triangular cycle then works very effectively. Public school funding is granted on a per capita basis based on the number of students, with a minimum sum guaranteed to ensure the normal operation of the school. Beyond this, the school will need to seek more funding by attracting additional students.

The principal can contribute to two aspects of the 'Survival Triangle'. First, the allocation of funding. The current Chinese Education Act makes provision for increased funding for schools but this is still allocated on a student per capita basis. Government grants remain the only source of funding. Charitable, personal donation is rare and schools are forbidden to charge extra fees. The principal decides on the most appropriate allocation of total funding within the school, excluding maintenance and equipment costs which are covered by the local government education department. The principal must ensure that his/her spending secures excellent teachers and promotes the school's overall development.

Secondly, the principal can make his/her contribution to funding by working hard to recruit more students: deemed 'fighting for students', 'making a bigger cake' and 'siphonage'. For example, recruiting the most able which both enhances funding and increases the popularity of the school.

Principals use various methods in an attempt to enrol additional students. Schools are supposed to recruit within regions determined by the local government. The Internet is, however, now used frequently to attract students from a wider area. Some schools target excellent youngsters well in advance and offer them 'advanced' or 'elite' classes.

On occasions, schools obtain permission to establish 'speciality' classes. In the event, with the pressures of all types of examinations, such classes often disappear once the students are recruited.

2. *The Development Triangle* *(below)*

In China, academic quality remains a key issue. Students are enrolled at all stages up to university level by single examinations. Affective/social development is largely ignored in this respect. Government policy is the key determinant in terms of quality. Considerable emphasis is placed by schools on recruitment handbooks which emphasise their success rates relating to student university entrance. Such information has a huge influence on parental choice. Success in inter-school academic competitions is also a very positive marketing factor, particularly if this achieves media publicity.

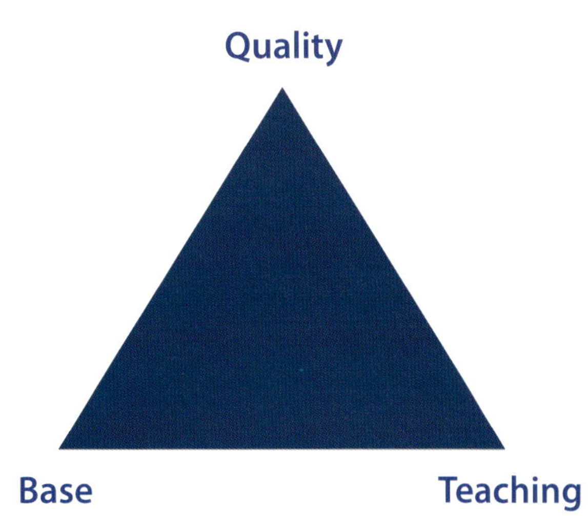

All this means that schools regard teaching and learning quality as a key issue. For principals, the main challenge is how to achieve ongoing improvement in this respect. This is not easy to achieve within a context of a very prescriptive curriculum, common/agreed textbooks and a tightly controlled examination system. The Government does not provide alternative supplementary teaching materials and schools cannot charge for the extra materials they purchase for students. Teaching hours for every grade and subject are determined by the local government education department. It is often stated that, in practice, the local education department is the 'first' principal of the school and the school leader the 'second' principal.

The limited school improvement strategies left for the principal include improving the teaching and learning process, increasing overall teaching efficiency in terms of examination requirements and focusing strongly on school self evaluation (see **Chapter 10**). Additionally, there is the (sometimes unpopular) approach of rigorously checking, for example, the teacher's implementation of the agreed standard classroom practices, (including lesson plans and teacher's marking) and the setting of student homework. Currently, there is more emphasis on preparing clearer pathways for teacher promotion, their professional development and payment by results. Emphasis is still placed, however, on teacher appraisal and detailed analysis of their students' examination performance. External experts are often involved in the latter process.

Continuity and progression in teaching and learning is regarded by many principals as a key factor in ongoing school improvement. We must always build on students' previous knowledge and understanding (see **Chapter 6.2**). Emphasis is placed on ensuring that students are well prepared for the transition between phases (for example some schools organise summer camps for this purpose). Some influential high schools work with kindergarten and primary schools in order to both select and improve their potential future students. Students are often forced to study for inter-school academic competitions, for example the chemistry contest for junior high school students is scheduled in the first semester of Junior Grade Three, only two months after the academic year begins. Schools have no choice but to 'focus on the best soldiers'.

Conclusion

The majority of Chinese principals work hard to 'make a difference'. They are, however, constrained in many respects by the educational management system.

Changes are taking place in the country's public education system. For example, with regard to student selection/allocation, teaching and learning materials and teacher professional development. Government schools are gradually meeting a wider range of educational demands and providing a more equitable system for their students.

Schools vary enormously across China. This one is in rural Guizhou Province.

(b) Co-principalship within the Xiehe Dual Stream School

Dr Roger Morgan and
Maxine Lu Hui Wen

Co-principalship is a key management dimension of the Xiehe Dual Stream School Model. It is, however, also a style of leadership which might usefully be considered with regard to single stream schools.

> ***'The core business of a school is teaching and learning: keep it central'.***
>
> Professor David Reynolds

With its two streams, local and international, the most effective form of leadership with respect to the Xiehe Dual Stream model has proved to be co-principalship, with a Chinese and a Western colleague working in partnership. We were co-principal partners in SUIS (Pudong) between 2008 and 2012.

Before exploring this innovatory but complex management style in detail there is a need to take account of two key factors : first, parental expectations within the Xiehe Global School and, secondly, the differing forms of international education within Shanghai.

Parental expectations

Broadly, these break down into three categories.

- Chinese parents who want their children to be prepared for life in a global society, with a sound understanding of English language. However, they wish their children to retain their Chinese cultural assumptions and pride in being Chinese. The vast majority of these parents prefer their children to enter the local stream.

- Chinese parents who are returnees to China, they may have been out of the country for more than ten years. They wish their children to be reassimilated into the Chinese environment and become fluent in Chinese but receive an education in the international stream.

- Expatriate parents who want a Chinese dimension to their children's education, including a high standard of Chinese language teaching, in the international stream.

The three forms of international education in Shanghai

1. 'Imported' international schools with only an international curriculum.

These schools only recruit foreign students and have little interaction with local schools. Their teachers are mainly Western, with additionally Chinese language teachers. The Chinese language teachers and Chinese administrators in these schools are not normally familiar with the local education system and its educational reforms and their career opportunities here are often limited.

2. International departments of local schools.

Overall, these schools are managed by Chinese Principals and the Western educational philosophy is, generally, not given a high profile. Foreign teachers in these schools are usually limited in number and most are in lower management positions. Chinese staff here follow the traditional Chinese routes in terms of professional development.

The 'East meets West' Xiehe Global Schools, with their local and international streams.

Here both Chinese and Western teachers need to be aware of both Chinese and Western educational and management systems. There are good career opportunities for both these groups of teachers in these dual stream schools. For example, Maxine Lu Hui Wen progressed from being an Assistant Head in an international stream to the Principal of a 6-19 years primary, middle and American high school within less than a decade. Western colleagues have made similar progress within Xiehe.

The co-principal management model

The co-principal management model has been pioneered extensively in the latter of these three types of schools.

The following are felt to be the key characteristics of a successful co-principal partnership in the Xiehe Dual Stream Schools.

- There is mutual 'cultural respect' between the Chinese and Western co-principals.

- Their professional relationship is based on total trust and open communication.

- There is a willingness to share and value their respective previous educational and management experience in what has usually been a very different environment(s) and to mutually respect these differing backgrounds (for example, Maxine Lu Hui Wen was able to share with Dr Roger Morgan her knowledge of local government relationships, Chinese educational reforms and experience of integrating international dimensions into the local stream curriculum. In turn, Dr Morgan was able to offer advice on Western curricula and the processes of curriculum and staff development. A key area for mutual exchange was support when dealing, respectively, with Chinese and expatriate parents).

- The Western co-principal, in particular, must appreciate that the West has by no means 'all the right answers' in educational and management terms and that his Chinese colleague has much to offer in both respects.

- There is a need to value both the differences in educational philosophy between the two streams but also the many similarities.

- There must be clarity with respect to their respective roles and goals. Some of the former will be very separate, others will be shared.

- There is a need for regular consultation, mutual support and joint decision making.

- There needs to be recognition that some roles are likely to be very separate and others can be shared.

- Both colleagues need to appreciate that the complexities of co-management need to be addressed, for example with respect to:
  - decision making processes;
  - overlapping responsibilities;
  - unnecessary competition and potential friction;
  - other complicated inter-stream management links.

- There must be a willingness to share their professional workloads.

- The co-principals should be regularly observed working together across the school.

- They should co-present on occasions, for example, at assemblies, events and functions.

- It has proved crucial, in terms of the geography of the school, to locate the co-principals and the other senior staff from both streams in adjacent offices.

- There may be a need to share particularly difficult issues with a third party (for example an inspector or consultant) when seemingly unreconcilable differences occur between them.

- It helps greatly if both co-principals are bilingual in Chinese and English but, interestingly, this has not always proved to be essential.

Some tips on daily working in the roles

About decision making

- Consult each other before making decisions on important or sensitive areas.
- Know where the 'bottom line' lies for both sides.
- Clearly present advantages and disadvantages.
- Be open minded.
- Do not presume any result.
- Know your partner.
  - 'Leave it to me'.
  - 'May I draft a plan for you to consider'?
  - 'Provided …., please go ahead …'.
  - 'If you agree, I would like to …'..
  - Be a friend of your partner and assume you are on his/her side.
  - Spend as much time and effort as possible on communication.
  - Write down important areas of consensus.

About meetings

- What should be on the agenda?
- Information sharing and discussion: different agendas need different organisation.
- How long will the meeting last?
- Record clearly decisions made and the follow up action plan.

About disagreement

- It naturally exists and is a learning opportunity.
- Give both parties 24 hours for some slow thinking.
- Understand the reasons for disagreement (e.g. Values? Cultural differences? Professional backgrounds? Parent needs?)
- Ensure disagreements don't become conflicts.
- Compromise is another way of being insistent.

Try your best to avoid

- Raising an 'irresolvable question'.
- Using vague deadlines.
- Translating directly without analysis.
- Criticising his/her professionalism.

On occasions people have questioned whether or not this shared management model is achievable in practice: who on earth is in charge? In fact, the Chinese and Western co-principal work as 'parents', like a mother and father, undertaking their own duties and trying their best to co-operate in harmony. This can be achievable within the 'school family'.

Dr Roger Morgan has held senior management positions in the United Kingdom and principal positions in the Middle East and South East Asia but found adaptation to the Chinese educational environment the hardest he had to face and understand. However, this was his most rewarding post career-wise.
Currently, when 'internationalised' education has been written into the medium and long term Education Reform and Development Plan of the Shanghai Municipal Government, Chinese senior managers with international experience in the Chinese context are extremely scarce. Importantly, the Xiehe system of co-principalship is an excellent way for such colleagues to become experienced in this regard.

Conclusion

The success or otherwise of the Western/Chinese co-principal role in the Xiehe Dual Stream School fundamentally determines the school's overall quality. Developed at its best the role exemplifies for students, staff and parents a number of key global learning concepts, such as co-operation and equality.

Also, if successful, it enables the best features of Western and Chinese educational practice to be fully developed within the curriculum and management systems of the school as a whole. Is there any other more exciting job, worldwide, in education than this one?

(c) Leading through values

Rob Bowden

In this final perspective, the author describes a project he is co-ordinating which focuses on the importance of values in a leadership context.

> ***'The only thing of real importance that leaders do is to create and manage culture … the unique talent of leaders is their ability to work with culture'.***
>
> Peter Schein

In close fitting with Schein's quote above, this perspective on leadership focuses on the form and function of school cultures that adequately respond and adapt to the challenges of 21st century learning. Three core concepts are offered for consideration, before sharing insights into a project that has been exploring how they interweave to present both challenges and opportunities for practice.

The first concept is that of **leadership** and in particular the 'leadership of schools' (a collective cultural process) as distinct from more common conceptions of 'school leadership' as individualistic.

The second concept is that of **change** and the capability, or otherwise, of schools and their leadership to respond to changes in the needs of learning and the wider societal context of our education systems.

The third concept is that of **values** and the ways in which values underpin learning and leadership within a school community, whether consciously or otherwise.

The nature of leadership

The first concept for consideration is that of leadership. There is no shortage of discussion on leadership whether in relation to education or otherwise. In fact leadership advice is an industry in its own right and my bookshelves groan when I attempt to squeeze the latest 'must have' publication on leadership into an already overloaded space. Whilst the nuances of a new perspective are always of interest, there is something remarkably consistent about the majority of these 'guides' and that is their almost universal treatment of leadership as an individual pursuit.

This has always made me feel uncomfortable, for it sits uneasily with my own understanding and experiences of what I deem to be effective leadership. My own interpretations rest far more in a collective and collaborative endeavour whereby leadership is a cultural process involving an entire community in what I suggest is the central tenet of leadership: learning.

I find it impossible to think of leadership without also thinking of learning, and yet regularly encounter leaders who seem either immune, or actively resistant to learning. I am not talking here of the learning that may (or may not) occur on a day course, but of the learning opportunities that present themselves daily in our own settings and with our own peers. The absence of learning within educational leadership is all the more surprising given its apparently obvious association, but in many settings education remains extremely hierarchical in both structure and practice, with an overwhelming focus on incremental school improvement, the parameters of which are prescribed from on high. Such environments are not always conducive to learning.

Whilst no-one involved in education, including myself, is against improvement per se, it seems that the conservative nature of education (in England at least) leads few to ask 'improvement in what?' Should a hierarchical, linear, didactic and rigid form of education be the focus of this improvement? Many, including myself, would argue not. Instead I would advocate a process of thinking about what education is for and devising a form of education and leadership better suited to our aspirations for its function. Whenever this question is embraced by educationalists I have worked with, they quickly identify shortfalls in the ability of the current system to meet the needs of 21st century learners growing up in a complex and uncertain world. But this recognition needs to look inwards as well as outwards because as West-Burnham asserts:

'It is not just the global context of schools that demands change – it is both the nature of schools themselves and the nature of the clients they serve that demands profound rethinking.' [1]

This will inevitably demand a concurrent rethinking of the leadership needed to support such change for:

'If we are to transform children's lives then we need leadership that is transformational.' [1]

This is especially true for schools committed to enabling, and further preparing, their learners to survive and thrive as 21st century citizens.

Global learning is often identified or advocated as the vehicle for fulfilling such a transformation, but in my experience frequently flounders in its application. The reasons for this may be multiple, but foremost among them for me is the error of seeing global learning as simply another 'function' to fit into an existing 'form'. It is much more than this, or at least should be.

Quality global learning is dependent on dialogue, multiple perspectives, critical thinking and creative responses around a series of complex and ever-changing issues. These approaches require the nurturing of a safe, open, and dynamic learning environment, at odds with conventional models of leadership. In short, they require a form of leadership appropriate to the function of the learning and the learner. This is the necessary transformation.

It is a transformation in thinking, power, responsibility, ownership and spirit. It is a shift from school leadership, to the leadership of schools; from an individualistic to collaborative state; from a role within an organisation to a process of the organisation – its culture.

The table in **Figure 1** on the next page breaks down some of the elements of a school system and suggests the dominant characteristics of the two approaches.

Fig 1: Contrasting leadership characteristics

	A transformational journey...	
	...from leadership as ***individual*** pursuit	...to leadership as ***cultural*** process
Structure	*Hierarchical*	*Related systems*
Ownership	*Individual*	*Shared*
Creativity	*Limited*	*Maximised*
Communication	*Manufactured*	*Organic*
Resilience	*Low*	*High*
Innovation	*Minimal and slow*	*Significant and fast*
Learning	*For a purpose*	*State of being*

Seeing the school as a system

How do you approach leadership as a cultural process? There is a growing body of support for this, but in my work I have found the most useful and engaging stimulus to be that of living systems thinking. Drawing from ecological principles or 'lessons from nature' this approach has proven highly effective in helping to better understand the complexity and interdependencies of a school (or any system) and through doing so, nurture leadership as a cultural process. Looking to nature for advice is not new (though perhaps forgotten) and has a record of transformational impact such as through the work of John Muir (1838-1914) who was instrumental in establishing the National Parks of the USA. Muir famously stated that, *'when we try to pick out anything by itself, we find it hitched to everything else in the Universe',* long before systems thinking emerged as a field. It is a statement well suited to global learning and this association is further enhanced by the Center [sic] for Ecoliteracy whose work on systems thinking has found that:

> *'A systems approach helps young people understand the complexity of the world around them and encourages them to think in terms of relationships, connectedness, and context.'* [2]

Systems thinking also enables a shift in perceptions (through learning), to a more holistic and dynamic understanding of our schools, that is highly complementary to leadership as a cultural process.

The Center [sic] for Ecoliteracy identifies six key shifts for schools as: [3]

- ***From parts to the whole,*** with implications for how we build a whole-school culture and develop authentic integrated curricula.
- ***From objects to relationships***, with implications for the pedagogies we use and our perceptions of knowledge creation and acquisition.
- ***From objective knowledge to contextual knowledge,*** with implications for how we resource learning and see the role of teachers (as co-learners).
- ***From quantity to quality***, with implications for how we assess learning and perceive school improvement.
- ***From structure to process***, with implications for how we manage the system and for our understanding of where and how learning occurs.
- ***From contents to patterns***, with implications for how we plan/share learning and for what we perceive to be core transferable skills and knowledge.

Living as change

A fundamental principle within systems thinking is the ability to respond and adapt to change and it is to this that I turn as the second concept for consideration. Change is nothing new in education. In fact a senior leader of 40 years experience in England, told me in a recent project *'change is the only thing that has been consistent in my career'* [4] (Peacock, per com 2011).

The issue with change in education is that it is often 'change to' and 'change of', and is normally given or expected. This situates schools, leaders, teachers and learners as 'living with change', which is at best passive, and at worst (and it often is), disruptive, confusing, upsetting and alienating. Change is therefore overwhelmingly associated with the negative and people are often perceived as not liking or resisting change, with obvious implications for the leadership of schools.

In my work on change with schools and other organisations, the key to unlocking an alternative and more transformational understanding of change has been the issue of ownership. Where people own change it can be a force for empowerment, learning, creativity, innovation, achievement and drive, but this is not a simple task for as Sir Ken Robinson identifies:

> *'...a key can be turned in two directions. Turn it one way and you lock resources away, even from those they belong to. Turn it the other way and you release resources and give people back themselves.'* [5]

The way in which change is approached is therefore important, and I would argue core to the effective leadership of schools. As with the application of systems thinking, change not only relates to the form of the school (changes in structure and management etc) but also to its function (how does change interface with learning). This is again, especially relevant to global learning as former head teacher and author of 'Change' and 'Creating Tomorrow's Schools Today' points out:

> *'Our schooldays shape what we become, and the system itself is not designed to prepare us to live with change and uncertainty. Quite the opposite. Days are highly structured and ordered; we are trained to function in a framework of regime and familiarity'.* [6]

The motivation for improving the way we approach change is twofold. The first is to better embrace changes in the operational environment of a school - government policy, assessment criteria, initiatives, funding etc. The second is to help learners (including teachers) better adapt to the changing and uncertain reality of 21st century living. In terms of global learning, this second motivation is a major driver for as Bauman asserts in his influential works on living in an age of uncertainty:

> *'Forms ... are unlikely to be given enough time to solidify, and cannot serve as frames of reference for human actions and long-term life strategies because of their short life expectation: indeed, a life expectation shorter than the time it takes to develop a cohesive and consistent strategy'* [7]

Bauman refers to this as 'liquid modernity' and it is a notion that has proven very useful in enabling educators to see and 'own' the challenge of preparing learners for living such futures. The necessary learning for this is often contrary to that of the existing system however. Conventional understandings of knowledge as fixed and certain, and of the teacher as arbiter of this, are at odds with a world in which information is everywhere, knowledge is relative and transient, and learning is increasingly a social enterprise with teacher as facilitator.

The transformation needed then is for schools to engage change not as something to live with, but as a manifestation of life in its own right – living ***as*** change. This should not be a difficult transition for education, for if reduced to its basics, education is fundamentally about making a change. The question is about the nature of the change we want to see and it is for this that I turn to the third and most important of my core concepts – values.

Finding a common core

In England at least, there is an increasingly varied debate about what is variously (and I believe unhelpfully) called virtues, moral, character or values education. Leaving debate around the nuances of these differing terms to one side, I want to focus on a general discussion around values. Ask any educator about values and you will almost certainly receive a positive response as to their importance and presence. That this is so, should not be a surprise for as Will Ryan reminds us:

'Most teachers join the profession to make a difference for the future. They are energised by a compelling moral purpose to do the right things for children.' [8]

This moral purpose, more often than not, will extend to the school as an institution and there will be some form of values statement or vision to assert this. At the risk of being controversial, I would suggest that this is sometimes as far as an engagement with values extends into the life of the school. In one recent project, a teacher in a school that named its houses after values – loyalty, friendship, respect etc –recounted that she had never known any discussion with staff or pupils as to what these stood for. This is what we might call surface or shallow values.

The relentless pressure of changes, locally and globally, provides a compelling argument for moving beyond such a shallow engagement with values and I am not alone in making this case:

'It is time to recapture that moral purpose. There is a very real world out there.' [8]

The recapturing that Ryan talks of requires not just a deepening of our engagement with values, but a profound dialogue; a dialogue that is crucially about self, but also about our relationships with others and the wider world in all its forms (social, economic, environmental, spiritual, cultural etc).

This dialogue will need time and resourcing and in my own work I encounter leaders who say they have neither time or resource to devote to this. I would suggest that is short sighted and others with far more experience allude to the same:

'...if you want to be a leader, you have to be a real human being. You must recognise the true meaning of life before you can become a great leader. You must understand yourself first.

In this sense the cultivated self is a leader's greatest tool...It's the journey of a lifetime.

...that cultivation, 'becoming a real human being', really is the primary leadership issue of our time, but on a scale never required before.' [9]

Where leaders have been bold enough to embark on this journey, starting with themselves and rippling outwards, the impact (through almost any measure) has been profound:

'Adopting a values-based approach to teaching and learning can radically change relationships, and how the school functions, within a short space of time.' [10]

'I need to have a word with myself'

This subtitle comes from a colleague of mine and powerfully sums up what I believe to be central to effective leadership – constant critical reflection. At the core of this we find values – our values. Values underpin all that we are and can/will be, and are intimately connected to processes of thinking and learning as neatly stated by the educational thinker Edward de Bono:

'We think so that we can arrange the world, either in our minds or outside of our minds, in a manner that satisfies our values.' [11]

That this is true for ourselves is also true for all those we work with, and in the context of schools, for all those we seek to educate. It therefore has considerable light to shed on our relationships with others and the world around us, especially in the context of global learning. Values are not always easy to examine however, as they reside deep beneath the opinions, attitudes and behaviours that are the more familiar expressions of our identity. Moreover, our values normally occupy the sub-conscious realm, so that even when we directly question them we may struggle with the language and capabilities to adequately discuss them.

Thankfully, a growing body of research and understanding around values is helping to address these challenges, and pedagogies and processes are being developed to apply this in educational settings and to the leadership of schools (and global learning) in particular.

Common to much of this work is a set of 'universal human values' that have been collated through research with over 65,000 people across 68 countries. These 60 or so values have been formulated into a values map that shows not only their existence, but also their relation to one another. This map (see **Figure 2**) is helping people to explore their values, develop a shared values language, and better understand how values work and how they can be (and are) influenced, even manipulated.

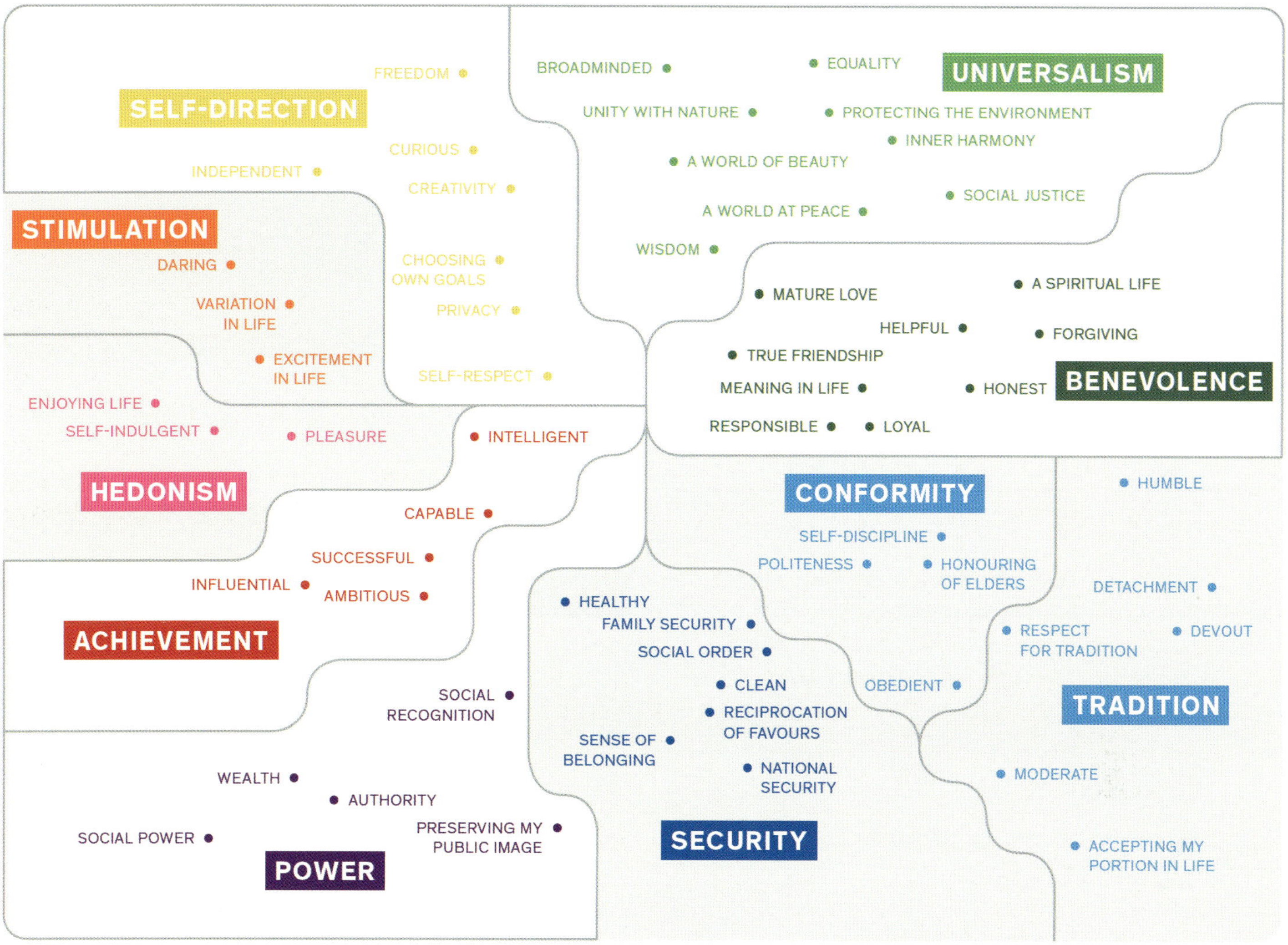

Fig 2: A map of 'universal human values' and their organisation into value groups. [12]

When applied within organisations at the cultural level, this fresh thinking around values can have a transformational impact as within several UK schools that have implemented the process (see 'Leading Through Values' (LTV) case study below).

There are many inter-related factors that drive this transformation, but the key ones would include:

- **Recognition of a shared set of universal values**, (held by all, but prioritised and 'lived', through our opinions, attitudes and actions, differently).

- **An awareness of how values work**, leading to greater understanding of where our own perspectives on self, others, and the wider world, come from, and how they are formed and influenced.

- **An emerging values language** that enables more complex and explicit dialogue around values-laden issues (many global issues are values-laden) and the values dilemmas that inevitably occur within any system (organisation).

- **Improved identification and understanding of the connections between the elements of a system** (i.e. a school and its curriculum) through a shared values pedagogy that transcends specialisms and inter-system boundaries.

These, and other factors combine to provide what Mezirow[13] terms a 'disorientating dilemma', which in his own seminal work on 'learning as transformation', is considered the first of ten phases that typify any transformation (see below).

The ten phases of transformation:

1. a disorientating dilemma;
2. self-examination with feelings of fear, anger, guilt, or shame;
3. a critical assessment of assumptions;
4. recognition that one's discontent and the process of transformation are shared;
5. exploration of options for new roles, relationships and actions;
6. planning a course of action;
7. acquiring knowledge and skills for implementing one's plans;
8. provisional trying of new roles;
9. building competence and self confidence in new roles and relationships; and
10. a reintegration into one's life on the basis of conditions dictated by one's new perspective.

Such a dilemma can be particularly powerful within educational settings and has led many educators to recognise the distance between the learning they believe is necessary for their learners to survive and thrive in the 21st century and the education that they actually receive. Global learning can provide much of the content and many of the approaches to foster this shift, but I would suggest that without the values perspective to guide the process there is a risk of 'innovation without change'.

It is the awareness and exploration of values that provides ownership of a shared challenge and helps to transcend power differentials (or at least more explicitly acknowledge them) in order to achieve systemic cultural change.

A particular strength of learning through values is that its holistic nature and motivating energy (see online paper Motivating the Core)[14] has shown that it directly contributes towards school development with improvements in attainment, behaviour and attendance all noted outcomes from across a wide range of studies. In the context of developing global schools, values have also proven highly effective in building confidence in teachers and school leaders to engage with global issues more regularly (and sometimes for the first time).

Leading Through Values: bringing it all together

Having shared these three core concepts, the final part of this section turns to a discussion of how these can come together within a formal education setting. This is done through sharing an action-learning case study called 'Leading Through Values' that was implemented in nine primary schools in the UK in 2012-13. It was driven by the idea that a values-led pedagogy could inspire a more critical and creative learning environment for teachers and students alike and that this environment would be naturally more conducive to engaging in the Bigger Than Self issues (see box, right) that continue to shape the 21st century.

The action-learning project took participating schools through a values-led journey over a period of around six months, during which there was a mixture of working together (peer learning), working alone (school-based experimentation) and working in partnership with a delivery partner (team-teaching and professional co-learning). The journey had six key steps as outlined in **Figure 3** (right) that combined the ideas of leadership, change and values outlined earlier in this section.

The project was a small-scale pilot working in just nine active primary classrooms, but its findings have attracted significant interest from a diverse range of educators in England and beyond. These findings are too detailed (and perhaps too context specific) to enter into fully in this contribution, but I share some key findings on pages 191-192 that may help readers to reflect on the implications of such an approach in their own setting.

Bigger Than Self (BTS) issues.

Bigger Than Self (BTS) issues is a means of referring to a range of topical and critical issues that have shaped, and continue to shape 21st century for ourselves, others and the wider world. It incorporates issues such as global inequality, climate change, human rights and international conflict. These are all in themselves complex, and for teachers and students, sometimes daunting areas of learning. Their scale alone can deter engagement with such issues, or reduce it to over-simplistic treatment that ignores the range of perspectives and degrees of uncertainty that more accurately characterise such topics. Using the idea of BTS issues has enabled us to bypass these 'barriers to engagement' and to instead focus on the shared elements of these disparate issues such as their local to global scale, their interconnectedness, their links to individual choice, and their lack of single black and white solutions. This approach has led teachers to more confidently engage with BTS issues and helped students to look beyond their teacher for the necessary answers, forming a genuine learning community. It has created higher levels of dialogue in the classroom and increased critical engagement through the use of approaches such as P4C (see **Chapter 5.3**). Most importantly however, this approach has been driven by a more explicit focus on the values associated with BTS issues and this emerging process and language has enabled teaching and learning around BTS issues to fit more naturally with existing areas of study, rather than as 'one-off' or 'extra' interventions consigned to specific weeks or themed days.

Fig 3: Key steps for transformation of practice [15]

1 *Thinking about values*

- Values and how they work
- Personal values
- Community/school values
- Values and learning

2 *Seeing the BIG issues*

- Exploring Bigger Than Self issues
- Me and my world
- Connections for learning
- BTS and values

3 *Learning for change*

- What do we want for the future?
- Who should we ask?
- Understanding how change happens
- Making change stick

4 *Stimulating learning*

- BTS as a context for learning
- Curriculum connections
- Asset mapping
- External support

5 *Making it work*

- Appropriate methods
- Thinking about pedagogy
- Monitoring and evaluating
- Patience and risk-taking

6 *Sustaining leadership*

- Action learning
- Community of being
- Models of leadership...
- ...leaders as models

Key findings reported by the project…

…in relation to teachers:

- increased confidence in the ability of primary learners (as young as Y2 (6-7 years old) in complex and sometimes controversial issues;
- greater understanding of values, including their own, and of how values intersect with teaching, with school and with the wider society;
- more willingness and ability to include Bigger Than Self issues into everyday teaching and learning;
- a permanent shift in pedagogy and teaching philosophy. Teachers spoke of a new ways of seeing the world and of their role as a teacher;
- reinvigoration of their teaching and more critical insight into the education and learning that their learners need as 21st century citizens; and
- opportunities to refresh existing curriculum content and make it more relevant and meaningful by connecting it to values and BTS issues.

…in relation to learning:

- higher levels of engagement in the classroom. Observers (including head teachers and governors) noted the genuine interest of learners in the values and BTS issues being explored;
- marked improvements in the speaking and listening skills of students;
- connecting values and BTS issues to the 'day-to-day' learning (as opposed to an add-on) supports learners to begin identifying these links for themselves;
- the active development of a values language in the classroom is key to deepening learners' understanding of and engagement with values and BTS issues;
- the most successful learning was observed where teachers 'walk the talk' and use values to support a more active student voice in the classroom environment;
- a safe space in which learners can confidently express their thoughts and ideas without judgement is essential for critical engagement;
- learning through values has a direct and positive impact on classroom behaviour and on the attainment of learners. Teachers spoke of the values work spilling over into the playground, community and all areas of learning; and
- supporting the evolution of values through classroom dialogue that creates ownership is essential to the sustainability of learning through values.

... in relation to leading through values:

- greater values awareness (through professional learning) is critical for the effective implementation of learning through values;
- the direct or indirect support of leadership is a major factor in the success of learning through values;
- teachers who are supported to 'take risks' and 'let go' achieve more and gain greater confidence in these approaches than those who 'play it safe';
- the engagement of an external provider and/or resources to support values and BTS approaches has a significant positive impact;
- the most successful teachers were those who were able to critically reflect on their own values and on the values that permeate and govern their professional role in school;
- the opportunity for peer learning around values and BTS issues is critical for teachers' own development and reflection in an area of complex and controversial learning;
- teachers need structured reflection time to unpack the true meaning and potential of learning through values;
- connecting values and BTS issues to existing curricula and planning is empowering for teachers;

- values and Bigger Than Self issues can act as a core driver of school improvement. Five of the nine pilot schools stated a commitment to adopting this approach for their own schools.

- a more explicit values language across the school (at all levels) is key to greater understanding of the potential of values and Bigger Than Self issues; and

- all schools have identified the need to discuss greater community engagement.

'That Values Education can simultaneously provide strong direction, a unifying ethos and maintain and enhance achievement, makes it an attractive pathway. Furthermore, its emphasis on dialogic and critical pedagogies goes a long way in fostering the dynamic and resilient leadership required to sustain direction in an age of uncertainty.' [16]

Conclusion

The Leading Through Values pilot project suggests that bringing change (as a process and reflection of society), leadership (by all for all) and values (our own as well as those of others and the wider world) together can support significant and positive transformation for schools and their wider communities. It points towards a careful balance of these components and to the need to think, explore and reflect on all of these carefully before embarking on any such journey.

At the final meeting of the project group, the teachers and schools leaders involved were asked to reflect on what they thought would strengthen or weaken the attempts of a school to enact such a transformative process. They used a continuum to record their responses and this is repeated in **Figure 4** below. Their reflections will give readers points of familiarity and perhaps echo practices in their schools, but there are likely to be one or two that give pause for thought and reflection. This is not because the teaching profession is inherently lacking in values – far from

Fig 4: Responses from teachers when asked "What would strengthen or weaken learning around values and Bigger Than Self issues?" [17]

Strengthens .... Weakens

* allowing time for children to reflect and discuss ideas
* children's enthusiasm for themes/topics (BTS issues)
* support from school leadership
* bank of resources
* opportunities to share ideas for values activities
* keeping it positive - ensuring BTS issues are not all 'doom and gloom'
* students that can think critically
* involving parents

* creativity in teachers and learners
* incorporating learning across the curriculum
* fresh ideas for teaching through values
* children confident and able to articulate their feelings
* providing inspiring learning opportunities
* keeping content current and relevant - the world does not stand still!
* engaging wider community

* labelling values as right or wrong
* just teaching 'safe' topics - never challenging values!
* embedded views and beliefs - children, staff and parents
* resistance from staff
* keeping it going when there are other (competing) priorities
* lack of resources and knowledge of where to find them
* not involving the wider community

it. It is more, I would suggest, because values are often assumed and implicit in schools and education and may even be prescribed and defined for learners in very distinct moments of learning (assemblies, topic work etc). My experience suggests that a shift towards a more explicit and less certain engagement with values is far more effective and far-reaching.

At the same final project meeting, participants also reflected on the qualities needed to lead through values. Their responses are shown in **Figure 5** (below) and for some models of school leadership these present a considerable challenge to received wisdom.

To me, they make a lot of sense and I would echo many of these if given the opportunity of defining my own list. The challenge for many in leadership positions in schools is how to enact these ideals amidst the very real pressures of day-to-day management and the wider education system. I would like to end by suggesting that a values-led, change-aware process that is truly inclusive and open to learning can achieve a culture of leadership within schools that enables the realisation of such ideals. It is when the culture and system are ignored and the responsibility too heavily vested in one or two individuals, that the pressures suppress the ideals, and the vision of learning that many will share, can be lost.

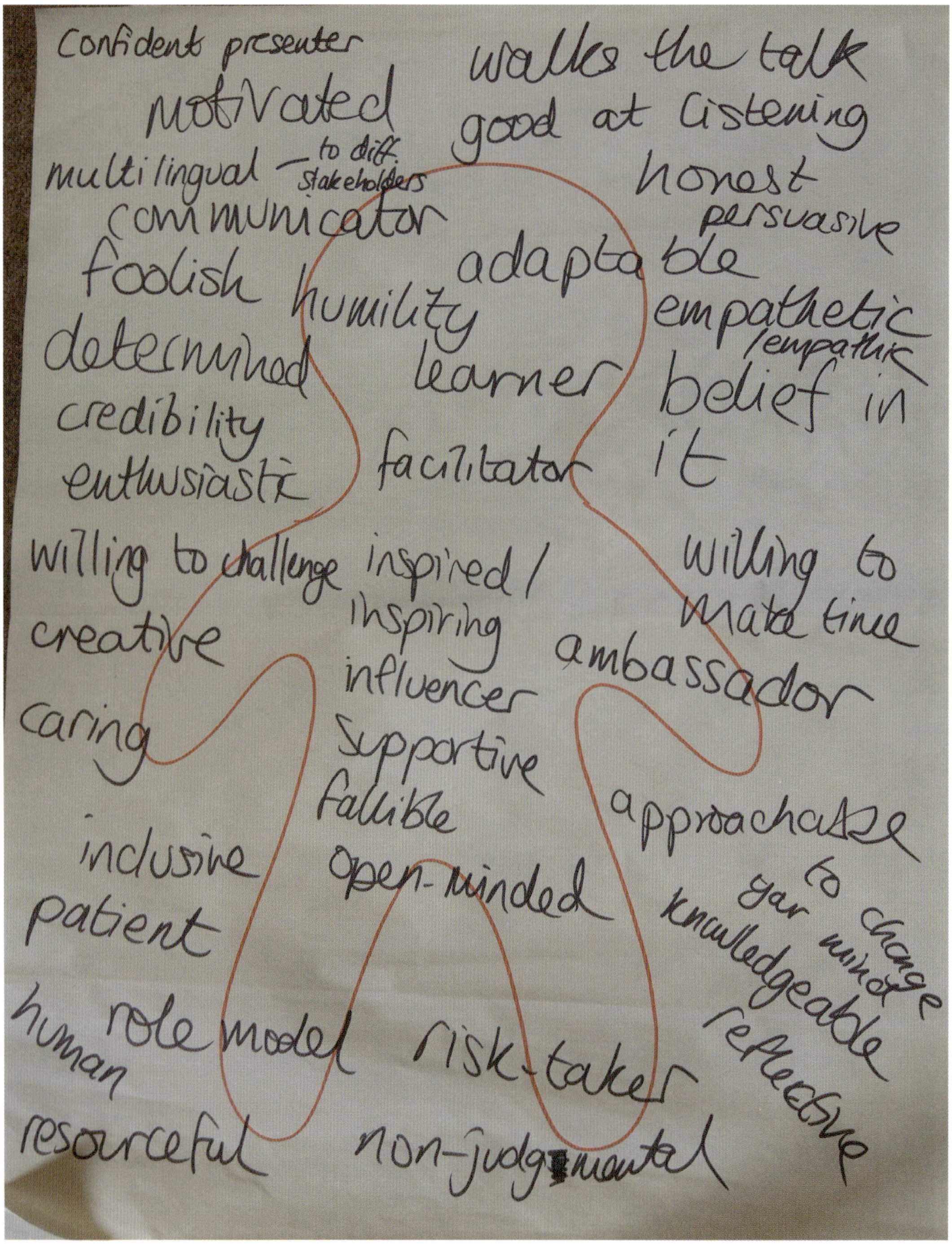

Fig 5: Project group responses to the question: "What qualities are needed to lead through values?" [17]

Talkabout

- *Devise strategies for evaluating the leadership in your school and/or organisation, for example a 'school leadership culture' survey.*
- *Use one of these strategies to gather evaluative evidence on leadership and analyse the outcomes.*
- *Devise indicators of excellence and observable features to define outstanding practice in school leadership, using information from this chapter.*
- *Consider the advantages of adopting the co-principal model of educational leadership in your own school or schools within your organisation.*

Acknowledgements

[1] West-Burnham, J. (2009). *Rethinking Educational Leadership: from improvement to transformation.* London: Continuum.

[2] Center for Ecoliteracy (2013). *Systems thinking.* [available from http://www.ecoliteracy.org/essays/systems-thinking - accessed 05 October 2013]

[3] adapted by author from Center for Ecoliteracy (2013). *Systems thinking.* [available from http://www.ecoliteracy.org/essays/systems-thinking - accessed 05 October 2013]

[4] Peacock, R. (2011). per com during *What is Education For? Study Visit Project.* Lifeworlds Learning

[5] Robinson, K. (2011) *Out of our minds: learning to be creative.* Chichester: Capstone

[6] Gerver, R. (2013). *Change: learn to love it, learn to lead it.* London: Penguin

[7] Bauman, Z. (2007). *Liquid Times: living in an age of uncertainty.* Cambridge: Polity Press

[8] Ryan, W. (2008). *Leadership with a moral purpose: turning your school inside out.* Bancyfelin: Crown House Publishing

[9] Senge, P. et al (2004). cited in West-Burnham, J. (2009). *Rethinking Educational Leadership: from improvement to transformation.* London: Continuum.

[10] Duckworth, J. (2009). *The Little Book of Values: Educating children to become thinking, confident, responsible and caring citizens.* Bancyfelin: Crown House Publishing.

[11] de Bono, E. (2005). *The six value medals: the essential tool for success in the 21st century.* London: Vermillion

[12] diagram reproduced from Blackmore, E. et al (2013). *Common Cause for Nature.* Machynlleth: Public Interest Research Centre

[13] Mezirow, J. (ed.) (2000). *Learning as transformation: critical perspectives on a theory in progress.* San Francisco: Jossey-Wiley.

[14] Bowden, R. (2013). *Motivating the core,* Think Global Thinkpiece (available from www.learningthroughvalues.org/resources.html)

[15] adapted from Bowden, R. (2013). *Leading Through Values: Six Steps for Change.* Lifeworlds Learning

[16] adapted from Bowden, R. (2013). *Buillding a Case for Change.* Lifeworlds Learning (available from www.learningthroughvalues.org/resources.html)

[17] Bowden, R. (2013). *Leading Through Values: Final Project Report.* Lifeworlds Learning (available from www.learningthroughvalues.org/resources.html)

8.2 Creating whole school policies in Xiehe Global Schools to ensure consistency in excellence

Trevor Higginbottom and Richard Hine

This chapter is concerned with a key strategy for maximising student attainment: policy formulation and implementation as the basis for ongoing school improvement.

> ***'The senior management team should implement curricula and other policies for the whole school to ensure consistency of students' experience and performance throughout the complete age range.'***
>
> Her Majesty's Inspectorate for England and Wales

In Xiehe Global Schools, the following appear to have been the benefits of whole school policy development.

- To provide a clearer view of the meaning of *'East meets West'* in the context of the process of teaching and learning.
- To enhance/ensure consistency of excellent whole school practice in teaching and learning across the curriculum (lesson by lesson, the students' curriculum should surely not be a 'lottery' for them in terms of quality?)
- To define excellent practice in this respect for the benefit of newly appointed teachers. This helps them to learn, quickly, what the school regards as quality education.
- To ensuring greater continuity in the process of teaching and learning both within and across the age ranges.
- To enhance, overall, the student's cognitive and affective attainment.
- To provide a clear agenda for whole school evaluation and related external inspection/accreditation of the school's education.
- To share such policies with governors/advisory groups and parents, as part of the 'partnership' with them in the education process.

Much thought has been given to the processes of whole school policy formulation in order to ensure that such statements become reality rather than mere rhetoric: 'it is vital that policies should not become the destination rather than the starting point for change.'[1]

This chapter is devoted to three case studies of policy development in Xiehe Global Schools.

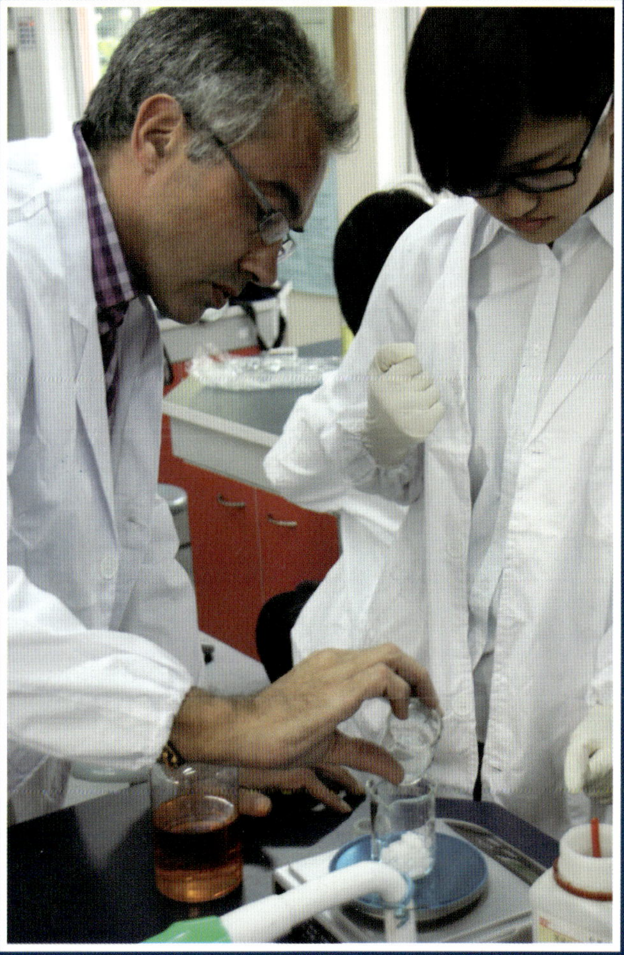

Teaching and learning at SUIS (Gubei): a key policy dimension

Case Study 1: An holistic approach to whole school policy development

In the first Xiehe Global School, Xiehe Bilingual School (which opened in 2003), an attempt was made to create a policy framework for whole school development.

Initially, a consistent approach to curriculum planning was adopted by means of the model illustrated in **Figure 1** (below). It was felt that this was a means of promoting inter-departmental dialogue and of ensuring continuity and progression in the curriculum.

Subsequently, this consistency in planning was adopted for the whole school by means of the framework summarised in **Figure 2** (right). This was an attempt to ensure the highest possible education standards.

The framework was devised by staff and shared with parents, on an ongoing basis, as it was implemented.

There were two key components. First, considerable emphasis was placed on the process of whole school policy development. Secondly, it was felt important to create an unthreatening but demanding climate of self review and evaluation within the school. Chinese and Western teachers contributed their own professional strengths in the staff discussions.

Fig 1: A model for curriculum planning

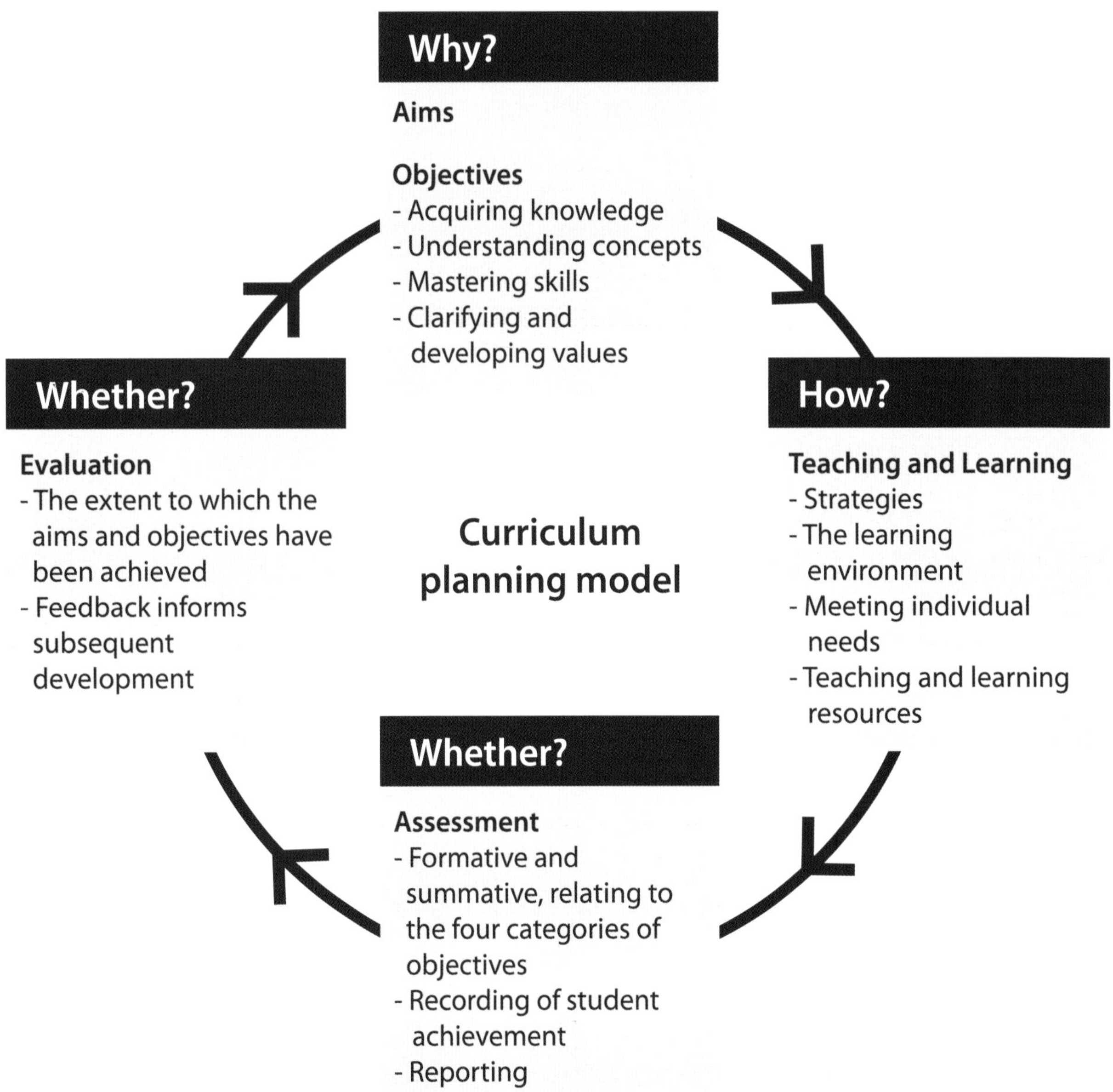

For example, at that stage the Chinese teachers had far more experience of school self evaluation and summative assessment. The Western teachers were more familiar with differentiation in the teaching and learning process and with formative assessment.

From the outset, therefore, Chinese and Western teacher collaboration was seen to be a key dimension of the policy development process.

The seven stage process for developing individual whole school policies is summarised on pages 199-200 of this chapter, which follow.

Fig 2: The development of a whole school planning policy

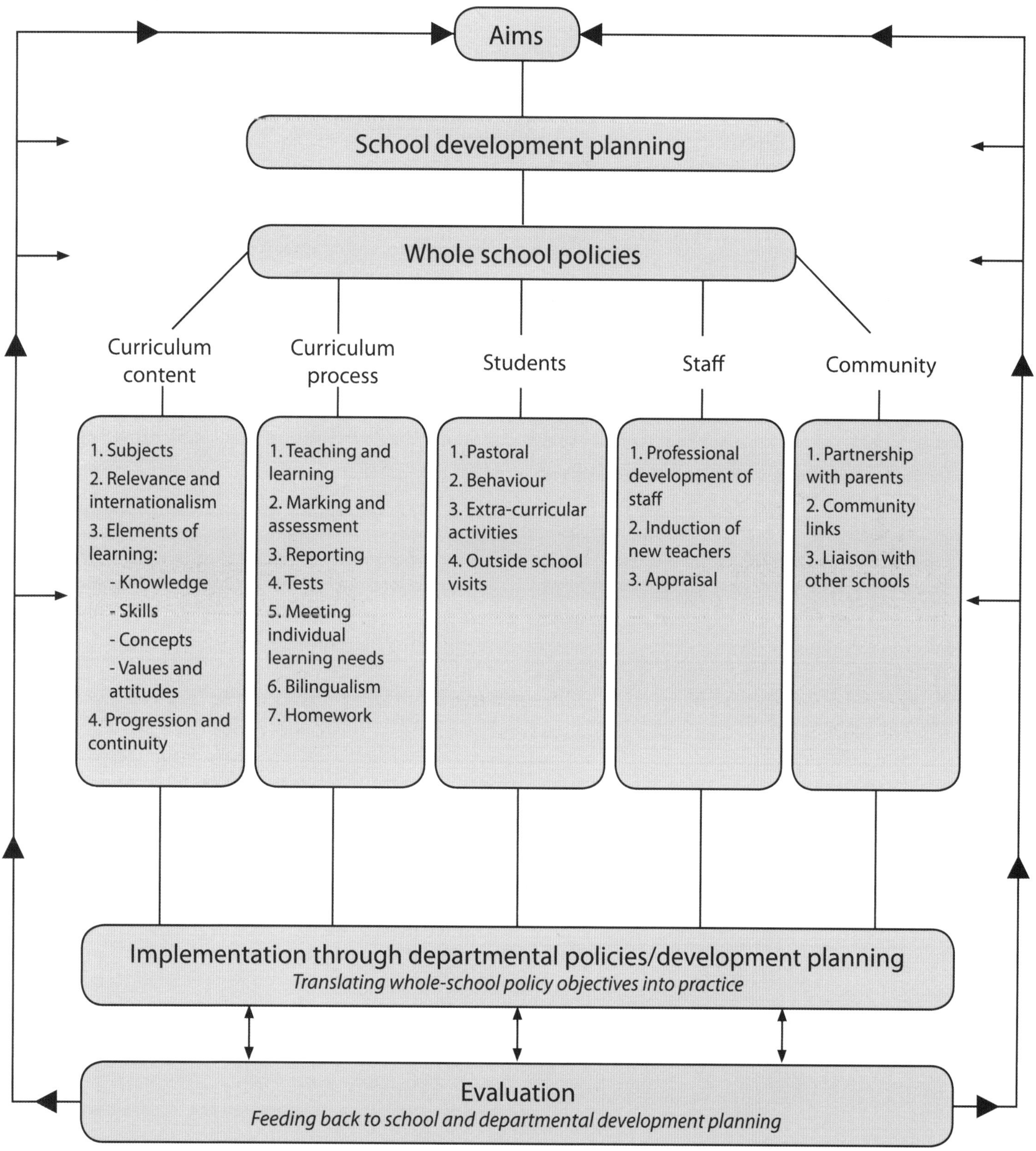

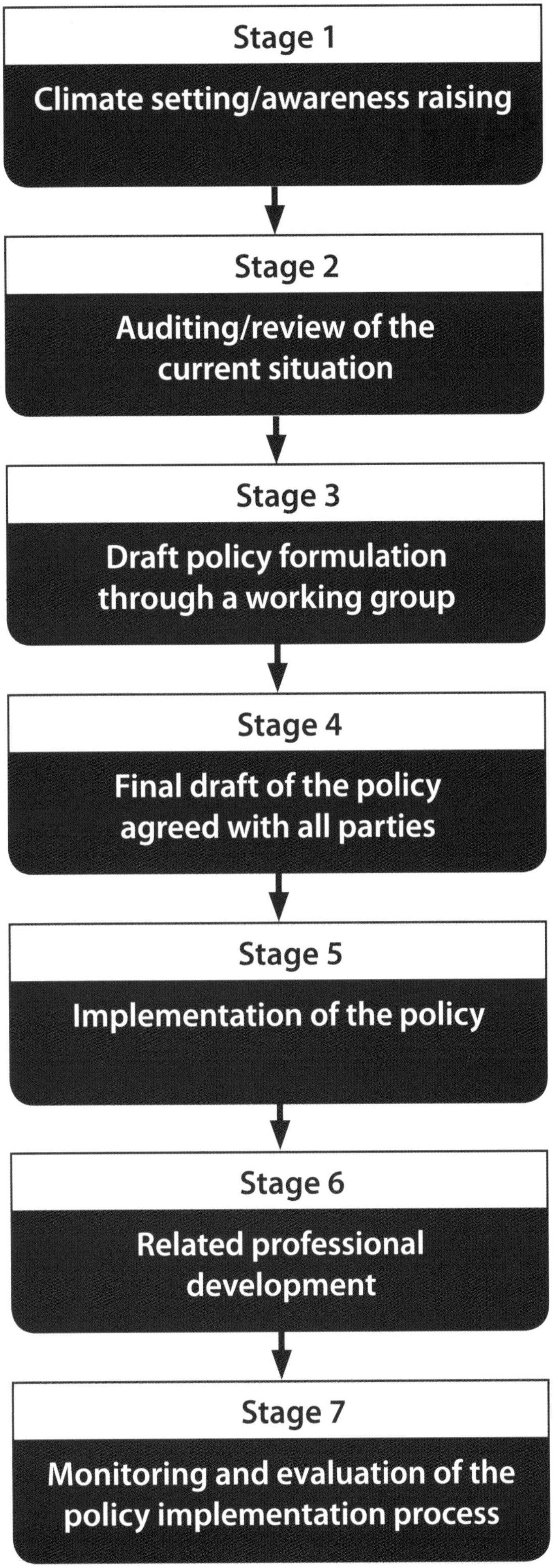

The following were issues raised relating to each of the development stages

Stage 1

- From the outset, purposeful leadership from the senior management team.
- An initial meeting of the whole staff to establish the purposes of any policy and stages in the formulation and implementation process.
- Identification of the issues which need to be addressed.
- Consideration of links with the existing school aims and objectives as reflected in policies and with Xiehe's mission statement and policies.
- Where the size of the school makes it desirable, consideration of the need for a Policy Co-ordinator with a clearly defined job description, sufficient status, appropriate skills and time to lead and help staff.

Stage 2

- Auditing with respect to current practice in the school relating to this policy area.
- Review of management structures associated with this area of the curriculum.

Stage 3

- Formulation of a draft policy; work which could be undertaken by a small representative working group from within the school. Possible external consultancy involvement.
- It may be helpful to produce a brief written statement of intent for internal circulation incorporating immediate aims and objectives and those who are to be involved at this stage. This statement can then be used to form the core of the initial school policy statement.
- Initial drafting of a comprehensive policy statement.
- The policy should not be too long.
- It may be helpful to include examples of good practice.

Stage 4

- Initial draft discussed with all teaching and non-teaching staff, students, parents, School Advisory Group members, the wider community and possibly the Xiehe senior management team.
- Revisions/additions made in the light of this wide ranging discussion.
- Once finalised the policy statement should be made available to all teaching and non-teaching staff, students, parents and School Council. School Advisory Group members and included in the school information brochure. There will be a need for a bilingual (Chinese and English) translation.

Stage 5

- Briefing of specific groups of staff regarding their roles in policy implementation, for example senior management team, co-ordinators/heads of department, pastoral staff, classroom teachers.
- Assumption that the new policy has implications for all staff and students.
- Note the importance of 'the hidden curriculum' within the school's ethos: words (in the policy) and actions across the school should not be at variance.
- If relevant, procedures for dealing with incidents, or alleged incidents of discrimination should be clearly identified.
- The process of implementation of the newly developed policy should be integrated into the school's development plan.
- The aspirations of the policy should be reflected in year group/departmental handbooks, syllabuses and schemes of work.

Stage 6

- Professional development may be required for all colleagues, including the senior management team.
- This should be planned collaboratively.

Stage 7

- Implementation of the policy should be subject to systematic monitoring and evaluation.
- Responsibility for evaluation should be clearly identified in the job descriptions of the senior managers and the Policy Co-ordinator.
- As stated in Stage 3 above, the policy statement should provide at least some of the evaluative criteria.
- Feedback from monitoring the evaluation should inform subsequent review and revisions of the policy.

The school felt that a useful way of thinking about whole school policy development was to consider the process in terms of three phases of educational change (right), as recommended by the 'Improving the Quality of Education for All' Project (IQEA).[2]

Both the seven stages of policy development and the three phases of educational change, summarised right, significantly informed the process involved in establishing Xiehe Bilingual School's policy framework, as described in **Figure 2**. Overall, the framework provided a firm foundation for the school's subsequent development.

The initiation phase

The initiation phase is about deciding to embark on innovation and of developing commitment towards the process. The key factors making for success at this stage are:

- that innovation should be tied to a local agenda and high profile local need;
- have a clear, well-structured approach to change;
- an active advocate or champion who understands the innovation and supports it;
- active initiation to start the innovation (top down is acceptable under certain conditions); and
- good quality innovation.

The implementation phase

Implementation is the phase of attempted use of the innovation. The key factors making for success at this stage are:

- clear responsibility for orchestration/co-ordination;
- shared control over implementation (top down NOT ACCEPTABLE);
- a mix of pressure, insistence on 'doing it right' and support;
- adequate and sustained staff development and in-service; and
- rewards for teachers early in the process.

The institutionalisation phase

Institutionalisation is the phase when innovation and change stop being regarded as something new and become part of the school's usual way of doing things. Key activities at this stage are:

- an emphasis on 'embedding' the change within the school;
- the elimination of competing or contradictory practices;
- strong and purposeful links to other change efforts, the curriculum and classroom teaching;
- widespread use in the school and local area; and
- an adequate bank of local facilitators, (e.g. advisory teachers) for skills training.

Case Study 2: External advisor led policy development

In 2012, an external accreditation team recommended that there was a need for SUIS (Hong Qiao) to have more inter-stream curriculum policies which reflected the best of Chinese and Western educational practice. Generic teaching and learning was chosen as the policy area because: (i) this was felt to be the school's most central curriculum activity; and (ii) there was evaluative evidence available which showed some particular strengths of classroom practice in the respective streams.

The processes involved

- The school's senior management team decided that an external adviser should chair an inter-stream Working Party to formulate a draft policy. It was agreed that the membership of the working party, eight in total, should represent a cross section of the staff, including middle managers and newly appointed teachers.
- The Working Party's view was that the policy should be based on evaluative criteria expressed in terms of:
    - 'Indicators of excellence': specific examples of good practice which might be seen in the teaching and learning; and
    - 'Observable features': what might be seen in a lesson to suggest that the indicator of excellence was being achieved.
- In order to inform the Working Party's discussions, the external adviser and other members observed lessons in both streams. Classroom responses to a wide range of potential indicators of excellence were evaluated. Extracts from the follow-up report to the Working Party are included below.

Draft indicator of excellence relating to:	Evidence from evaluative data:
Lesson management to ensure all students are on task	• All the outstanding lessons were characterised by extremely high concentration levels. • Usually created by a wide range of competitive and 'control' strategies. • A critical criterion but this needs careful definition.
Balance of the four types of teaching and learning strategy	• Whole class teaching was generally effective. • Even in the outstanding lessons there was a need for more structured paired and group work. A critical policy issue. • Overall, individualised learning was neglected.
Differentiation in the teaching and learning	• Only in one lesson was there any evidence of differentiation by task. A critical policy issue. • Differentiation could usefully be extended particularly in (i) team teaching and (ii) individualised learning.
The overall lesson structure	• In the most effective lessons the students were clearly aware of the learning targets. • In over half of the lessons there was a need for some improvement in the lesson structure. Eg A rigorous concluding review.
The pace of the lesson	• The best lessons were all characterised by a fast pace. • Usually created by a carefully planned range of tasks. • Another critical policy issue.
Student confidence and self esteem	• Virtually all the lessons were characterised by very good teacher/student and student/student relationships. • The use of praise words is an important policy dimension. • The self esteem/confidence of the least successful students needs more emphasis
A classroom environment supportive to learning	• Most of the classroom environments were highly conducive to learning but there is some unevenness in quality. • Observable features relating to this criterion could be formulated from existing excellent practice.

Defining the learning outcomes	• See points above in relation to lesson structure • Clearly, in any learning experience, the students must be aware of the targets for learning. • However, the policy must make clear there are a variety of ways of achieving this.
Lesson content which promotes global learning	• A Chinese lesson was a superb example of how global learning can be used to promote language acquisition. • This is, obviously, a very important criterion which would be easy to define.
The adoption of both co-operative and competitive learning strategies	• Competitive learning was used extremely effectively in several lessons and, undoubtedly, aided both concentration and motivation. • Co-operative learning (as a concept) needs more emphasis/ discussion.

A draft policy statement was presented by the Working Party to the school's senior management team.

What is excellent practice in teaching and learning within our school's classrooms, combining the best of Chinese and Western practices?

In all our classrooms the teaching is characterised by the following indicators of excellence.

- An attempt to meet the differentiated learning needs of individual students, as far as is practicable. An observer in the lesson is likely to see:
  - » clear targets in this respect within the teacher's(s') lesson plan;
  - » evidence of differentiation by either outcome or task and possibly both;
  - » the teacher being overtly conscious of the needs of the least and most successful students; and
  - » if homework is set, some attempt at differentiation in the task(s) set.
- Classroom management which attempts to ensure that, at all times, the students are on task in their learning.
- Teaching which reflects both careful planning but also opportunism in the actual lesson context.
- An appropriate balance between whole class, paired and group work and individualised learning.
- A planned structure to the paired and group work, which ensures that all students are involved appropriately.
- Planning which promotes both co-operative and competitive learning.
- A teaching ethos which supports the confidence and self esteem of individual children, including the maximum use of praise.
- A pace within the lesson which ensures that students of all abilities are appropriately challenged in their learning.
- The use of tablet-based e-books and search-based, immersive, experiential and collaborative online courses (dependent though on the resources available to schools).
- Evidence that the students are well aware of the learning objectives of the lesson.
- Lessons that are structured in order to ensure that the learning is sequential.
- Planning which maximises the students' opportunities to create, inquire, investigate and problem solve.
- Lesson content which is interesting and motivational for the students (e.g. through the use of ICT and visual aids such as PowerPoint and DVD).
- When set, carefully planned homework with appropriate time being given for pre-instructions during the lesson. Also, homework content which is a natural extension of the lesson and is both interesting and challenging to students of all abilities.
- Formative and summative assessment strategies which both carefully monitor the attainment of individual students and are also supportive to ongoing learning (where appropriate, assessing knowledge, ideas, skills, values and attitudes).
- An ethos that ensures rigorous evaluation of the teaching and learning, as a key catalyst for ongoing school improvement.

In all classrooms the learning is characterised by the following indicators of excellence.

- Well motivated students.
- Evidence that students are very willing to create, inquire, investigate and problem solve.
- The willingness of students to communicate verbally with their peers in a confident manner.
- Students learning in an ethos which reflects the school's values eg relating to honesty, fairness and justice.
- The willingness of students to express and to defend their opinions but also to respect the views of others.
- Empathy and respect for differing nationalities and cultures and a willingness to learn more about similarities and differences in this respect.
- Ability, on occasions, to take control of their own learning.
- Caring students who show compassion for other people and the natural environment.
- Students who are prepared to take risks in their learning and to accept that learning involves uncertainty and difficulty.
- Students who have sufficient self esteem to cope with failure.
- Reflective learners who are prepared to think carefully about their successes and failures and to consider ways of seeking self improvement.

RIGHT: SUIS (Hong Qiao) Senior management team discuss the draft teaching and learning policy

In their Final Report, the Working Party made a number of key points, as follows.

- 'The policy content needs to be carefully formulated in such a way that ensures colleagues do not feel they are teaching within 'a professional strait jacket'. Rather it must be regarded as a strong, positive reflection of whole-school culture: 'the way (professionally) we do things around here'. (Research tells us that those organisations with a clearly communicated and fully understood and implemented mission statement are usually the most successful).'
- 'All the school's teachers will need to appreciate that they have a contractual obligation to do all that they can to implement the whole school teaching and learning policy, given that it has been approved by the school's senior management team and all other colleagues.'
- 'It is fully accepted, however, that some staff might feel that they need further professional development in order to effectively implement some dimensions of the policy. (Two possible examples of these might be the development of students' individual needs and structured group work).'
- 'The Working Party's view is that it would be interesting to present the whole staff with a selection of indicators of excellence relating to (a) teaching; and (b) learning. Then to ask them, in a workshop to:

  - identify three or four more indicators for each area; and

  - devise a maximum of four observable features for all the indicator features.

  It is felt that this might be a means of ensuring that colleagues have a 'sense of ownership' for the final version of the policy'.

At the time of writing, the Working Party's Report was continuing to inform the work of the school.

Case Study 3: Teacher led whole school curriculum policy development

This case study relates to curriculum policy development in the International Stream at SUIS (Gubei). Here, the Principal felt that evidence from his lesson observations suggested that the students were too passive in their learning. While many teachers dreamt of passive classes, it was unlikely that this attitude supported a Western style education which involved English GCSE or IGCSE exams at 16 years of age and then the International Baccalaureate diploma as a pre-university course. The Principal therefore decided to ask a newly appointed, but highly experienced, teacher to lead a Working Group to review this major curriculum issue.

The Group was established using volunteers from as many departments as possible. Many different dimensions of teaching pedagogy were considered and it was decided that a whole staff INSET day would be devoted to the exploration of different aspects of active learning. The day was broken down into sections, starting with an introduction, which summarised some of the research into active learning, mainly based on Prince (2004), Niemi (2002) and Geoff Petty's website. Following this introduction, teachers participated in a carousel of discussions delivered by the volunteers. The topics under discussion were culture, language, conversation, group work and games.

The feedback from this discussion emphasised a number of issues that teachers faced in the school. Language was a key issue. If students struggled to access the curriculum, then effective learning was not taking place. Either the teaching style needed to adapt to this or the students were not getting the education they deserved. Another aspect of language was the amount of teacher talk taking place. A school senior manager stated *'after this training I noticed that I talked too much in my lessons and tried to change this, by embracing activities such as think, pair, share'.*

During subsequent whole staff meetings, feedback was received from departments as to activities they had been exploring in the area of active learning. This is still taking place with many excellent ideas being shared.

Perhaps the most important outcome of this training was the decision that the school needed to have a better definition of what styles of teaching and learning should take place in the classroom. With this in mind, a second INSET day was devoted to exploring the definition of a good lesson. In order to vary the style of discussion a 'speed dating' format was used. Following discussions with the working party members the following topics were chosen.

Classroom organisation	Learning activities
Groups	Differentiation
Timing	Learning objectives
Language	Pace and challenge
Subject knowledge	Assessment
Praise/rewards	Homework

Each member of staff had an individual timetable for the INSET day. They went through ten periods of ten minute discussion groups, always with a different membership and no designated leader in place. Colleagues went to a room where there was a piece of paper with the topic to be discussed. Minutes of the discussion outcomes were collected and collated later. At the end of each ten minute session, a whistle blew and everyone moved around to their own next discussion. This had the additional benefit of highlighting how the experience of a student is influenced by the structure of the school timetable.

The feedback from these activities provided the basis of an 'our good lesson' definition. This information was fed back to the senior management team. The 'our good lesson' definition was broken down into two sections: teaching and learning.

These sections were noted so that they could be used as part of a teacher appraisal system or as a training session for new staff to inform them as to the whole school idea of what a good lesson is: in effect a lesson charter.

In a good lesson at SUIS (Gubei) the following can be seen.

- The quality of learning is excellent.
- Students are doing rather than listening (active).
- Students can demonstrate they are independent learners.
- Students show resilience when tackling challenging activities and co-operate to progress.
- Students are keen and pursue opportunities to extend and improve their learning.
- Progress is good or excellent. The lesson time is exploited fully by the student.
- Students understand the point of this lesson in the subject and can describe what they are learning, not just what they are doing.
- Student feedback can influence the lesson.

The teacher supports this by ensuring the following.

- Teaching is of a high quality.
- Students are enthused. The lesson is structured and has a variety of activities.
- Excellent subject knowledge is applied.
- Resources, including new technology, are utilised. The teacher demonstrates control of the workspace.
- Teachers are aware of prior learning and use this to plan effectively. Specific needs of the student are catered for.
- Dialogue, either verbal or through marking, is of a high quality and positive in nature. Exemplars of good work are displayed with feedback in the classroom. Formative and summative assessments are being used.
- Material to aid student understanding is available in the workspace.

Group work at SUIS (Gubei)

The next step was to further define some of the more general definitions that were used such as 'the quality of teaching is excellent' and 'the quality of learning is excellent'. Subsequently, a toolkit of teaching techniques was made available for use by teachers to enable them to meet the needs of all students. A further INSET day was planned for the next school year and this topic provided a key focus for subsequent management development.

One of the most rewarding aspects of this process was that it was undertaken and 'owned' by the staff themselves with quality time being made available by the senior management to allow them to explore these key professional issues. It was felt that significant progress had been made in developing a whole stream policy on how to teach in their school in order to meet the individual learning needs of their students. Additionally, a teacher appraisal system closely related to such a policy would have far more acceptance by the staff than one imposed by the senior management team.

Conclusion

It is regrettable that policies are often viewed negatively by teachers for two reasons: first, on occasions they feel these are 'imposed' on them; and, secondly, such statements frequently fail to inform schools' day-to-day practice. However, when developed and managed in the ways outlined in this chapter, policies can be an invaluable catalyst in helping to create 'outstanding' schools.

Talkabout

- *Complete the SUIS (Hong Qiao) draft generic teaching and learning policy by listing four observable features for each of the indicators of excellence, apart from the initial exemplar provided.*
- *Evaluate the success, or otherwise, of one of your whole school policies. How might it be implemented more successfully?*

Acknowledgements

[1] Hargreaves, D. H., and Hopkins, D. (1991). *The Empowered School: the Management and Practice of Development Planning.* London, England. Cassell.

[2] Centre for Teacher and School Development (1998). *Improving the Quality of Education for All.* University of Nottingham.

Richard Hine is Head of Science at SUIS (Gubei).

9. Strategies for teacher professional development within the Shanghai Xiehe Education Group

This chapter includes two examples of how Xiehe has attempted to provide in-house support for teachers facing the challenges of preparing young people for the rapidly changing world of the 21st century.

9.1 The Stars Project

Cathy Wang Yi and James Waldron

This first example of professional development within Xiehe is an ambitious and highly innovative initiative aimed at supporting staff already identified as 'high flyers' (or 'stars') within the Organisation.

> ***'The irony is that schools are organisations devoted to learning, but they are not by any means always learning organisations for their staff'.***
>
> Professor Andy Hargreaves

Xiehe believes that an outstanding educational organisation is a learning place for staff as well as for its students. The Group's unique mission *'East meets West'* demands ongoing professional development. Colleagues already showing sound knowledge, understanding and experience need further training to provide a solid foundation to ensure their own and Xiehe's future success.

The Stars Project: Aims and Curriculum

As stated in earlier chapters, Xiehe has developed a wide variety of curricula in its Global Schools: an important aim of the Stars Project is to review these in the light of the *'East meets West'* mission.

A second key aim is to consider how to combine the best of local and worldwide educational practices.

Well qualified, high standard teachers will ensure that the Group has a very bright future. Our teachers need to be well versed in the theory and practice of global education and to be prepared to develop it at

Stars trainees learning with Professor Hu Wei.

the classroom level. Only if this happens will Xiehe's *'East meets West'* mission make sense.

The Project's curriculum is designed to meet the above aims. It is implemented in a nine month course beginning in October in each academic year. A cohort of approximately twenty trainees is accepted in each round. Twelve keynote sessions are organised during the course either once or twice a month, at weekends, led by the Group's senior managers, external consultants, professors from both local and overseas universities and local educational representatives. The first course was held in the academic year 2008-9.

Specific sectional themes thus far have included:

- curriculum planning and development;
- global comparative education;
- learning assessment;
- school self evaluation;
- time management and conflict management;
- administration;
- organisational change and personal development;
- China's curricula development and reform;
- Chinese non-government education development;
- school development planning; and
- community service.

The course is very participative: all the trainees are required to lead a session, either individually or as part of a team. This provides them with an opportunity to share their educational practices with their peers.

The trainees also have an opportunity to attend external training courses, to visit other educational organisations and institutes and to participate in international and local education forums and seminars.

Over the last four courses they have attended, for example, the Carnegic Coursc and the Yangtze River Delta Educational Forum and undertaken school visits in Nanjing, Hainan, Shandong, Guangzhou and Zhuhai. All these activities have greatly extended the trainees' knowledge of global education in particular.

ABOVE: Sharing experiences and developing communication skills.
BELOW: Team building through activities in the Stars Project

Stars Project networking

The Project is not only a training programme, the trainees are regarded as 'a family'. Course members are invited to participate in social evenings, dinners, field trips and outward bound training. Such activities help to promote team building and working relationships.

Learning strategies

As well as listening and presenting, trainees are expected to read widely and to prepare educational case studies. Their listening, communicating, reflecting, sharing and co-operative skills are developed during the course.

Assessment

Formative and summative assessment strategies are adopted within the Stars Project. All the trainees must complete the following tasks:

- create a personal blog for sharing assignments or case studies;
- provide three case studies (one for teaching/ learning, one for management and one for another area);
- organise or participate in a working group on a research topic based on the course members' practical demand;

- host at least one seminar attended by group trainees; and
- edit and publish a newsletter relating to part of the training course.

All the assignments are assessed by course trainers, the students themselves and their peers. The assessment programme is 60 per cent formative and 40 per cent summative.

The examination lasts for half a day, in June. It includes theme based interviews with four examiners (20 per cent) and three group discussions assessed by observers (20 per cent)

All the training activities are free of charge. Trainees who attend all the sessions and complete the assignments successfully are awarded certification. Trainees can apply for Stars Project research funding on successful completion of their course. Those who rank in the overall top three in the assessment programme receive an extra financial reward. Trainees enjoyed free lunches and a transportation allowance for attendance at the weekend.

Star Project outcomes

Seventy two trainees have graduated from the Stars Project since 2009. **Figure 1** below gives details of the trainees' profile over the four years (2009-2013).

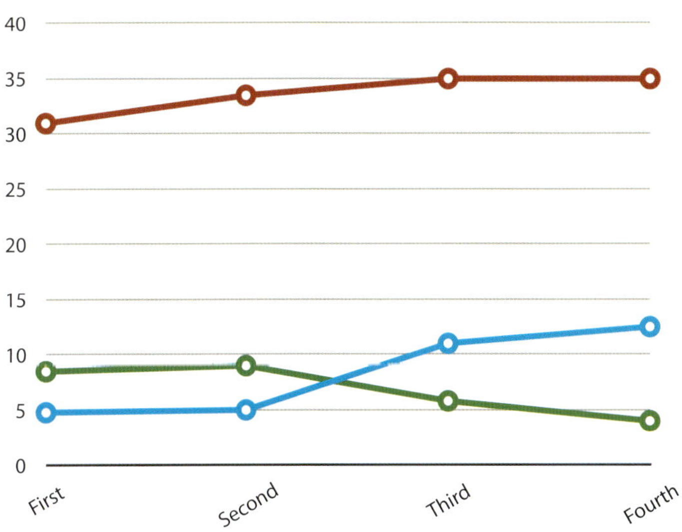

Fig 1: Trainee profile

The trainee's average profile has been as follows:

- average age 33;
- representing more than ten subject backgrounds;
- average teaching experience 10.39 years;
- average length of time with Xiehe 4.59 years.

Many of the trainees have had wide ranging teaching and management responsibilities in schools. All have expressed the need for professional development, 80.95 per cent felt this was an urgent issue for them.

Figure 2 provides a summary of the trainees' post course destinations for the first three courses (up to June 2013).

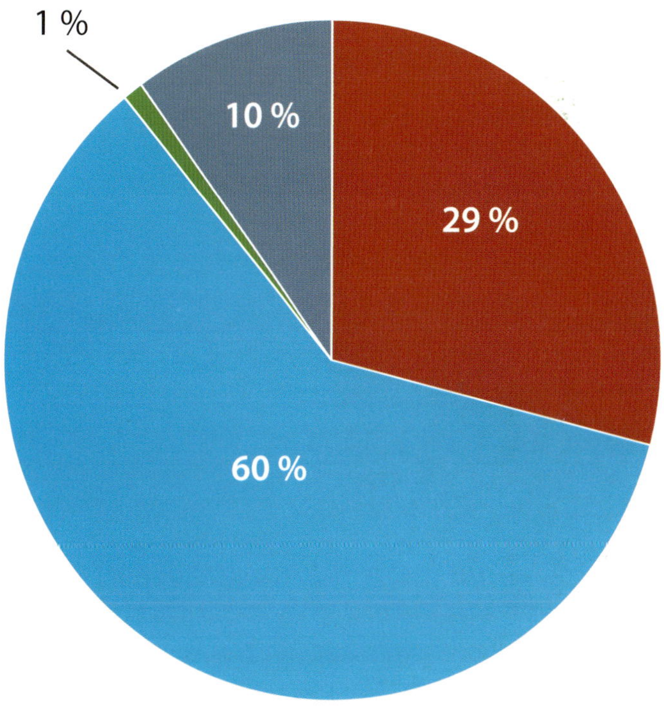

Fig 2: Trainee destination

Over the next three years Xiehe will be opening at least three new schools and Stars Project graduates are likely to fill a significant number of leadership roles in them, both in educational management and administration.

Graduate networking

Post-course the graduates join a Stars Project network across the Group. Research has suggested that a cadre of like minded graduates are now working collaboratively in many Xiehe campuses, which is having a very positive influence on educational quality.

Reflections on the course from four Stars Project graduates

'A first native Indian saying is : 'if you are moving too fast, hold on and give the soul time to catch up'. Above all, the course gave me time to think where I was, where I wanted to go and how I was supposed to get there'.
Yang Yinshuo

'I was able to think about education in a fresh, new way, beyond my teacher perspective'.
Bright Liu

'I became more mature, confident, open minded, patient, caring and willing to learn. As the course progressed I was less afraid to do my homework!'
Helen Liu

'I developed a deeper understanding of global education. The course helped me to devise my personal professional development plan. I now feel more confident to take on bigger challenges in the future'.
Lily Xue

James Waldron's research has suggested that the biggest impact in this respect has been a clearer understanding of the ways of implementing the Xiehe *'East meets West'* mission. The following are extracts from James Waldron's research on the Stars Project.

Methodology

Guskey [1] describes five levels of evaluation to improve professional development:

- participants' reactions;
- participants' learning;
- organisation support and change;
- participants' use of new knowledge and skills;
- and student learning outcomes.

This is similar to the requirements of the Kirkpatrick Model, but without the Kirkpatrick Model's focus on the strategic outcomes of training.[2] However, the Guskey model does have a focus on student outcomes, something which the more business-orientated Kirkpatrick Model does not.

Both models are interested in the outcomes: the changes that happen. We are also interested in the outcomes, in this case of the Stars Project: for example, if the students applied what they learned on the course and what issues they are encountering in the experience of this knowledge.

The Kirkpatrick Survey
The following are some of the results of the Kirkpatrick Survey as they apply to the learning environment, relevance of the programme and delivery of the programme.

Fig 3: The learning environment

The class environment helped me to learn

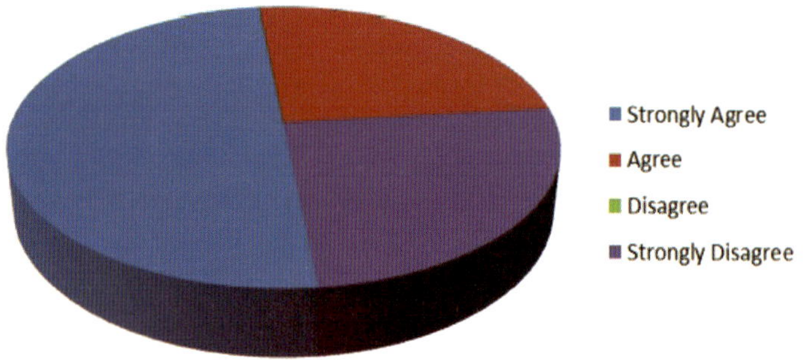

All students either agreed or strongly agreed that there were no major distractions that interfered with their learning. Additionally 75 per cent of students agreed (**Figure 3**) that the learning environment helped them but there was a significant minority that disagreed that the learning environment was good enough. From analysis of the survey it appears to be that, though overall the facilities are good, the students feel that more use of the Xiehe classrooms could be supportive.

Fig 4: Relevance - using the learning

I will be able to immediately use what I learned

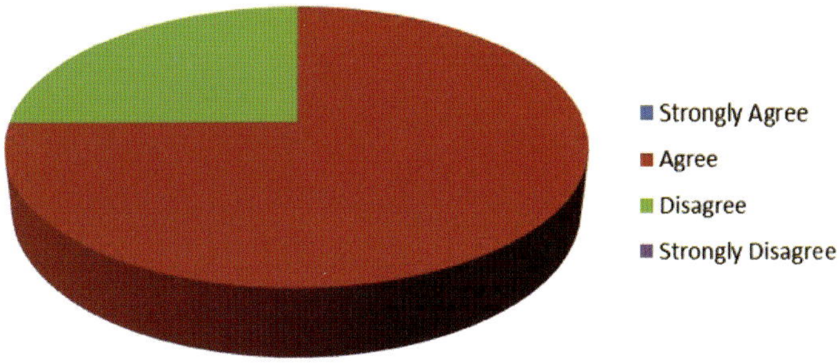

The programme was, overall, felt to be relevant as 75 per cent of students agreed that they would be able to immediately use what they learned with 25 per cent disagreeing that they would immediately be able to use this (**Figure 4**).

All students agreed that the programme material would be helpful for their success in the future. With nearly 70 per cent of students strongly agreeing (**Figure 5**)

Fig 5: Relevance - future success

The programme material will be helpful for my success in the future

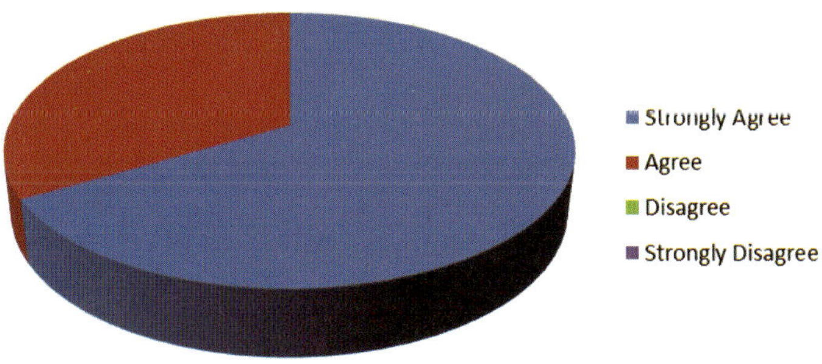

Encouragingly, all students either strongly agreed or agreed that the programme met their expectations (**Figure 6**, right). More than three quarters strongly agreed that they would recommend the programme to their co-workers (**Figure 7**, right). However, one comment in this area of the survey was '*the Stars Project would be even better if it was linked more clearly to external standards*'.

The Kirkpatrick survey also asked students to rank two items that measure *'energy for change'* (see table in **Figure 8**, below). These show that the majority of participants felt that they were able and willing to enact change as a result of their participation in the Stars Project.

Fig 6: Overall satisfaction

The programme met my expectations

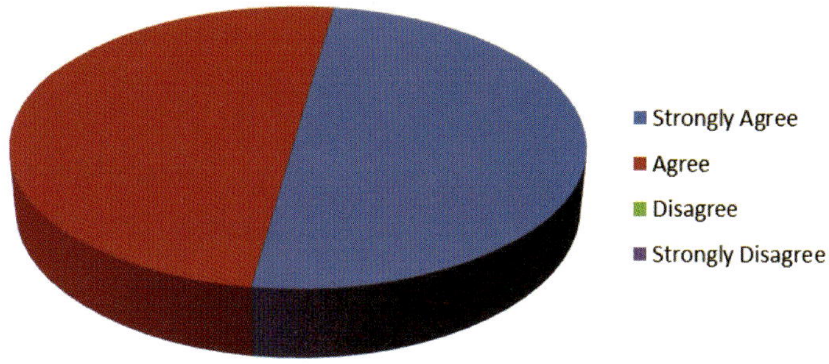

Fig 7: Recommendation

I would recommend this programme to my co-workers

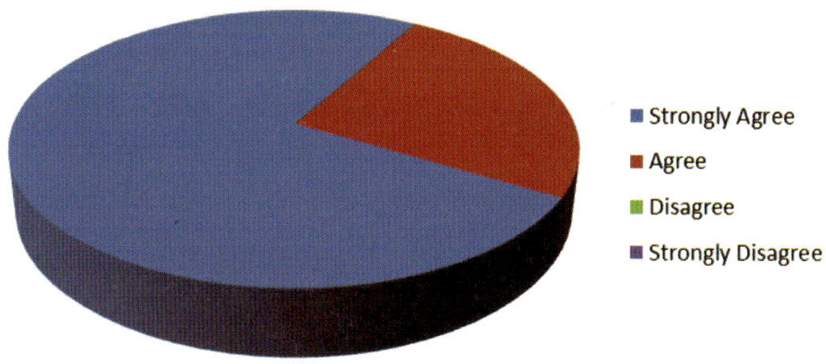

Fig 8: Energy for change

Question	Average
How confident are you that you will be able to apply what you have learned back on the job? (Select a number, with 1 the lowest and 10 the highest)	7
How committed are you to applying what you learned to your work? (Select a number, with 1 the lowest and 10 the highest)	7.75

The Guskey Survey

The Guskey Survey focuses on the acquisition and application of skills.

All students agreed that they acquired the intended knowledge and skills (**Figure 9**, below). Almost 75 per cent of them had already effectively applied the knowledge and skills acquired with just over 25 per cent unable to do so at the time of the survey (**Figure 10**, below).

Fig 9: Aquired knowledge and skills

I acquired the intended knowledge and skills

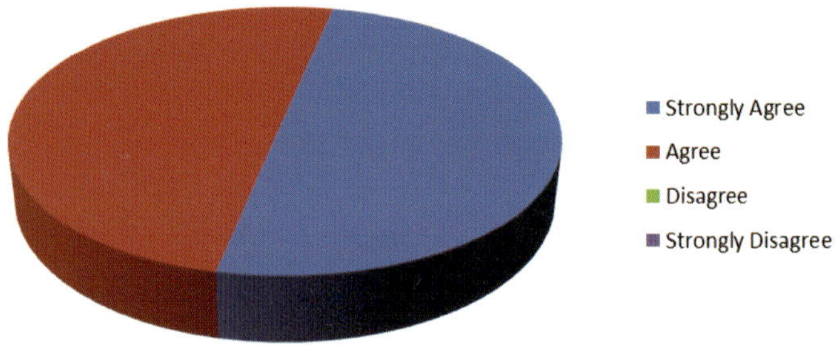

Fig 10: Applied knowledge and skills

I have already effectively applied the new knowledge and skills

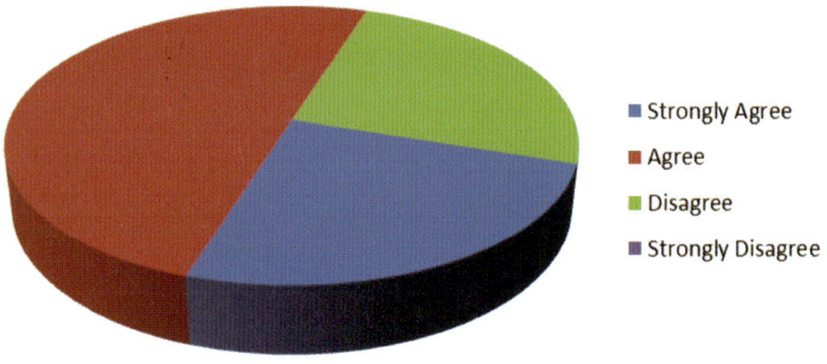

Fig 11: Applied knowledge and skills

I'm encountering challenges in applying what I learned

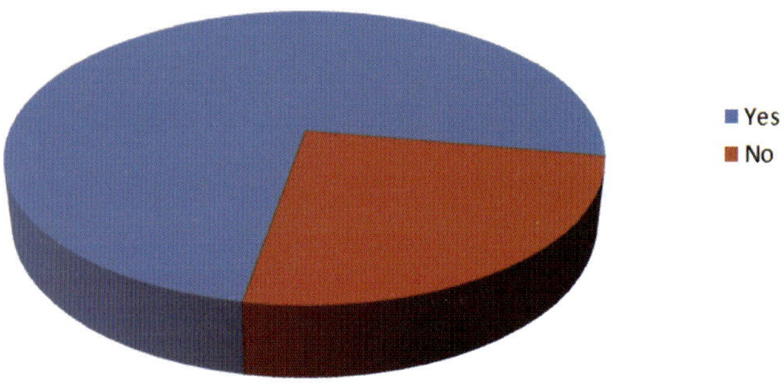

More than 25 per cent of the students stated that they were having difficulties in applying what they had learned, back in school (**Figure 11**, below left). This is a significant proportion.

Perhaps there is scope for the Stars Project to insist upon both students and presenters being able to apply what they are learning on the job during the year long course.

In the future, students could be asked to undertake projects aimed at changing internal school systems with the aim of enhancing both their knowledge and skills and those of the organisation to which they belong.

Conclusion

The Stars Project is an example of a professional development programme that has successfully fast-tracked staff into both understanding the culture of the Group and allowing them to network effectively with other people throughout the Group. It also enables Xiehe to identify future leaders. Although, as with all professional development programmes there are areas for development, these areas are surprisingly few given that this is such a new programme.

One key area for development is the possible linking of the Stars Project more firmly with recognised national and international standards. Perhaps the standards contained within international educational leadership bodies such as the International Baccalaureate Organisation or the (English) National College of School Leadership could be a guide. Additionally, there could be space for the students to specify what it is they intend to achieve by the end of the course and then for them to be assessed upon this at its conclusion. This might help to ensure that the students can apply what they have learned during their studies.

The Stars Project graduates now play an important role in influencing the overall culture within Xiehe, both within schools and the Group as a whole. They also exemplify what the Group wants to see achieved, within its *'East meets West'* mission in particular.

Talkabout

- *Discuss the advantages and disadvantages of the Stars Project as a major professional development initiative. Decide on whether or not a similar course could be introduced into your own organisation, giving reasons for your decision.*
- **Figure 11** *in the chapter suggests that a significant minority of course graduates have faced constraints back in school when trying to implement what they have learned. Suggest what Xiehe could do to try to address this problem.*

James Waldron is Secondary Vice Principal at SUIS (Wuxi).

Acknowledgements

[1] Guskey, T. (2002). *'Does It Make a Difference? Evaluating Professional Development.'* in Educational Leadership, Vol.59, No.6, pp.45-51.

[2] Kirkpatrick Partners. (2012). *Our Philosophy.* Available at: http://www.kirkpatrickpartners.com/OurPhilosophy/tabid/66/Default.aspx [accessed: 19 Dec 2012].

9.2 Xiehe teacher involvement in external degree courses

Aivlys Hardy

Under the leadership of Dr Roger Morgan, Chief Inspector/Advisor, Shanghai Xiehe Education Group and Co-Principal SUIS (Pudong), Xiehe teachers and other practitioners in Shanghai have had an invaluable opportunity to participate in a range of external degree courses provided internationally by a number of universities. This has been a key dimension of Xiehe's teacher professional development programme. The initiative has also helped, greatly, to promote Xiehe Global Schools as learning organisations for staff as well as students.

> *'It is no good encouraging children to collaborate in their learning if teachers don't act as good role models in this respect themselves.'*
>
> Edward Sarason

China is vast beyond imagining, with sandy deserts and snow capped mountains, oceans and lakes, mystical waterfalls, mythical landscapes, caverns and rock stacks, ancient hanging temples, modern towering temples of commerce and industry, motorways, speed trains and space rockets. It is vast, diverse and steeped in history and culture. An industrious nation: energetic, united and confident in its identity. There is an unquenchable thirst for discovery and an enthusiasm to explore.

As an outsider it is hard to imagine why anyone would want or need to look beyond this amazing country; and yet it looks beyond, exploring and embracing opportunities and ideas from around the globe that can be added to its reservoir of knowledge and understanding and further enrich this vibrant society.

There is a sense of confidence in China's historic position and the role and purpose of the present that catapults thinking forward to shape the future. Behind The Great Wall is a fertile land where ideas are incubated, skills nurtured and education flourishes.

A city hungry for learning

Shanghai is part of this and in a city of over 27 million people, demand for high quality is fierce and competition for high skills and qualification are self evident. It is this spirit that I believe has made external degrees such a successful venture in Shanghai. Reasons to come and teach here are various and expatriates find themselves faced with the inescapable truth that Shanghai is one stop on a learning journey: and opportunities are here. If they need convincing then they need look no further than the example set by their Chinese colleagues who pursue the external qualifications that are professional currency worldwide.

Both the present and future are made of many parts and many peoples and in Shanghai the presence of expatriates is apparent. China has attracted global attention with its phenomenal growth and potential. With these developments come the demands and expectations for a different style of education, one that will provide a world class education for the childrens' future. The foreigners here want education that is familiar, not least of all because of the language barrier that exists for many : they demand 'Western style' international schools and qualifications that have universal recognition. Many expatriates are contracted workers and will either return to their homeland or move to other world locations : they are a transient population but one which is regularly replenished. These parents want their children to not only know and understand the language and culture of China but also to have an international education.

Expatriates intending to reside permanently in Shanghai make a similar demand because 'who knows what the future may bring' and their children may choose to attend overseas universities.

Similarly, many Chinese families, who having lived and worked abroad and have returned here, are used to international 'Western style education' for their children and demand quality international schools. It is no longer acceptable that a graduate with a specific subject skill can simply stand in front of a class and proclaim themselves to be a teacher: they need to prove it with a first class professional qualification. A discerning market knows that teaching is a profession, not a job!

Rising to the challenge

Overall, many expatriate and Chinese parents in Shanghai, where *'East meets West',* require a unique blend of education. This is provided within Xiehe's Global Schools.

The Shanghai Xiehe Education Group was quick to recognise the fundamental and emerging needs of the market and actively supported the external degree courses proposed and directed by Dr Roger Morgan, in 2007, to enhance the quality of teaching and educational provision in their schools and *'to establish a learning organisation ethos in the schools'.*

Dr Morgan believes that the most valuable resource in any school is the teaching staff. Without well qualified teachers there is little chance of high quality education. In a rapidly changing world, teachers must be confident professionals prepared to adapt to meet the needs of their students, *'at any moment ... a new step in understanding be taken'.*

With many years experience in international education, higher education and teacher training, Dr Morgan knew only too well the importance of providing teachers with the opportunity to become qualified educators. He rapidly made links with the University of Sunderland in the UK and the Post Graduate Certificate in Education (PGCE) course started with 11 national and international graduates working together. During a six year period over 200 graduates have successfully completed these external courses. The reputation spread, as did the catchment, to include graduates from schools across Shanghai and beyond. SUIS (Pudong) became a natural hub for graduates pursuing qualifications with top American, Canadian and Australian Universities joining the steady stream of those taking external degree courses.

Graduates who imagined they could simply arrive in Shanghai and teach found that without a professional qualification this was not the case. Here, quality in education is a highly prized commodity, there is no compromise on the standards expected of teachers entrusted with the education of national or international children in Shanghai. The future is too important.

Some graduates who intend to make China a brief stop over in their teaching career frequently find they simply do not wish to leave. Any opportunities that may lie beyond these shores are dwarfed by the dynamic potential of the country and they opt to make their future here for themselves and their families. To be successful they need qualifications that match any in the world and so the demand for external professional and higher degrees increases: *'I was working in Shanghai for three years teaching English as a second language. I knew I wanted to become a qualified teacher and thought I would have to return to England ... then I heard from a friend working in SUIS (Pudong). I was given a fantastic opportunity to continue working in Shanghai whilst getting qualified.'* [1]

The PGCE course process

The University of Sunderland PGCE course has become extremely popular in Shanghai and many graduates from this continue with their studies on Masters and Doctoral Degrees programmes.

The PGCE is a rigorous and well established course for graduate teachers overseas. A one year course, it has two, six week practical experience placements, one running from September to December of the academic year and the other from February to March. Graduates must successfully complete these practical teaching sections of the course and tutors from the University participate in the evaluation during a one week visit to Shanghai.

Additionally, the graduates complete regular written assignments that are submitted direct to the University for marking. As National Tutor for the PGCE, Dr Morgan provides participating schools with a comprehensive overview and documentation and is the point of contact for trainees, mentors and school staff. His experience in higher education provides expertise, stability, continuity, support and guidance for all trainees on three external degree courses. Before each teaching practice, the trainees are brought together for introductory seminars and prepared for the course. During the practice Dr Morgan arranges and coordinates the programme of visits for the University tutors.

The University appoints mentors in each school to help a trainee to learn how to carry out their job within the context of the school's systems and culture. *'They provide guidance and advice. It is a relationship which is outside the normal hierarchical structure and mentors are experienced educationalists, knowledgeable of the trainee's subject and phase, helping trainees to develop their own approaches and to make their own decisions.'* [3]

For the practical teaching placement, trainees have to sustain the learning of a class or classes of students for two, six week periods. This is complemented by written assignments marked and assessed externally by the University. This practical experience gives trainees the opportunity to work with a mentor, discuss teaching and learning, build and sustain effective relationships, increase their competence in planning and teaching lessons and understand the processes of classroom management and control. *'I grew more confident in my teaching methodologies and this inspired me to try new things and push myself.'* [1] Trainees develop the habit of reflecting on and evaluating their practice as a basis of modifying and improving their effectiveness. As one trainee remarked *'I have essentially been transformed as a planner and a thinker.'* [1]

There is no doubt that this is a demanding course for the trainees, both academically and practically. Many trainees teach full-time and all have responsibilities above and beyond commitments to school. For an academic year their life is the PGCE. During the practical element there are Teaching Experience files to be constructed and maintained in addition to a Teaching Standards File that requires robust and regular evidence of all aspects of the skills and crafts demanded of a qualified teacher. Without successful completion of these documents, the practical element would fail. Trainees have the responsibility *'to ensure that school placements are fruitful experiences for the school as well as themselves.'* [4] The Xiehe trainees certainly fulfill this requirement, not only during their practice but beyond, in their influence on teaching and learning standards as full time teachers in the schools: *'I am more aware of the expectations of an exceptional teacher and continue to find ways to achieve this.'* [1]

Remarkably, the Shanghai PGCE trainees have achieved a 100 per cent success rate on the teaching practice for the duration of the course. Amongst the trainees there has been a yearly average of 12 Xiehe teacher participants. Of these, approximately half have elected to continue with a higher degree in education, enrolling on UK Masters and Doctorate courses with Sunderland, Warwick or Leicester Universities. On completion, several have moved to work overseas and to other schools in Shanghai and China. However, many have elected to remain in the ever expanding range of Xiehe Global Schools and several have been promoted to senior and management positions. The PGCE course is not student 'age specific' and it attracts a diverse range of trainees working in kindergartens, primary and secondary schools across a complete range of subject areas.

In addition to Sunderland University's Post Graduate, Masters and Doctorate Courses, SUIS (Pudong) is the Shanghai destination for students coming to

Graduates from the Sunderland University PGCE course celebrate the completion of their studies.

study in China from The University of Warwick for the practical element of their full time PGCE course in the UK. These students come on an annual basis, for six weeks in February, and are affectionately known as 'the Shanghai Five'. For three years SUIS (Pudong) has mentored them and one has returned to take up a full time teaching position within the school. The Warwick post graduate students have made a very significant professional contribution within the school as trainee teachers. Like the Sunderland trainees, the Warwick students' University Tutors visit SUIS (Pudong) to check progress, liaise with Dr Morgan and ensure University standards are met. Teaching placements and mentoring for teachers also occurs at SUIS (Pudong) for trainees working with Universities in Australia and America.

Benefits for all

It is obvious that all the trainee teachers derive considerable benefit from these external courses, the most apparent being that, on successful completion of the PGCE, they are awarded a professional qualification that is recognised worldwide: *'I was particularly attracted to the opportunities it would create for living around the world and in a sense it acts as a relative guarantee of good work for the foreseeable future.'* [1] They broaden their opportunities to work in any global location.

For the transient teacher this provides them with a passport to travel and earn. For Chinese teachers it gives them the chance to work in another country and gather Ideas to contrIbute to the melting pot of ideas simmering with respect to the future of China.

Other National trainees are committed to knowing and understanding about education in the broadest terms and to contributing positively to the changing and emerging needs of their school in Shanghai. Teachers change their perspective as they work towards the PGCE: *'The degree has exceeded all my expectations in terms of its benefits to my general teaching and my outlook on the profession. I find myself at the end of the course with a genuine enjoyment in what I do.'* [1] They discover not only the value of education but also an awareness of their professional responsibility to ensure their students receive a high quality education. They identify with and choose to make their professional commitment here in Shanghai.

Similarly, expatriate trainees who have lived in China for several years (some of whom are married and believe their children will have a better life in Shanghai than elsewhere) recognise the benefit of having access to higher education to improve their career opportunities and the contribution they can make: *'it was extremely beneficial for me, it enabled me to continue living in Asia. It also gave me the opportunity to work full time, alongside my studies, which of course helped me pay my fees. The PGCE route I took gave me credits toward my Masters Degree, reducing the course from three years to two.'* [1]

The following summarises some of the main advantages of the external degree course programme for Xiehe Global Schools through a consideration of eight different elements.

1. **Building a quality work force for the schools.**

    a. The programme provides high quality professional qualifications for teachers.

    b. The quality of school based and inter-school in service training improves. Newly qualified teachers are encouraged to share 'good practice' by actively contributing to regular in service sessions. They also participate in reciprocal observation of one another's teaching to enable valuable discussion and the exchange of ideas.

    c. PGCE students return to the schools with new skills of 'international' co-operation and mutual respect.

2. Providing quality staff for new and expanding schools.

a. Staff recognise career opportunities expand within the Group for those with good qualifications. There is mobility between the various school campuses and a flexibility that allows for skills to be shared between them.

b. Well qualified staff from other schools participating in the Shanghai PGCE programmes are attracted to work in Xiehe schools.

c. Teachers formerly on placement for external degree qualifications frequently return to work in Xiehe schools.

3. Enhancing the reputation of the school.

a. Parents recognise that the investment in well qualified teachers will benefit the investment they make in their children's education.

b. External higher degree providers are attracted to work in tandem with Xiehe and further extend their professional programmes.

4. Improving the work environment of the school.

Teachers who have worked together for professional qualifications become empathetic co-workers. They learn to co-operate, collaborate, evaluate and solve problems. They form a cohesive workforce with common goals and standards.

5. Building a cohesive curriculum and approaches to teaching and learning with common goals and appreciation of values and standards.

a. Western teachers have different cultural and educational backgrounds : there can be a tendency for some staff to cling to programmes of teaching and learning that are familiar to themselves, rather than understanding broader curriculum issues: *'the degree has transformed my teaching to something which I now consider to be a daily set of opportunities. The broader picture of teaching and new aspects have been revealed to me.'* [1]

b. Input from the trainees on external degree courses helps change the views on curriculum and teaching, opening up new possibilities.

c. Teachers participating in external degree courses are equipped to confidently articulate curriculum and teaching issues to parent groups. This enhances the quality of provision for parents and encourages cohesive expectations.

d. With more PGCE trained teachers forming a major element of Xiehe Global Schools' staff at all levels, new strategies have been implemented to provide more robust, relevant and sustainable curriculum approaches: *'the PGCE has really enabled me to critically evaluate my teaching and has taught me a variety of different strategies for teaching. The written assignments gave me background knowledge on critical elements of the curriculum, whilst the teaching practices gave me the opportunity to try out these strategies with regular feedback from an experienced mentor. Each week I felt I was learning something new about myself personally and professionally.'* [1]

6. School management improves.

One pioneer PGCE trainee, currently enrolled on an external Doctoral programmed stated *'I have a Chinese Education Bachelor Degree and Masters of Business Administration, which fit me well for working in Chinese schools. However, this is not enough to enable me to become an expert in international education. I want to further my study in overseas university programmes so I can support my co-principal better in running an international curriculum.'* [1]

7. Graduates emerge with a clearer understanding of the *'East meets West'* concept.

One PGCE trainee commented *'I have found co-teaching with a Chinese teacher both insightful and challenging, combining two very different attitudes and teaching styles … trying to find a balance that we were both happy with and one that worked for the children…. It was a good opportunity to talk and evaluate together.'* [1]

8. Broadening opportunities for students and creating a culture of excellence.

It is said that 'education is a window to the world' and teachers and institutions that value further education can inspire students to work hard and aspire to achieve higher. Education is simply the soul of a society as it passes from one generation to another.[5] Last year history was made in Xiehe with the hosting of the joint STARS and PGCE Graduation Ceremony. The visiting speakers were the Pro Vice Chancellor of the University of Sunderland, who conferred the external degrees and the Principals of Bader College UK and Queen's University of Canada. Queen's University offers higher and graduate degrees and the Principal visited Xiehe secondary campus schools to talk with senior students about these courses.

If you teach students facts, you give them a glimpse of a garden; if you teach students to learn then you enable them to create their own garden for a lifetime. Teachers on external education degree courses learn how to teach students to learn; they become educators and education is the route to the future: *'the quality of an education system cannot exceed the quality of its teachers.'*[6]

Aivlys Hardy is a Xiehe Education Consultant and Inspector and has responsibilities for mentoring PGCE students.

Conclusion

The initiatives summarised in this chapter have brought together Chinese and Western teachers in what has been a major professional development strategy for Xiehe. This has helped to further promote the growth of a learning culture for staff in the Group's Global Schools.

Talkabout

- *Consider what more could be done to enhance your school's and/ or organisation's professional development programme.*
- *How does your school attempt to ensure that feedback from colleagues involved in external degree courses is shared with the rest of the staff? How might more be done in this respect?*

Acknowledgements

[1] University of Sunderland and University of Warwick PGCE Trainees.

[2] Isaacs, S. *'The children we teach'.*

[3] Faculty of Education and Society University of Sunderland Document: *'Staff Guidance and Trainee Support 2012/2013'.*

[4] Faculty of Education and Society University of Sunderland Document: *'Practice of Teaching Guidance ED 2008'.*

[5] Chesterton, G. K.

[6] Rose, J. *'Independent Review of the Primary Curriculum'* (McKinsey and Company. 'How the world's best-performing school systems come out on top')

10 Self evaluation as a key school improvement strategy in the Xiehe Global School

Trevor Higginbottom and Cathy Wang Yi

Over the last decade school self evaluation has been regarded as a key curriculum management strategy in Xiehe Global Schools.

> ***'The essence of a successful organisation is the search for improvement, to which self evaluation is the key.'***
>
> Michael Barber

School self evaluation has been a constant theme throughout this book, frequently as a natural follow up to policy formulation and implementation (for example with respect to bilingual education (**Chapter 4.3**), generic teaching and learning (**Chapter 5.5**), and continuity in the 2-19 years curriculum (**Chapter 6.2**).

In this chapter the authors provide a summary of the various processes of self evaluation which have been developed by Xiehe schools over the last decade. Also, of the ways in which these processes have been used as a key school improvement strategy, not least in ensuring that the benefits of Chinese and Western inter-stream professional teacher collaboration have a positive impact at the classroom level.

Self evaluation and development In Xiehe's first Global School based on 'outstanding schools' criteria

Prior to the opening of the first Dual Stream School Xiehe Bilingual School, in September 2003, the Chinese and Western senior managers across the two streams agreed on two key management principles, as follows.

There should be an attempt to develop the school based on eleven agreed criteria for defining outstanding schools, based on worldwide research on school effectiveness.

Self evaluation should be regarded as the key to school improvement, with every attempt being made to evaluate the extent to which these 'outstanding schools' criteria were being implemented, in a carefully planned manner and an ongoing basis.

The table in **Figure 1** (opposite) is a summary of the link which the school established between the agreed outstanding schools criteria and the self-evaluation process.

The criteria are highly summarised in the table, for implementation purposes they were expressed in a much more detailed form.

Fig 1: Self evaluation and outstanding schools

Characteristics of 'Outstanding Schools'	How self evaluation within the Xiehe Bilingual School promotes these characteristics
There is strong professional leadership from both senior and middle management.	Teachers are given an opportunity to evaluate the school's leadership.
All the staff have shared vision and goals which creates a consistency of approach across the school.	'Vision' and 'goals' are defined and shared by all staff (by means of evaluative criteria) and then promoted through school self-evaluation/ improvement. A consistent approach ensures that all students receive a quality education.
There is concern for the quality of the learning environment.	'Quality of the learning environment' can be defined through evaluative criteria.
There is emphasis on teaching and learning as the school's key focus.	Defining criteria and using them as the basis for ongoing school self-evaluation/school improvement ensures that the staff focus on the teaching and learning process.
Staff have explicit high expectations of their students.	'High expectations' need to be defined in terms of evaluative criteria within the school self-evaluation/ improvement process.
Students receive positive reinforcement from their teachers.	This is an important dimension of the school's framework for evaluating teaching and learning.
There is ongoing self-monitoring and evaluation of all aspects of the school's work.	This is a key ongoing task within the school.
Students know and understand their rights and responsibilities.	Students are involved in the evaluation process.
There is purposeful teaching.	'Purposeful teaching' is defined by means of evaluative criteria within the process of school self-evaluation/improvement.
The school is a learning organisation for the staff as well as the students.	Establishing a climate/ethos of school self evaluation/improvement creates a learning organisation for staff within the school.
There is a strong, effective home-school partnership.	Parents are involved in the evaluation process.

The aims of self evaluation

The following were regarded as the main aims of self -evaluation within the school.

- To define what the school regards as 'quality education' and to ensure that the students benefit from it.
- To support policy formulation and implementation.
- To support development planning which ensures that the pace of change is realistic.
- To establish a spirit of ongoing improvement, inquiry and investigation amongst the staff which ensures that the school is a learning organisation.
- To ensure that the school feels a sense of ownership and accountability for its own development.
- To provide the school with its own research data to enable it to judge its own effectiveness.
- To complement any external quality assurance process, for example inspection or accreditation.
- Overall, to promote the school's development and thereby enhance student achievement.

A climate of self-evaluation

To establish a supportive climate of self evaluation within the new school, the Chinese and Western senior managers felt that the following were required.

- A commitment from the leadership to the value of self-evaluation and the principles summarised below.
- Understanding of the need for all staff to feel empowered and to be involved.
- Clear understanding by all staff of the processes involved in 'monitoring' and 'evaluation'.
- Appropriate whole school co-ordination of 'monitoring' and 'evaluation' by a member(s) of staff.
- Acknowledgement of the importance of these processes in the job descriptions and working practices of all managers within the school.
- Quality time available both for the processes to be undertaken and for the essential review and follow up planning.
- Formulation of clearly defined evaluative criteria relating to policies associated with the main dimension of the school's work and to its development planning targets.
- An agreed framework of decision making which ensures that all staff feel a sense of ownership regarding the evaluative criteria.
- Recognition that change is most effective when there is an appropriate balance between 'top down' and 'bottom up' pressures.
- Acknowledgement that students, parents, community representatives and external consultants, as well as staff, might usefully be involved in the evaluative process.
- Appreciation of the important 'ethical' dimensions of the process: for example, the need for trust and clear understanding of the destinations of any published outcomes of evaluation.
- Publication of outcomes of specific school based monitoring and evaluation exercises, incorporating clearly outlined recommendations. The readership of the publication is always agreed and fully understood beforehand by all participants in the exercise.
- Recognition that there must be follow up to evaluation which ensures that feedback informs subsequent practice.
- A clearly established interface between the school's monitoring and evaluation work and any external accreditation or inspection.
- Recognition of the value of sharing good practice with other schools, for example, through guideline documentation on evaluative criteria.
- Appropriate induction for new staff on the school's 'monitoring' and 'evaluation' procedures.
- Incorporation of the above principles in a whole school policy on monitoring and evaluation.

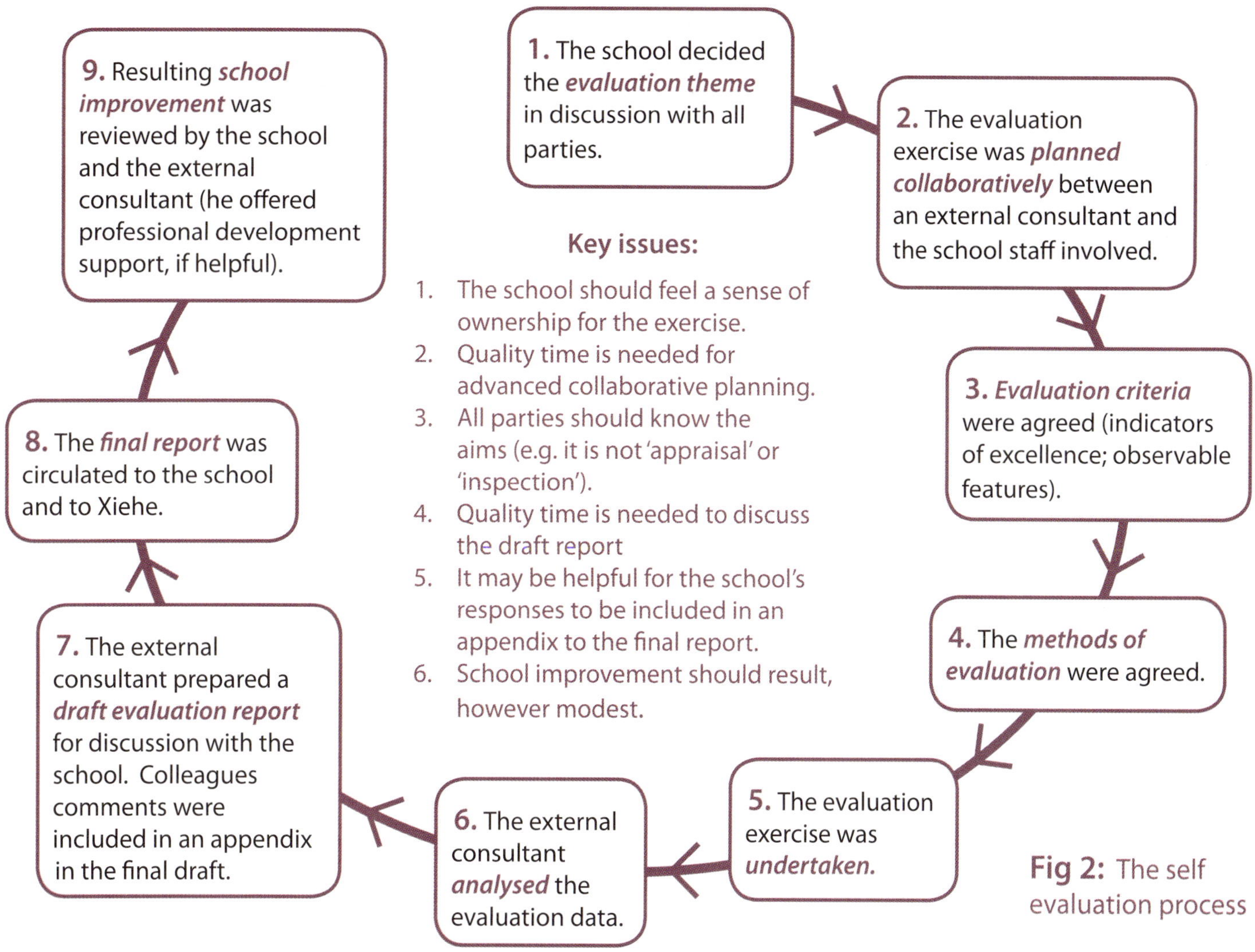

Fig 2: The self evaluation process

A climate of self-evaluation

Three terms required definition as part of the evaluation process.

Monitoring: What is happening? What are we doing? Collection of data on starting points and the position over time. Seeking patterns.

Evaluation: How does this fit with our intentions? How does this compare with our baseline? Making comparisons. Making judgements.

Follow up review: What shall we do about this? Making decisions about changing plans.

The diagram in **Figure 2** (above) is a summary of the way in which the school related self evaluation to its ongoing strategies for development and improvement.

Developmental planning

Policy formulation, implementation, monitoring and evaluation were regarded as a key feature of school development. Each policy was formulated after consultation with staff, which ensured that teacher colleagues felt a sense of ownership for the school's development.

The policies were defined in terms of evaluative criteria, expressed as 'indicators of excellence' and 'observable features' (as outlined in **Chapter 8.2**).

Any evaluation process undertaken within the school should never simply be regarded as 'an event'. It was clearly agreed by the combined Chinese and Western senior management team that there must be clear outcomes from evaluation, as a result of rigorous subsequent development planning.

The school's development plans included the following.

Fig 3: A framework for evaluating teaching and learning

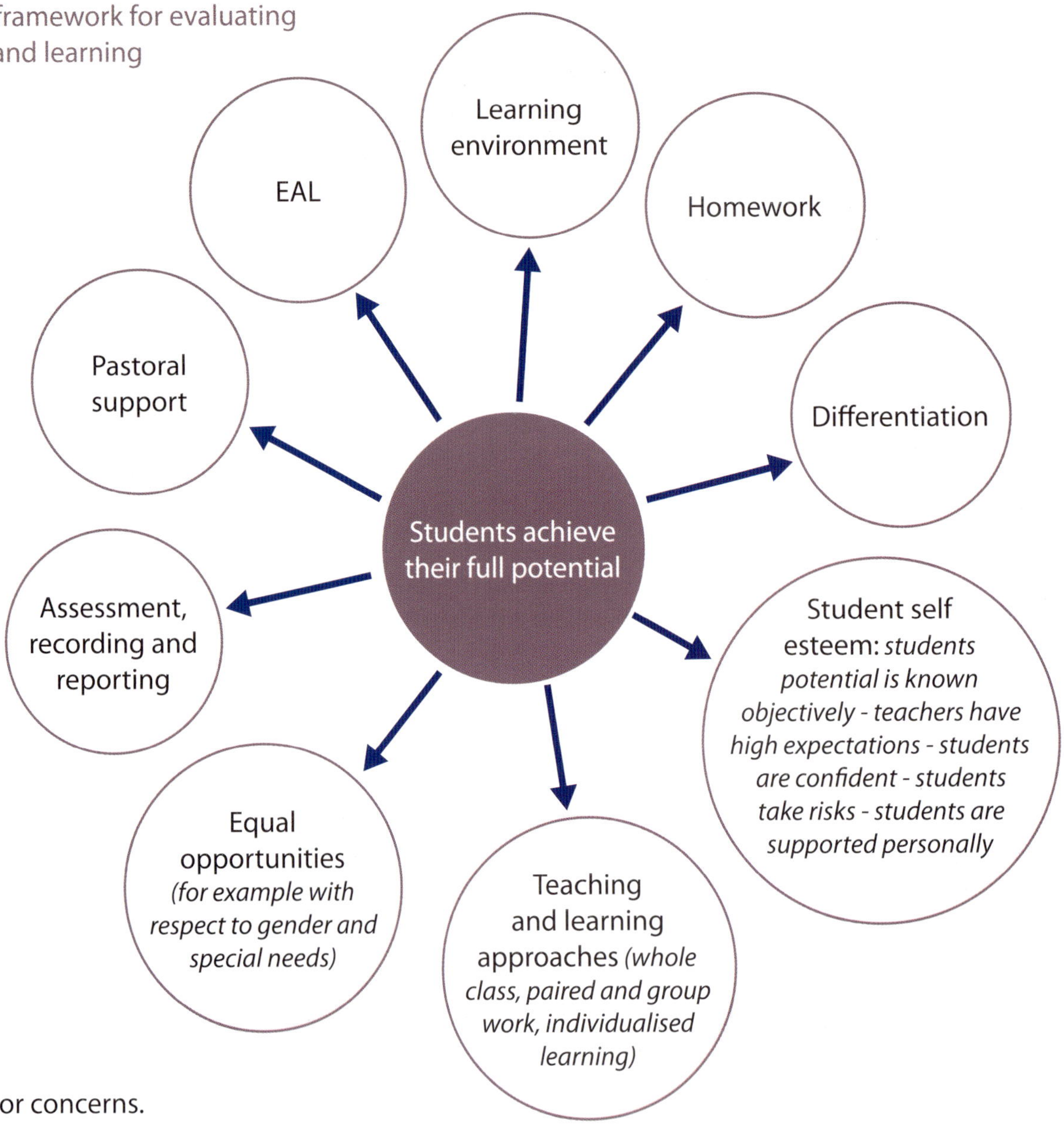

- Major concerns.
- Strategies and specific tasks.
- Timescales.
- Success criteria.
- Methods of evaluation.
- Staff responsible.
- Resources required.
- A budget summary.

The key focus in the self-evaluation was on what happens in the classroom, in relation to the school's detailed teaching and learning policy, which was expressed in terms of indicators of excellence and observable features.

As Professor David Hopkins has stated *'ultimately the only way to judge the effectiveness of a school is what happens in the classroom'.* [1]

Figure 3 above is a summary of the framework the school used for evaluating its teaching and learning.

Self evaluation strategies

The school developed a wide variety of self-evaluation approaches, adopting the best of Chinese and Western practice in this respect. For example:

- individual and group annual teacher research;
- observation of 'open lessons';
- departmental and stream evaluation exercises;
- analysis of student work;
- and micro-teaching (analysis of videos of individual lessons).

Additionally the school adopted many of the following methods of self-evaluation summarised by Professor John Macbeath.[2]

1. Asking

- Interviewing, Questionnaire, Surveying } e.g. students, teachers, parents

2. Observing

- Lesson observation
- Shadowing a student through e.g. a day

3. Collecting

- Analysing student work
- Keeping an ongoing portfolio of student work

4. Discussing

- With a group of students
- With fellow teachers (either an individual or a group)

5. Measuring (Quantifying)

- Measuring student performance

6. Imaging

- Taking photographs throughout a class, the school; for subsequent analysis
- Videoing lessons

7. Diarying

- Keeping a personal diary e.g. of an ongoing lesson sequence

A major strategy was the whole school inter-stream evaluation exercise. The aims of such an exercise were as follows.

- To provide an agenda for the teachers' individual/group research exercises, which followed.
- To provide the school with future development planning targets, particularly with regard to staff development.
- To share good practice in teaching and learning across the local and international streams (*'East meets West'*).
- To promote the idea of the whole school as a learning organisation for teachers as well as students.
- To support the implementation of the whole school's teaching and learning policy and therefore to improve the quality of the teaching and learning.

In one particularly successful exercise undertaken the processes involved were as follows:

- Eighteen colleagues (working in nine pairs) observed 31 lessons, chosen at random: 17 lessons in the local stream; 14 lessons in the international stream.

Lesson observation at SUIS (Hong Qiao).

- Nine members of the evaluation team were from the local stream, seven were from the international stream and two from the Xiehe Group.
- The school colleagues represented a complete cross section of roles, from the principal to teacher colleagues.
- The lesson evaluation proforma was based on the evaluating criteria contained in the school's teaching and learning policy (see **Figure 4** which follows).
- The evaluation was conducted in five stages: (i) prior notice of the evaluation; (ii) prior briefing to all staff; (iii) lesson observation; (iv) presentation of the written evaluation report to the individual colleague(s) being evaluated; and (v) verbal feedback to these individual colleagues.
- The evaluation exercise was evaluated, comments were received from:
  - those colleagues evaluated;
  - the evaluators.
- The evaluation report, based on the outcomes of the exercise, contained the following headings.
  - *What the school can be pleased about.*
  - *Some teaching and learning strategies which appeared to be particularly successful.*
  - *Four main areas which the evaluators identified as key areas for school improvement.*
  - *Suggested action to support future school development planning with respect to these four targets.*

  It was felt that four development targets were sufficient. As Professor David Hargreaves has stated: *'if a school has too many planning targets it may as well have none'.* [3]

Lesson observation

Lesson observation was regarded as a very important method of evaluation because teaching and learning is the most important activity undertaken in the school.

The process of lesson observation was very complex and required great skill from the evaluator(s). Successful observation needed careful preparation and a clear understanding, on the part of both the teacher being observed and the evaluator, of why the observation is happening.

There were three stages in the lesson observation process:

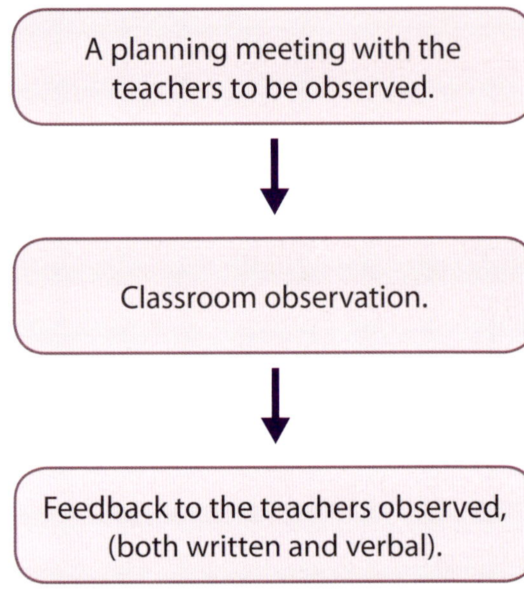

It was felt that, to be worthwhile, the evaluation needed to be structured in a way that enabled the observer to focus on agreed areas beforehand.

Figure 4 is an example of a lesson observation pro-forma which was used within the school. The evaluation criteria were taken from the school's teaching and learning policy. The evaluators' comments in **Figure 4** relate to a team taught lesson observed in the school. The lesson is not named in the interests of anonymity.

It was felt to be important that the observer ensured that the lesson proceeded in as normal an atmosphere as possible.

An attempt was made to ensure that full, constructive and timely feedback offered an opportunity to discuss what went well and what might be done differently or better next time.

Some lesson observation skills included:

- focusing on the task;
- watching very carefully;

Fig 4: Example of a completed lesson observation report using a standard evaluation pro-forma

Evaluation Pro-forma

Class observed : ______________________ Teacher(s):______________________

Subject : ______________________ Evaluator(s): ______________________

Date: ______________ Time: ______________

Evaluation criteria	Evaluator comments
Was the lesson planned appropriately, with clear learning outcomes and relevant teaching materials? (Including textbook adaptation).	Overall, lesson planning was appropriate. It would, however, have been useful to mention language (mainly English) learning outcomes. Very good range of teaching materials/visuals.
Were the students on task during the lesson, both overall and in significant parts? (In percentage terms). Was the lesson paced effectively?	Approximately 90 per cent of the students were on task, highly commendable. The lesson was very well paced, largely as a result of the variety of learning tasks employed.
Were the needs of individual students, including the most and least successful, being met appropriately? (State whether by outcome or by task).	The individual learning needs were being met by outcome, which was largely successful. Children of all abilities were coping well with the lesson content.
Were the relationships in the lesson, teacher(s)/student and student/student, appropriate? Did the teacher(s) make appropriate use of praise?	The overall classroom ethos was relaxed but purposeful. (The class appears, in this respect, to be developing with a nice 'east meets west' methodology). Both teachers/students and students relationships were excellent. There was appropriate use of praise.
Was there an appropriate balance of teaching and learning approaches? (Whole class, paired and group work, individualised learning).	Whole class and paired work strategies were used. There was a good balance in this respect. The whole class teaching was, overall, more impressive than the group work. However, in both cases the team teaching dimension was excellent.
Did the lesson promote cooperative and/or competitive learning?	There was a good balance between co-operative and competitive learning. The former could be strengthened with more structured group work.
Was there (i) an opening introduction; (ii) a central section; and (iii) a concluding section? (Comment on the effectiveness of each).	The overall lesson structure was very satisfactory. The learning was an excellent reflection of the compromise between subject and thematic work. Children were learning English as a result of the latter, very effectively (particularly in the whole class work).
Did the teacher(s) use inquiry, investigating and/or problem solving approaches?	There was a good sense of challenge throughout the lesson: both investigation of several very appropriate geographical concepts and bilingualism. (English and Chinese in the language learning).

What were the main learning outcomes? Were these made explicit in the lesson? Were they achieved?	The students understood why certain areas of the world are hotter than others, as a result of very skilful teaching by the teacher using a careful whiteboard diagram. (Excellent geographical education).
Comment on any other evaluative criteria from the school's teaching and learning policy. (eg punctuality; national/international dimensions; use of audio visual aids and/or computers; whether or not the environment supported learning; quality of the homework set).	• The lesson was very well planned in terms of time. • The international dimension might usefully have been extended. (What type of people live where it's (i) hot and (ii) cold? But this is debatable: might have made lesson too complex?). • Good use of the visualiser. • Homework set in the other lesson? (Need to discuss)
Criteria from the school's teaching and learning policy which the teacher(s) wished the evaluators to focus on particularly during the lesson.	The teachers did not provide any criteria. It would have been helpful for them to have done so. (Uniquely relating to IPC and language links).
Strengths of the lesson	• The team teaching was very effective: genuinely shared, seamless teaching and learning. • Very encouragingly, there was evidence of the transference of English language knowledge from the specialist English subject lessons (e.g. one student, in the paired work, used the quite complex sentence 'I am sorry I don't know'). • The lesson was a model of its kind, thematic study being used to promote the students' language development.
Areas for future development	• In the paired work the students: - could have been given a more specific task relating to the geography; - their collaborative work could have been more carefully structured (think/pair/share); - and there should have been an insistence on the use of English (there was too much Chinese being used). • The bilingualism dimension needs review. (eg Key words displayed in English e.g. equator).

Signed (evaluator/s): ______________________________

- listening;
- recording quickly and accurately;
- clarifying the outcomes;
- being prepared to challenge the teacher about the outcomes;
- being supportive;
- being flexible;
- asking questions of the teacher(s); and
- 'leaving the teachers feeling better.'

The following were some other questions the school's evaluators asked about lessons in addition to those summarised in **Figure 4** (devised by Dr Alma Harris, University of Nottingham, England). [4]

Evaluating a lesson – some questions teachers should ask.

- How well did the lesson go generally? What were the highs and lows?
- What did the students learn in the lesson? How do I know what they learned?
- Were my intentions for this lesson met in full, in part, not at all? Why was this the case?
- Was any learner disadvantaged during the learning? How might this be avoided next time?
- What changes could be made to improve the lesson?
- Are there any immediate actions I need to take following the lesson?
- What did I learn from this about the way in which the lesson was structured, about the students, about the content, about the approach?
- How do I ensure that the learning which took place during the lesson is consolidated?
- Would I teach this lesson again?
- How might the lesson be taught differently? What might be the differences upon learners and learning?

Some key outcomes of Xiehe Bilingual School's self-evaluation work to 2006

A consistent outcome of the school's self evaluation was the identification of the specific strengths of the Chinese and Western teachers' methods of teaching and learning. It soon became apparent that both streams had much to learn from one another (see summary in Chapter 2, page 7).

School self-evaluation had a significant impact on the morale of the teachers: they enjoyed the creativity which the process brought to their day to day work and appeared to relish the contacts they made with colleagues with very different professional backgrounds, experience and nationalities (particularly when involved in the inter-stream self-evaluation exercises described above).

Considerable discussion took place regarding the link between these processes of school self-evaluation (when the school was 'inspecting itself') and the external accreditation/inspection process. The school's view was that, with respect to the latter, much emphasis should be placed on accrediting/inspecting:

(i) the accuracy of the school's view about itself, as represented in its evaluative evidence; and

(ii) the effectiveness of its evaluation strategies.

Overall, these developments in school self-evaluation in the early years of the Xiehe Bilingual School informed subsequent developments in this regard in the Group's growing number of Global Schools. Also, a number of the accreditation organisations employed by Xiehe (for example, the International Baccalaureate Primary Years Programme and the Advanced Ed) had adopted the approach described above.

Self-evaluation developments in Xiehe's schools

In recent years there have been a number of further developments in the processes of school self-evaluation within Xiehe, relating to evaluation strategies, the ways in which exercises are organised and evaluation themes. Two examples are given below.

Student Pursuits

Student pursuit evaluation exercises have proved to be invaluable in comparing the impact of Chinese and Western curricula in Xiehe's Dual Stream Schools. The following is an example of an exercise undertaken in this type of school by an external adviser and a school senior manager.

Aim of the exercise: To compare the curriculum experiences of two very successful girls studying in Grade 5: one in the International Stream, the other in the Local Stream (particularly with regard to the pastoral and teaching and learning dimensions).

Evaluation strategy: The two girls' curriculum activities were each observed for a whole day. Amy*, in the international stream, was following the International

Baccalaureate, Primary Years Programme (PYP). She was observed for a total of five lessons. Wei*, in the local stream, was following the Chinese National Curriculum. She was observed for a total of six lessons. One of the evaluators was Chinese, the other English. This meant that the evaluation team had both a 'Chinese' and a 'Western' educational perspective. **Examples of written evidence from the 11 lessons observed.**

* The names of the two girls involved in the Pursuit were changed in the follow-up Evaluation Report, in order to retain their anonymity.

Two of Amy's curriculum experiences in the International Stream, Grade 5, International Baccalaureate, Primary Years Programme (PYP).

Lesson 1 - Home Room Lesson

- There are 22 students in Amy's class from 10 different countries. She is regarded as one of the most successful students in her class and as a good team player. Her Chinese and spoken English are both good and her written English is above average.
- This is a Home Room lesson led by a Western and a Chinese teacher in a team teaching context. They both offer Amy pastoral support.
- Amy contributes well to a review of the class's weekend activities. There is further interesting discussion on the 'Rights of the Child', United Nations, and on the rights of children in the school. There is some indiscipline in the class which rather restricts Amy's contribution. Some students, not Amy, call out their responses.
- Preparation for 'International Day' follows which gives Amy a chance to work co-operatively in a team with her peers. This part of the lesson is somewhat dominated by extrovert children in the class, not including Amy.
- Amy benefits greatly and contributes well to a very useful discussion on 'leadership skills'. Amy is able to review her own strengths and weaknesses in this respect.
- Amy is not systematically engaged in the lesson activities. There needs to be more structure in the lesson planning.
- Clothes are to be sold at the 'International Day' but opportunities for Amy to engage with her local stream peers seem(?) restricted.
- Commendably, the Western teacher later gives an opportunity for Amy to take ownership of the activities. She receives good pastoral support from him.
- There is very helpful review by Amy, and her peers, of their useful PYP Journal.
- The Western teacher has dominated the teaching here, with the Chinese teacher very much in a 'teaching assistant' role. Arguably, this does not provide Amy with an effective perspective on the role of the Chinese staff or a good 'cultural' model?
- The classroom ethos has been pleasantly informal but at times too relaxed which has meant that Amy has not always felt confident in contributing amongst some of her very dominant peers.

Lesson 3 - Unit of Inquiry

- The lesson is team taught by Amy's two Home Room teachers. The Western teacher again dominates the teaching. There is no sense of team work in the team teaching.
- He provides a very helpful review at the outset on leadership and organisational skills. Amy listens attentively and contributes well.
- There is then further planning for 'International Day'. Groups are engaged in various tasks. Amy helps to sort out various clothes. The Western teacher provides helpful, detailed instructions. He also 'instructs' the Chinese teacher.
- Amy benefits from the fact that the students are given ownership of the activities. However, the fact that extrovert students tend to dominate the class is a hindrance for this self-effacing girl.
- The Western teacher suggests selling school lost property but Amy says this is not honourable ('A student may recognise his old jacket'), so the idea is dropped.
- Amy designs a very creative advertising poster. She benefits greatly from the Western teacher's considerable enthusiasm for and commitment to the initiative.
- Amy works in a small team of five girls. This appears to be a very positive social group and she benefits greatly from this.
- The lesson could have benefitted greatly from a concluding review but simply fizzles out.

Two of Wei's curriculum experiences in the Local Stream, Grade 5, Chinese National Curriculum

Lesson 3 -Science

- The lesson venue is a very pleasant science laboratory with a most supportive learning environment. Wei's teacher is a recently employed new graduate teacher.
- This is another bilingual lesson which Wei greatly benefits from. English is the main medium. The teacher has received excellent support from the Head of Bilingual Education in the Local Stream.
- The lesson content is 'Introduction to the use of the microscope'. There are clear targets at the lesson outset. The related skills are thoroughly explained by the teacher, she uses PowerPoint admirably.
- The pastoral teacher is here to provide support. Wei relates very well to her. There are three international students in the class.
- The Chinese evaluator suggests, at one point, that the teacher's instructions on the use of the microscope could be clearer.
- The classroom ethos is extremely purposeful. Concentration levels are never below 95 per cent.
- Competitive learning strategies are used, Wei is obviously motivated by these.
- Wei hugely enjoys being a young scientist. She observes insects, sharing the microscope with two other students.
- Wei and her peers are extremely friendly to the evaluators: 'would you like to come and look through our microscope?'
- The groups all work diligently.
- The concluding skills review is first class, Wei contributes very well. Perhaps there should have been more time for the students to comment, in a more relaxed atmosphere? The PowerPoint presentation here is excellent.
- The lesson ends with a spoken rhyme: 'Ten steps on how to use the microscope'. Very creative.
- Wei has learnt much in this lesson in a science context and has also acquired further bilingual skills. The pace of her learning has, notably, been extremely fast.

Lesson 5 - English

- This lesson is taught by Wei's pastoral/class teacher. The content is a very interesting attempt to differentiate by task.
- The theme is food with the students role playing a restaurant in two differentiated groups. They order food from one another. The students have prepared excellent PowerPoint's, showing teamwork skills. Wei has enjoyed this preparation greatly.
- The restaurant activities are both creative and challenging. Wei is a waitress serving her peers. She speaks English accurately and with great confidence. This is outstanding practice in English language education. All the students are extremely well motivated throughout: there is much informal English.
- It would have been interesting for the students to have self-evaluated after these very varied and challenging learning activities.
- The English/pastoral teacher enjoys excellent relationships with her students. She strikes an excellent balance of pressure and support for their language and affective work.
- There is then a very purposeful summary through a whole class brainstorm.
- Further group work follows. Group A prepares and waits for their customers; Group B decides which of the Group A restaurants they will visit. Wei is a customer this time. There is huge enjoyment. The teacher provides an outline framework from the PowerPoint, of key questions to ask, which means that there is an effective balance of both formal and informal English in the group dialogues. Wei is involved in both.
- The pace of learning is really fast. Here again, group numbers vary from three to six.
- The homework does finally involve evaluation: Group A students are asked to consider how they might have improved their restaurant; Group B students are asked to evaluate the restaurant they visited.
- Wei's English language acquisition has been significantly enhanced in an outstanding example of good practice in English language education.

Analysis of the evidence from the 11 lessons observed.

Analysis of the lessons was summarised in tabular form (see below) as the basis for follow up discussion with the school's senior management. The evaluators emphasised that the evidence base was small but those involved in the discussion accepted that many of the points in the above table confirmed trends which had been noted previously in the teaching and learning across the two streams. Of the 12 points highlighted in the table, (j) relating to the pace of the teaching and learning, proved to be the most contentious.

A summary comparison of the two girls' curriculum experiences in the two streams, based on an analysis of the evaluative data

	Amy's IB-PYP curriculum experience	Wei's Chinese National curriculum experience
(a)	She has physical activity (to be clarified)	She starts her day with a 20 minutes programme of physical activity.
(b)	She experiences 'implicit' national education.	She has 'explicit''national' education (e.g. through the flag raising ceremonies she joins in).
(c)	She experiences global education through day-to-day dialogue with students from ten different countries.	She has less contact in class with students from different countries. However, there are three international students in her class.
(d)	She experiences a rather more 'informal' classroom atmosphere.	She experiences a more 'formal' classroom atmosphere. For example, in most lessons she stands up when answering a question in whole class discussion.
(e)	She experiences a great deal of co-operative learning, there is rather less emphasis on competitive learning.	She experiences more of a balance between cooperative and competitive learning.
(f)	Overall, her curriculum provision is more thematically based. She has more opportunities to discover the relationships between subject areas.	Overall, her curriculum is more subject based and she has more opportunities to develop explicit specialist learning targets (e.g. in science).
(g)	There is a particularly strong emphasis on inquiry in her curriculum.	Inquiry does happen in some of her subject work but it is not a specific cross-curriculum aspiration/dimension.
(h)	She is given significant opportunities to review/reflect on the process of her own learning (e.g. through her PYP journal).	She is able to evaluate her process of learning in some lessons.
(i)	She is more sharply focused on the qualities she needs to become a very effective learner (through the PYP learner profile).	The learning qualities she needs are highlighted less formally and more implicitly within lessons.
(j)	On occasions, the pace of her cognitive learning is slower to give her more time for reflection on affective issues.	The pace of her cognitive learning is extremely fast in most of her lessons. Self reflection on issues is a less significant dimension of her day-to-day studies.
(k)	She has many opportunities to be creative and to problem solve in her learning.	She has fewer opportunities to be creative and to problem solve, but it appears that the number of these is increasing.
(l)	She has two pastoral/Home Room teachers	She appears to have more lesson-by-lesson contact with her pastoral teacher. The Homeroom Teacher is available for the students during morning exercises, break and homeroom time.

Follow up targets for school improvement

Five areas for follow up were identified.

- Further development of good practice in team teaching.
- A more effective balance of the four modes of teaching and learning.
- Enhanced structuring of the processes involved in paired and group work.
- Student self-evaluation of their learning.
- Identification of gaps which have been revealed in the teachers' initial professional training and how the Chinese and Western teachers can support one another in this respect. For example, with regard to co-operative and competitive learning activities.

Associated professional development was planned.

External adviser-led exercises

Reference was made on pages 226-227 to the advantages of undertaking inter-stream staff team self evaluation exercises in Xiehe schools.

A variation on this process has been the leadership of an external adviser in leading such a staff team. This model of evaluation has nine stages.

Stage One: The external adviser meets all the school staff to review the processes involved in the exercise, to consider the evaluative criteria and to deal with any queries.
Stage Two: The external adviser meets the four teachers who will be in the evaluation team to prepare for the exercise. They represent a cross section of the management structure, including a person who was not a senior or a middle manager. There are two aims in this meeting. First, to refine/finalise the evaluative criteria; and secondly to review the evaluation processes.
Stage Three: The external adviser teaches an open lesson, observed by as many staff as possible, aimed at demonstrating good practice in the evaluation theme. The lesson is evaluated by the evaluation exercise evaluation team, but other staff are also invited to do so.
Stage Four: There are two days of lesson observation by the evaluation team.
Stage Five: The evaluation team meets to consider the outcomes of the exercise and to plan the follow up staff workshop.
Stage Six: The evaluation team presents its evaluation report and leads the staff workshop.
Stage Seven: The external adviser prepares a first draft policy (or revised policy) based on the staff workshop outcomes for the school to consider.
Stage Eight: Final policies are subsequently agreed by the school, implemented and used as the basis for ongoing review, evaluation and school improvement.
Stage Nine: The external adviser writes a report on the whole exercise with the aim of sharing any perceived good practice with other Xiehe schools.

Xiehe has found that this model of school self-evaluation has a number of key advantages.

- The staff feel a sense of ownership for the exercise because they have an opportunity to be involved in devising the evaluative criteria.
- The external adviser's involvement reduces the workload for busy staff, for example with respect to the overall organisation of the exercise and draft report and policy writing.
- Stage Three, the lesson taught by the external adviser, is a key dimension: this helps to build trust between this person and the staff, not least when they appreciate that all lessons reveal areas for improvement!
- The staff evaluators are involved, in effect, in a training for trainers' course on evaluation.
- Policy development, as part of the follow up, supports the ongoing school improvement process.
- All the evidence suggests that this model of school evaluation is a particularly useful and creative professional exercise for the staff evaluators.
- The external adviser's involvement ensures that any good practice is disseminated effectively to other schools within the Xiehe Group.

Evaluation of teacher questioning

School self-evaluation within Xiehe over the last decade has involved the investigation of many aspects of the curriculum. One popular theme has been a consideration of the process of teacher whole class questioning, informed considerably by one of the author's previous involvement in the University of Nottingham, England 'Improving the Quality of Education' (IQEA) Project. [5]

The ability to question is a vital skill teachers should have.

- Questioning is an essential, integral part of virtually all models of teaching and learning across all subjects.
- It is a means of transferring ownership of knowledge and understanding from teacher to the student.
- It is a key determinant of the level of challenge provided and progress made in lessons.
- Questioning is one of the most accessible and immediate ways for a teacher to assess the effectiveness of learning.

The purpose of questioning is as follows.

- To check on the extent of prior learning.
- To check on or stimulate recall.
- To stimulate interest, engagement and depth of thinking.
- To pinpoint future learning needs.
- To review and consolidate the main 'learnings' in a lesson.
- To diagnose learning difficulties.

It might also:

- provide an active warm-up activity;
- focus attention on the teacher or a particular resource;
- draw on the ideas of some students for the benefit of others;
- allow and encourage the expressions of feelings or opinion; and
- stimulate language development and reasoning skills.

Types of questions

Building the skills of 'question selection' is an important part of a teacher's professional development. This involves the selection of open or closed questions but also choosing the most appropriate starting point for particular purposes.

Selecting a CLOSED question

- May be more useful in judging prior knowledge
- May be more useful for testing precise recall.
- May aid rapid repetition of key facts (to help memorisation).

Selecting an OPEN question

- May provide greater opportunities for a child to show the full extent of their understanding.
- May be more useful in diagnosing lack of understanding/learning difficulties.
- May stimulate higher order thinking and learning.
- Will tend to encourage language development because it requires a lengthier response.
- May be more useful in encouraging the expression of feelings and emotion.

There have been a number of revealing school self -evaluation exercises on whole class questioning in Xiehe Dual Stream Schools. The diagram in **Figure 5** (opposite) provides a summary of the evaluative data which emerged from one such exercise.

Analysis of this type of data has enabled teachers to review good practice with respect to this key teaching and learning activity. The following are examples of indicators of excellence which have been highlighted.

- Differentiation should be regarded as a key issue within whole class questioning. For example, are the most successful students being asked challenging questions?
- One gender within the class should not be dominating the student responses.
- Individual teachers need to recognise that they may have a tendency to concentrate their questioning in one geographical area of the classroom.

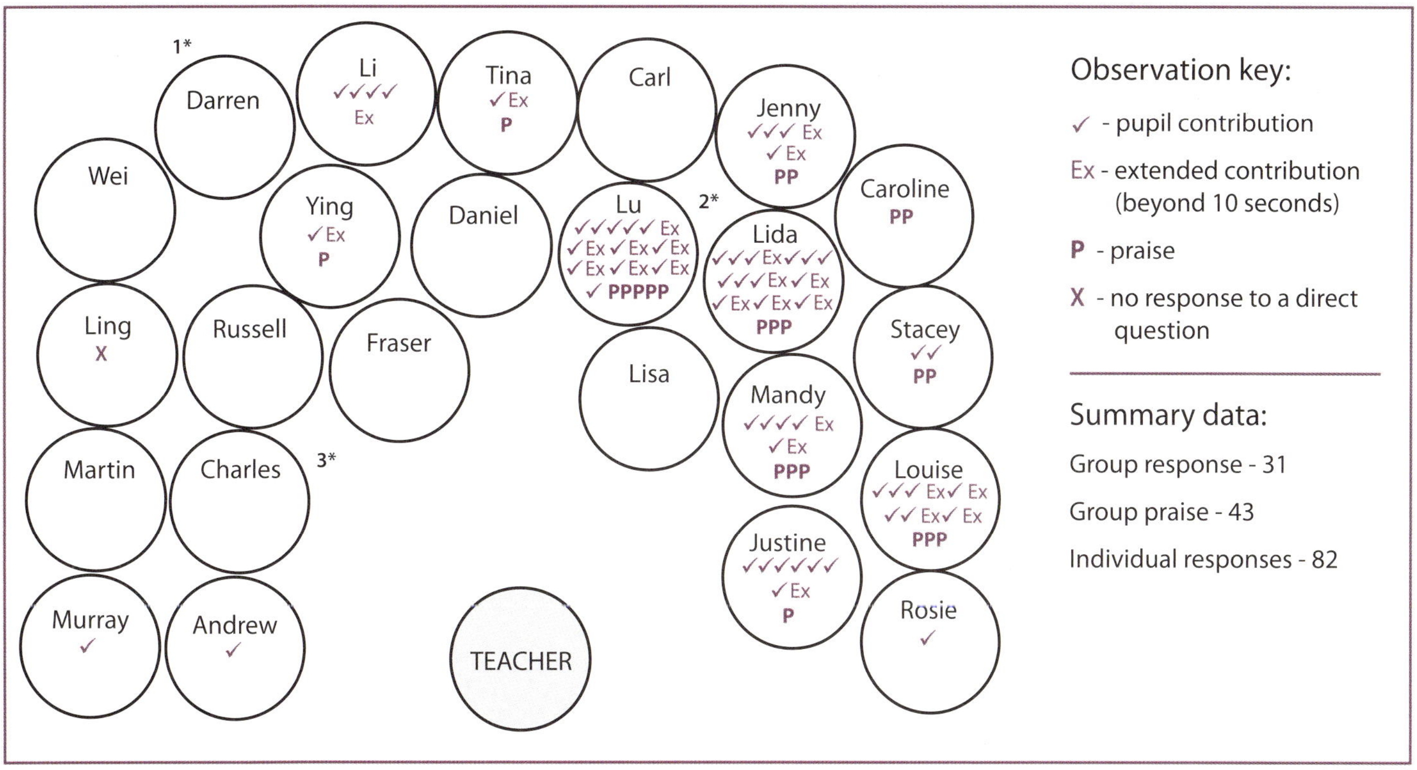

Fig 5: Example of questioning analysis

- The teacher needs to consider the balance between asking students to 'volunteer' the answer or whether they are 'conscripted to do so'.
- Extrovert/over-confident/outgoing students must not be allowed to dominate.
- Effective class questioning can do much to enhance student self esteem and confidence.
- Self-evaluation should include reviews of concentration levels within a teacher's whole class questioning. Could these be enhanced? If so, how?
- Are the students being asked to ask each other questions?
- Are the students being encouraged to take risks in their responses?
- What strategies is the teacher using to encourage shy students?
- Overall, the process requires careful planning.

Here again, Chinese and Western teachers have much to learn from one another in this regard. For example: the former often involve students as whole class questioners, in the role of 'little teachers', which promotes individual student self esteem and supports the development of a collaborative learning culture within the class; there is evidence within Xiehe classrooms which suggests Western teachers over-praise and Chinese teachers under-praise.

A significant school self-evaluation outcome: concentration in the Chinese classroom

In working together for almost a decade on school self evaluation in Xiehe's Dual Stream Schools, the authors of this chapter have been able to explore the distinctive 'classroom cultures', respectively, of the Chinese classroom in the local streams, and the Western classroom in the international streams. There are many interesting differences but the most significant comparison is in terms of student concentration levels.

In the local stream concentration levels are rarely below one hundred per cent throughout the lessons, some of which are one hour in duration. In contrast, although the international classroom culture has some excellent, distinctive features, the average concentration levels are approximately seventy five per cent. These very significant differences in concentration levels between the Chinese and Western classrooms can, arguably, be partly explained by cultural and values driven factors but also by a number of classroom management dimensions.

Several striking cultural differences between China and the West appear to affect classroom attitudes: in China parental authority is sacrosanct rather than negotiable as it is in the West. If children are given too many choices, for example what to eat, how to amuse themselves, perhaps they regard classroom concentration as a matter of choice. Also, Chinese parents have very high expectations of their children, much higher than in the West, and consequently demand much more of them in terms of study and achievement. Chinese children are expected to listen very carefully when their elders are speaking and to respond quickly to them if elders ask. Traditionally, they treasure the knowledge of their elders. Chinese parents also lay down much clearer moral guidelines in terms of behaviour and responsibility, in contrast to the more laissez-faire Western mentality. Also the Chinese family is given much more importance within society, with parents expected to assume greater responsibility for their children.

Considerable attention is given to classroom concentration by Chinese society. There has been much study in China on different perspectives of this issue. For example, with respect to physiology, psychology, behaviouristic issues and nutrition.

Within Xiehe, however, very successful classroom management also appears to be a critical factor in ensuring high concentration levels. Lessons in these local streams are now far removed from the often stereotypical Western educator's view of Chinese classrooms: a punitive ethos, extensive drilling, and an over-reliance on the textbook and whole class learning approaches. Generally, in local stream lessons the pace of learning is extremely fast and even within forty minutes the teaching and learning can involve carefully structured whole class, paired, group work and individualised approaches. There is a good balance between the learning of subject objectives and their application in day-to-day settings. Relationships between teacher/student and student/student are excellent overall.

High concentration levels also appear to be promoted by often very creative competitive learning techniques which reward differing groups of students for their attitudes to learning, in particular. Such techniques, as well as enhancing motivation, also foster student enjoyment which is another characteristic of many lessons. Overall, ensuring students' attention is a key indicator of classroom management for Chinese teachers.

The vast majority of the local stream lessons are rigorously planned with particular attention being paid to progression in the learning. There is nearly always initial review of previously learnt targets and a concluding summary of those attempted in the current lesson, but rarely in a regimented manner. Crucially, a key aim of the planning is to ensure that students are fully aware of the learning objectives within lessons.

Two external factors appear to further promote concentration levels. First, the pastoral/class teacher, who usually does not teach the class extensively, plays a key role in supporting his/her students by frequently being present at the start and conclusion of many lessons. Secondly, students in the local stream begin most days with at least a twenty minutes spell of rigorous physical education drills. There might well be a link between their physical well being and mental alertness?

This is just one glimpse of the Chinese classroom within Shanghai's education system. If, however, it is at all typical it might well help to explain the now well known fact that the city leads the world in the performance of fifteen year olds in maths, science and reading, according to recent OECD PISA surveys.

There are surely messages here for Western teachers, educational administrators and politicians. As in so many other respects (for example, social cohesion, crime, delinquency and the care of the elderly), Western educators need to take a far less Western-centric view of education. Just as the West has exercised great influence on other cultures in the past two centuries, there is no reason, in principle, why China should not do the same in future, in an increasingly globalised world.

Clearly, the issue of concentration is a critical issue in any school classroom and a key factor with regard to student academic attainment. It is, arguably, a dimension worthy of further extensive study within the context of comparative educational evaluation and research.

Conclusion

Xiehe Global Schools continue to learn much about the benefits, for both students and teachers, of the Dual Stream Model through the self-evaluation process.

Increasingly, there is now also an interest in evaluating how students can be most effectively prepared for global citizenship.

Experience within Xiehe over the past decade with respect to school self-evaluation suggests that there are two key dimensions to the process:

first, evaluating should be linked, overall, to the cycle of policy development and implementation within the school; and

secondly, it needs to be fully accepted that without rigorous follow up in terms of ongoing school improvement, evaluation is a fruitless activity.

Undoubtedly, evaluative inquiry is a process which benefits teachers as well as students within these Xiehe 'educational learning laboratories'.

Talkabout

- *Consider why school self-evaluation, if conducted rigorously, can lead to school improvement.*
- *Review the current strategies your school adopts regarding self-evaluation and suggest areas for improvement.*
- *Discuss the ways in which an external evaluator might be most usefully involved in a specific self-evaluation exercise in your school. What expertise and professional skills should this person possess in order to undertake this work successfully?*
- *Study* **Figure 5** *on page 236. From this evaluative evidence suggest six areas for improvement that the teacher should consider in his questioning strategies.*

Acknowledgements

[1] Hopkins, D. (1989). *Evaluation for School Development.* Open University Press.
[2] Macbeath, J. (1998). Extending Opportunity. DFEE
[3] Hargreaves, D. H. (1991). *The Empowered School.* Cassell Educational Limited.
[4] Harris, A. (1998). The Centre for Teacher and School Development.
[5] IQEA, School of Education, University of Nottingham, England.

An '*East meets West*' approach to Maths provides an educational theme for evaluation in the Xiehe Global School.

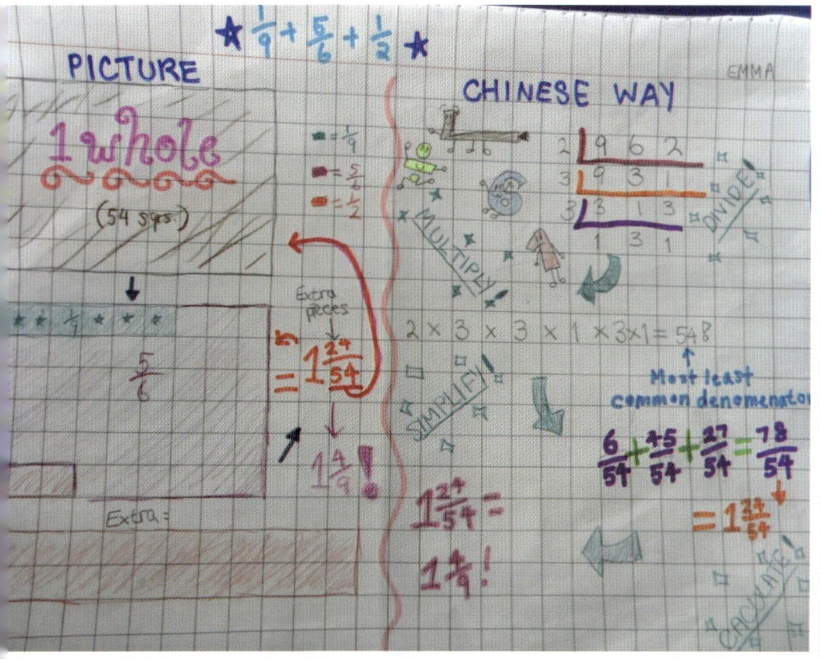

11 The Shanghai Xiehe Education Group's future mission

Professor Hu Wei

Xiehe's founder describes the Group's future aspirations.

> ***'Ensure you have a clear mission, owned by all in your organisation, constantly evaluated in terms of impact and reality not rhetoric'.***
>
> Lingbiao Hu

Looking towards the next ten years, Xiehe will push forward with both the modernisation and globalisation of its education system. The emphasis will be on further development, on enhancing quality and on specific educational innovations. New strategies for resource allocation will be considered. A key aim for our students will be to better equip them to become global citizens.

In order to achieve these objectives we will need to accomplish the following.

- The Group's management relationship with individual schools will be clarified: it will offer professional service rather than prescriptive administration and be a reactive rather than a pro-active planner with schools.
- The central management structure will be reviewed with greater clarity in terms of the management, school operation and quality assurance dimensions.
- There will be a more holistic approach to the management of our kindergartens, primary and secondary schools; to local and international streams, and to academic and non academic education.
- More staff with an international background will be appointed.
- Education should not be isolated from the rest of society. The Group, therefore, will strengthen its interaction with government, social groups, local communities and overseas agencies. Resources will be made available for this purpose.
- There will be further improvements in the structure and layout of all our education campuses, given that this factor obviously impacts on the quality of education. Each campus building will relate to historical heritage, culture, regional location and curriculum innovation.
- Innovation will continue at the same speed as in the last two decades. Traditional ideological, institutional and regulation barriers will be removed as far as possible.
- The Group will continue to promote and combine the very best of Chinese and Western educational practice. Teacher-centred, classroom-orientated and textbook driven education will be further removed from Xiehe teaching and learning at all levels.
- School quality, the enhancement of social awareness and the development of Xiehe's reputation as a global education provider will be key priorities.
- It is felt that future progress will be achieved particularly through sharper target setting,

the further implementation of school self evaluation and the involvement of government, the community and parents in quality assurance within the process of overall development.

- Greater continuity in education from kindergarten to higher education will be sought, together with improvements in the English as an additional language (EAL) centres and the process of allocation of students to our schools.
- There must be a more inter-related, collaborative system of cross phase education and management (see **Chapter 6.2**).
- We will take care to preserve the unique characteristics of individual schools whilst ensuring that all of them focus on globalisation and environmental protection.

In order to achieve the above, we will ensure that the following happens.

- We must view Xiehe's *'East meets West'* approach to education less in terms of the best characteristics of each but more holistically as simply what is best for students in enabling them to be effective 21st century citizens.
- We will continue to develop a three step approach to the curriculum: the Local Stream Chinese National Curriculum, the hybrid *'East meets West'* Pioneer Curriculum and the International Stream curricula, such as the International Baccalaureate, the English National Curriculum and the American High School curriculum. The local streams will focus more on the transdisciplinary thematic approach (see **Chapter 5.1**) and the Pioneer Stream will be expanded based on the principles outlined in **Chapter 5.5**. There will be more emphasis in the international streams on the advantages of China's traditional education and on our children learning more about the host country of China, for example its culture, society, history and geography. In taking this three dimensional approach, we shall be moving closer towards our goal of excellence in global education.
- We will ensure that our schools are not merely preparing students for overseas education. We will maintain our practice of not selling international educational qualifications to intermediary organisations or businesses. Xiehe's aim will be to develop its own distinctive 'brand' of global education, including inquiry methodology. Our students will be educated, as far as is feasible, to develop individual personalities with vision, competence in analysis and the ability to make sound judgements.
- The extended use of information technology will be a key feature of the teaching and learning process in Xiehe classrooms. This will enable us to promote educational innovation, digital teaching, online teaching, enhanced EAL acquisition and, significantly, sharper differentiation in the learning process. This will lead, overall, to the more effective development of 'well rounded' students.

Our combining of Chinese and Western cultures, in the educational interests of all our students, remains the eternal dream of the Xiehe Education Group. This can only be achieved through continuing mutual collaboration worldwide with all our education partners.

Talkabout

- *Discuss the benefits of having a school mission statement.*
- *What are the most effective ways of ensuring that the aspirations of a mission statement are achieved in practice?*
- *If you have a school mission statement, review this in light of the need to prepare your students for both national and global citizenship.*

12 Two external perspectives on the publication: 'East meets West'

The Future of Chinese Education: integrating Local and Western approaches to teaching and learning

Professor Gu Zhiyue
East China Normal University, Shanghai

Introduction

The basic education history of China has witnessed two foreign educational and cultural influences. First the 'Western Learning Spreading to the East' in the early 20th century, when new schools and modern subject teaching broke the previous traditional educational pattern of academic study which focused on the imperial examination-oriented education: 'Four Books and Five Classics'. This introduced modern scientific subjects such as geometry, algebra, physics, and biology, thus achieving the 'First Industrial Revolution of Chinese Education'. The second influence occurred in the 1950's, the early period after the foundation of the 'New China', when it was urgent to cultivate a great number of constructions and successes for the socialist cause. Experts from the former Soviet Union assisted us in compiling the first set of textbooks for primary and middle schools of the 'New China' featured in the six-three-three-year system. Kairov's educational thoughts cultivated the first-generation people's teachers of the 'New China' and guided its education to develop gradually from nothing into a fairly complete system and to achieve the socialist transformation of Chinese education.

At present, Chinese basic education is largely the derivative of these two foreign educational ideas and systems. All educators in primary and middle schools, from the principals to the teachers, still promote subject-oriented teaching concepts, taking the completion of teaching programmes, curriculum standards and learning tasks regulated by the textbooks, as the primary tasks of the schools and the starting points and destination of all their work. All affairs of the schools are focused on completing the tasks of lesson standards and textbooks. School students are mainly challenged with these demands. Can you learn and grasp them? If yes, then you can follow the curriculum of the higher level; if no, in failing the exam, you have no other choice but to undertake pre-job training and then to look for a job.

Though revised nationwide many times since 1949, the textbooks in Chinese primary and middle schools are still the products of the planning system. Before 2000, primary and middle schools throughout China used the unified textbooks, which are published by the People's Education Press. The new curriculum reforms in 2000 changed the nationwide unified teaching programme and textbooks and adopted a method whereby the country compiled the unified curriculum standard and the publishers published textbooks which were approved by the government and adopted by the local governments. There were textbooks of different editions offering options. The latter, however, were not decided by schools but by local educational administrative authorities.

It is common for a province to act as a whole to choose one or more kinds of textbooks. This approach to the content of textbooks of primary and middle schools still has its origins in the subject curriculum that the Soviet Union experts assisted China to compile in the 1950s, except that parts of its content have been deleted, some of the orders have been changed and the attainment levels revised. Because the subject construction of pedagogy in Chinese higher education did not begin until 1980, there have been no real curriculum experts in universities until the present day. The review of primary and middle school textbooks is now undertaken by experts in all subjects. These experts are often influenced by what they learnt in their primary and middle schools, and pay much attention to the inheritance of the knowledge associated with traditional subjects. Compared with those of Western primary and middle schools, the textbooks in Chinese schools focus more on the integrity of subject knowledge, however this is not fully expanded and there are insufficient opportunities for this knowledge to be applied.

Teacher Training in China

The training system of present primary and secondary school teachers in China is strictly in accordance with the requirements of subjects and disciplines. Throughout the training of four-year higher normal education, what these new teachers master, from basic courses to theory courses of a programme, is basically in the realm of professional knowledge of one discipline.

The differences between 'normal' education and 'non-normal' education lie in that two additional subjects, education and psychology, are learnt in the third year for normal students and they also take a six-week internship in primary and secondary schools. The primary and secondary school teachers in China are responsible solely for subject teaching correlated with their own programme; the organisational structure for such work is the 'teaching and research' group. Teachers from each subject group work in the same office. Here various activities are carried out among the teachers, such as formal or informal exchanges, about the topics of subject teaching, the review of disciplinary problems, the interchange of teaching skills, discussion about teaching experiences and exploration of teaching methods. Thus, in comparison with teachers in Western countries, Chinese teachers are given more opportunities to exchange, discuss and exchange professional ideas relating to one specific subject.

Primary and secondary school teachers engaged in specialized teaching are more inclined to fall into a phenomenon called 'professionalisation in a narrow sense', which means that the professional knowledge and teaching experiences of individual teachers is totally constrained to teaching materials and practices of one semester and one subject. This tends to be repeated year after year and this can result in teacher 'burnout' as no new points of growth are found and the plateau period for individuals professionally is reached.

Teaching in China

As a result of being taught by full time subject teachers, primary and middle school children in China tend to have greater mastery of subject knowledge and skills.

The preferred methods for Chinese teachers in terms of whole class teaching are as follows:

(a) Example.

To help students to understand abstract and complex concepts, the teacher will cite some visual examples which are very familiar to them, usually taken from their daily lives. Citing is one of the commonest ways for Chinese teachers to develop classroom instruction. The quality of teaching depends largely on the quantity and quality of the examples they provide.

(b) Scaffolding.

Chinese teachers tend to divide a complex and inexplicable problem into a combination of several simple ones and to ask the children to solve these simple problems one by one. Not until a series of simple problems are resolved individually and then combined once again will the complex problem be fully explored.

Let us take an example to illustrate this point:

What is 1/2 plus 1/3?

This is a classic and difficult arithmetic question in some Western countries. Why does a 1/2 plus a 1/3 not equal 1/5? Though this is a wrong answer, most teachers cannot explain the reason. How do Chinese teachers teach this? Usually, they take out three pieces of round paper with the same size but different colours, then fold one in half and cut it apart, thus creating two semicircular papers. This explains what is 1/2 and then the students understand the concept. Secondly, the second piece of round paper is cut into equal parts on a 120 central angle basis, thus explaining what 1/3 is to the students. The teacher then divides the third piece of round paper, on a 72 central angle basis, into five equal sectors. When the teacher puts the 1/2 piece of paper together with the 1/3 piece of paper and compares it to the 1/5 piece of paper, obviously the students will understand why 1/2 plus 1/3 does not equal to 1/5. This is a visual example and the students are given sensory experience of why 1/2 plus 1/3 does not equal to 1/5. Subsequently, the teacher explains the reasons: the circle is divided into several portions, one portion constitutes the basic unit of the whole body. If the whole is divided equally into two portions, 1/2 is the basic unit of the bisector; if the whole is divided equally into ten portions, 1/10 is the basic unit of the whole body. The basic unit is the dimension in this equal division.

There is a basic principle in real addition and subtraction arithmetic: only numerical values with the same attribute and dimension are able to be added or subtracted, those values with different attributes and dimensions cannot be added and subtracted arithmetic directly. For example, what is one cow plus one horse? This addition cannot hold water because the two factors have different attributes and dimensions. Even two values with the same attribute, such as one metre of cloth and ten feet of cloth, one kilogram of oil and one ton of oil, are unable to be calculated in addition and subtraction arithmetic because of their different dimensions. The teacher will further explain, after the basic principles of addition and subtraction have been discussed, that the first priority is to normalize the dimensions of the two numerical values with the same attribute, as if they are in real addition and subtraction. As far as the fractional addition and subtraction is concerned, dimensional unity refers to the reductions of fraction to a common denominator; that is, the fractions will be normalized in accordance with one single unit.

To illustrate this point, the teacher introduces two concepts: the greatest common division and the least common multiple. By using these two concepts, this complex problem can be resolved as follows: first, two denominators can be multiplied through scaffolding and their greatest common divisor divided in order to calculate their least common multiple; this is also a common denominator of the two denominators. After the fractions are calculated by this common denominator, addition and subtraction can be undertaken because there is the same denominator and dimension.

Such teaching and learning ideas are often developed in China by a small number of distinguished teachers before being included, as for example in the case above, in Chinese primary school arithmetic textbooks. Fractional addition and subtraction is a unit comprising five or six class hours of teaching content and includes fraction addition and subtraction of the same denominator, greatest common divisor, least common multiple, reduction of fractions to a common denominator and fraction addition and subtraction of different denominators.

A proportion of Chinese primary and secondary school textbooks contain problem solving exercises. Some are devised as precise formulas, such as those for abacus, multiplication and triangular induction. The students are asked to recite these formulas to the extent that they become an automatic 'mental reflex', which means that instant recall will then be expected once a signal is given. Other formulas are written as very distinct procedural steps, which may be followed by students very systematically in resolving specific problems. This phenomenon is called 'learning by standing on the shoulders of teachers'.

Such study methods can shorten students' study time and improve their learning efficiency. However, such methods require teachers to have precise professional skills. Highly qualified teachers can help their students to achieve their full potential. On the contrary, if teachers are not sufficiently well qualified they may just repeat what the textbook tells them by rote, with the background theory unexplained. This study method is far too rigid: knowledge is still knowledge while experience is still experience. Knowledge cannot be absorbed into students' personal experience if it is just for examination purposes.

Changes to Education in China

More than ten years ago, many overseas-funded enterprises entered China's major cities as part of the country's economic reforms. Many foreign parents' children came to live in these cities, forming a significant school education market. International educational organisations from many Western countries have taken up these business opportunities. In turn, this Western education is slowly influencing Chinese education.

Compared to the Chinese knowledge based curriculum, Western curricula have shown Chinese teachers how to develop new educational pedagogies. For example, in the International Baccalaureate's PYP course now adopted by many international schools in China, one dimension of the course content is 'human beings and the environment'. This focuses on six themes, 'who we are, where we are, how to express ourselves, how this world is operating, how to organize ourselves and how to share this planet'. Teachers have to develop thematic activities based on experiential learning and clearly articulated values.

The financial management course in European primary schools is similar, it requires teachers to design activities relating to 'self-acknowledgement, rights and duties, saving and consuming, planning, budgeting and the establishment of children's businesses'. These five themes enable the students to acquire very interesting and important 'economic' skills and concepts.

In the FOSS (Full Option Science System) science courses developed by the American University of California Berkeley Lawrence Hall of Science, there are 36 researchable scientific theme units for kindergarten to grade eight students (five for kindergartens, 22 for primary schools and nine for secondary schools). In each theme unit, there are four to six sets of exploring activities and three to four experiments. Each theme unit is of eight to ten weeks duration. The content of such study is concentrated, in-depth and focuses on students' course experiences, from Western primary and secondary textbooks. From these courses Chinese teachers can appreciate that Western teachers are emphasising basic but very relevant themes. There is less knowledge content but every theme enables the students to adopt problem solving and subject modelling approaches. Consequently, the Western teachers' emphasis is on knowing how to study as well as simply to acquire knowledge. If students have mastered the study method, they can learn at any time when they need knowledge. The acquisition of knowledge will never be enough if they do not know how to study.

Chinese teachers' classroom teaching is commonly named 'teaching first, learning second' since they are used to transmitting their prepared teaching contents. 'Teaching first' means teachers will understand the textbook first by lesson preparation then explain to students their understanding. Students just need to memorize and to use the textbook. In 'learning second' the students just review and finish their homework after class and no high quality conceptual work is involved. In essence, therefore, the students are following only their teachers' thought. In contrast, Western teachers' classroom teaching is 'learning first, teaching second'. Students preview and raise questions by self-studying. They discuss their points of view with others in the class. Teachers advise, develop, debate, judge, evaluate and plan curriculum activities to ensure students' knowledge acquisition, conceptual understanding, skill development and value clarification/development. In essence teachers boost the students' learning.

'Classroom reversal' was a teaching reform slogan which appeared in China in 2013 to encourage teachers to stand aside and to return the studying process much more to their students. However, such action is difficult to develop on a large scale because Chinese textbooks focus too much on knowledge acquisition. Also classroom teaching time is limited and teachers have no way to allow their students more space for discussion, problem solving and inquiry.

Next steps for education in China

A combined approach to subject and thematic work is slowly emerging in some Chinese primary and secondary schools. Team teaching between Chinese and Western teachers in Xiehe has supported this new development in its Local Streams. The hybrid Pioneer Curriculum, as outlined in **Chapter 5.5**, is another highly commendable attempt to combine the advantages of both subject based and thematic learning, as well as the best parts of Chinese and Western education. Students are provided with a solid subject knowledge foundation as well as with many opportunities to explore cross-subject issues and/or problems. Diverse curricular choices and differentiated teaching and learning methodologies enable every student to learn according to their individual interests and talents. This is an obvious and considerable benefit from the *'East meets West'* Xiehe approach.

The Shanghai Municipal Government proposed a basic course, an extension course and a research course in its second stage course reform which started in 2000 in order to enrich the students' overall education. Additionally, Shanghai has further proposed the implementation of a half day 'happy period' in every primary school every week. Primary schools are not allowed to arrange teaching courses during this time but are required to organise comprehensive thematic practical activities in order to discover and develop students' potential in undertaking activity tasks, integrating them with what they have learnt and relating them to their experience and capabilities. Also, every semester, teachers are requested to develop a free researching homework not restricted by time and space. This allows students to have enough time to experience both enjoyable and productive learning.

From September 2014 a half day activity has been extended to every Government secondary school and the integration of subject and comprehensive thematic courses is a target for the compulsory education stage. All these developments mean that China's basic education reform is gradually beginning to reflect the *'East meets West'* education integration approach, advocated by the Xiehe Education Group.

Subject courses and comprehensive practical thematic courses represent opposite educational approaches for many Chinese educators. The country's traditional philosophy proposes moderation and opposes extremes. Xiehe's creative and brave attempt to combine the most valuable parts of Chinese and Western education together in its 'global approach' is inspiring. Hopefully, more Eastern and Western educators will have the vision to participate in this exciting development in order to enhance educational quality worldwide.

Professor Gu Zhiyue

Emeritus Professor of Education
East China Normal University

Former Dean
Shanghai Pudong Institute of Education Development

Deputy Head
Shanghai Teachers' Study Association

Interculturalism, capabilities and teacher development: towards a progressive curriculum future

Professor David Lambert
Institute of Education, University of London

Introduction

In this contribution to *'East Meets West'* I want to stand back, ponder, and then offer some personal reflections on the significance of what is being attempted in this provocative, informative and inspiring book. I do this mainly 'looking in from the outside' which has at least the potential of fresh perspective. I am a geography educationalist (and a former school teacher) with enormous passion for the subject and belief in its educational possibilities to nurture and develop global perspectives. Geography enables us to gain a sense of the global and according to Doreen Massey to 'take on the world' [1]

I fully acknowledge that a lot has to be right, and be in place, for such educational possibilities to be realized. Geography taught badly can reinforce stereotypical categories, rigid boundaries and hurtful prejudices, partly because of its (understandable) intellectual heritage of regional classification based on difference. Geography taught well however can be transformative: it can teach us to be suspicious of stereotypical half-truths; it can teach us to understand the porosity of borders and boundaries and what we can gain from a 'relational' understanding; and it can teach us always to be surprised about the world in which we live and its rich and amazing diversity – a kind of global 'open mindedness' that is the prerequisite to prejudice reduction.

Interculturalism and capabilities

I am excited to be given this opportunity to reflect on this book. It is so very ambitious in its scope. As pointed out in the introduction the book takes on aspects of teacher development, school management and improvement, curriculum design and planning, pedagogic innovation and of course global learning. It carefully and expertly takes us through pedagogic materials and techniques as diverse as philosophy-for-children, differentiation, progression in learning, language development, intellectual skills development, values, creativity... This is not an exhaustive list and it serves to remind us just how capable and competent all teacher practitioners have to be no matter what they teach, and especially if they take global education seriously.

But what interests me most about the book are the profound ideas that underpin the practical outcomes featured so brilliantly. Many of these are explicit but some are less so. For example, it is certainly the case that 'inter-culturalism', or what Bhikhu Parekh calls 'interactive multiculturalism' [2] is a concept that implicitly underpins the entire project. There is not the space here to unfurl inter-culturalism fully (see James 2008[3] for an excellent summary), but it is worth noting that Parekh is keen to show that there are benefits available to all if people can participate in their lives in a spirit of openness and dialogue – even though he would not require this. It would be oppressive, Parekh argues, to require people to diminish their local cultural allegiance, even if this is inward looking, closed and against reason. Now in saying this Parekh is placing inter-culturalism in relation to the state. In this book, however, we are interested in education. This means, in my view by definition, that we are against indoctrination, coercion of thought and other forms of oppression. We are for human freedom in the broadest sense and one of the things this implies is that we are very much interested in introducing children to the 'formation of reason.'[4]

We can see that various strategies developed in this book have been designed to do just this and thus to expand students' capacities to think for themselves. This contributes to their agency and their ability to function as human beings: I like to think of this as contributing to children's 'capabilities' development.[5]

The 'capabilities approach' has its origins in Amartya Sen's important and influential work theorizing human development and welfare economics. This helped us grasp the significance of poverty being in the way it deprives us of human freedoms and potentials. Understanding this provides an unassailable rationale for poverty eradication. The capabilities approach to humanizing economics has clear educational applications – again, by providing a rationale for educational activities in terms of their outcomes in contributing to human flourishing.[6] Thus, doing mathematics or geography lessons may be a good thing in itself, like poverty reduction, but the real significance of specialised knowledge learned in school is in the ways it enhances a person's capabilities set (partly, but by no means only, denoted by qualifications). So, we may say a 'sense of the global' is a good thing to develop in itself: the capabilities approach encourages us to say why and in what way this is the case.

One contribution to the debate on inter-culturalism is Sen's work on identity and human freedom and the need to counter the widespread tendency to 'miniaturise' people through the reductive processes involved with categorization and classification.[7] We all need to be aware of such tendencies not least in my own subject, geography, as noted in my initial remarks above. Sen urges us to challenge those who 'partition the people of the world into little boxes of disparate civilisations' [7] which is in a way what Doreen Massey also argues for in asking geography to 'take on the world'. In a slightly different way Mary Biddulph, as editor of the professional journal Teaching Geography, reminds us of the danger of the 'single story'.[8]

One danger Sen alerts us to, epitomized by Huntingdon's notion of the 'clash of civilisations', [9] is that singular, boxed thinking may result in and explain Western aggression toward Islam for example - and its rising anxiety over China. Huntingdon's clash of civilisations seems to fulfill the West's apparent need to replace the Cold War 'world order' with new fixed and oppositional (and grossly over-generalised) categories. Part of what is meant by Massey's 'sense of the global' is to appreciate that the boundaries and borders that make up the world map are not fixed or unchanging; neither are they sealed or impermeable, but porous (this is so even when the state takes steps to impose isolation: in January 2014, Prospect magazine in the UK reported the estimate that half of North Koreans have now watched foreign television). The capabilities approach to education can be used to bolster and communicate global learning in schools: thus, time young people spend in school should be used to build in them a sense of the global, and an understanding of the planet as a whole.

Young people who do not have such knowledge and intellectual capacity are, according to such thinking, deprived or diminished in certain aspects of their capability as global citizens. If this sounds like an overreaching claim then compare for a moment with the case of Jeanne described touchingly in Sebastian Faulks' 2012 novel 'A Possible Life'. Set in post revolutionary France, she is introduced to us as 'the most ignorant person in the Limousin village where she had lived most of her life'.[10] She is honest, warm hearted and hard working, but nevertheless the butt of jokes and unkindnesses partly as a result of her lack of learning; born into poverty and an orphan she had never been to school. It is interesting how Faulks depicts the deficiencies brought about by these circumstances on Jeanne's capacity to understand anything beyond her daily routine and encounters: 'She made no judgement on what she had seen in her life, but each experience affected her idea of what the world was'.[10] Even in those days, 200 hundred years ago, education was seen as more than merely access to learning how to read and write. Jeanne could do neither, but also we learn that she '... lived her life from one minute to the next, with no plan for the future and no sense that she would one day grow old or weak ... Her time at the orphanage had given her a fierce sense of the supernatural … She understood so little of the material world – how water boiled, why a walnut fell from a tree – that she had had to take almost everything on trust'. [10]

In 21st century economically prosperous and technologically advanced societies where education is virtually universal, and information about how the material world works is freely available to anyone with electricity and access to a computer, we might argue that the conditions of ignorance that condemned Jeanne to such a closed existence – and a prey to those who would exploit her over-dependence on the supernatural to explain her world - no longer exist. We should not underestimate how many millions of people wordwide are still condemned in this way. However, the point I really wish to stress is equally important. The capable citizen is not simply a person armed with information and a marketable skill-set. After all, we could argue that even Jeanne possessed such basic attributes as these. What Faulks pointed to was Jeanne's lack of knowledge beyond her everyday life – what the British sociologist Michael Young calls 'powerful knowledge'. [11 & 12] This is knowledge that is derived in the disciplines. It is thus specialized knowledge and exists beyond the everyday experience of people: it is often abstract, being theoretical or conceptual, and it is enabling. It is argued that a sacred purpose of schooling is to provide access to powerful knowledge for all young people – precisely because like Jeanne, without it we are condemned to ignorance. In the 21st century, I would argue that a crucial aspect of powerful knowledge is to provide a 'sense of the global'.

A capabilities approach to education encourages us to understand and deliberate on the learning outcomes envisaged by the methods and principles advocated in *'East meets West'.* Their significance lies in extending the freedoms of young people to think: to discern, to select and to make informed and healthy choices. In my subject I like to refer to such goals in terms of 'geo-capabilities'.

Curriculum

If capabilities and **inter-culturalism** are implicit concepts that drive the *'East meets West'* project, then 'curriculum' is a far more explicit idea. Curriculum design and curriculum planning pervade the book, and rightly so. If ever there is an idea that forms the ethical heart of a school, or of an individual teacher's identity, it is the curriculum. The distinguished UK educator Lawrence Stenhouse, quoted early on in the book, concluded that curriculum development went hand-in-hand with teacher development – and vice versa. In other words, we cannot expect meaningful teacher development to take place without curriculum development resulting (the latter is, in this sense, a kind of 'measure' that teacher development has taken place); and, if we want teachers to develop then the way to engineer this is to engage them in curriculum development. Though easy to assert, this is a profound relationship to realize and not in any way straightforward to achieve.

In England, partly because the Stenhousian approach is quite a challenging notion, teacher development has often been conducted in more recent times in a rather impoverished and diminished form. We have not the space in this essay to explore the full extent of this claim, save to say that for the last 15-20 years teacher development in England has been dominated by improving technical teaching proficiency (or 'competence') - which frequently and unfortunately is ultimately reduced to teaching-to-the-test. The curriculum, the idea that lies at the ethical core of education, has been left to founder as a taken for granted and common sense idea. This is partly associated with the introduction of a national curriculum (which in England did not happen until 1991) which seemed to sub-contract curriculum thinking to agencies other than schools and individual teachers. It is at about this time when curriculum 'delivery' became the dominant metaphor in schools. The fact that it still seems to be would have Stenhouse 'turning in his grave'.

Thus, for the remainder of my contribution I want to acknowledge and applaud that *'East meets West'* is not described by, or aligned to, 'delivery' in any way. If this book has any single metaphorical tone it is 'engagement' not delivery. This is part of the significance of this book: it is using the concept of curriculum as the prime site for teacher and educational development. I want also to provide a wider theoretical framework for curriculum thinking which may strengthen the way this book is used, and to give durability to the ideas it is promoting. To do so we need to go right back to square one, and ask why exactly curriculum is such a special idea. I answer with another question, for the curriculum is concerned ultimately with a single, deceptively tricky question: what shall we teach?

I do not think we ever come to a final answer to this question, at least not in terms of specifics. However, for reasons touched on in the previous section I believe it is important for educationalists (as distinguished from politicians, business people and other interest groups besides) to argue for the importance of knowledge as the main building block of the school curriculum.

Access to knowledge is what makes schools special settings (as distinct from hospitals, factories, shopping centres, families or even the wordwide web). If we accept that children and young people are highly unlikely in their daily lives to encounter sustained engagement with ideas and processes that make up 'powerful knowledge' (which frequently is counter intuitive, abstract and requires some effort to grasp) rather than information to consume (which is often fragmented, accessed on demand and lacks 'systematicity' or a conceptual connectedness to 'what is known') then the question of what to teach in school cannot be answered without great care. Not least, care to distinguish the different, albeit very complementary emphasis connoted by pedagogy and curriculum.

We have to be cautious about bringing the everyday into the classroom – wholly justified pedagogically, but in curriculum terms too heavy an emphasis on everyday relevance can undermine the significance of disciplinary knowledge. We have to be cautious about the balance between generic skills (including unanchored 'critical thinking skills') and specialized knowledge as the main building blocks of the curriculum (we need both of course, but not one without the other).

We need to be cautious about the degree to which the 'social construction' of knowledge is adopted as a curriculum principle: again, in pedagogic terms it is highly justified to think in terms of providing opportunities and scaffolding (and the time and space) for children to make meaning from data of all kinds, and furthermore, to argue about meaning. But in curriculum terms it is distracting and misleading to imply that the only meaningful knowledge available to young people is that which is 'constructed' on site. To do so may unintentionally exclude them from disciplinary knowledge which has been created by a community of scholars: from a social justice point of view we may wish to ask why we would ever want to do that!

One of the difficulties of discussing, or promoting, knowledge (or powerful knowledge) as a curriculum principle is that it has to many ears a back-facing tone to it. Boring classrooms led by 'authoritative' teachers who talk too much; copying down and rote learning; disengagement and disillusion. I hope there is nothing in what I have written in the previous paragraphs to even suggest that this is what is implied by powerful knowledge. The following framework may help make some distinctions to consolidate the place of knowledge in a progressive, future-facing curriculum (future three or F3).

Knowledge and three alternative curriculum 'futures' [12 & 13]

F1: subject 'delivery' – of knowledge for its own sake; organised by traditional subjects; stable, enduring, 'given'. This is under-socialised knowledge.

F2: skills and 'learning to learn' – knowledge is constructed; subject divisions are artificial and arbitrary; integrated themes and or 'issues' are preferred. This is experiential and over-socialised knowledge.

F3: subjects are not given (as in F1), but not arbitrary either (as in F2) – knowledge development is led by '... the epistemic rules of specialist communities' to provide ways to understand the world and take students beyond their everyday experience.

Conclusion

I have tried to say why I think *'East meets West'* is an interesting and important contribution to educational advancement. I make no apologies for doing this through my geographer's eyes, though I have wrapped up my thoughts in three even bigger ideas: inter-culturalism, capabilities and curriculum.

Is it possible to identify a curriculum in which *'East meets West'*? Is it possible to envision a knowledge-led curriculum that takes pedagogy seriously? This book shows that it is. But the responsibility to make this happen rests with the creativity of teachers, as it always has done.

Acknowledgements

[1] Massey, D. (2014). *Taking on the World*, in Geography, Vol 99, No.1, pp.36-39.
[2] Parekh, B. (2007). *Multiculturalism,* in Baggini, J. and Strangroom, J. (eds) *What more philosophers think.* London: Continuum, pp.45-56.
[3] James, M. (2008). *Interculturalism: theory and policy.* London: The Baring Foundation (available at www.baringfoundation.org.uk).
[4] Backhurst, D. (2011). *The Formation of Reason.* Chichester: Wiley-Blackwell.
[5] Lambert, D. (2011). *Reframing School Geography: a capabilities approach*, in Butt, G. (ed) *Geography, Education and the Future.* London: Continuum.
[6] Solem, M., Lambert, D. and Tani, S. (2013). *Geocapabilities: Toward An International Framework for Researching the Purposes and Values of Geography Education*, in Review of International Geographical Education Online (RIGEO), Vol 3, No.3, pp.214-229 (available at http://www.rigeo.org/).
[7] Sen, A. (2006). *Identity and violence.* London: Penguin Group
[8] Biddulph, M. (2011). *Editorial: the danger of a single story*, in Teaching Geography, Vol 36, No.2, pp.45.
[9] Huntingdon, S. (1997). *The Clash of Civilizations and the Remaking of World Order.* New York: Simon and Schuster.
[10] Faulks, S. (2013). *A Possible Life.* London: Random House/Vintage.
[11] Young, M. (2008). *Bringing Knowledge Back In.* London: Routledge.
[12] Young, M. and Lambert, D. (2014). *Knowledge and the Future School: curriculum and social justice.* London: Bloomsbury.
[13] Young, M. & Muller, J. (2010). *Three Educational Scenarios for the Future: lessons from the sociology of knowledge*, in European Journal of Education, Vol 45, No.1, pp.11-27.

Bilingual global education.